D1555665

# Equity in the Workplace

# STUDIES IN PUBLIC POLICY

## Series Editor: Paul J. Rich, Policy Studies Organization

Lexington Books and the Policy Studies Organization's **Studies in Public Policy** series brings together the very best in new and original scholarship, spanning the range of global policy questions. Its multi-disciplinary texts combine penetrating analysis of policy formulation at the macro level with innovative and practical solutions for policy implementation. The books provide the political and social scientist with the latest academic research and the policy maker with effective tools to tackle the most pressing issues faced by government today. Not least, the books are invaluable resources for teaching public policy. For ideas about curriculum use, visit www.ipsonet.org.

*Analyzing National and International Policy: Theory, Method, and Case Studies*,
    by Laure Paquette
*Developmental Policy and the State: The European Union, East Asia, and the
    Caribbean*, by Nikolaos Karagiannis
*Policymaking and Democracy: A Multinational Anthology*
*Policymaking and Prosperity: A Multinational Anthology*
*Policymaking and Peace: A Multinational Anthology*
    Three-volume set edited by Stuart Nagel
*Equity in the Workplace: Gendering Workplace Policy Analysis*, edited by Heidi
    Gottfried and Laura Reese
*Politics, Institutions, and Fiscal Policy: Deficits and Surpluses in Federated States*,
    edited by Louis M. Imbeau and François Pétry
*Innovation and Entrepreneurship in State and Local Government*, edited by
    Michael Harris and Rhonda Kinney
*Comparative Bureaucratic Systems*, edited by Krishna K. Tummala
*Public Policy in Israel: Perspectives and Practices*, edited by Dani Korn
*The Struggle of Soviet Jewry in American Politics: Israel versus the American
    Jewish Establishment*, by Fred A. Lazin
*Foreign Policy toward Cuba: Isolation or Engagement?*, edited by Michele
    Zebich-Knos and Heather N. Nicol
*The Work of Policy: An International Survey*, edited by H. K. Colebatch
*The Politics of Biotechnology in North America and Europe: Policy Networks,
    Institutions, and Internationalization,* edited by Éric Montpetit, Christine
    Rothmayr, and Frédéric Varone
*Local Government Reforms in Countries in Transition: A Global Perspective*, edited
    by Fred Lazin, Matt Evans, Vincent Hoffmann-Martinot, and Hellmut Wollmann
*Beyond Realism: Human Security in India and Pakistan in the Twenty-First
    Century*, by Rekha Datta

# Equity in the Workplace

## Gendering Workplace Policy Analysis

Edited by
Heidi Gottfried and Laura Reese

LEXINGTON BOOKS

A division of
ROWMAN & LITTLEFIELD PUBLISHERS, INC.
*Lanham • Boulder • New York • Toronto • Plymouth, UK*

BLACKBURN COLLEGE
LIBRARY

Acc. No. BB46575

Class No. 331.4133.Got

Date 21-10-13

LEXINGTON BOOKS

A division of Rowman & Littlefield Publishers, Inc.
A wholly owned subsidary of The Rowman & Littlefield Publishing Group, Inc.
4501 Forbes Boulevard, Suite 200
Lanham, MD 20706

Estover Road
Plymouth PL6 7PY
United Kingdom

Copyright © 2004 by Lexington Books
First paperback edition 2008

*All rights reserved.* No part of this publication may be reproduced, stored in a
retrieval system, or transmitted in any form or by any means, electronic,
mechanical, photocopying, recording, or otherwise, without the prior permission of
the publisher.

British Library Cataloguing in Publication Information Available

**Library of Congress Cataloging-in-Publication Data**
The hardback edition of this book was previously catalogued by the Library of
Congress as follows:

   Equity in the workplace : gendering workplace policy analysis / edited by Heidi
Gottfried and Laura Reese.
      p. cm. — (Studies in public policy)
   Includes bibliographical references and index.
   1. Sex discrimination in employment—Government policy.  2. Sex discrimination
against women—Government policy. I. Gottfried, Heidi, 1955–    II. Reese, Laura A.
(Laura Ann), 1958–   III. Series.
HD6060.E67  2003
331.4'133—dc21                                                                2003007312

ISBN-13: 978-0-7391-0688-4 (cloth : alk. paper)
ISBN-10: 0-7391-0688-0 (cloth : alk. paper)
ISBN-13: 978-0-7391-2907-4 (pbk. : alk. paper)
ISBN-10: 0-7391-2907-4 (pbk. : alk. paper)

Printed in the United States of America

∞™ The paper used in this publication meets the minimum requirements of
American National Standard for Information Sciences—Permanence of Paper for
Printed Library Materials, ANSI/NISO Z39.48–1992.

To my son, Bernhard, who dares to be different.
—HG


To the most influential women in my life, Janet B. Reese
and the late Margaret T. Reese.
—LAR

# Contents

# Foreword

## Gender and Civil Society

*Paul Rich*

Here is a timely book if there ever was one. This policy series by Lexington Books and the Policy Studies Organization claims to cover the major policy issues of our day, so it could hardly make such an assertion without a consideration of gender.

It seems that every conference now has gender on its mind, and rightly so. The recent focus in political science on social capital and civil society has increased the importance of gender scholarship, as gender issues increasingly interface with discussions of trust, social capital, and civil society: "In the world of ideas, civil society is hot. It is almost impossible to read an article on foreign or domestic politics without coming across some mention of the concept."[1]

There is little doubt that the building of social trust through the fostering of gender equity is contributory to democracy:

> In a society that is looking for alternatives to a way of life dominated by corporations and state, social movements suggest other choices. A network of organizations that encompass broad constituencies can change our understanding of what is possible and desirable. Little by little we can build a new political culture based on our own questions about the existing order. Meeting human needs neglected by the state and the market is the basis for social movements. By working together they promote positive change and stretch our understanding of democracy and justice. The values of the everyday world, including friendship, respect, and concern for others, combined with shared hopes and aspirations, and healthy doses of courage and patience, characterize what is best about the culture of social movements.[2]

Associations and volunteerism that influence gender equity are getting more attention partly as a consequence of the end of the Cold War:

> The renewed interest in civil society first emerged in Eastern Europe after communism crumbled. Leaders like Vaclav Havel wanted to go beyond establishing new governments and create a culture that could sustain political and economic liberalism. They looked for help to those private groups beyond the reach of the state—citizens' associations, churches, human-rights chapters, jazz clubs—that had nourished dissident life. Around the same time, the victorious Western democracies found themselves confronting sagging economies, a fraying social fabric, and the loss of national purpose. Here too, the experts and statesmen agreed, revitalizing civil society would overcome our malaise.[3]

Obviously the debate about the contribution of intermediate organizations to democracy should also include a discussion of the contribution of such organizations to gender issues. More attention is needed to the contributions of nongovernmental organizations (NGOs) to the gender discussions.[4] Not always are these contributions positive. Indeed, some NGOs were reactionary and did not build trust or social capital. Studying American fraternal orders, William D. Moore writes:

> The lodge room then can be understood as a place in which masculine values which were disappearing in the outside world were preserved. It was a theater in which millions of American men entertained each other by acting our morality plays, and a hallowed space where the same men found spiritual meaning and perpetuated what they unconsciously recognized as a disappearing social order.[5]

Gender issues are controversial. Recently, there has been an increase in male movements that emphasize supposedly traditional sex roles. American salvation, some like Robert Bly claim, is via a renewal of male ritual, and that ritual centers on initiation with the involvement of a mentor or "male mother." A necessary part of a male-dominated society is "Iron John," a male authority figure. Much nonsense like this is being written today about male initiation and bonding.[6]

In the *New York Times*, Professor Hal Foster of Cornell University has described this development as "celebration of the masochistic man" and relates it to the growth of "the cult of abjection" with an oscillation between sensitivity and sadism, adding, "God save the women who get caught in between."[7]

While perhaps overstated, it does seem that a corollary to the new male ritualism in more than a few cases is a viciously reactionary male chauvinism that would see that women are again relegated to the kitchen, de facto deprived of their civil rights. Those who think gender has become an obvious civil rights issue will be surprised to learn how, once again,[8] at least according to Martin Green in *The Adventurous Male* (1993), "politics is a male group phenomenon" and that "Seymour Lipset's *Political Man* naturally deals with men and not with women."[9] (I know Dr. Lipset, a friend, and hasten to add that he is not a chauvinist, whatever Mr. Green is.)

Much of the growth of nongovernmentals worldwide is prompted by the missionary zeal of American organizations, including those oriented toward women. For example, Soroptimist International, a women's professional club similar to Lions or Rotary, reported chartering new clubs in Japan, the Philippines, Taiwan, Korea, the Czech Republic, Norway, the Netherlands, Austria, Sweden, Lithuania, Germany, Turkey, and Australia. The Soroptimists have more than 3,000 clubs in 112 countries.[10]

Common sense about gender has been a long time coming. But today the Internet is almost gender blind. As for higher education, 57 percent of university students in America are women. The percentage is even higher when it comes to minorities—60 percent of Hispanics and almost two-thirds of black university students are women. There are old-girl networks aplenty. Women are found in many occupations that were once closed to them. As child-care services become more of a right than a privilege, the remaining obstacles to careers will disappear. Family structures have become far more diverse, and single-sex relationships have increasingly been given legal recognition.[11]

Victor Hugo is often credited with saying that "Stronger than all the armies is an idea whose time has come." Actually this is a paraphrase from his *Histoire d'un crime*, a protest against the coup of Louis-Napoléon in 1851. But paraphrase or not, it is true about gender and gender's place in policy scholarship. Its time has come, as the essays in this impressive study show.

Paul Rich is Titular Professor of International Relations and History, University of the Americas-Puebla, Visiting Fellow at Stanford's Hoover Institution, and President both of the Policy Studies Organization and of Phi Beta Delta, the international honor society.

## NOTES

1. Fareed Zakaria, "Bigger Than the Family, Smaller Than the State: Are Voluntary Groups What Make Countries Work?" *New York Times Book Review*, August 13, 1995, 1.

2. Duncan Cameron, "Civil Society," *CUSO Forum* 12, no. 3 (December 1994): 4.

3. Zakaria, "Bigger Than the Family," 1.

4. For example, see "Research Conferences at ILAIS," Newsletter, Fall 1995, 1.

5. William D. Moore, "Masonic Lodge Rooms and their Furnishings, 1870–1930," *Heredom: The Transactions of the Scottish Rite Research Society* 2 (1993): 125.

6. "By the mid-1970s, men's conferences were being held and organizations formed to respond to a growing list of male concerns, ranging from divorce and

alimony rights, parenting, and job situations to sexual fulfillment and, especially, gay rights, which dominated the early movement. A men's liberation movement had been born. The basic focus was a recognition of the shortcomings of playing the traditional masculine role of always getting ahead and staying cool." Joe L. Dubbert, *A Man's Place: Masculinity in Transition* (Englewood Cliffs, N.J.: Prentice-Hall, 1979), 286.

7. Hal Foster, "Cult of Despair," *New York Times*, December 30, 1994, A17. "Related to the celebration of the masochistic man is the success of failure: in the last few years, an esthetic of the pathetic—an ethic of the loser—has emerged in contemporary art and music. . . . With its initial contempt for pop success and good looks, grunge music tapped into this resignation." Ibid.

8. However, even without considering the male "backlash" that Iron John may represent, the progress made in achieving sexual equality is open to doubt: "Taken as more or less functioning wholes, the institutional structures of the United States and other societies are organized along lines of gender. The law, politics, religion, the academy, the state, and the economy . . . are institutions historically developed by men, currently dominated by men, and symbolically interpreted from the standpoint of men in leading positions, both in the present and historically. These institutions have been defined by the absence of women. . . . In spite of many changes bringing women into all institutions, and the reclaiming of women's history that shows their earlier important participation, males still dominate the central institutions." Joan Acker, "Gendered Institutions: From Sex Roles to Gendered Institutions," *Contemporary Sociology* 21, no. 5 (September 1992): 567.

9. Martin Green, *The Adventurous Male: Chapters in the History of the White Male Mind* (University Park: Pennsylvania State University Press, 1993), 145. Here he is relying heavily on Lionel Tiger's *Men in Groups* (New York: Vintage, 1970): "In fact, Tiger says, armies, sports, secret societies, training patterns, and economic and religious power-structures all offer data to prove the importance of this male bonding. These activities are linked to each other by the importance of the kind of bonding in all of them. For instance, the basis of most sports is a preparation for or rehearsal of war. The same is more obviously true of hunting. Initiation ceremonies, with their pains and humiliations, separate the initiate from home and family and generate strong new bonds that enable adventurers—for we hardly need to point out that all these are forms of adventure. . . . Tiger suggests that we could call secret political societies the demi-monde of politics. The two things—the demi-monde and the secret societies—are both partial withdrawals from the light of social day and are often felt by women (the guardians of that daylight) as inimical."

10. "New Clubs Chartered," *The International Soroptimist* 23, no. 3 (September 1995): 12.

11. Marvin J. Cetron and Owen Davies, "Trends Shaping the Future," *The Futurist* (January–February 2003): 35–36.

# Acknowledgments

The articles in this volume emerged out of an ongoing research agenda on women, work, and public policy undertaken by several working groups: Research Group on Gender and Workplace Issues, CULMA at Wayne State University, and the Globalization, Gender, and Work Network. Additional research and input has contributed to the ongoing work represented by this volume; we would like to thank Dean Alma Young for her generous endorsement; Bill Cooke and Willie McKether of the Fraser Center for Workplace Issues for their institutional support; Heather Kahn and Irene Knokh for their help with the index; and Mari Osawa, Kazuko Tanaka, Keiko Aiba, Makiko Nishikawa, Yuko Ogasawara, Monika Goldman, and Karen Shire of the International Network. David Fasenfest deserves special recognition for his continuous efforts in support of this research project. Thank you to both Serena Krombach and Brian Richards, who shepherded the text through the publication process. We would like to thank Paul Rich of the Policy Studies Organization and David Feldman, editor of the *Review of Policy Research*, for their permission to include articles from the symposium on Gender, Policy, Politics, and Work, volume 20, number 1, spring 2003. This volume also includes Heidi Gottfried and Jacqueline O'Reilly's "Re-regulating Breadwinner Models in Socially Conservative Welfare Regimes: Comparing Germany and Japan," *Social Politics* 9, no. 1 (spring 2002): 29–59, by permission of Oxford University Press.

# Introduction

## Gendering Workplace Policy Analysis

*Heidi Gottfried and Laura Reese*

The last two decades of the twentieth century saw the rise of new policies, ranging from equal opportunities, and parental and family leave, to regulation of working time and sexual relations, that have made the workplace more hospitable to women workers in many industrialized countries. The analyses in this volume illustrate a number of contemporary workplace issues that have both gendered causes and/or gendered effects and provide an assessment of extant public policies to address gender-based workplace issues. By highlighting the gender dimensions of workplace policies in a comparative context, the treatment integrates usually separate bodies of research on welfare-state developments, employment transformations, workplace policies, and work experience through a gender lens. The recurring themes of globalization, changing markets and systems of production, an evolving relationship between women and the marketplace, and the attendant effects on the work/home balance clearly indicate that industrialized nations share a common set of environmental forces and hence can learn from each other's experiences with workplace gender policies.

However, the countries represented in the research here—the United States, the U.K., Germany, Japan, Canada, and the EU more broadly—embody some important contrasts. The U.S., Canada, and the U.K. are, in some typologies of industrial relations and welfare-state regimes, placed together as "liberal" as compared with the more "corporatist" Germany and Japan, and the social democratic Swedish model (Crouch and Streeck, 1997; Esping-Andersen, 1999). Germany reappears in many of the chapters as a socially conservative welfare regime undergoing change, while the U.K., Canada, and the U.S. as liberal welfare regimes appear to diverge with respect to the development of social rights and civil rights respectively. And, for U.S. audiences in particular, the explicit comparison of gender-based workplace policies among

1

the nations noted presents a picture that can only raise concerns about the state of U.S. workplace policies vis-à-vis other industrialized countries.

Taken as a whole the chapters in this book suggest substantive change, but also continuity in the pathways of contemporary workplace policy. On the one hand, all of the countries examined have extended regulation over gender relations in the workplace. On the other, there appears to be a high degree of path dependency. Historical, economic, social, and legal systems continue to color workplace policies in the nations considered here. These systems lead to differences in the nature of workplace policies among industrialized nations and within nations with federal systems.

Yet, the categorizations above may be too simplistic. Feminist-inspired social-policy analyses have refined distinctions within and between clusters of cases (O'Connor et al., 1999; Daly and Lewis, 2000; Gottfried and O'Reilly, 2002; Mutari and Figart, 2002), recasting welfare-state typologies in terms of gender-sensitive categories that bring into focus social care, sexuality, reproduction, and the body. The gender focus sheds light on changing relationships both *between* and *within* families, states, and markets and highlights attendant public-policy implications.

As the chapters show, the increasingly public gender regime with a dual-earner family has not yet uprooted the female-carer arrangement. Sweden has moved closest to the gender equity model while Germany and Japan continue to rely on women's unpaid labor for care in the family, saving taxpayers' money that would otherwise be absorbed via expensive institutional care. The U.S., on the other hand, has lagged behind many EU nations in the implementation of fully woman-friendly policies in the workplace. The extent that this is due to national or political systems and culture and/or the absence of pressure from regional or global bodies is unclear. However, the issues raised and comparisons posed in the chapters provide essential input into the debate surrounding gender and workplace issues by making explicit often implicitly constituted systems of gender relations at the societal and workplace levels. Policy debates can only become more refined and better informed as a result.

The following sections briefly summarize issues raised in this volume, providing a review of the contextual factors that shape national approaches to gender and workplace policies and help to explain cross-national variation in perceptions of, and approaches to, workplace policy.

## CENTRAL ISSUES IN UNDERSTANDING GENDER AND WORKPLACE POLICY: CROSSCUTTING THEMES

### Feminist Comparative Research

The majority of chapters in this volume approach gender and workplace policy from an explicitly feminist and comparative perspective providing a unifying theme for understanding national trends in gendered workplace issues. Feminist policy research brings gender into analytical focus, asking "how gender is constructed in welfare-state policies and how these policies are a force in ordering gender relations through an examination of a wide range of contexts" (Sainsbury, 1999: 4). Gender enters into both the framing of policy and its differential impacts. Comparative policy research from a feminist perspective has moved beyond case studies published side by side in edited collections devoid of the common theoretical framework needed to make sense of both similarities and differences. Recent studies have compared a single policy area such as child care (Michel and Mahon, 2001), job training (Mazur, 2001), and equal pay (Kahn and Meehan, 1992), and/or analyzed structural features such as state feminism (Stetson and Mazur, 1995) and welfare regimes (O'Connor et al., 1999) cross-nationally.[1] Amy Mazur (2002) demarcates four different areas of feminist comparative research: gender and the welfare-state, feminist policy formation, state feminism, and women's movements and policy. The chapters in this volume cut across these overlapping approaches and contribute to the broad range of literature on these topics.

Nonfeminist theorists recently have integrated feminist insights into their welfare-state models (Korpi, 2000; Esping-Andersen, 1999). Revisiting his three models of welfare capitalism (Esping-Andersen, 1990), Gosta Esping-Andersen's (1999) analysis of the postindustrial state borrows the feminist concept of "defamilization" to denote provision of services outside the family by either state or market. But, as Ann Orloff (2002) suggests, he misses another key aspect of feminist theorizing that considers how policies decrease women's economic dependence. On the other hand, Jane Lewis's concept of the male-breadwinner model highlights the gendered assumptions of policy makers about family forms, and the ways in which this contributed to the social organization of care. Women's access to benefits has been derived from and mediated by their relationships to men (in Orloff, 2002). Current policies supporting women's labor-force participation and reconciliation of work and family life have modified, eroded, and weakened the male-breadwinner model. Still the legacy of the male-breadwinner model continues to inform policy formation.

Case studies have also contrasted countries with different gender regimes. Feminists have elaborated on either Connell's or Walby's concept of gender regime for comparative and transnational research (Ostner and Lewis, 1995; Fagan and O'Reilly, 1998; Walby, 1999). Gender regime refers to "a system of gender relations in the market and household economies, the polity, and in civil society, that includes interpersonal violence and sexuality" (Walby, in this volume). Modernization of the gender regime entails women's increasing participation in public spheres and expanding civil, social, and reproductive rights.

Feminist policy formation overlaps with the state-feminism approach since both analyze policy processes and structures internal to the state.

They attempt to unravel the comparative puzzle to explain the extent to which the contemporary welfare-state pursues feminist/women-friendly policies (Mazur 2001, 2002; Stetson and Mazur, 1995; Kahn and Meehan, 1992). The state-feminism approach first noted the emergence of women's policy machineries and examined the array of institutional arrangements inside the state devoted to women's policy questions across a range of issues and countries and asked what accounts for the effectiveness of feminist policies to improve women's social status (Stetson and Mazur, 1995). Feminist comparative policy theorists credited the role of femocrats[2] and feminist organizations in bringing feminist issues to bear on political institutions at multiple levels of polities (Mazur, 2001). Extending this approach further, Mazur (2002) uses the secondary literature to elaborate eight subsectors of feminist policy to explore whether, how, and why governments pursue purposely feminist actions. Three of the eight subsectors, specifically equal employment, reconciliation of work and family life, and sexuality and violence policies, are particularly relevant to the study of gender, policy, and work.

These approaches, while sharing common concerns, have different foci and have different understandings of the state. Welfare-state theory typifies national cases through excavation of regime and/or policy logics. In contrast to welfare-state theory, feminist policy formation and state-feminism approaches treat the state as internally differentiated structures and processes (Stetson and Mazur, 1995; Mazur, 2001). Neither expects coherence nor unity across policy areas, yet state feminists avoid welfare-state theories' generalizing about national policy styles.

Feminist theorizing also explores how women's mobilization, either through autonomous movements or within larger organizations (such as unions) and political parties, affects the type, locus, and effectiveness of policy. Working women's self-organization, as indicated by their absolute increase and relative share in trade unions, has pushed the development of equality policies (Walby, 1999). Peggy Kahn and Elizabeth Meehan (1992) found that unions influenced the path of equal-pay initiatives; the strength of the labor movement affects change on the national level in the U.K. and it is largely confined to the public sector in the U.S. Unions have not always recognized the gender impacts of issues that are not framed in gendered terms such as job training (Mazur, 2001). Women's movements also are adopting new spatial forms of politics through transnational networks. Networks as organizational forms aggregate micropolitical processes, mobilize horizontal channels of information, foster communicative action, and facilitate pooling and sharing of resources over time and space (Lenz, 1999). Policy transfer has occurred through international organizations (particularly, the UN women's conferences, specifically Beijing and Beijing plus) and cross-fertilization among women's groups. NGOs and transnational women's networks translate and transform feminist goals into actual policy-making process at multiple levels (Gelb, 2003).

Feminist comparative policy research represents a rich and growing field of study. The integration of gender into policy research illuminates areas often hidden from view and indicates differential impacts between men and women and among groups of women. Through examination of changing relationships within and interaction between private and public spheres, feminist analyses examine how policies affect intimate practices in everyday experiences to broader social changes. Many of the authors in this volume pursue a comparative feminist approach to better understand the theoretical underpinnings of changing gender and workplace policies such as the forces of globalization, transnational women's organizations, and the effects of supranational governing bodies such as the EU. The comparative feminist approach is also evident in chapters that assess and compare different public stances toward gender and workplace policy and how policy is intricately embedded in social, economic, and historical forces that vary by nation or regime.

### Doing Comparative and Transnational Research

The chapters here present original, cutting-edge research on policy, politics, and work and evaluate some of the most current policy developments cross-nationally. A variety of research methods and methodologies are used, including process tracing, life-course analysis, participant observation, correlational analysis, survey research, content analysis, and the comparative method. All of the articles examine processes in flux, over the long haul, either through overtly longitudinal analysis of data or process tracing over time. Examination of process over time is central to understanding and theorizing policy processes and dynamics in any setting.

The impulse for comparative study extends beyond the usual and more narrowly bounded research communities. Comparative research increasingly dominates earlier styles of area studies conducted on the basis of in-depth analysis of a single case. There is a growing recognition that real qualitative changes have altered political-economic institutions and that greater interconnectedness between subnational, national, and supranational levels increasingly compels consideration of comparative and transnational studies that pay close attention to relationships between and within cases. Comparative research must be distinguished from transborder or transnational research: comparative research may or may not be transnational; the former does not necessarily entail comparisons between more than one country/region.[3] A study may compare subnational units within a country or examine a process over time within a single case.

Richard Locke and Kathleen Thelen (1995) design research around "conceptualized comparisons" by conducting in-depth case studies analyzed in relationship to each other. This approach typically uses "thick" description and "thick" theory toward developing a comparative contextualized account (Thelen, 1999). Such contextualized comparisons are sensitive to both history and culture, and

> demonstrate how various international trends are not in fact translated into common pressures in all national economies but rather are mediated by national institutional arrangements and refracted into divergent struggles over particular national practices. . . . Contextualized comparisons are meant not to displace but rather to complement traditional matched comparisons; they bring new insights to labor scholarship by highlighting unexpected parallels across cases that the conventional literature sees as very different and, conversely, by underscoring significant differences between cases typically seen as "most similar." . . . By focusing on the way different institutional arrangements create different sets of rigidities and flexibilities, we can identify the range of possible "sticking points" or potential sources of conflict between labor and management in a particular country (Locke and Thelen, 1995: 228, 342).

The contextualized comparative method, however, can reify national institutions in its attempt to look deeply at cases. As several chapters demonstrate, contextualized comparisons detail factors that lead to divergent pathways and convergent policy directions.

Comparative and transnational researchers have acknowledged regionalization of policy formation and practice especially for the study of the EU. To study the EU vis-à-vis member states, political theorists consider the relationship between national and supranational (including regional) levels and units of analysis. The metaphor of "multi-levels" was introduced by Wolfgang Streeck (1998) to analyze the relationship between national and supranational governance institutions Europe wide. The European Union, however, should not be studied in isolation, despite its considerable peculiarities. The EU possesses characteristics loosely resembling those of other political systems, and these systems can usefully be compared. For example, the multitiered decision making by the European Commission is likely to create quite distinctive pressures and constraints on social-policy development by national actors (Pierson and Liebfried, 1995) and this point is made in several of the analyses here.

More comparative research stretches beyond the usual Western cases. One innovative approach by T.J. Pempel (1998) derives a puzzle from comparative analysis of welfare-states, asking, how can we explain phenomenal economic growth, low unemployment, and a low degree of social inequality given that the postwar features of Japan deviate from patterns noted in European welfare-states? Pempel situates Japan in broader contexts to understand particular changes within Japan and revise understandings of welfare-states typically based on either intra-European comparisons or U.S. and European comparisons. As a non-Western, industrialized country, Japan can reveal comparative insights about significant similarities and differences that may go unnoticed when studying countries that share a common historical background (Peng, 2003; Gottfried, 2000; Gelb, 2003).

The comparative literature on policy developments increasingly pays attention to globalization, changing the context and content of policy formation and implementation.[4] Many analyses of globalization have assumed that there is a process of deregulation as national economies attempt to compete in increasingly globally integrated markets. The emphasis on deregulation has occurred in part because of the absence of a feminist analytics. Specifically, feminist analyses uncover the process of re-regulation. Globalization has altered the sites, the subjects, and the ways of doing politics and has rescaled political institutions and arenas to expand the field of politics in which women's movements can make claims integrating concern with networks and agency with the more structural approaches. Globalization is seen as an open-ended process, which is subject to negotiation by a variety of political actors. This has important policy implications, since changing regulations are framed by global connections, with the UN system and its conferences as a key element in the diffusion, development, and hybridization of gender equity policies. Such comparisons raise several questions. How and why are countries, like Japan and Germany, differently affected by global feminism? Is Germany buffered from the global by the EU, whereas Japan is not? And, how does the global system frame the possibilities for and nature of workplace policies that address gender differences?

The EU has opened a new political space for organized interests to influence policy making at the national and subnational level constituting an emerging polity, which has had a significant impact on modernizing gender regimes both at the EU level and within member nations (Walby, 1999). The EU is becoming a driving force in developing a wide range of policies that address women's inferior position in paid labor:

> The Community has brought about changes in employment practices which might otherwise have taken decades to achieve. Irish women have the Community to thank for the removal of the marriage bar in employment, the introduction of maternity leave, greater opportunities to train at a skilled trade, protection against dismissal on pregnancy, the disappearance of advertisements specifying the sex of an applicant for a job, and greater equality in the social welfare code (O'Connor cited in Orloff, 2002: 21).

The shift from a national to a multilevel governance structure offers new opportunities for democratic politics especially for those groups formerly excluded from, or marginalized in, corporatist structures (Bergqvist, 2001). Women's groups have found room to maneuver in local and national politics due to changing regulation on the EU level.

The EU has advanced regulation, via its legally binding directives on equal treatment of men and women and in the Treaty of Amsterdam and the more recent development of "gender mainstreaming." To what extent is "Europeanization" of policy formation (and identity formation) taking place (see Liebert, this volume)? There seem to be greater obstacles in the way of building a social-policy union that can harmonize historically different pathways taken by member states than faced by monetary-union architects of the Eurozone. Past policy frameworks continue to shape implementation and interpretation of directives issued by various bodies of the European Commission. Still, the effects of EU directives can clearly be seen in changes in workplace policies suggesting that regionalized policy stances can impact member nations. At the EU level the directive on parental leave in 1996 has pushed countries to adopt leave policy.[5] The comparison also indicates that parental- and family-leave regulations have advanced further than child-care support, highlighting the underdevelopment of a social infrastructure of care services with the exception of Sweden. The EU's failure to issue a binding directive on child care has left the question of reproductive work to be resolved in the mixed economy of privately and publicly provided care (Gottfried and O'Reilly, this volume). Still, EU institutions, ranging from the European Commission, European Parliament, and the European Court of Justice, appear to be more open to feminist input and the emergence of supranational state feminism.

As a group, the chapters in this volume illustrate the richness of understanding that can be gained through the juxtaposition of a variety of research methodologies focused on a common theme. The side-by-side presentation of single case studies—Canada, the U.S., Germany, Japan—focusing on specific workplace policies places in stark contrast the differing approaches to gender and workplace issues, often viewed myopically in research focusing on one system alone thus narrowing the range of policy options. The more explicitly comparative focus within the EU allows not only for an assessment of how the global affects the "local" but also illustrates clearly that national approaches to gender and workplace policy form a spectrum of approaches that, while rooted in the historical and social cultures of individual nation-states, are also subject to similar international global and economic forces albeit with varying policy results.

### Reconciliation of Work and Family Life: Maternity, Parental, and Family Leave

One of the most far-reaching workplace policies related to gender has been the extension of parental and family leave. Its initial conception as maternity leave enabled mothers to take time off before and after child-birth. In response to increasing female labor-force participation, especially among mothers with young children, and changing norms about work and family, all industrialized countries have moved from some sort of maternity leave to either parental- or family-leave policy. The chapters in this volume examine the least developed Family and Medical Leave Act (FMLA) in the U.S. as well as family leave in Germany. The U.S. and Germany contrast with the model family-leave policies in Sweden, which pioneered parental leave in 1974. As the national cases illustrate, social policy influences paths to and shapes patterns of women's employment, especially the continuity of their participation over the life course (Orloff, 2002).

The policy examples explored by authors in the volume suggest the importance of being cognizant of the extent to which welfare-states promote familialism versus women's employment; that is, the relative extent of defamilization (Orloff, 2002). Defamilizing policies make possible relatively high female employment levels and generate employment by increasing demands for child-care services; public in Scandinavia and France and market based in the U.S. and Canada. In many countries care is provided privately with little development of public services for the care of children, but general support to families with children is high (Germany and Japan). Another way to characterize differences relates to whether care is organized either as a transfer-intensive system as in Germany or as a service-intensive system as in Sweden. Sweden has retained and strengthened universalistic, egalitarian principles despite neoliberal pressures to privatize. Privatization of child care has not abrogated public responsibilities, but rather, "private" child care is "publicly regulated and financed" in Sweden. The Swedish state, despite devolution of responsibility from the national to the municipal level, has spurred growth of high-quality child-care services (Bergqvist and Nyberg, 2001). By contrast, Germany "more readily gives direct financial assistance to those taking on the tasks of child or elder care in the family, rather then investing in an expansion of public social services" (Gottschall and Bird, this volume). To ensure quality and more universal access, Sweden moved preschool from the Ministry of Health and Social Affairs to the Ministry of Education and Science in 1996 (Bergqvist and Nyberg, 2001), whereas Germany has kept child care separate from public education. Japan offers an example of a different mix of private provision with public guidance; relaxation of state control in 1996 freed child care from regulation to encourage the expansion of private for-profit child care (Peng, 2001). The result has been more, but inadequate, child-care facilities and hours unable to accommodate full-time work schedules for both working parents in both Germany and Japan. Sweden represents the case with the most extensive degree of defamilization.

Further, Gornick, Meyers, and Ross distinguish between support for mothers' employment, measured in terms of policies that provide care for young children and allow women to maintain employment continuity (through paid leaves), and general support to families with children. Care for children under three, which is essential for mothers' employment, is less developed outside of Nordic countries and France (see Orloff, 2002). A higher percentage of mothers drop out of the labor force to take care of young children in countries like Germany and Japan that provide general family support. Care has shifted to some extent to institutions other than the families. Yet policies often do not attend to either the quality of care or the quality of care work (in terms of wages and benefits). Care work, especially in the private sector, often pays low wages and is undervalued. The quality of care work is likely to be associated with the quality of care. By focusing specifically on leave policies, a set of chapters in this volume shows how the global and international forces can have both strong effects on policies in some countries (EU) but relatively little on others (U.S.). Further, the focus on leave policy provides a lens to illustrate how such policies reflect social norms and/or perpetuate historical gender imbalances.

## Regulating Sexual Relations in the Workplace and Standards of Equity

Equal opportunity and antidiscrimination policies were "a watershed in the history of welfare-state egalitarianism" (Esping-Andersen, 1999: 43). Studies show that success, implementation, and enforcement of these policies have varied widely at the organizational level (Reese and Lindenberg, 1999) as well as cross-nationally due to differences in legal systems and legal strategies. For example, legislation and enforcement practices of sex equality law are embedded respectively in German labor law in the form of workers' protection laws versus civil rights law in the U.S. (Zippel, this volume). Thus, in the latter, the dynamics of implementation have emphasized individuals' legal redress, individual reporting, and lawsuits that have affirmed employers' responsibilities to prevent sexual harassment by institutionalizing policies and educational programs. In contrast, in the absence of strong antidiscrimination laws in Germany, the implementation of policies against sexual harassment depends on the political will of unions, employers, and emerging state equality offices for women—offices that are often stronger in the public sector (see Gottfried and O'Reilly, 2002). The approaches to sexual harassment mirror the different ways that women's movements have pursued their agendas in the two countries (Young, 1999). U.S. women's groups have relied on the court for extending rights, whereas German women's groups have worked through organized political actors (political parties and unions) to effect change. Thus, the courts have been an important mechanism for social action in the U.S. absent other political vehicles in Germany and other European countries.

Thus, legal systems can significantly affect the implementation of workplace policies as the case of sexual harassment policy illustrates. For example, large settlements either through individual or class-action suits are rare in Germany. The legal arena exerts less pressure on German employers to take action on issues of sexual harassment or discrimination. Class-action suits have been more successful in the U.S. in terms of settlements than in more collectively oriented countries like France or Germany (Mazur, 1995). In Japan, a U.S.-style legal strategy is more evident whereby women's legal advocates bring suits against companies. These widely publicized trials serve a symbolic function to shame companies and the state into addressing sexual harassment rather than seek to win large monetary rewards (Hirakawa, 1998).

Different political opportunity structures have shaped the "access" of women to the state and/or courts, and thus also the priorities and agenda of women's movements, thereby influencing whether sexual harassment law came mainly through changes in case law (U.S.) or by the passage of new laws (Germany). In both the United States and Germany, the federal systems of government have created tensions between state and national regulations. In the United States, some states have enacted more extensive provisions and have experimented with initiatives aimed at paying a portion of family leave, but no state mandates paid leave. Similarly, Lenz notes the more progressive development of Equal Opportunity Law in the federal state of Nordrhein Westfalen, with a long history of progressive politics (this volume).

A rights revolution has spread across the globe, yet the extension of formal equality has not eliminated gender inequality. Feminist research attempts to evaluate the extent to which policies make societies more gender just/equal. However, there isn't a single feminist standard of gender equity or even agreement over what constitutes a women-friendly policy. Women-friendly policies should promote feminist goals and principles of gender justice by breaking down gender-based hierarchies (Mazur, 2002), enhancing women's independence, increasing their capacity to support and sustain an independent household, empowering women, and ending unequal burdens of labor (Orloff, 2002).

Focusing solely on sexual harassment policy, the studies in this volume suggest that both the U.S. and German models are deficient when evaluated against a norm of gender equity. An effective policy aims to protect women's rights to sexual self-determination and nondiscrimination, and interventions should combine both individual and group-based responses and remedies, offer multiple routes and forms of complaints, and provide training that changes gender workplace culture.

It is not possible here to sketch either a blueprint of or a pathway for realizing gender equality. However, the chapters in this volume, among other feminist comparative research, critically evaluate existing policies for transforming asymmetrical gender relations and suggest feminist principles of and strategies for achieving gender equity. The increasingly public gender regime with a dual-earner family has not yet uprooted the female-carer arrangement.

## ORGANIZATION OF THIS VOLUME

Focusing on the central themes just discussed, the chapters in this volume are organized into four sections: theoretical perspectives on gender and workplace policy focusing on global forces, making explicit the implicit gender equity effects of workplace policy, a comparative examination of work/family or wage-earning/caregiving balance, and an examination of approaches to sexual equity in the workplace in the form of sexual harassment policy.

### Theoretical Perspectives on Gender and Workplace Policy

A relatively new area of comparative policy research concerns regionalization and globalization of policy formation and gender politics. The chapters in this section analyze the policy-making process that has developed through extranational institutions and the emergence of feminist transnational networks. Both the European Union and the United Nations appear as determinants of and arenas for successful feminist coalition building and policy making. Regionalization and globalization can be positive forces to the extent that they present new arenas for feminist actors in governments and society to mobilize around effective women-friendly policies.

Walby and Lenz challenge gender-blind globalization theories in their analyses of policy developments for workplace gender equity. In these chapters they argue against the standard view that globalization is principally associated with deregulation. Walby presents evidence suggesting that many of the new employment forms, which have been associated with a new economy, are actually related to regulation or re-regulation of the workplace and that globalization does not necessarily weaken the role of government in bettering workplace policies for women. Thus, the gender lens enables a clearer understanding of the way in which globalization involves not only deregulation, but also re-regulation and how the larger forces of economic and societal globalization can affect the nature and quality of workplace policies. More specifically, Walby shows how EU policies have stimulated changes and, indeed, improvements in women's work policies within the U.K. Pursuing similar themes, Lenz adds to the reconsideration of the globalization process by arguing that it does not inherently spell doom for a consideration of gender issues. Indeed, she highlights aspects of globalization that well suit the abilities of women's organizations to gain and foster influence both at the international level within nations—in these examples, Japan and Germany.

Woodward maps the transmission from various international and supranational institutions and systematically studies gender-mainstreaming policies as they have been translated into national and subnational practices. The case of "gender mainstreaming" illustrates both the transformative promise and pitfalls of state feminism. Implementation of gender mainstreaming varies from locale to locale within countries as well as across countries in the EU.[6] One reason for this is the ambiguity of the language of mainstreaming itself. This ambiguity is evident in the confusion over the meaning of the term and the wide disparity of practices under the same rubric. The language is ambiguous in another sense; mainstreaming is a policy tool that attempts to use the "language of the state against the state." Thus, the ambiguity or paradox leads to the same policy tool being viewed as both an innovation and a deception by different actors and in different places. The scope and scale of gender mainstreaming seems to be broadest where femocrats exercise the "power of definition"; that is, the ability to define what gender mainstreaming means in practical terms. Women's policy machineries are also important to the success of feminist policies. While not all women's policy machineries have the mission of mainstreaming, many of these agencies and femocrats pursue effective mainstreaming practices.

Woodward's cautionary tale suggests that gender mainstreaming as an instrument and a discourse can either promote gender equality or serve as window dressing. As a consequence, equal opportunity offices should not be abandoned but rather supplemented by this new policy toolkit. Gender mainstreaming has both innovative and deceptive potentials depending on the success of gender politics, and the issue of nomenclature or "naming" has important policy implications at both a symbolic and practical level. The language of debate about the appropriate policy frame for gender and workplace policies carries embedded implications for policy outcomes.

### The Implications of Gender in the Workplace: Making the Implicit Explicit

Several chapters in this volume very clearly illustrate that approaches to workplace policies can have unequal gendered effects even when that is not the intent of the policy. Indeed, there are many forces not explicitly related to gender issues that can affect the playing field for men and women in the workplace, and indeed often work to the detriment of women's job opportunities and/or their ability to balance work and family. The chapter by Gottfried and O'Reilly situates the comparison of workplace policies in Germany and Japan within the feminist comparative tradition. In doing so the authors show how state policies can serve to sustain the male-breadwinner model even though that is not the publicly stated or even intended purpose of the policies. Many seemingly gender-neutral policies regarding taxes and social security continue to embed the legacy of the male-breadwinner model. Working-time policies, particularly important given the high incidence of maternal part-time employment, have not uprooted familialist biases in policy inherent to socially conservative welfare-states. The analysis documents recent reforms aimed at harmonizing work and family in the context of demographic and economic pressures. It is too soon to assess the impact of this accumulation and acceleration of gender policy making but their analysis strongly suggests that a careful assessment of the often hidden gender implications of workplace and other social policies is critical for a complete understanding of potentially unequal gender effects.

In a similar vein, Hassett illuminates the societal, governmental, and historical forces that, while not appearing to be explicitly gendered, nevertheless serve to limit the number of women managing cities in the United States. Limited representation of women in city management positions is not without important implications, both for local governance and for the local public policies that result. The chapter has broader implications in that it shows how the glass ceilings in many work organizations are the result of the complex interaction of the culture of organizations, the perceived "differentness" of women, and even the perceptions of what it means when women exercise or use gender-based policy protections such as those dealing with sexual harassment. The lessons about how government structure, historical political relationships in communities, and social views on breadwinning and caretaking impact women's representation in high-level public management are ones that can be applied to settings beyond the U.S. public-sector workplace.

On the other hand, Berggren's analysis of the male-breadwinner model in the United States suggests that some progress is being made in bringing the reality of gender and work more in line with feminist policy and that the sometimes hidden gender implications of workplace policies are becoming more explicitly integrated into public debates. Over time it appears that the benefit structures of some male- and female-typed occupations are becoming more similar with respect to generalized insurance and health and vacation benefits. Women in professions such as nursing receive benefits in line with skilled blue-collar workers such as mechanics. Nurses have a high level of organization in unions or professional associations and have experienced labor shortages, which may account for the generous benefits and relatively high wages. However, it also appears that several critical health benefits—hospitalization, surgical, and catastrophic medical—in "female professions" remain lower, thus perpetuating one significant barrier to an effective shift from male to universal breadwinning. Despite this area of inequity, the language and dialogue about workplace policies at the national level in the United States appear to have become more sensitive to gender issues over time. This suggests some progress in making the implicit explicit, although the persistence of explicitly "male" and "female" language suggests that policy debates, at least in the United States, still have a long way to go.

## Addressing the Tension between Wage Earner versus Caregiver

In her comprehensive and up-to-date review of parental-leave policies, Haas compares the fifteen EU countries in terms of key policy features, including the length of leave, payment, flexibility, and incentives for fathers. Five clusters of countries range from traditional to egalitarian based on the extent that each parental-leave policy helps mothers combine work demands and family responsibilities. Parental-leave and maternity programs play an important role in allowing women to take up employment on more equitable terms by guaranteeing income security when they must attend to caregiving. In countries where leave provisions are generous but other employment supports are not well developed, leave may reinforce traditional division of labor and women's nonemployment (Germany, Italy). A major shift in policy debates among EU nations discussed by Haas has been the recognition of the need for incentives to encourage fathers' participation in caring labor. Sweden comes closest to an egalitarian society in that policies effectively provide male employees incentives to share in the care of young children. In Sweden the nontransferable entitlement to fathers has not only significantly increased men's use of the benefit, but also has positively affected their time at work. The persistence of sex-based occupational segregation not only indicates trouble in Swedish feminist paradise, but also points to the deeply entrenched gendered power relations resistant to policy innovation from above.

Wisensale's chapter on the history of the FMLA implies that the United States is an outlier when compared to other industrialized nations. The timing of the regulation in the United States lagged behind other countries, although debate over leave began much earlier, in 1984. It was the 1987 U.S. Supreme Court case *California Federal Savings and Loan (Cal Fed) v. Guerra* that brought to light inconsistent provisions between, and minimal coverage of, state and federal laws. At issue was the conflict between many state-law requirements that pregnant employees be treated in a special manner and the federal mandate that they be treated the same as other workers. When the U.S. Supreme Court upheld California's maternity law providing for special benefits to pregnant workers, feminists directed their attention to arguments both for and against special treatment and the framing of pregnancy as a disability. The FMLA is both a continuation and a departure from earlier laws: it is a continuation as an individual-based entitlement, but it is a departure in providing a federal standard, albeit with significant exemptions, for family-based leave. The policy differs from other countries, not only in the lack of remuneration, but also by combining leave for child and elderly care. Further, the case highlights the impact of the U.S. federal system on the implementation of workplace policy that allows for significant variation among states in the quality and content of family-leave regulations. Adding another consideration not explicitly addressed in the chapters on EU leave policies, Wisensale provides a specific focus on the need for and impacts of policy on the increasing reality that workers—particularly female workers—must balance work and elder care in addition to child care. With an aging U.S. population, the need for working women to also provide care for elderly relatives will become a more pressing public-policy issue and one that current legislation is not well adapted to address.

In a companion chapter, Trzcinski provides a history and assessment of Canadian workplace policies focusing specifically on a variety of leave programs—maternity, parental, and sickness—and highlights comparison with U.S. approaches. In addition to providing a window on the Canadian policy approach to balancing breadwinning and caregiving, this chapter also specifically addresses the balance in cost between public and private wage replacement programs and allays concerns that governmental wage replacement programs will be used to the exclusion of private programs with large attendant societal costs. Instead, it appears that privately financed programs are preferred. Still it appears clear that market responses are not sufficient to meet needs and/or demands for leave. Thus, even the more generous leave policies in Canada do not fully address the needs of female workers to create an optimal work/family balance.

Gottschall and Bird offer an innovative contribution to welfare-state theory by combining life-course and labor-market approaches to better understand how policies affect the patterns of women's labor-force participation and the gendered division of labor. The public-education and dual-vocational-training systems that are unique to Germany are important background conditions. The former because of the short hours and lack of after-care programs and the latter because of the gender bias in training toward men in manufacturing and devaluation of traditional women's work in the service sector. Through empirical analysis, the authors construct motherhood cohorts based on the birth of the first child in order to determine the impact of the four important policy reforms (mother allowance, maternity leave, family leave, and parental leave) on women's work choices and chances in Germany. The progression from mother allowance to family leave has had the effect of shoring up the male-breadwinner, female-carer model despite the diversification of family forms and increased female labor-force participation. Essentially, leave regulations have standardized a "baby break" among women. Thus, the findings are contrary to the standard employment relation and corresponding labor-market theory, which never fully addressed women's labor-force positions and participation. Policy has likewise tended to address issues that affect men in core manufacturing sectors. Further, Gottschall and Bird's analysis indicates a strong path dependency to the development of regulation and, perhaps more critically, shows how changes in workplace policy can directly impact, for good or ill, leave-taking behaviors on the part of female employees.

Finally, the chapter by Roberts provides an assessment of policies to balance work and family in Japan providing a case where entrenched social values clearly run counter to the application and use of leave policies and flexible work arrangements. A variety of dynamics are converging in Japan that portend changes in work/life balance, particularly for women. Educated, younger women are putting off marriage and the government is becoming increasingly concerned about declining birthrates, giving rise to various legislative initiatives to create "gender-equal" workplaces. Despite these trends, the societal value placed on corporate men supported by stay-at-home wives renders real change slow and marginal at best. It remains to be seen whether the globalization processes facilitating greater women's group pressure described by Lenz (this volume) will facilitate societal support for more substantive gender equality in Japan.

### Specific Applications of Workplace Policies: Gender Equity in the Workplace

The chapters in this section provide an examination of the application of a different set of workplace policies than those described above regarding the work/family balance, specifically focusing on gender equality and sexual harassment policies. Sexual harassment policies represent a uniquely problematic aspect of gender relations in the workplace because they operate at the intersection of public and private or social and workplace norms. Further, they are embedded in the most problematic of gendered relationships—sex. Germany and the United States provide an interesting comparison in approaches to workplace sexual harassment policies.

In a broader sense, the application of gender equity policies in the German military provides a focus on how the goal of gender justice is applied in a very particular type of workplace setting. The chapter by Liebert provides a bridge between the forces of globalization, gender dynamics, and workplace policies in the EU and the quest for policies that increase gender equity in actual workplaces. She describes the role of the EU court and the German state in applying equal gender opportunities in the German military. Unlike the case of Japan, here the EU court appeared to be a catalyst for gender equality processes already fermenting within the German state. Rapid and apparently full compliance with court directives within Germany suggests that both the government and social system were ready for such changes. This chapter then focuses on the application of policy to ensure gender justice or equality in the workplace through the means of equal access to jobs. The next two chapters focus on approaches to achieving gender justice by ensuring a harassment-free workplace once women are employed.

In an explicitly comparative approach, the chapter by Zippel provides the theoretical or conceptual underpinnings of sexual harassment policy in the two nations. The German definition of sexual harassment as mobbing redefines the issues in gender-neutral terms focusing on fairness and respect for all workers and favoring work-group or organizational cultural solutions to harassment. Because the approach in the United States is legally and individually based, the focus is on individual behaviors, formal reporting, and often adversarial investigations, and ultimately punitive solutions. Zippel suggests an alternative approach to sexual harassment that would combine the advantages of the U.S. and German models in an effort to set a conceptual framework for sexual harassment policy that might ultimately deal with both organizational and individual behaviors and cultures.

The chapter by Reese and Lindenberg more explicitly focuses on sexual harassment policies as they are applied and implemented in actual public-sector workplaces. The authors find that, regardless of the model employed (either individual or organizational approaches), sexual harassment policies tend to be infrequently used, are widely disliked by employees, and represent implementation nightmares for organizations. The study asks what kind of sexual harassment policies would employees willingly use and which would actually reduce sexual harassment. A survey of public-sector employees provides answers to these questions. The findings highlight the importance of organizational climate, the role of supervisors, and the necessity of training and education in developing and implementing effective sexual harassment policies.

## SUMMARY

The chapters say much about the central themes addressed in this volume—comparative approaches to understanding gender and work, using feminist analysis in comparative perspective, the current state of social-care and gender equity policies in the countries studied. They ultimately provide lessons for understanding gender and work and policy alternatives that can be applied to many national settings but are particularly interesting for scholars and policy makers in the United States, where debates often appear to take place in isolation from the experience of even other "developed" or "Westernized" countries.

By using a contextualized comparative approach, the studies compiled in this volume provide in-depth descriptions of the policy-making process in particular countries over time and help to assess the relative weight of global, national, and subnational forces in explaining the presence or absence of particular policies. When read side by side, the case examples here indicate both convergence and divergence with regard to policy sets across countries. Clearly, there is a general tendency toward path dependency, indicating the resilience of the nation-state and national institutions in shaping the policy process. The attention to historically specific contexts helps gauge why some policies are more resistant or open to negotiation, compromise, and change.

Yet, regional and global institutions and organizations increasingly appear as arenas for, and exert influence on, policy formation at the national and subnational levels. Several of the case studies provide strong evidence for arguing that feminist movements influence policy making through the election of feminist representatives (femocrats), lobbying efforts, and the shaping of political discourse. Transnational feminist networks also are found to affect the success of women-friendly policy making; for example, gender mainstreaming developed in the context of international conferences was diffused through NGOs before national and local governments took up the issue. This finding has particular relevance for theories of the state, which have neglected the role of women's mobilization on the making and unmaking of policy. It provides a corrective to influential state-centered arguments. Theories of the Japanese developmental state focused on how bureaucratic-led policy making operates with minimal transparency and narrow input. These accounts failed to take account of femocrats in the Diet and in the Ministries, along with women's organizations, initiating gender policies and shaping the direction of reforms (Gelb, 2003; Osawa, 2003). As Lenz suggests, transnational feminist networks were a potent force for the adoption and reform of equal opportunity laws and for the passage of the Basic Law for a Gender-Equal Society in Japan.[7]

A new emphasis on social care and the need for workers of both genders to balance family and work life is evident in chapters reviewing the proliferation of policies on child care, elder care, and leave schemes. An edited volume published by the International Labor Organization frames care as a human right and as a basic human need to compel policy makers to consider both care receivers and caregivers (Daly and Standing, 2001: 2–4). As the comparisons highlight, the relative roles of the state, the market, the family, and "civil society" networks (Daly and Standing, 2001: 3) shift the boundaries between public and private responsibility over time and vary across countries. All the countries discussed have pursued care policies, but few have either "promoted the capacity of men and women to engage in and share it" or addressed the quality of care work (Daly and Standing, 2001: 10). Who will provide care and under what conditions will depend on the outcome of future political negotiations, economic pressures, and possibly the recognition of substantive benefits—to both workplace and home—of creating and implementing policies that facilitate the caring and working balance.

While the comparisons in this volume are instructive for scholars across countries, they highlight some particular lessons for the United States. First, it is clear that market solutions have prevailed over social benefits in the United States to a greater extent than in most of the other nations examined. The U.S. state provides income transfers to poor women in need of child care but does not support the building of new child-care centers. For-profit childcare tends to yield a continuum of care services in accord with consumers' ability to pay, leading, in many cases, to low-quality care for those without the means to pay and low wages to child-care workers. The FMLA, while a step forward, does not offer income replacement for parents to care for children and dependent adults. One small step was taken by the California state legislature in provision of paid leave, yet the lack of remuneration elsewhere prevents many men and women from taking leave and burdens men and women with fewer resources to cushion time off for the purpose of caregiving. The corollary of this market dynamic is seen in the individualistic and legalistic approach to sexual-harassment policy, tending to shift the focus from organizational and work-group norms and thus minimizing the capacity of the workplace as a vehicle for gender justice. Finally, the research from Canada and the EU indicating substantial productivity and cost reduction benefits to firms from more comprehensive and less market-driven caregiving policies as well as the minimal burden placed on the private sector should provide fodder for political and social debate within the United States, over the FMLA as well as other social-care policies.

## DIRECTIONS FOR FUTURE RESEARCH

While there may be heuristic value in differentiating between policy types, this book shows that the analysis of gender policy should be drawn broadly and not ghettoized. Simply put, while it is clear that there are gendered effects of sexual harassment, family-leave, and child- and elder-care policies, there are gender justice implications to a broad range of policies beyond those that are often characterized as "women's issues." Workplace policies encompass areas directly and indirectly affecting both men's and women's conditions of work, and policies that impact work-life quality for both men and women do not exist solely within the realm of "workplace policy." These broader connections should be the focus of future research extending the effort begun in the chapters here to make explicit the often implicit gender effects of a spectrum of public policies.

For example, the political backlash against policies like affirmative action, particularly in the United States, has significant potential effects on gender as well as racial balance in the workplace and may also affect how other gender-related policies are interpreted in social science. These issues need to be explored to examine how race, gender, and workplace equity are connected both socially and politically, although those connections may not be clear in public discourse. Along the same lines, there are a number of other feminist-inspired issues such as domestic violence and reproductive rights (abortion, access to contraceptives, family planning, the side effects of contraceptives) that have significant impacts on women and their ability to work. Research should make these impacts more explicit. Comparative policy analysis of seemingly gender-neutral workplace policies such as the minimum wage and tax policies would be well served by "mainstreaming" gender into the analysis of alternative policy options and attendant policy outcomes. Such policies often affect women more than men because of gender-based hierarchies and the concentration of women in low-wage jobs. These types of policies, while not explicitly tied to gender, have differential effects on male and female workers and without a consideration of such effects policy research will be missing important potential externalities, opportunity costs, and inequities in impact and outcome.

Finally, research is needed on enforcement of and compliance with public policies. As many of the chapters make clear, merely having national or even local policies to address gender equity and work/family balance does not mean that policies are fully implemented or implemented in a meaningful way. Research should not stop at the adoption or even the substance of policy—implementation is also a critical factor.

A compelling cultural turn in state theory reminds theorists not to take for granted any key concepts. Adams and Padamsee (2001: 16) argue contra Esping-Andersen that policies "both reach beyond and operate within recognized national and local state boundaries, and . . . even contribute to creating our perceptions of those boundaries—our ideas, for example, of what counts as 'public' and 'private.'" One important direction for feminist comparative policy research involves reading for the gender subtexts by examining the language of policy to ascertain the construction of women as mothers and/or workers, as either individuals or dependents. The chapters in the volume serve as a critical beginning and set a coherent context for future comparative efforts.

## NOTES

1. Feminists have established transnational infrastructures for doing research, linking individual efforts, building institutional bridges cross-nationally, and creating virtual research communities. Such affiliative mechanisms foster dialogue among scholars in distant localities and provide the context for intellectual exchange. Transnational

research networks compose interpretive communities well suited to carry out comparative and transnational research. The process of globalization provides opportunities and technologies for the establishment of transnational networks. International conferences and computer technologies push the frontiers of networks by intensifying interactions at the local level and enabling sustained connections by the Internet.

2. Australian feminists coined the term "femocrats" to describe feminist state bureaucrats who work in women's policy offices and who advocate gender equality policies (Stetson and Mazur 1995, 10; Mazur 2001, 4).

3. Barbara Stallings made this distinction during a workshop on the third case sponsored by the Social Science Research Council in cooperation with the Japan Foundation, 1999.

4. Globalization affects a growing number of chains of economic, social, cultural, and political activity that are worldwide in scope and promotes an intensification of levels of interaction and interconnectedness between states and societies (Amin, 1997: 129).

5. A recent study of the Parental Leave Directive, the first collective agreement adopted by the European Commission, found that many member states' standards surpassed the minimum requirements. The detailed study of the process and impact of the directive on member states rejects arguments correlating misfit with adaptations and demonstrates the importance of national contextual variables (e.g., interest-group pressures, administrative capabilities, party politics, issue linkage, and gold-plating) (Falkner et al., 2002).

6. At the first meeting of the newly formed Employment, Social Policy, Health, and Consumer Affairs Council, ministers took up the issues of gender mainstreaming in relationship to social exclusion issues (Employment and Social Affairs, 2002).

7. Gelb (2003) aptly uses the term *kansetsu gaiatsu* to describe the influence of external norms and movements on gender policy making in Japan.

## REFERENCES

Adams, Julia, and Tasleem Padamsee. 2001. "Signs and Regimes: Rereading Feminist Work on Welfare States." *Social Politics* 8, no. 1: 1–23.

Bergqvist, Christina. 2001. "Gender (In)equality and the Transition of Swedish Corporatism." Paper presented at the ECPR Conference, Canterbury, September.

Bergqvist, Christina, and Anita Nyberg. 2001. "Alive and Fairly Well: Welfare State Restructuring and Child Care in Sweden." In *Child Care and Welfare State Restructuring: Gender and Entitlement at Crossroads*, ed. Rianne Mahon and Sonya Michel. New York: Routledge.

Crouch, Colin, and Wolfgang Streeck. 1997. *Political Economy of Modern Capitalism: Mapping Convergence and Diversity*. London: Sage.

Daly, Mary, ed. 2001. *Care Work: The Quest for Security*. Geneva: ILO.

———. 2002. "Care as a Good for Social Policy." *International Social Policy* 31, no. 2: 251–70.

Daly, Mary, and Guy Standing. 2001. "Introduction." In *Care Work: The Quest for Security*, ed. Mary Daly. Geneva: International Labor Organization.

Daly, Mary, and Jane Lewis. 2000. "The Concept of Social Care and the Analysis of Contemporary Welfare States." *British Journal of Sociology* 52, no. 2: 281–98.

Employment and Social Affairs. 2002. "Employment, Social Policy, Health and Consumer Affairs Council Meets in Luxemburg." At http://Europa.eu.in.

Esping-Andersen, Gosta. 1990. *The Three Worlds of Welfare Capitalism*. Cambridge, U.K.: Polity.

———. 1999. *Social Foundations of Postindustrial Economies*. Oxford: Oxford University Press.

Fagan, Colette, and Jacqueline O'Reilly. 1998. "Conceptualizing Part-Time Work: The Value of an Integrated Comparative Perspective." In *Part-Time Prospects: An International Comparison of Part-Time Work in Europe, North America, and the Pacific Rim*, ed. Jacqueline O'Reilly and Colette Fagan. London: Routledge.

Falker, Gerda, Miriam Hartlapp, Simone Leiber, and Oliver Treib. 2002. "Transforming Social Policy in Europe? The EC's Parental Leave Directive and Misfit in the 15 Member States." MPIfG Working Paper 02/11, October.

Fraser, Nancy. 1997. *Justice Interruptus: Critical Reflections on the "Postsocialist" Condition*. London: Routledge.

Gelb, Joyce. 2003. *Gender Policies in Japan and the United States: Comparing Women's Movements, Rights, and Politics*. New York: Palgrave.

Gottfried, Heidi. 1998. "Beyond Patriarchy? Theorising Gender and Class." *Sociology: Journal of the British Sociological Association* 32, no. 3: 451–68.

———. 2000. "Compromising Positions: Emergent Neo-Fordisms and Embedded Gender Contracts." *The British Journal of Sociology* 52, no. 2: 235–59.

Gottfried, Heidi, and Jacqueline O'Reilly. 2002. "Re-regulating Breadwinner Models in Socially Conservative Welfare Regimes: Comparing Germany and Japan." *Social Politics* 9, no. 1: 29–59.

Grauerholz, Elizabeth, Heidi Gottfried, Cynthia Stohl, and Nancy Gabin. 1999. "There's Safety in Numbers: Creating a Campus Advisers' Network to Help Complainants of Sexual Harassment *and* Complaint-Receivers." *Violence Against Women* 5, no. 80: 950–77.

Hirakawa, Hiroko. 1998. "Inverted Orientalism and the Discursive Construction of Sexual Harassment: A Study of Mass Media and Feminist Representations of Sexual Harassment in Japan." Ph.D. dissertation, Purdue University.

Hoskyns, Catherine. 2001. "Gender Politics in the European Union: The Context for Job Training." In *State Feminism, Women's Movements, and Job Training: Making Democracies Work in a Global Economy*, ed. Amy Mazur. Routledge: New York.

Kahn, Peggy, and Elizabeth Meehan, eds. 1992. *Equal Value/Comparable Worth in the UK and the USA*. New York: St. Martin's Press.

Kitschelt, Herbert, Peter Lange, Gary Marks, and John D. Stephens. 1999. *Continuity and Change in Contemporary Capitalism*. Cambridge: Cambridge University Press.

Korpi, Walter. 2000. "Faces of Inequality: Gender, Class and Patterns of Inequalities in Different Types of Welfare States." *Social Politics* 7, no. 2: 127–91.

Lenz, Ilse. 1999. "Globalization and the Formation of Semi-Publics." Paper read at international Conference on Rationalization, Organization, and Gender Proceedings. Sozialforschungsstelle Dortmund.

Lewis, Jane. 1992. "Gender and the Development of Welfare Regimes." *Journal of European Social Policy* 2: 159–73.

———. 2001. "The Decline of the Male Breadwinner Model: Implications for Work and Care." *Social Politics* 8, no. 2: 152–69.

Liebert, Ulrike. 2000. "Europeanizing the Military: The ECJ as a Catalyst in the Transformation of the Bundeswehr." Paper prepared for Joint Workshop on Europeanization in Transatlantic Perspective, Institute for European Studies, Cornell University and Jean Monnet Centre for European Studies, University of Bremen, Bremen.

Locke, Richard, and Kathleen Thelen. 1995. "Apples and Oranges Revisited: Contextualized Comparisons and the Study of Comparative Labor Politics." *Politics and Society* 23, no. 3: 337–67.

Katzenstein, Peter. 1999. "Regional States: Japan and Asia, Germany in Europe." Paper prepared for Germany and Japan: The Future of Nationally Embedded Capitalism in a Global Economy, Max-Planck Institute, Cologne, Germany, June.

Mazur, Amy. 1995. *Gender Bias and the State: Symbolic Reform at Work in Fifth Republic France*. Pittsburgh, Pa.: University of Pittsburgh Press.

———. 2001. "Introduction." In *State Feminism, Women's Movements, and Job Training: Making Democracies Work in a Global Economy*, ed. Amy Mazur. New York: Routledge.

———. 2002. *Theorizing Feminist Policy*. Oxford: Oxford University Press.

Michel, Sonya, and Rianne Mahon. 2002. *Child Care Policy at the Crossroads: Gender and Welfare State Restructuring*. New York: Routledge.

Mutari, Ellen, and Deborah Figart. 2001. "Europe at a Crossroads: Harmonization, Liberalization, and the Gender of Work Time." *Social Politics* 8, no. 1: 36–64.

O'Connor, Julia, Ann Shola Orloff, and Sheila Shaver. 1999. *States, Markets, Families: Gender, Liberalism and Social Policy in Australia, Canada, Great Britain, and the United States*. Cambridge: Cambridge University Press.

Orloff, Ann Shola. 2002. "Gender Equality, Women's Employment: Cross-National Patterns of Policy and Politics." Paper prepared for Workshop on Welfare, Work, and Family: Southern Europe in Comparative Perspective. European University Institute.

Osawa, Mari. 2003. "Japanese Government Approaches to Gender Equality Since the Mid-1990s." Working Paper Series, Wayne State University.

Ostner, Ilona, and Jane Lewis. 1995. "Gender and the Evolution of European Social Policies." In *European Social Policy: Between Fragmentation and Integration*, ed. Stephen Leibfried and Paul Pierson. Washington, D.C.: The Brookings Institution.

Pempel, T.J. 1998. *Regime Shift: Comparative Dynamics of Japanese Political Economy*. Ithaca, N.Y.: Cornell University Press.

Peng, Ito. 2001. "Gender and Generation: Japanese Child Care and the Demographic Crisis." In *Child Care and Welfare State Restructuring: Gender and Entitlement at Crossroads*, ed. Rianne Mahon and Sonya Michel. New York: Routledge.

Pierson, Paul, and Stephan Leibfried. 1995. "Multi-tiered Institutions and the Making of Social Policy." In *European Social Policy: Between Fragmentation and Integration*, ed. Stephan Leibfried and Paul Pierson. Washington, D.C.: The Brookings Institution.

Reese, Laura, and Karen Lindenberg. 1999. *Sexual Harassment Implementation in the Public Sector Workplace*. Thousand Oaks, Calif.: Sage Publications.

Sainsbury, Diane. 1999. *Gender Regimes and Welfare States*. Oxford: Oxford University Press.

Sassen, Saskia. 1996. "Toward a Feminist Analytics of the Global Economy." *Indiana Journal of Global Legal Studies* 4, no. 1: 7–41.

Stetson, Dorothy McBride, and Amy Mazur. 1995. "Introduction." In *Comparative State Feminism*, ed. Dorothy McBride Stetson and Amy Mazur. Thousand Oaks, Calif.: Sage.

Streeck, Wolfgang. 1998. "The Internationalization of Industrial Relations in Europe: Prospects and Problems." *Politics and Society* 26, no. 4: 229–459.

Thelen, Kathleen. 1999. "Historical Institutionalism in Comparative Politics." *Annual Review of Political Science* 2: 369–404.

Walby, Sylvia. 1999. "The New Regulatory State: The Social Powers of the European Union." *British Journal of Sociology* 50, no. 1: 118–40.

Young, Brigitte. 1999. *Triumph of the Fatherland*. Ann Arbor: University of Michigan Press.

# I

## THEORETICAL PERSPECTIVES ON GENDER AND WORKPLACE POLICY

# 1

# Globalization, Gender, and Work: Perspectives on Global Regulation

*Ilse Lenz*

## GLOBALIZATION AND COMPLEX INEQUALITIES

Globalization processes interrelate with gender in various and contradictory ways. On the one hand, they contribute to the erosion of national hegemonic gender orders. Thus, they are part of the social transformations, which may open futures for new gender contracts. On the other hand, they are forming in the context of deep historical inequality. As they originate in the context of the capitalist and patriarchal world system (Wallerstein, 1975; Leacock, 1981), they are prestructured by long-term power relationships between the North and South, dominant men and women, workers and subordinated ethnicized and racialized groups. This inequality is indicative of the access to new chances and risks in the context of globalization. To be a player in the global game requires considerable material resources (i.e., financial assets, organizational efficiency, and information) and adequate personal capacities.

Globalization processes are shaped by power games under circumstances in which women as well as other subordinated groups have fewer resources and less power. But I will argue that existing power relations do not automatically determine the result of these processes in ways "globalization determinists" seem to assume. Neither does globalization lead to prosperity for all, as the neoliberal proponents have advocated, nor does it simply intensify capitalist rule over the Third World, workers, women, and nature as some critical authors have argued. Rather, I conceptualize globalization processes as contradictory and potentially open to the formulation of strategies leading toward gender equality.

In the following I propose a working definition of globalization in order to substantiate this approach. Then I link its elements to the options of diverse

29

actors such as feminist networks, supranational and state institutions, and en-terprises. In conclusion, I seek to illustrate the argument by looking at processes of feminist regulations that were negotiated by women's move-ments that relate global influences to the state level.

## A WORKING DEFINITION OF GLOBALIZATION

Novel sociological approaches have broadened the narrow economic focus of the first rounds of debates on globalization. Without neglecting the crucial role of the globalizing economy, they highlight the new quality of interde-pendence on a global scale (Giddens, 2001: 59), opening new options as well as risks. Giddens considers globalization as a "two-way flow of images, information and influences. . . . A 'decentred' and reflexive process charac-terized by links and cultural flows which work in a multidirectional way" and as "the product of numerous intertwined networks" (Giddens, 2001: 59–60). These new forms of information and interdependence result in reconfigura-tions of time and space, transcending the order of the nation-state, thus lead-ing to transformations in which "established boundaries between 'internal' and 'external,' 'international' and 'domestic'" are breaking down (Ibid.).

Information technology and network organizations are also highlighted in Urry's "mobile society" (2000). Urry proposes a broad concept of scapes and flows: "Scapes are the networks of machines, technologies, organizations, texts and actors that constitute various interconnected nodes along which flows can be relayed" (Urry, 2000: 193). Scapes can be understood as techno-organizational networks because they connote "inhuman hybrids," but Urry cautions against "conceptions of agency that specifically focus upon the ca-pacities of humans to attribute meanings to a sense or to follow a social rule" (Urry 2000: 194). These notions are fleshed out by references to multina-tional enterprises such as American Express, McDonald's, or Sony, which "are organized on the basis of a global network of technologies, skills, texts and brands" (Ibid.).

A marked structural perspective underlies this focus on information technologies/networks and flexible and effective organizations. In these ap-proaches, globalization appears "as a dynamic and open process that is sub-ject to influence and change" (Giddens, 2001: 59) and the crucial factors are information and communication as well as flexible network organizations. In their working definition, therefore, globalization is conceptualized as open-ing new horizons of options and also of risks by the creation and appropri-ation of information and communication in the context of global space and "timeless time" as well as by the effective utilization by flexible network or-ganizations. But from a gender perspective, information-based concepts should be related to *embodied subjects*. Persons with minds, emotions, and bodies will want and need to live, work, and reproduce in the context of globalization. Furthermore, they need to be historicized in relationship to the long-term contradictory dynamics of internationalization, which has been going on since the fifteenth century.

In the following, I want to propose a working definition of globalization integrating the economic, political, and informational aspects of globalization. This is a highly risky venture on account of the immense range of publications and debates on this topic. The classical approach of critical theory is still valuable and emphasizes three epistemological dimensions of definitions in social theory: (1) They should encompass a system and its elements in a holistic way; (2) They should be grounded in a historical perspective of contradictory, dialectical developments; and (3) They should be dynamic in looking at changes and factors of change in contradictory human practice (Adorno, 1969).

Thus, globalization is a qualitatively new stage in a long, ongoing process of the development of the capitalist world system, which was promoted by Western modernization and colonialism. Whereas Western states colonized large parts of the world, they also transformed internally into modern neopatriarchal nation-states. The anticolonial and socialist liberation movements then also formed nation-states and thus contributed to a pervasive diffusion of the nation-state. The "nationalization of the world" into national states formed the other side of internationalization. Whereas internationalization has been proceeding since the sixteenth century, globalization seems an adequate term for a new quality of interdependence in a hierarchical unequal postcolonial world system. Following this hypothesis, unilateral dominance is being replaced by interdependent inequalities.

Also, it is important to see globalization not so much as a new structure but rather as a *set of interlinked, often contradictory, and open processes*. The debate on global governance suggests, contrary to the structural prognosis, that global fields are emerging that are prestructured by power relationships, but still relevant for agency (Held, 1999). Especially in the context of gender, we also observe new global processes and frameworks relevant for developing institutions and regulations. Whereas globalization is crossing and reorganizing boundaries formerly set by nation-states, the basic differentiation between the fields of economy, politics, and culture, which is characteristic of modernity, has been maintained with modifications. As globalization processes induce increasing economic and political interdependence and create new spaces of cultural and informational exchange, these fields are extending from the global to the national and local spaces. Globalization processes are changing the following four fields of action and imply increasing interdependence.

1. Politics: growing international political interdependence.
2. Economics: growing economic interdependence.
3. Information, communication, and mobility: increasing information and communication by new and old media and by personal mobility (migration, tourism, scientific exchange/conferences).
4. Ecology: ecological interdependence with new risks and chances.

The first three of these global fields of action[1] will be briefly discussed now from a gender perspective: In the political field, the importance of supranational global or subregional organizations—like the United Nations (UN) or the European Union (EU)—has grown. The UN Decade for Women has been fundamental in creating a global gender-policy arena. At its Fourth World Conference, gender mainstreaming was recognized as a basic strategy for equality. Gender mainstreaming attempts to change the functioning of organizations and institutions towards equality based on the image of gender-free organizations based on two propositions. First, women have an equal participation in decision making at every level, including the top level. Further, *all* strategies and measures of the organization should be evaluated for their impact on gender relations (not only those stereotyped as concerning women, like child care, etc.), thus aiming at policies promoting gender justice.

The EU is becoming very crucial for gender policy in member states. For example, about 60 to 70 percent of political decisions relevant in Germany are predicated on or influenced at the EU level. Another reason is the prominent integration of gender equality and gender mainstreaming in the 1997 Amsterdam treaty and its transfer into some national legislation. Whereas the nation-state is changing its functions, it is by no means evaporating. The regional and local levels of decision making are becoming more important. The region in particular turns into a space of negotiation and intersection while global enterprises and regional strategies attempt to build clusters of economic innovation, science and technology transfer, and human-capital development. While competitive regions develop clusters of high-tech industries, science and technology institutions, in order to attract multinational investors, also seem to demand "flexible personalities" irrespective of care relationships who can adapt to changing demands (and who also employ a mostly migrant serving class). The competition of regions enhances regional disparities.

Political globalization is marked by a dual democracy deficit: accountability and representation become diffuse or nonexistent in view of nonelected supranational political decision-making organizations. The gender democracy deficit is also dramatic as women are pervasively marginalized or excluded from formal leadership positions. In the UN, women in leadership positions were nearly nonexistent in the 1960s and accounted for 13 percent in 1995. Women's membership in the European Parliament grew from 16.1 percent (1979) to about 30 percent in 2000 (Lenz, 2001a).

Economic globalization has been at the center of debate. One important aspect is the anonymous power of dynamic financial markets. Another crucial development is the ascendancy of transnational corporations (TNCs) as powerful visible global actors. Their number has increased tenfold from about 7,000 in 1969 to about 60,000, with 800,000 affiliates abroad, in the year 2000 (UNCTAD, 2001: 1; Lenz, 2000: 28). Ninety of the largest 100 TNCs are headquartered in the Northern Triad of the United States, the European Union, and Japan. The top ten TNCs from developing countries originate mainly from east Asia[2] (UNCTAD, 2001: 7). In 1999, the world's largest TNCs employed an estimated 5.82 million persons (UNCTAD, 2001: 6). But in spite of the large number, it should be kept in mind that it is small compared to the labor force in OECD countries, which was an estimated 372 million in 1995, and in east Asia and the Pacific (an estimated 963 million) (Filmer, 1995: 18). Also, many dynamic TNCs are much smaller.

The quantitative impact of transnational employment appears less important than the qualitative effects, especially the increment of TNCs' power due to their global organizational capacities and their contribution to modernized gender segregation.

1. The globalization of labor markets by the TNCs has led mainly to an intensification of segregation (Lenz, 2002; Anker, 1998). As Anker demonstrated in his pioneering study, management is predominantly male (more than 80 percent) nearly all over the world[3] and foremen/supervisors globally have a male share of at least 90 percent (Anker, 1998: 263, 274–76).[4] In many TNC offshore industries, segregation is rigid with young women working at unskilled jobs without chances of training or advancement. On the other hand, many large TNCs have adopted affirmative action or diversity schemes to mobilize and effectively utilize a transnational workforce, including skilled women in middle management.
2. A marked global trend is the flexibilization of the labor force, especially among women, but in some regions slowly spreading to men. Part-time work, self-employment, or new forms of contract or registered work have been increasing, involving less skilled as well as skilled women.[5]

Thus, the impact of TNCs on gendered labor markets has been contradictory and differentiating. Large-scale segregation and sex stereotyping has characterized offshore production in the South and parts of the East, while a modernization of gender roles can be observed in the middle ranges of management and skilled work especially in more qualified portions of the service and knowledge sector. Flexibilization affected women initially, but it is proceeding to men as well (Lenz, 2002).

The general impact of economic globalization on the gender division of labor extends beyond the roles of TNCs for labor markets. Globalization also strongly influences welfare states in their regional context. It may be surmised that this influence on welfare states will lead to rearrangements of paid, unpaid, and civic work. Diane Elson has designed a useful scheme to outline the relationships between gender and work in the global economy (cf. Diagram 1, Unifem, 2000: 30). The global private sector is positioned at the center; it is based on formal paid work as well as on informal paid or unpaid work, such as subcontracting of work by unpaid family workers. The public sector undertakes paid care work, but relies on unpaid care work mostly by women in the domestic sector in the North and South. The NGO sector is composed of contributions by volunteer "civic" and unpaid work. Financial restructuring, especially in the form of IMF measures, exerted strong pressure on public sectors in the South. Public health and education was cut back and was partially or largely relegated to the domestic sector and some NGOs. In the North, the reorientation of welfare states from subsidies to promotion of employment neglects the issue of who will perform unpaid care work now. New evidence shows some success for integrating women into the new dual-career working patterns as well as into the "working poor," but it also hints that some women become "welfare drop-outs" now concentrating on informal work and unpaid care work.[6] Unpaid work and care work may become invisible again in view of the political priority of wage work and the labor market.

Finally, globalization of communication and media made it possible to be informed in real time about major developments on a global level. The image of the reconfiguration of time and space strongly relies on these new opportunities of "simultaneous ubiquity" or the image of getting access to information "all over the place at all times." The Internet is a current symbol for the new global modes of communication. But to perceive and to use these new options, organizations and persons need access, resources, and power on the one hand. Existing evidence suggests large but complex patterns of inequality according to world region, development level, class, and gender. According to the *Human Development Report 1999*, "industrial countries—home to less than 15% of people—had 88% of Internet users. By contrast South Asia is home to over 20% of all people but had less than 1% of the world's Internet users" (UNDP, 1999: 63). Furthermore, "current access to the Internet runs along the fault lines of national societies, dividing educated from illiterate, men from women, rich from poor, young from old, urban from rural" (UNDP, 1999: 63). The largest groups of Internet users are highly educated, white, under thirty-five years old, and male (cf. UNDP, 1999, 63). The billions of poor people with little access to education, especially poorer and elderly women, tend to be marginalized or excluded.

But whereas access is still concentrated on groups that are also global or national elites, one example may show that access and use of global communication is not determined unilaterally by world region, class, or gender. In the Philippines, less than 1 percent of the entire population has Internet access, but women make up 43 percent of the users, compared to 35 percent in Germany (UN, 2000: 96; UNDP, 1999: 63). Whereas participation of women on the Internet tended to be reluctant at first and then grew rapidly at least in the North, feminist networks all over the world have increasingly, sometimes enthusiastically, used the Internet as a medium of information, exchange, and strategy coordination during the UN decade for women. Global networks are forming based on decentered multilocal forms of communication and organization, and feminist networks have been playing the role of pioneers.

Global communication is not limited to technology transporting information, but migrants with their minds and bodies are also on the move. The new mobility and migration patterns promoted the formation of transnational migrant networks and communities (Pries, 2001). Furthermore, migration has been feminized: the share of women has increased and women are visible and have a voice in migration networks. Two groups have new potentials and capacities for developing new approaches to transnational communication and networking. Some groups of "second-generation migrants" develop complex and flexible identities and look for new integrated perspectives on gender democracy.[7] They have important positions in communicating international perspectives to the women's movement and they play crucial roles in transnational antiracist- and feminist-policy networks. The second group is transnational diaspora intellectuals who have proposed creative and very influential feminist approaches toward economic, political, and cultural globalization.[8]

Discourses on human/women's rights and global democracy have evolved with the formation of feminist networks and action groups. People and ideas have met in global or transnational feminist networks. These networks experienced an opening of political opportunities during the UN decade for women (from 1975 to the present) and grew rapidly in scope. By discussing the issues that they brought from local or national contexts or from global developments and by learning through "conflicts in sisterhood," they have placed a multifocal set of issues on an expanding transnational agenda. In a process of communicating and network organizing, feminist networks were able to create consciousness about and discourses on a variety of issues, for instance, inequality in work and education, violence against women, ecology as a gender issue, and the equal participation of women.

For this mobilization, they had to find shared or common concepts in which their differences could be respected. For example, women's movements from different sociocultural backgrounds came to share concepts like equality in work or struggling against violence against women or women's empowerment on a global level; but they give different meanings and develop different strategies for realizing these concepts in their contexts. The approach of women's/human rights proved very productive in finding a shared language. This approach made it possible to bridge differences and to develop convergent strategies of women's movements in the South, East, and West. And it also could be translated into the global discourses on human rights and social issues. Thus, global feminist and transnational networks and women's movements could influence the UN processes around the decades of women and the UN social conferences—from the Rio conference on ecology in 1991 to the world social summit in 1996—as well as put pressure on governments.

I argue for a broader understanding of globalization and for overcoming its narrow economic focus. The working definition proposed for globalization sees it as an ensemble of interlinked processes with possibly open results characterized by

- increasing economic, political, social, and ecological interdependence
- increasing global communication and mobility
- increasing influence of new actors—especially supranational organizations, transnational enterprises, and civil-society organizations (CSOs) or NGOs.

These new actors can expand and promote the range of *their options according to their material, organizational, and power resources as well as their capacity and potential for orientation, reflexivity, and learning in the new complex global games.* Global orientation and communication capacities become crucial for organizing in globalization.

The globalization of communication, discourses, and social movements, especially women's movements, suggests that new actors besides nation-states and corporations enter the international stage in unprecedented numbers and diversity. Whereas the first international feminist networks until 1940 had professional or upper-class women at their core and were centered on the West (Rupp, 1997), now representatives of working women, female farmers, or students and "everyday feminists" or lesbians without a large bank account have joined international meetings. Feminists developed agency on a global and transnational level. They participated in the emergence of international gender politics and gender policy networks by negotiating with or entering into strategic coalitions with supranational organizations such as the UN or the ILO, with state institutions such as the women's offices established during the UN decade for women, and with NGOs in global civil society.

## NEW INEQUALITIES AND NEW OPTIONS
## IN THE EMERGING GLOBAL MULTILEVEL SYSTEM

Options of actors are changing as a consequence of globalization processes. Some actors can enlarge and differentiate their options, playing at once in many fields and spaces. Other actors experience shrinking options with the decreasing relevance of the nation-state and its corporatist forms of regulation or with the stronger impact of market forces. This dynamism in the range of options is related to interchanges between the new forms of communication/ information that extend into simultaneous ubiquity and the concurrent increasing potential of organizations. Castells (2000) suggests that flexible network organizations can develop and use these options especially well, as they tend to show reflexive potential by rapidly and effectively processing knowledge and reflecting changes in their own setup as well as in their environments.

The options that actors can envision and realize in the global game relate to their resources, power, and capacities. Of course, financial resources are important in globalization, but the capacities for communication/ information bridging global times and spaces and organizational capacities are also crucial factors. The capacity of transnational and global orientation is crucial for developing options by communicating and forming transnational coalitions as well as organizational innovation, resiliency, and efficiency. For example, TNCs as powerful enterprise organizations could claim their leading role in globalization in view of their financial assets, their organizational efficiency, and their global information management. Women's movements, like other social movements, have less access to resources, but they were able to develop transnational capacities of communication and orientation. The UN Decade for Women and transnational feminist networks provided spaces for learning by negotiating and bridging conflicts as well as developing strategic sisterhood in diversity. And feminist networks tend to function in horizontal, flexible ways that may provide specific advantages such as flexibility, intensive communication, and creativity, but may pose special problems of organizational efficiency and resource mobilization.

Furthermore, women's movements' access to resources is also dependent on class, ethnicity, or cultural milieu. For feminist migrant groups or local projects in poor regions, it is very difficult or impossible to finance activities, to find organizational space, and even more, to pay for Internet access and computers or airfare to international meetings. These differences between women according to class, ethnicity, or cultural milieu also raise questions of new emerging hierarchies of accountability. Professionalization and specialization of activities was very important to increase efficiency and to influence global gender policies. But the danger of feminist jet-setting without clear representation or accountability to grassroots movements cannot be over-looked (Wichterich, 2001).

Therefore, globalization processes do not simply reinforce and carry on ex-isting power relationships in deterministic ways. Even from asymmetric posi-tions, actors can develop capacities for international orientation, communica-tion, and organizing that can support them in entering the global games. International orientation in this sense means knowledge of global economic, political, and cultural structures and institutions, and of global or transnational communication. As the global feminist networks and women's movements have shown, negotiating in asymmetric power relationships can bring incre-mental results. These negotiating processes also suggest that global and na-tional levels should not be dualistically juxtaposed in discussing globalization. Rather, the former monopolistic regulatory power of nation-states is receding and becoming relative whereas other levels of action are gaining in impor-tance. The saying "Think globally, act locally!" reflects this emerging global multilevel system (*Mehrebenensysteme*). The most important levels are the

- global level
- subregion (EU, southern Africa, east Asia; NAFTA, Mercosur)
- nation-state
- local community
- household.

Globalization means not a simple top-down process, but rather processes of interplay in this multilevel system. For example, the Convention for the Elim-ination of all Forms of Discrimination of Women (CEDAW) (global level) was established in the first UN Decade for Women in 1979 and was ratified by most nation-states (national level).[9] At present, NGOs from regions or enter-prises can contact the CEDAW committee with grievances (meso-level of or-ganizations or regions). The Working Women's International Network (WWIN) in Japan directed a petition to CEDAW as a part of their national strategy to fight against discrimination in wages and sex stereotyping of job allocation. The network mobilized public opinion and was able to attract many interested women; also, the appeal to an international highly legiti-mate UN institution such as CEDAW strengthened their negotiation standing vis-à-vis the firm. Because of this "articulation" of the global and the local, some authors speak of glocalization (Robertson, 1995). Virtual global flows need to be located—to be incorporated, processed, redirected—in a con-crete region where embodied subjects are living. As the local level is the space of everyday experience and interaction of many women, it is compar-atively open to feminist organizing.

In the following sections, I first discuss the changing opportunity struc-tures for women's movements. After summarizing some results of global gender politics and the impact of global feminist networks, I illustrate the global regulation processes towards gender equality and the interplay in the multilevel system by comparing some developments in Germany and Japan.

## GLOBALIZATION AND CHANGING OPPORTUNITY STRUCTURES

Sylvia Walby (2001) emphasizes the connections between modernization and globalization. Both trends work towards a public gender order, integrating women in work, social movements, and politics. In the wake of both interrelated processes, the former hegemonic gender orders are eroding or changing. But globalization is seen as a set of contradictory processes that enhance inequalities immensely while also opening spaces for global negotiations. A critique of globalization, however, which turns to the protected space of the nation-state with a nostalgic gaze, tends to neglect the state's underlying neopatriarchal gender order. The division of public and private and the allocation of women to the domestic sphere is characteristic of Western hegemonic national gender orders. While including men and women of the dominant cultural or ethnic group, they were exclusive toward minorities and black or migrant groups.[10] Political and social citizenship is still not fully realized for women with national membership, as can be seen from their low representation in political decision making and top positions in social institutions and management, even lower for migrants who do not even have full political rights.

But globalization and modernization also are effecting changes in the social and political opportunity structure for gender politics and women's movements. The level of female education has increased dramatically in some world regions, coming up to or slightly surpassing that of men in some, even if growth is slow in other areas. Also, women's integration into the labor market has led to a silent revolution in many regions (except the Near East) (UN, 2000: 90). Women's access to political decision making and functions, especially their share of parliamentarians, has increased as well (Unifem, 2000: 76–80; UN, 2000: 163–68). Except for some countries in the Near East, we are in a transition toward a public gender order on a global scale in which women have entered the public spaces of work and politics while the unequal division of labor in care work and parenting is modernized.

## UN PROCESSES: SEARCHING FOR EGALITARIAN REGULATIONS AND GLOBAL GENDER DEMOCRACY

The UN process toward women's equality, development, and peace can be seen as one pioneering experiment in developing flexible modes of regulations sensitive to different cultural contexts. Therefore, I think it is highly relevant in thinking about strategies for egalitarian regulation and their limits. The UN Decade for Women and the social UN conferences from 1991— from the Rio conference on ecology to the world social summit in 1996, but especially the Fourth World Conference on Women in Beijing in 1995— opened spaces for different feminists from around the world. They provided spaces for communication and a highly visible agenda setting that was influential in the formation and development of international feminist networks. They opened up arenas for changing norms without, however, providing the power of implementation.

The UN processes also contributed to the establishment of gender policy institutions and new legal instruments or measures; they led to new global norms and the entry wave of femocrats into national and supranational governance institutions. In other words, the results were norms (some of them with the force of international law) on gender equality. These norms, of which CEDAW is the most important, had been established in global negotiations with the world's nation-states and supranational governing bodies. At the same time women's political machineries—women's offices or ministries, EO departments, etc.—were enlarged or established in these negotiations and their tasks included implementing these norms (Unifem, 2000: 37–61). From the first stage of the Decade for Women (1975–1985) these norms and institutions contributed to an expansion of the political opportunity structure as femocrats were established in state and supranational bodies as potential allies.[11]

Building on this groundwork, the women's movements in South Africa, east Asia, and Latin America, as well as from Europe and North America, influenced the UN Fourth World Conference on Women in Beijing in 1995 (UN, 1995; Wichterich, 2000). The Beijing conference came up with a declaration that established basic norms and steps for gender equality in a process of international negotiating between governments and feminists from very different regions and approaches. Its goals of empowerment and autonomy, including the body and sexuality, equality in work and society, development and structural change, peace and nonviolence, and personal relationships and political participation, can be seen as a feminist formula for global gender democracy. Feminist networking thus put on the agenda the issue of developing concepts of inclusive global gender democracy with respect to gender and international justice, the differences between women and women's movements, and connection to a nonviolent and sustainable development based on the empowerment of women and marginalized people.

The declaration also proposes goals, strategies, and measures for gender equality in twelve fields of action and gives detailed time frames with specific targets for supranational organizations, national governments, and organizations from economic and civil society.[12] Gender mainstreaming is a further strategy from the Beijing declaration. The responsibility for realizing gender mainstreaming lies with supranational institutions such as the UN, the EU, etc., and with governments of nation-states who signed the Beijing declaration. At the Beijing conference, women's movements had gained great potentials and achievements: They had created global and transnational discourses that respected difference and created a fundament for common action and they had agreed on a common feminist charter for the world in the form of the Beijing declaration and platform for action. They developed capacities for global orientation and could communicate around the world on the waves of the Internet. They also formed various transnational and global networks and organizations and forged coalitions within UN institutions (the UN, the ILO, the World Bank) and supranational institutions. Finally, they had achieved women's political machineries in global and regional institutions and national governments.

But women's movements had gained little autonomous resources and still had to rely on external opportunity structures like state funds or women's offices. They had entered political governance structures and organizations, but had not gained a firm foothold or a clear power base. The public gender order still relied on integration into marginality. Furthermore, while taking advantage of horizontal network flexibility, they also had to face concurrent problems. Sometimes the democratic issues of accountability and representation tend to become rather diffuse and elitism is not absent from feminist circles (Lenz, 2001a; Wichterich, 2001).

However, the development of a global program and vision for gender equality is different from its incorporation into the national and local contexts which will be selected and shaped by the national or local relationships of interest and power, by the political opportunity structure, and by political culture. Selection and incorporation is negotiated and the approaches will be reevaluated during these processes by femocrats and gender politicians, as well as by women's movements. The results are shaped by political power constellations and sociocultural contexts. This contradicts the assumption that globalization promotes uniform and standardized patterns as implied by the catchword of McDonaldization in globalization (Ritzer, 2000). Rather, I prefer to speak of national or local *regulation.* Regulation is not seen as a top-down state action, but rather as the outcome of social negotiations by state governments, interest groups (as enterprises and other organizations), and social movements (Lenz, 2001a).[13]

## PROCESSES OF FEMINIST
## REGULATION IN GERMANY AND JAPAN

I will now consider regulation processes on the national level under the influence of global norms and institutions in reaction to the UN Decade for

Women, in light of the gender approach and gender mainstreaming in Germany and Japan. These countries were selected as examples for a number of reasons: Both are late developmental states in which a neopatriarchal and community-oriented political culture has put up barriers to public participation of women and individual women's rights.[14] Furthermore, they demonstrate that international gender regulations can become relevant for gender politics in the North[15] and they highlight the different strategies of the Japanese and German women's movements toward globalization and regionalization.

The different political opportunity structure is briefly outlined by pointing to the gender empowerment measure (GEM)[16] in Germany and Japan and other postindustrial countries (table 1.1). The GEM does not show the quality of gender relations per se, but gives some indication of the access to public chances. For example, the high rate of female employment, the outstanding female participation in tertiary education, and the long life expectancy of women in Japan are not visible. The share of women in parliament and management is higher in Germany: Women are integrated in several ways in a subordinate position into German corporatism and national politics. In Germany, the establishment of women's political machinery and equal opportunity officers at the communal and regional level was strongly linked with national party politics and federal states' legislation; therefore the mainstream of EO and the gender policy field was characterized by a dominant national orientation.

### Feminist Regulation in Japan

In Japan, the women's movement showed a marked international, somewhat pan-Asian, and national orientation in the 1950s and 1960s, which then switched to a high global interest especially after the start of the UN Decade for Women in 1975. In postwar Japan, women controlled the purse strings in the household and the network strings in the neighborhood, but were kept away from the ropes of political alignments and factions. This de facto exclusion from all spaces of national corporatism and power politics changed only during the past years.

**Table 1.1.  The Gender Empowerment Measure for Selected Postindustrial Countries**

|                        | Great Britain | Germany | Japan | USA  |
|------------------------|---------------|---------|-------|------|
| Fem. members of parl.  | 17.1 %        | 33.6    | 9.0   | 12.5 |
| Fem. adm./ managers    | 33.0          | 26.6    | 9.5   | 44.4 |
| HDI rank               | 10            | 14      | 9     | 3    |
| GEM rank               | 15            | 6       | 41    | 13   |

In Japan, the small feminist movements had participated in the UN Decade for Women from its very start in 1975 with energy, enthusiasm, and rapidly increasing international expertise.[17] The established wing and the new autonomous movement met in preparation, and some activists went to the starting conference in Mexico in 1975. These groups used the new opportunities of the high UN prestige in Japan and the new global and highly visible public spaces of the UN decade for agenda setting and developing international networks. In view of the UN decade, the groups also consolidated their organizational structure. Activists from the autonomous groups formed a network for getting active in the UN International Year of Women (abbr. *Kôdô suru kai*). A hotbed for many of the later leading feminist lawyers, medical doctors, scientists in women studies, and politicians, this group had a long and successful career with some changes that ended in the late 1990s.

The international orientation of the Japanese women's movement was broadened from the former pan-Asian focus or the parallel focus on the West to a more detailed consciousness of global gender issues especially in the South. This growth of global consciousness was limited to a few internationally oriented activists or experts until the mid-1990s. Then, the Fourth World Conference on Women in Beijing in 1995 worked like a magnet, attracting more than 5,000 Japanese feminists—experts as well as grassroots activists, networks from the metropolitan areas as well as from the countryside. The Beijing Conference and its preparatory and follow-up processes marked the mass arrival of the Japanese women's movements in the regional east Asian context as well as its turn to politics and lobbying (Lenz, 2000a).

The UN Decade for Women and the influence of the different currents of the women's movement resulted in the establishment of women's political machinery, the former Women's Office in the Prime Minister's Office. Two important legal reforms relevant for gender and work have been achieved. The passing of the Equal Employment Opportunity Law (EEOL) for Men and Women (*Danjo koyô kikai kintô-hô*) in 1986 grew out of a reform coalition of progressive social scientists, bureaucrats interested in a regulation under the auspices of the Labour Ministry, and some feminist groups (Lam, 1992). The women's movement was split on the reform issue as the law rationalized the former menstruation leave which was seen as a recognition of female difference in work as well as some basic protective measures in view of hard working conditions. For the first time in Japan, the EEOL contained provisions for equal chances of men and women in recruitment, job allocation, and training even if it relied on administrative guidance and did not include sanctions. The reform of the EEOL (enacted in June 1997, enforced in April 1999) showed that it had taken roots in feminist networks on gender and work. Feminists in the women's movement and trade unions lobbied widely for a more effective law. The committee in the Labour Ministry, which was in charge of the reform, had a remarkable share of women. The revised law shows clear progress in such matters as prohibition of discrimination against female workers armed with sanctions, settlement of disputes and complaints, measures for actively promoting equal treatment (so-called positive action), and measures against sexual harassment (Osawa, 2000a: 14).

Japanese feminist networks and established women's groups took the Beijing declaration back home and started lobbying. They formed an umbrella network, called Beijing JAC (Beijing Japan Accountability Caucus), which had twelve working groups, one for each of the issues in the declaration. Beijing JAC brought together feminist experts and grassroots activists from all over Japan with long experience. They framed demands for the twelve issues in the Japanese context and have been negotiating with state and regional government on them.

Several issue-oriented networks are regularly connecting and exchanging with women's movements in east Asia so that regional horizontal integration is increasing. In December 2000, the Violence-Against-Women Network (VAW-net) organized a tribunal on Japanese responsibility for the issue of sex slaves in the Japanese army in the Pacific War, together with east Asian women's action groups, including for the first time the cooperation of North and South Korean as well as Chinese and Taiwanese groups. In contrast to the NGO policy network of Beijing JAC, these currents are rather critical of the legal reforms by the government fearing co-optation in the Japanese system of dominance in east Asia.

In 1999, the Japanese conservative LDP government passed the Basic Law for a Gender-Equal Society. Mari Osawa, a highly astute participant and observer of the legislative process and member of the preparatory committee, sees the significance of the law in its basic concept of a gender-free society and the respect for individual human rights. As the law also regards gender equality as a means to overcome crucial economic problems such as the low birth rate or the coming labor-market constraints by using women workers' potential it appeals to broader economic and political interests in order to promote realization and concrete results (Osawa, 2000a). The Basic Law gives a general framework to be operationalized by specific laws and rules on the national, prefectural, and communal level (Osawa, 2000b). It also strengthens the focal position of the Gender Equality Bureau in the Cabinet Office in administrative reforms.

In the Japanese terms of the law, gender equality is called "joint participation of men and women" (*danjo kyôdô sankaku*), which is related to equality of opportunities. The term equality (*byôdô*) was eschewed by conservative politicians, as it is associated "with equality of outcome and . . . hence the paraphernalia of 'Western-style' feminism: quotas, affirmative action, positive discrimination, etc." (Osawa, 2000a: 6). Osawa discusses the language politics of incorporating gender mainstreaming into the Japanese context of political regulations. This concept of gender equality had the merit of overcoming the narrow focus on women and difference of the former laws and institutions. The interpretation of "gender free" and "individual human rights" is epochal indeed in Japan.

Several factors account for the passage of the law: When the conservative LDP president Hashimoto was planning administrative reform, female politicians and external and internal lobbying by feminists convinced him to integrate the concept of the gender-equal society into the reforms. The feminist networks were able to mobilize well-known female researchers and prestigious female leaders for the government commission preparing the law and supported its debates with public lobbying and events. The small femocrat core in the Office for Gender Equality in the Prime Minister's office—women's political machinery in Japan—played an important role in coordinating efforts, especially in internal lobbying and serving as a counterpart to the feminist NGOs. The committee came to compromises by integrating Japanese and global concepts (Osawa, 2000a). Despite various problems, the Basic Law provides a framework for more equal gender regulations in work, family, and politics. It also achieves institutional development by expanding gender policy machineries at the national cabinet level and at the prefectural and communal level.

### Feminist Regulation in Germany

In Germany, EO policy showed a marked orientation towards integration into the national corporatist structures during the 1970s and 1980s. The relative success in creating several thousand EO posts integrated into local administrations or in social organizations may have confirmed this orientation. Gender mainstreaming was received in the context of the European Union. As a result of intensive lobbying by the European Women's Lobby (EWL), the principles of gender mainstreaming were incorporated into the EU Amsterdam treaty of 1997 and thus became obligatory for the member states (Schmidt, 2000: 218–20). In spite of its stronger legal foundation by the EU subregional context and thus rather far-reaching potential, at first gender mainstreaming was received rather reluctantly by the women's movement in Germany. Feminists feared that the equal opportunity offices and instruments like quotas might be abolished under the slogan of gender mainstreaming; furthermore there was concern that the visibility of women's policies might suffer under a general rhetorical smoke screen of "gender."[18] Furthermore only some wings of the new women's movement mobilized for the UN Decade for Women or discussed their results in view of political action in Germany. Exchange on gender policies in Europe is growing mainly in research networks, but there is still no systematic networking, for example, between France and Germany, who count among the "EU big shots."

Until 1995, the feminist mainstream considered global networking and regulations somewhat matronizing rather than useful for the South. The established wing (*Deutscher Frauenrat; German Council of Women*) had the connections to official international gender policies of the national government and the EU. But until the mid-1990s it did not give high priority to spreading global concepts of gender mainstreaming or mobilizing for their incorporation into German policies. The new feminist movements formed an NGO Women's Forum (*NRO Frauenforum*) as a broad and vital network, which, however, had few resources or lobbying energy. There is no coordinating network for information or lobbying on global gender issues and regulations in Germany.

This may also be due to the closing of political opportunities during the liberal conservative government of Helmut Kohl, who was called a patriarch even by party friends. But the new coalition of the Social Democrats and the Green Party, although owing its ascendancy to female voters, has not promoted gender equality very actively either. In view of the slow reaction of the women's movement to gender mainstreaming mostly femocrats and feminist politicians as well as some researchers have worked for a more positive incorporation of gender mainstreaming. It has been integrated into gender policies in some federal states (Lower Saxony, Saxony-Anhalt), and into the Equal Opportunity Law of the federal state of North Rhine-Westphalia. However, the plan for a comprehensive Gender Equality Law of the national government based on gender mainstreaming failed in 2001, due to enterprise resistance and lack of support by the chancellor and the cabinet. The measure has been framed in terms of voluntary affirmative action.

As EO officers and feminist networks get more information and expertise about gender mainstreaming, the approach appears less top-down, but is rather seen as a horizontal concept empowering feminists in organizations and at the local level. The principles of gender mainstreaming can be turned to great advantage for new regulations on work as they can be related to concepts of organization reform and flexibility and of organizational learning. The gender concept can appeal to feminist or liberal men's interests for gender justice and thus be conducive to coalitions with reform-oriented male colleagues in management and trade unions. Claiming one-half of decision-making posts for women is an engine for change and its inclusion in the Equal Opportunity Law of the federal state of North Rhine-Westphalia has had an impact in public institutions and corporations. For example in the university the EO policies were reframed according to the law which prescribed one-half of the seats on all posting committees for female professors. As the share of female professors is still about 10 percent, the university administration now realizes that gender equality is an organizational and not only a rhetorical issue. In Germany and Japan, both gender-conservative societies and nation-states, global norms and regulations of gender equality were incorporated into national, regional, and communal gender policies. In

Germany, the new women's movements, after concentrating on national gender policies from the 1990s, are discovering the EU level and gender mainstreaming. In Japan, the women's movements could refer to the UN Decade for Women and its results in opening political spaces in national and local governments and in participating in legal reform. From an extremely asymmetric position, they could deploy capacities for international orientation, communication, and organizing that supported them in entering national and local negotiations for gender equality in work, everyday life, and politics and achieving new regulations.

## CONCLUSION

This chapter aimed to propose a broader understanding of globalization that, while realizing the power asymmetries and risks, focuses on the changing options of actors. These options are related to their resources, power, and capacities. The UN Decade for Women provided a dramatic opportunity for the global women's movement that could enlarge and diversify their options. They had developed a common charter while respecting differences and capacities for global orientation. They also established transnational and global networks and organizations and worked within and from outside of UN institutions (as the UN, the ILO, the World Bank) and supranational institutions (as the EU). Women's political machineries have been established in global and regional institutions and national governments. As Alison Woodward points out, the institutions of the European Union and other units of international governance have been instrumental in creating new sorts of "velvet triangles" around women's issues in a field that is normally characterized by informal relationships. The velvet refers to the fact that almost all of the players are female in a predominantly male environment. The softness offers considerable vagueness about inputs and loyalties. The poles are held down by feminist bureaucrats and politicians (femocrats), trusted academics, and formally organized voices in the women's movement (Woodward, 2001).

The legislation of the EEOL and the Basic Law for a Gender-Equal Society in Japan is one example of regulation toward gender equality in the interplay of the global and the national level and the working of (a conservative) government, academic experts, femocrats, and women's movements. While the Basic Law is a rather symbolic and soft regulation without the bite of tough sanctions, its focus on convincing language and cultural politics and the implementation in local society by the input of local forces, such as committed women, can promote a self-sustaining or reinforcing dynamism.

In Germany, after the turn to gender mainstreaming, strategies are focusing on organizational change in administration and public and private enterprise. Gender mainstreaming provides a general regulatory frame, whereas the content is filled with targets, aims, and policies from the context of the organization and with the support of its top. Again regulation is rather soft without legal sanctions, but also aims for a self-sustaining or reinforcing dynamism.

Both cases suggest that negotiations and regulations in the global context are possible from an asymmetric position and that innovative capacities for transnational and global orientation and horizontal organization are crucial. Further research is necessary on innovative and egalitarian forms of regulation in globalization. The first wave of the globalization debate, which pronounced the abdication of politics, supranational institutions, and states in the face of the increasing power of TNCs, has subsided. The writing on the wall warns of the potential immense catastrophes of global conflicts. It is finally becoming visible to dominant powers, a large part of business, and traditional social organizations, after it has been recognized and called out by global institutions, visionary politicians, entrepreneurs, intellectuals, and global civil society. The approaches to global regulation for gender equality may prove a fruitful research issue of general interest.

## NOTES

1. Due to limited space it is not possible to discuss the field of ecology, in which feminist networking has been important and intensive.

2. Fifty transnational corporations from developing countries originate mainly from east Asia, Latin America, and South Africa and they concentrate in construction, food and beverages, and diversified industries (UNCTAD, 2001: 5).

3. Only in five OECD countries (including Canada and the United States) is the male share in management less than 60 percent (Anker, 1998: 263–69).

4. Only in six countries (among fifty-four) is the male share of foremen/supervisors slightly lower than 90 percent; they have a large export-oriented textile industry (Anker, 1998: 274–76).

5. For an overview of the literature, cf. Wichterich, 2000; Lenz, 2000a.

6. Personal communication with Joan Acker about her project on welfare reforms and gender.

7. Research on the migrant women's movement in Germany found that about one-half of the groups were transnational in the sense that their members came from different countries of origin; cf. Schwenken, 2000. These studies also show that trends toward fixed national identities or cultural nationalism are also present, but that transnationalism is an influential approach.

8. One fascinating example is the edition of *Signs* on globalization; cf. *Signs* 26, no. 4 (summer 2001).

9. CEDAW became effective in 1981 and was reinforced by an optional protocol in 1999 that allows groups in countries that ratified it to bring complaints directly to the CEDAW committee (Unifem, 2000: 43–44).

10. See Lenz, 1999, for a discussion of hegemonic national gender orders.

11. The first UN conference in Mexico in 1975 and the World Action Plan passed at the conference contributed to the establishment of women's policy machineries in

the nation-states. The Research Network on Gender, Politics, and the State (RNGS) does comparative research on the relations between women's movements and women's offices (or women's policy machineries) in Western postindustrial countries on a number of crucial issues; see Mazur, 2001.

12. See UN, 1995, and Unifem, 2000: 47–60, for a brief overview of developments since the Beijing conference.

13. By focusing on negotiations and various actors in developing international norms in the context of globalization, the concept of regulation is similar to *global governance* (Held, 1999). But it is has a clearer focus on power relations and actor's interest (Lenz, 2001a).

14. Therefore they offer an interesting comparative perspective in spite of the differences in their development path and culture. See Lenz, 1999, for a discussion of the merits of comparing gender politics in Germany and Japan.

15. Especially in Germany gender politics in the 1980s and 1990s tended to concentrate on the national level of the "German model" and the UN Decade for Women was perceived as mainly important for the South. The reception of and implementation of the UN decade in the United States is also an important issue, especially after the more national turn of the Bush government.

16. The gender empowerment measure of the UNDP is a useful index for *public participation* and the public gender order (GEM, cf. UNDP, 2000: 165). It is based on four criteria: (1) the share of female members of parliament, (2) the share of female administrators and managers, (3) the share of female professional and technical workers, and (4) women's GDP per capita. The data are rather fragmentary and the measure may be somewhat homogenizing the differentiation of female employment mentioned above. Still, the GEM provides a broad comparative framework.

17. The following report on Japan is based on fieldwork by the author in 1994 and 1997 (with about seventy expert interviews) as well as continual evaluation of sources and documents. Cf. the extensive source collection: Miki et al., 1992–1995, and as overview publications: Osawa, 2000b; Hara and Osawa, 1996; Khor, 1999; Yokohama fôramu, 1992; Kokusai fujinnen Nihon taikai no ketsugi o jitsugen suru tame no renrakukai, 1989. Current developments are reflected in the yearly white book of the Office for Gender Equality in the Prime Minister's Office (*Danjo kyôdô sankaku no genjô to shisaku*) and the journal of the Asia Japan Women's Resource Center (*Women's Asia*). The *US Japan Women's Journal* is a very valuable source for information and exchange between feminist studies in Japan and the English-language community.

18. This skeptical view was corroborated by the abortive attempt to abolish the committee for women's right in the European Parliament by appealing to gender mainstreaming. Gender mainstreaming has since substantially advanced in the EU Commission (Schmidt 2000; 2001).

## REFERENCES

Adorno, Theodor W. 1969. *Der Positivismusstreit in der deutschen Soziologie.* Neuwied et al: Luchterhand.

Anker, Richard. 1998. *Gender and Jobs: Sex Segregation of Occupations in the World.*

Geneva: International Labor Office.

Castells, Manuel. 2000. *The Rise of the Network Society*. 2d rev. ed. Oxford: Blackwell.

Filmer, Deon. 1995. *Estimating the World at Work*. The World Bank, Policy Research Working Paper 1488.

Giddens, Anthony. 2001. *Sociology*. 4th ed. Cambridge, U.K.: Polity Press.

Hara, Hiroko, and Mari Osawa. 1996. "Joseigaku to joseiseisaku." In *Ajia—Taiheiyô chiki no joseiseisaku to joseigaku*, ed. Hiroko Hara and Mari Ôsawa. Tokyo: Shinyôsha, 1–25.

Held, David. 1999. *Global Transformations: Politics, Economics and Culture*. Cambridge, U.K.: Polity Press.

Khor, Diana. 1999. "Organizing for Change: Women's Grassroots Activism in Japan." *Feminist Studies* 25: 633–61.

Kokusai fujinnen Nihon taikai no ketsugi o jitsugen suru tame no renrakukai, ed. 1989. *Rentai to kôdô. Kokusai fujinnen renrakukai no kiroku*. Tokyo: Ichikawa Fusae kinenkai shuppanbu.

Lam, Alice. 1992. *Women and Japanese Management: Discrimination and Reform*. New York: Routledge.

Leacock, Eleanor. 1981. *Myths of Male Dominance: Collected Articles on Women Cross-Culturally*. New York: Monthly Review Press.

Lenz, Ilse. 1999. "Politische Modernisierung und Frauenbewegungen in Japan und Deutschland. Zum Versuch einer vergleichenden Perspektive." In *Ostasien verstehen. Peter Weber-Schäfer zu Ehren. Festschrift aus Anlaß seiner Emeritierung*, ed. Andreas u.a. Pigulla. BJOAS Bd. 23, München: 217–31.

———. 2000a. "Globalisierung, Geschlecht, Gestaltung?" In *Geschlecht—Arbeit—Zukunft*, ed. Ilse Lenz, Ursula Müller, Hildegard Nickel, and Birgit Riegraf. Münster: Westfälisches Dampfboot, 16–49.

———. 2000b. "What Does the Women's Movement Do, When it Moves? Subjektivität, Organisation und Kommunikation in der neuen japanischen Frauenbewegung." In *Frauenbewegungen weltweit. Aufbrüche, Kontinuitäten, Veränderungen*, ed. Ilse Lenz, Michiko Mae, and Karin Klose. Opladen: Leske+Budrich, 95–133.

———. 2001a. "Globalisierung, Frauenbewegungen und internationale Regulierung." *Zeitschrift für Frauenforschung und Geschlechterstudien* 1+2: 8–29.

———. 2001b. "Bewegungen und Veränderungen. Frauenforschung und Neue Frauenbewegungen in Deutschland." In *Zwischen Emanzipationsvisionen und Gesellschaftskritik: (Re)Konstruktionen der Geschlechterordnungen in Frauenforschung—Frauenbewegung—Frauenpolitik*, ed. Ursula Hornung, Sedef Gümen, and Sabine Weilandt. Forum Frauenforschung Band 14. Münster: Westfälisches Dampfboot.

———. 2002. *Geschlechtsspezifische Auswirkungen der Globalisierung in den Bereichen Global Governance, Arbeitsmärkte und Ressourcen*. Gutachten für die Enquete-Kommission Globalisierung der Weltwirtschaft—Herausforderungen und Antworten des Deutschen Bundestags.

Lenz, Ilse, and Michiko Mae, eds. 2000. *Frauenbewegungen weltweit. Aufbrüche, Kontinuitäten, Veränderungen*. Opladen: Leske+Budrich.

———, eds. 1997. *Getrennte Welten, gemeinsame Moderne? Geschlechterverhältnisse in Japan*. Opladen: Leske+Budrich.

Mae, Michiko. 2000. "Wege zu einer neuen Subjektivität. Die neue japanische Frauenbewegung als Suche nach einer anderen Moderne." In *Frauenbewegungen weltweit: Aufbrüche, Kontinuitäten, Veränderungen*, ed. Ilse Lenz, Michiko Mae, and Karin Klose. Opladen: Leske+Budrich, 95–133.

Mazur, Amy, ed. 2001. *State Feminism, Women's Movements, and Job Training: Making Democracies Work in a Global Economy.* New York: Routledge.

Miki, Sôko, et al., eds. 1992–1995. *Nihon ûman ribu shi.* Kyoto: Shôkadô shoten.

Osawa, Mari. 2000a. "Government Approaches to Gender Equality in the Mid-1990s." *Social Science Japan Journal* 3, no. 1: 3–21.

———, ed. 2000b. *Danjo kyôdô sankaku shakai kihon-hô.* Tokyo: Kyôsei.

Pries, Ludger. 2001. *Internationale Migration.* Bielefeld: Transcript.

Ritzer, G. 2000. *The McDonaldization of Society.* 3d ed. Thousand Oaks, Calif.: Pine Forge Press.

Robertson, Roland. 1995. "Glocalization: Time-Space and Homogeneity-Heterogeneity." In *Global Modernities*, ed. Featherstone, Michael, et al. London: Sage.

Rupp, Leila. 1997. *Worlds of Women: International Women's Organizations 1888–1945.* Princeton, N.J.: Princeton University Press.

Schmidt, Verena. 2000. "Zum Wechselverhältnis zwischen europäischer Frauenpolitik und europäischen Frauenorganisationen." In *Frauenbewegungen weltweit*, ed. Ilse Lenz, Michiko Mae, and Karin Klose. Opladen: Leske + Budrich, 199–232.

———. 2001. "Gender Mainstreaming als Leitbild für Gechlechtergerechtigkeit in Organisationsstrukturen." *Zeitschrift für Frauenforschung und Geschlechterstudien* 1+2: 45–63.

Schwenken, Helen. 2000. "Frauen-Bewegungen in der Migration. Zur Selbstorganisierung von Migrantinnen in der Bundesrepublik Deutschland." In *Frauenbewegungen weltweit*, ed. Ilse Lenz, Michiko Mae, and Karin Klose. Opladen: Leske + Budrich, 133–67.

Sôrifu danjo kyôdô sankakushitsu (yearly): *Danjo kyôdô sankaku hakusho.* Tokyo.

UNCTAD. 2001. "Promoting Linkages, overview." In *World Investment Report 2001.* New York, Geneva.

UNDP. 1998. *Human Development Report.* New York.

———. 1999. *Human Development Report.* New York.

———. 2000. *Human Development Report.* New York.

Unifem. 2000. *Progress of the World's Women: Unifem Biennial Report.* New York: United Nations.

United Nations. 1995. *Report on the Fourth World Conference on Women (Beijing, 4–15 September 1995).* A/CONF.177/20.

———. 2000. *The World's Women 2000: Trends and Statistics.* New York.

Urry, John. 2000. "Mobile Sociology." *British Journal of Sociology* 51, no. 1: 185–203.

Walby, Sylvia. 2001. "Analysing Social Inequality in the Twenty-first Century: Globalisation and Modernity Restructure Inequality." Unpublished paper.

Wallerstein, Immanuel, ed. 1975. *World Inequality: Origins and Perspectives on the World System.* Montreal: Black Rose Books.

Wichterich, Christa. 2000. *The Globalised Woman: Reports from a Future of Inequality.* London: Zed Press.

———. 2001. "From Passion to Profession. Mehr Fragen als Antworten zu Akteurinnen, Interessen und Veränderungen politischer Handlungsbedingungen der neuen internationalen Frauenbewegung." *Zeitschrift für Frauenforschung und*

*Geschlechterstudien* 1+2: 128–38.
Woodward, Alison. 2001. "Die McDonaldisierung der internationalen Frauenbewegung: Negative Aspekte guter Praktiken." *Zeitschrift für Frauenforschung und Geschlechterstudien* 1+2: 29–45.
World Bank. 2000. *Entering the 21st Century: World Development Report 1999/2000.* New York: Oxford University Press.
Yokohama fôramu, ed. 1992. *Shinpan. Onna no netowâkingu. Onna no grupu zenkoku gaido.* Tokyo: Yokohama Forum.

# 2

## Policy Strategies in a Global Era for Gendered Workplace Equity

*Sylvia Walby*

Policy toward gender relations in the workplace lies at the center of debates about the social relations in the workplace, the impact of globalization, and the nature of the gender regime. Is policy toward gender relations in the workplace changing in Western countries or is it a static feature of entrenched gender regimes? Are there nationally entrenched paths of development, or parallel, if differently timed, trajectories of change? Does globalization inhibit the range of possible policies by undermining the capacity of the nation-state to act, or does globalization restructure rather than erode polities?

This chapter investigates these issues with a focus on gendered workplace policies in the U.K. It examines the correlates and causes of gender inequality in the workplace in the U.K., and the nature and causes of the recent changes in policies that affect them.

### THEORIZING CHANGES IN GENDER RELATIONS

There are three important, if quite different, forms of analysis of gender relations relevant to gender relations in the workplace. First, the explanation of gender relations in employment within labor-market theory. Second, the theorization of the gender regime in terms of path-dependent forms of national development. Third, theorization of the gender regime as a form of social relations in transition.

First, there has been a considerable debate as to the explanation of gender differences and inequalities in the labor market within labor-market theory. It has been conventional, especially within economics, to understand differences in gender relations primarily in terms of the relative significance of two elements, differences in human capital and sex discrimination. Changes in women's position in employment have focused on changes in human capital, especially in educational qualifications and labor-market experience (Joshi and Paci, 1998), and in the extent of discrimination (Wright and Ermisch, 1991). Both elements are subject to policy intervention, ranging from education and maternity leave to improve skills and labor-market experience, and equal opportunity laws to engage with discrimination. Most analysis of the role of legislation in reducing sex discrimination in the U.K. has concluded that it made a significant difference (Joshi and Paci, 1998; Jones and Makepeace, 1996; Wright and Ermisch, 1991), as has maternity leave (Dex et al., 1998; McRae, 1993; Rees, 1998). The role of labor-market structures, especially that of occupational segregation (Rubery et al., 1999), is usually though not always seen as a special type of discrimination, best addressed by equal opportunities policies. However, there has been some attempt to view women's lesser engagement in employment than men as primarily an issue of choice rather than constraint (Hakim, 1996).

However, it has been argued that there are social processes more fundamental than these to understanding gender inequality in the workplace, such as an overarching pattern of gender relations in each country, which is key to understanding specific elements. This has involved discussion of a typology based on a strong or weak male-breadwinner model (Lewis, 1992, 1997). The body of literature on the gendering of the welfare state has typically assumed that the most important aspect of state intervention is whether or not it provides substitutes for domestic forms of caring. This has involved a sophisticated discussion as to the variety and implications of the ways in which such interventions are made, not least around the extent to which women are constituted as mothers, wives, or workers, and whether the care substitute is provided via cash and the tax/benefit system or via services (Hobson, 2000; Jenson, 1997; Sainsbury, 1996).

However, while making a claim to an overarching account of gender relations, these writers have typically considered only a limited number of elements of gender relations to be key. In particular, it is assumed that the most important way in which the state impacts on women's employment is by the provision or absence of welfare provisions related to caring (Ostner and Lewis, 1995). This is a limited account of the powers of the state and an even more limited account of the constitutive dimensions of gender relations. In these accounts gender has been effectively reduced to a reflection of gender relations in the family, as in the gendered welfare-state typology of the degrees of male breadwinnerhood. However, more recent writers have considered a wider range of state interventions, in particular regulation of the labor market, the family, and fertility (O'Connor et al., 1999; Gottfried and O'Reilly, 2000).

Underlying the theorization of gendering of the state labor market is the theorization of gender. There is a need for a more complexly constituted conception of gender. This should invoke not only the family and care, but also the state and labor market. I (1990) constitute gender in terms of six domains: household, employment, state, violence, sexuality, and culture. These may be seen as the economy (household and market), polity, and civil society (sexuality, violence) (Walby, 2004). There is an ongoing transition from a domestic to a public gender regime in most Western countries (Walby, 1990, 1997, 2004). The gender regime is a system of gender relations in the market and household economies, the polity, and in civil society, which includes interpersonal violence and sexuality. The modernization of the gender regime, its transition from a domestic to a public form, is taking place in most Western countries. It includes not only the move of women's labor from the household to the market, the increased presence of women in the state, and the increased permeability of the family, but also the criminalization of men's violence toward women and the increase in rights to bodily integrity including control over fertility (Walby, 2004). This transition is producing complex new forms of inequality, not least around age, as well as articulating traditional forms of inequality around class and ethnicity.

An analysis that is based on transition rather than on national specificity may bring into focus a different set of mechanisms and processes of social change. For instance, this shift in focus highlights the need to address the question as to whether there are changes in the political representation of what women see as their interests.

## THE IMPLICATIONS OF GLOBALIZATION

There are many attempts to innovate policy that would achieve gender equity in the workplace. Are such policies limited by globalization? Does globalization erode the power of nation-states or does it merely restructure polities? By globalization I mean a process of increased density and frequency of international or global social interactions relative to local or national ones. This includes economic, political, and cultural dimensions. This closely follows the definition of Chase-Dunn, Kawano, and Brewer (2000: 78). I resist a definition in terms of supraterritoriality (Scholte, 2000), as this underestimates the extent to which global processes still have a territorial component (Sassen, 1999).

Globalization sometimes has been seen to curtail ambitions for equity in employment because of the increased power of global capital as compared with labor. Does globalization remove the capacity of nation-states, especially welfare regimes, to develop policies which can confront markets sufficiently to deal with social exclusion? Some have held that the power of global economic markets reduces the political capacity of nation-states (Crouch and Streeck, 1997; Ohmae, 1995) because of increasing competition

between states to deliver environments of lower state expenditure in order
to attract footloose capital (Cerny, 1996; Hay, 1997; Wickham-Jones, 1995),
leading to the flexibilization and degradation of employment (Standing,
1999) and a decrease in living standards especially for the poor (Martin and
Schumann, 1997). However, this scenario is contested on the grounds that
there are insufficiently new global linkages to explain decreased state capacity (Hirst and Thompson, 1996). The above argument also overstates the
power of the economic over the political (Taylor-Gooby, 1997).

While globalizing processes have often been considered to have a tendency
to erode nation-states, there is a more diverse range of relationships between
globalization and political entities. Globalization does not simply entail an economic process that diminishes the political capacities of nation-states (Cerny,
1996; Ohmae, 1995), but rather more complexly is implicated in the restructuring of regional polities (Hettne et al., 1999) such as the European Union
(Walby, 1999a), and the development of multilevel (Ruggie, 1998) and global
(Held, 1995; Robinson, 2001) forms of governance of the system as a whole,
and of global civil society (Berkovitch, 1999). The changes in time-space relations involved in globalization can produce contradictory effects.

The most important issue for the analysis of gender relations in the workplace in the U.K. is that of the role of the European Union. The relatively
small countries of western Europe do not engage with the issues of globalization in isolation, but rather as part of an emergent polity of the European
Union. The relationship of the U.K. to globalization is significantly mediated
by the EU. The EU has accrued powers as part of its response to the challenge of globalization and is arguably part of the globalization process itself
(Hettne, et al., 1999). Whether or not the EU is a state, it is a polity which has
been restructured in the context of globalization. Its effects on gender relations in the workplace will be considered below.

Much of the debate on globalization has focused on class relations, on
whether the balance of power between labor and capital in the workplace
and the state has shifted toward capital. This has tended to neglect the significance of changes in gender relations, raising several questions: What are
the implications of globalization for gendered relations and policies in the
workplace? Are women entering degraded flexibilized jobs (Standing, 1999)?
Or, does globalization result in better jobs for women (Castells, 1997)? What
are the implications for gender relations in a global era?

## GENDER INEQUITY IN THE WORKPLACE

In this new context of both globalization and a transition to a more public
form of gender regime, what are the prospects for policies to enhance

workplace gender equity? This chapter relates the proximate causes of gender inequality in the workplace in the U.K.; considers the main policy options to engage with them—education, social infrastructure, redistribution, and regulation—and examines the reasons for these developments in the U.K. The central argument is that elements of the state related to the regulation of the labor market and the provision of education are at least as important as support for care work for the modernization of gender relations in the workplace.

Gender inequality in the workplace is most obvious in the case of pay. In the U.K., women who work full-time earn 82 percent of men's hourly pay, while those who work part-time earn only 61 percent (*New Earnings Survey*, 2000). Women are less likely than men to receive fringe benefits such as occupational pensions; less likely to be in jobs that have security; and more likely to be in a restricted range of occupations (*Labour Market Trends*, 2001; Walby, 1997). The correlates of the wage gap are varied. They include: fewer educational and vocational qualifications; lesser labor-market experience; interruptions to labor-force career; part-time working; occupational segregation; and discrimination (Dolton et al., 1996; Harkness, 1996; Jones and Makepeace, 1996; Joshi and Paci, 1998; Wright and Ermisch, 1991). These may be understood as the result of the gendering of the household, labor market, polity, and civil society.

### Education and training

Women have on average fewer educational and vocational qualifications than men. Among men, 13 percent have higher-education degrees, as compared to only 8 percent of women; while 34 percent of women have no qualifications, as compared to 27 percent of men (figures for 1996) (ONS, 1998). See table 2.1 below.

**Table 2.1.  Highest Qualification Level Attained by Sex, 1996**

| *Persons Aged 16–69 Not in Full-Time Education* | *Men* | *Women* |
|---|---|---|
| Degree | 13% | 8 |
| Higher education below degree | 12 | 10 |
| "A" level (exam at 18 years) | 14 | 10 |
| GCSE grades A–C (exam at 16 years) | 21 | 24 |
| GCSE grades D–G/apprenticeship | 10 | 12 |
| No qualification | 27 | 34 |

Source: Adapted from Office for National Statistics, 1998, table 7.1.

In recent years younger women have closed the gap in educational qualifications with young men; however, a gendered education and training gap
remains among people from their middle years onwards. Gender differences
in education and training remain an important element in the gender wage
gap (Harkness, 1996).

## Labor market experience

Women often have less labor-market experience than men. This is typically related to women's work as carers of children and also as carers of
elderly, sick, and disabled people, husbands, and home, though the role
of carer does not always reduce labor-market experience. The impact of
being a carer on employment depends both on the level of wages and on
social policy, both of which affect the possibility of finding substitutes for
women's care work. Women who are more educated and in higher socioeconomic groups are much more likely than poorly qualified women in
lower socioeconomic groups to have near continuous employment even
if they have children. Table 2.2 illustrates this point by showing the variance in employment rates by education, while table 2.3 shows the association of employment rates of mothers of young children with socioeconomic group.

**Table 2.2.  Economic Activity of Women and Men by Highest Qualification Level Attained**

| Age and Economic Activity Status | Persons of Working Age Not in Full-Time Education, Great Britain: 1996 | | | | |
|---|---|---|---|---|---|
| | Higher Education | GCSE "A" Level or Equivalent | Other Qualifications | No Qualifications | Total |
| Women | % | % | % | % | % |
| 20–29 | | | | | |
| Working | 90 | 80 | 68 | 35 | 70 |
| Unemployed | 2 | 3 | 5 | 8 | 4 |
| Inactive | 7 | 17 | 27 | 58 | 25 |
| Women | | | | | |
| 16–59 | | | | | |
| Working | 81 | 77 | 70 | 51 | 67 |
| Unemployed | 3 | 4 | 4 | 5 | 4 |
| Inactive | 17 | 20 | 25 | 45 | 29 |
| Men | | | | | |
| 16–64 | | | | | |
| Working | 89 | 87 | 80 | 62 | 79 |
| Unemployed | 3 | 6 | 8 | 11 | 7 |
| Inactive | 8 | 7 | 12 | 27 | 14 |

Source: Adapted from Office for National Statistics, 1998, table 7.6.

**Table 2.3. Economic Activity of Women, Percentages Working Full Time, Part Time, and Unemployed by Own Socioeconomic Group and Age of Youngest Dependent Child**

*Women Aged 16–59, Great Britain: 1994–96 Combined*

| Age of Youngest Dependent Child and Economic Activity | Socioeconomic Group | | | | | |
|---|---|---|---|---|---|---|
| | *1* | *2* | *3* | *4* | *5* | *Total* |
| | Percentages | | | | | |
| Youngest child aged 0–4 | | | | | | |
| Working full time | 39 | 17 | 20 | 9 | 2 | 17 |
| Working part time | 25 | 37 | 41 | 25 | 47 | 34 |
| All working | 64 | 54 | 61 | 34 | 50 | 51 |
| Unemployed | 3 | 6 | 3 | 6 | 4 | 5 |
| Economically active | 67 | 60 | 63 | 40 | 53 | 56 |
| No dependent children | | | | | | |
| Working full time | 78 | 56 | 48 | 41 | 9 | 53 |
| Working part time | 8 | 22 | 25 | 25 | 50 | 23 |
| All working | 87 | 79 | 74 | 67 | 60 | 76 |
| Unemployed | 2 | 4 | 5 | 7 | 5 | 5 |
| Economically active | 89 | 83 | 78 | 74 | 65 | 80 |
| Total | | | | | | |
| Working full time | 68 | 40 | 39 | 27 | 7 | 39 |
| Working part time | 14 | 32 | 32 | 31 | 51 | 31 |
| All working | 82 | 73 | 72 | 58 | 59 | 70 |
| Unemployed | 3 | 5 | 4 | 6 | 5 | 5 |
| Economically active | 85 | 78 | 76 | 64 | 64 | 75 |

1 Professional or employer/manager
2 Intermediate and junior nonmanual (e.g., office workers, secretaries)
3 Skilled manual and own account nonprofessional
4 Semi-skilled manual and personal service
5 Unskilled manual
Source: Adapted from Office for National Statistics, 1998, table 5.5.

### Interruptions

Interruptions to a labor-force career can negatively affect earnings over and above the effect they have on total years of employment experience. This is partly because entry-level wages are significantly lower than average wages. Further, women who reenter the labor market after a period of child care in the U.K. often do so part-time and at a lower occupational level than they had before childbirth (Blackwell, 2001). When women reenter the labor market after unemployment they take a job that pays on average 16 percent less than their former job (Gregg, 1998).

### Part-Time

Women who work part-time get paid considerably less than those who work full-time, earning only 61 percent of men's hourly rates in the U.K. (*New*

*Earnings Survey*, 2000). The part-time sector is where many of the varied disadvantages that face women workers are clustered. The gap is significantly due to the lesser education and work experience of part-time workers (Joshi and Paci, 1998), but is compounded by lesser access to employer-paid training. As compared with the United States, it is a somewhat larger sector of the labor market (23 percent as compared with 13 percent in 1999) and was still growing during the 1990s, unlike in the United States. (See table 2.4 below.)

**Table 2.4.   Part-time as % of Employment**

| Country | 1983 | 1991 | 1999 |
|---------|------|------|------|
| U.S. | 15 | 14 | 13 |
| U.K. | 18 | 21 | 23 |

Source: OECD, 2000.

This sector has been developing since the Second World War and was, until very recently, largely outside much of the regulatory framework, including unfair dismissal or the provision of fringe benefits, such as pensions. Part-time work in the U.K. is primarily located in the low-productivity, low-pay sections of the economy. Many women enter part-time working in order to gain the time flexibility that they want to combine work and family, but get stuck there when their children have grown up. Nearly 40 percent of women working part-time do not have dependent children (calculations from Labour Force Survey data, *Labour Market Trends*, 2001).

### Occupational Segregation

Occupational segregation, in which women are to be found in a different and narrower range of occupations than men, is a marked feature of U.K. labor markets (Hakim, 1992; Siltanen, 1990) and a further source of unequal pay. Occupational segregation is at least partly a result of historical practices of discrimination, which have become sedimented into institutional structures (Walby, 1986, 1997).

### Discrimination

Discrimination is a significant element in gender inequity in the workplace. There is a continuing stream of legal cases through the Employment Tribunal system in the U.K.[1] Complaints about illegal and discriminatory dismissal due to pregnancy constitute the largest part of the complaints with which the Equal Opportunities Commission is asked to assist (Wild, 2001). The revision of pay systems negotiated before the Equal Value Amendment of the mid-1980s so as to bring them into line with current law remains incomplete.

Harkness (1996) estimates that in 1992 discrimination accounted for 22 percent of the wages gap for full-timers and 40 percent for part-timers.

## POLICY INITIATIVES

### Education and Training

One of the most important polices for gender equity in the workplace is that of education and training. Over the last two decades the once very considerable gap in educational qualifications between men and women has been significantly narrowed. The disadvantaged position of women among young people in relation to education has ended, although a gap remains among people over forty. However, as the gender gap has narrowed, the generation gap between younger and older women has opened up. The gender policy challenge concerning education and training today relates to women beyond the typical age of school and college. In particular, the women with the least qualifications tend either to work part-time or to not be employed.

Women in part-time jobs lack sponsors for training. Employers are more likely to provide training for full-time employees than part-time employees (Rix et al., 1999), while the most valuable employer-provided training, that leading to a formal vocational qualification, is more likely to be given to men rather than women (Blundell et al., 1996).

The U.K. government has developed policies on education that are intended to take into account the widely acknowledged challenge of the new economy and globalization (Department for Education and Employment, 1999). However, while there is a theoretical government commitment to "lifelong learning" (DfEE, 1999), in practice most of the money has gone to schools and thus to young, not older, women. There has been a series of initiatives (PIU, 2001), including LearnDirect and Individual Learning Accounts (Owens, 2001), but these are aimed more at developing the market for adult education than in substantially financing such education. For example, mature women seeking to go to university face serious financial barriers (Callender and Kemp, 2000). The U.K. has developed a set of active labor-market policies known as the "New Deal," which includes access to training and advice, in order to help the unemployed return to work. These programs have been tailored for the young, the over-50s, for lone parents, and disabled people and have generally been regarded as successful (HM Treasury, 2001a; Riley and Young, 2000). However, there are no programs specifically aimed at women seeking to return to work after a period of intensive child care.

Women returners or older women workers are not targeted in these policies. Yet, since people in these groups are relatively poor, they are unlikely to have the disposable income to self-fund their own training. For the considerable number of women who work part-time, there is little employer assistance for training. Thus, while earlier policy development eliminated the gender gap among young women, older women are likely to lack effective access to education and training.

## REDISTRIBUTION AND SOCIAL INFRASTRUCTURE

Several policies address the equalization of the length of men's and women's labor-market experience and the reduction of interruptions that occur for women as a consequence of their care for children and others. One involves access to quality affordable convenient child care, since many women break their employment in order to care for children. This is especially true for poorer women, since women in higher socioeconomic groups with high levels of education already take significantly fewer and shorter breaks from employment than those from lower socioeconomic groups.

In the late 1990s the U.K. underwent a very significant change in policy toward publicly funded child care, moving from a minimal one to the goal of ensuring that all parents have access to quality affordable convenient child care. What is known as the National Childcare Strategy is a major departure in U.K. government policy. The strategy primarily involves the expansion of for-profit child care, though additional resources are available to set up facilities in neighborhoods of great deprivations. Most of the financial support is paid directly to poor working parents, especially lone mothers, through the mechanism of tax credits. This includes a child-care element in the Working Families Tax Credit for up to 70 percent of the cost of registered child care, up to a ceiling in 2001 of £150 and £200 for one or two children respectively. By 2003 the Integrated Child Credit brings this together with other child-related benefits in a single tax credit (HM Treasury 1998, 1999, 2000). The new initiative supports the establishment of nurseries for three- and four-year-olds; child-care places attached to further-education colleges; and after school clubs, so as to provide "wrap-around care." Services are delivered locally primarily in the private sector by private nurseries and registered child minders. In poorer neighborhoods, public partnerships by Early Years Development and Childcare Partnerships are led by local authorities and involve a wide range of private and public bodies. By spring 2001 the government was able to claim that the National Childcare Strategy had created a net increase of places for 343,000 children (HM Treasury, 2001b). However, this policy has been implemented slowly. For instance, the Department for Education and Employment (DfEE) targets in 2000 were only that nursery places for three-year-olds should increase from 34 percent to 66 percent of relevant children by 2002 (DfEE, 2000). There have been reports of the insufficiency of nurseries to meet women's needs, so that three out of four parents say working mothers cannot find enough affordable child care, and that there was only one place for every 7.5 children under eight (Papworth, 2000). The National Childcare Strategy is a very considerable strategic shift toward state-supported child care. It constitutes both a significant redistribution of resources toward the women and the working poor as well as building social infrastructure. However, actual provision by the end of 2001 covers only a minority of children.

This U.K. child-care strategy is distinctive. The U.K. has abandoned the notion that child care is a private matter, which it once shared with the United States. It did not adopt the social democratic pattern established in the Nordic countries of publicly provided child care which is either subsidized or free for all citizens (Esping-Andersen, 1990; Sainsbury, 1996). Most of the assistance is highly targeted on child poverty and, as a consequence, the working poor. The method of disbursement is primarily through tax credits, itself part of a radical restructuring of the tax/benefit system in the U.K. The mode of delivery is predominantly private rather than public, and only in areas of very high deprivation do local public-initiated partnerships step in. The financial support for child care is aimed at supporting parents' employment and is not available to support women looking after children at home, as has developed in some European countries (Hobson, 2000). The new child-care policies are part of an employment-led strategy of reduction of child poverty, which has class and gender redistribution almost as a by-product.

## REGULATION

Three sources of gender inequity in the workplace are addressed by increased regulation: discontinuous work histories; part-time disadvantages; and discrimination. The regulation relates to working time, equal opportunities, and the minimum wage. Most of these regulations (with the exception of the minimum wage) emanate from the European Union, rather than originating in the U.K. It is at EU level, not state level, that markets for labor, goods, and services are primarily regulated.

The regulation of working time includes maternity leave, parental leave, and the regulation of excessive working hours. These are designed to make the time regime of the workplace more compatible with the time regime needed for caring, that is, to reconcile employment and caring, or to effect better work/life balance (Department of Trade and Industry, 2000b). Maternity leave enables women to bear children without interrupting their employment relation by taking a break of a few months from actual working for the employer. Women who use maternity leave do not suffer the large reduction in wages traditionally associated with having children. Women who have continuous work histories either as a result of not having children or by having access to appropriate maternity and parental leave avoid the serious problems consequent on labor-market discontinuity experienced by those mothers who interrupt their labor-market career and break their attachment to an employer (Dex et al., 1998; Joshi and Paci, 1998; Joshi, Paci, and Waldfogel, 1999; Joshi, Dex, and Macran, 1996; Waldfogel, 1995, 1997). The existing period of statutory paid leave in the U.K. of eighteen weeks is being extended to twenty-six weeks, the minimum amount of pay is being increased from £60 to £100 a week, two weeks of paid fathers' leave are being introduced, and the amount of unpaid parental leave is being extended to one year, all from 2003 (Women and Equality Unit, 2002). Further, the Working-Time Directive restricts the working of excessive hours on an involuntary basis to forty-eight hours a week.

The equal opportunity laws in the U.K. derive primarily from EU directives and treaties. Following the Directives on Equal Pay (1975), Equal Treatment (1976), and Equal Treatment in Social Security (1978) were those on Parental Leave (1984), Pregnancy (1990), and Dignity at Work (1992) (Hantrais, 1995; Hoskyns, 1996); Working-Time; and Part-Time Work (DTI, 2000a). These include laws on comparable worth and the equal treatment of part-time with full-time workers. While some have expressed skepticism about the impact of EU-led equal opportunities laws (Ostner and Lewis, 1995; Rossilli, 1997), the evidence shows that they have significantly narrowed the wage gap (Dolton et al., 1996; Jones and Makepeace, 1996; Joshi and Paci, 1998; Walby, 1999b; Zabalza and Tzannatos, 1985). The most rapid narrowing of the wages gap took place during the implementation of the 1970 Equal Pay Act (which came into force in 1975), between 1974 and 1977. Women working full-time increased their percentage of men's full-time hourly pay from 66 percent to 74 percent, while part-timers increased their percentage of men's full-time hourly pay from 54 percent to 60 percent. Zabalza and Tzannatos (1985) estimate that the effect of the 1970 and 1975 acts was to raise women's relative employment by 12 percent and relative pay by 15 percent, reducing the discriminatory component in the gap in wages by between 30 percent and 50 percent—this being "by all standards a remarkable performance for a policy of economic regulation" (15).

There are also some ostensibly nongendered regulatory policies that affect disadvantaged employed women. In particular, the introduction of the National Minimum Wage by the U.K. has disproportionately increased the wages of women working part-time on low wages (Low Pay Commission, 1998; HM Treasury 2001a).

The regulation of the labor market so that it better accommodates carers is a highly significant development for workplace equity. It challenges the notion that equal opportunities policies are only effective if women adopt "male" patterns of behavior (Ostner and Lewis, 1995), since it entails the modification of the employment environment to fit around the needs of carers. Its significance in the U.K. can be underestimated unless both very recent developments are taken into account and the role of the EU is brought into focus (as in O'Connor et al., 1999). Working time is an important arena where there has been an increase, not decrease, in the regulations affecting employment.

## GLOBALIZATION AND THE TRANSITION IN GENDER REGIME

The dominant view of globalization is that it is a major obstacle to women's equality because the increased power of economic markets at the expense of the state reduces the possibility of redistributive and regulatory interventions. However, the evidence for the U.K. in relation to gender suggests that this view is misplaced. Of course, prior to the change of government in 1997, there were changes in the balance between capital and labor in the workplace which were to the advantage of capital (Dex and McCulloch, 1997). But, there has been, especially since 1997, an increase of state expenditure for the provision of child care for poor working women and an increase in the regulation of the labor market, especially in relation to working time, in order to make the workplace compatible with caring.

There are two main reasons for these gendered changes. First, the transformation of the gender regime is generating a new political constituency, that of employed women, who have interests in public services and in the regulation of the labor market so as to facilitate women's employment, and who are increasingly articulating their perception of their interests in policy and political arenas. As women in the U.K. and other Western countries have increased their paid employment, they have also increased their involvement in collective institutions associated with it, such as trade unions and professional associations (Ledwith and Colgan, 1996; Gagnon and Ledwith, 2000; Shaw and Perrons, 1995). While men's membership in trade unions has been falling significantly, data from the Labour Force Survey and the Certification Officer for 1999 show a near convergence with women's rates of unionization. Young educated women in particular are joining trade unions. Among people under forty the rate of unionization of women and men is the same, though there is a gender gap among older people. Among those with degrees, women are significantly more likely than men to be in trade unions; 45 percent as compared with 30 percent (Hicks, 2000). Trade unions are now more likely to engage with issues of concern to women workers than they used to be, constructing an agenda of equality issues (Ellis and Ferns, 2000). The proportion of women in decision-making positions in unions, while not yet reflecting their membership proportions, has increased significantly. In UNISON,[2] which is the largest union in the U.K., the proportion of members who were women rose from 68 percent in 1994 to 72 percent in 1999/2000, while over the same time period the proportion of women who were members of the national executive rose from 42 percent to 62 percent; the proportion of female conference attendees, from 46 percent to 58 percent; and the proportion of female national full-time officers, from 20 percent to 21 percent (Ledwith and Colgan, 2000).

There are changes in the political representation of women's perceptions of their interests at the government level. There is support for expenditure on public services by working women in the U.K., as there is in other Western countries such as the United States (Manza and Brooks, 1999). Surveys in the U.K. have shown a pattern of young employed women being the group most politically supportive of parties and policies that facilitate women's employment (Women's Unit, 1999; Fawcett Society, 2000). Further, most prospective parliamentary candidates (PPCs) in the U.K. have paid work, and indeed have held professional or managerial jobs. In 1992, among Conservative PPCs 98 percent were in paid work and 92 percent held professional or managerial jobs, while among Labour PPCs 94 percent were in paid work and 90 percent were in professional or managerial jobs. Only 1 percent of candidates were "employed in the home" (Norris and Lovenduski, 1995: 112). There has been a significant increase in women elected to Parliament in the U.K. and elsewhere in the West. In the last two decades the proportion of women in Parliament has increased at the same time as there has been an increase in women's employment, as shown in table 2.5 below.

**Table 2.5. Percentage of Women in the Workforce and in Parliament, 1950–2000**

| % Female | 1950 | 1960/1961 | 1970 | 1980 | 1990 | 1999/2000 |
|---|---|---|---|---|---|---|
| U.K. | | | | | | |
| Employment | 31 | 35 | 37 | 40 | 43 | 45 |
| Parliament | 3 | 4 | 4 | 3 | 6 | 18 |
| U.S. | | | | | | |
| Employment | 27 | 34 | 38 | 42 | 45 | 47 |
| Parliament | 2 | 4 | 2 | 4 | 6 | 14 |
| Sweden | | | | | | |
| Employment | 26 | 36 | 39 | 45 | 48 | 48 |
| Parliament | 10 | 14 | 14 | 28 | 38 | 43 |
| Ireland | | | | | | |
| Employment | 26 | 27 | 27 | 29 | 33 | 41 |
| Parliament | 3 | 2 | 2 | 4 | 8 | 12 |
| France | | | | | | |
| Employment | 34 | 30 | 35 | 40 | 43 | 45 |
| Parliament | 7 | 2 | 2 | 4 | 7 | 11 |
| Germany | | | | | | |
| Employment | | | | | | 43 |
| Parliament | | | | | 21 | 31 |

**Table 2.5.** (*continued*)

| % Female | 1950 | 1960/1961 | 1970 | 1980 | 1990 | 1999/2000 |
|---|---|---|---|---|---|---|
| W. Germany | | | | | | |
| Employment | 33 | 37 | 36 | 39 | 41 | |
| Parliament | 7 | 9 | 7 | 9 | | |
| E. Germany | | | | | | |
| Employment | 45 | 40 | 45 | 46 | | |
| Parliament | 28 | 25 | 31 | 34 | | |
| Italy | | | | | | |
| Employment | 25 | 25 | 26 | 32 | 35 | 37 |
| Parliament | 8 | 4 | 3 | 8 | 13 | 11 |
| Spain | | | | | | |
| Employment | 16 | 23 | 20 | 29 | 32 | 37 |
| Parliament | 0 | 0 | 1 | 5 | 15 | 28 |
| Australia | | | | | | |
| Employment | 23 | 25 | 32 | 37 | 42 | 44 |
| Parliament | 1 | 0 | 0 | 2 | 7 | 23 |
| Finland | | | | | | |
| Employment | 41 | 39 | 42 | 47 | 48 | 48 |
| Parliament | 9 | 15 | 17 | 26 | 32 | 37 |
| Denmark | | | | | | |
| Employment | 34 | 31 | 34 | 43 | 46 | 46 |
| Parliament | 8 | 10 | 11 | 24 | 33 | 37 |

Sources: For parliamentary data: Inter-Parliamentary Union, 1995; Inter-Parliamentary Union website, 1999, 2000. For employment data 1961–1999: OECD, 1968, 1974, 2000; for employment data 1950: Mitchell, 1981.
Notes: Data for 1960/1961: employment is 1961, parliament is 1960. Data for 1999/2000: employment is 1999, parliament is 2000. The IPU reports all parliaments, whether or not the elections meet conventional Western standards of freedom.

There has been pressure across the Western world to introduce legislation to provide equal treatment for women at work, the implementation of which often depends on worker and other organizations (Rees, 1998; European Commission, 1999; European Parliament, 1994; Hantrais, 1995; Pillinger, 1992). The EU directives were passed, not merely as a result of the interest of the European Commission, but also as a result of pressure from women activists (Hoskyns, 1996; Liebert, 1999; Rees, 1998). Their implementation is uneven across the EU, generating more activity, both litigation and also more traditional forms of union action, in support of them in the U.K. than in many other member states (European Commission, 1999). Without trade union support these cases would be unlikely. There is increased representation of women and their interests in trade union activities at both national and EU levels (Pascual and Behning, 2000).

Secondly, the development of the European Union has been of enormous significance in the strengthening of the regulation of the labor market in relation to working time and equal opportunities. Without the EU, such policies would not have taken root in the U.K. to the same extent. The development of these policies can be best understood in terms of the EU's response to globalization. The EU is not a passive victim of globalization, but rather it assertively and aggressively increased its powers in order to rise to the challenge of globalization. Key political leaders in the EU, such as Jacques Delors, sought the creation of a single market and a distinctive kind of capitalism, different from that of either the United States or Japan, the other two regional capitalist hegemons (Bornschier and Ziltener, 1999). An aspect of the distinctiveness of EU capitalism was a commitment to social cohesion, which was absent in the United States. Equal opportunities policies are part of this commitment to social cohesion, and to a model of capitalism in which a degree of equity is seen to help the overall efficiency of the society and economy.

The development of the European Union has created growing internal convergence on certain dimensions, though not all. In particular, there is a common legal framework for the regulation of labor markets as well as markets for goods and services. This highlights the differences between the United States having one form of capitalism and gender regime, and the EU having another. There are some remaining differences within the EU that pertain to the role of national states in providing social security, that is, income maintenance in the face of the risks of old age, unemployment, and sickness, and in relation to tax/benefit systems. These lie at the core of the differences between countries highlighted in the feminist welfare-state-regime literature (Sainsbury, 1996). However, even these differences in welfare regimes are unstable, not least in the face of the development of a common monetary policy, with a common currency and central bank, and with concomitant pressures to develop a common fiscal and taxation regime within the EU.

The growth of equal opportunities policies in the U.K. can only be understood in the context of the superior power of the EU over the U.K. in matters of the regulation of labor markets. Since 1970 the EU has been responsible for many of the innovations in equal opportunities regulations that the U.K. has been obliged to implement. The implementation of EU equal opportunities law has depended on a range of pressures, not least from women in trade unions and their allies (Walby, 1999a). This legislation originated from EU pressure, brought to bear on the U.K. by the European Commission through the European Court of Justice on the legal basis of Article 119 of the Treaty of Rome. The U.K. and several other member states were taken to court by the European Commission for failing to have strong enough equal opportunities legislation and forced to revise their domestic legislation (Gregory, 1987; Hoskyns, 1996; Pillinger, 1992).

The U.K. government, during the 1980s and early 1990s, attempted to restrict the scope of these directives and related EU policy developments, instead prioritizing the deregulation of the labor market. They sought a model of capitalism closer to that of the U.S. than that of the EU. For example, the U.K. sought to remove parental leave for fathers from the scope of the Parental Leave Directive, and the U.K. did not sign the Social Chapter of the Maastricht Treaty until the change of government in 1997. Nevertheless, the U.K. was subject to Article 119 of the Treaty of Rome during this period and the U.K. courts routinely found in favor of equal opportunities cases argued under its auspices. In one case, the House of Lords (the highest court in the U.K.) drew on Article 119 in their 1994 ruling that it was discriminatory to treat part-time workers less favorably than full-time workers. Thus, during the 1980s and most of the 1990s the U.K. has implemented ever stronger equal opportunities law as a result of the supremacy of EU law over U.K. domestic law (within its areas of competence) (Hoskyns, 1996; Walby, 1999a, 1999b).

Most of the legally based equal opportunities policies before 1997 were imposed on reluctant U.K. governments by the requirements of membership of the EU. Without legally binding requirements stemming from EU treaties and directives it is unlikely that the U.K. would have implemented such strong equal opportunities laws. However, the process is more complex than a simple imposition of the will of the EU on a resistant U.K., since significant groups within the U.K. actively welcomed such EU interventions. Indeed U.K. women workers and trade unions actively sought EU assistance in their fights for equal opportunities in the workplace. U.K. women were active in taking test cases through the courts to seek European-style justice. This was a process of "leapfrogging," or jumping over, the national state to the European level in order to secure change within the U.K. This represents a politics of effective coalitions and alliances at a transnational level.

## CONCLUSIONS

The most important current policy developments for gender equity in the U.K. workplace are the national child-care strategy, which contains targeted assistance for poor working women, the regulation of working time and equal opportunities, and the minimum wage. Earlier decades had seen the closing of the education gap between young women and men, which has been important in the increased participation of women in employment. Current policies result from the increased political voice of employed women, the transformation of the gender regime, and the emergence of the EU.

Conceptualizations of the gender regime need to be broader than this focus on "male breadwinners" and include gender relations in employment, including the regulation of working time and the democratic involvement of women, as well as in the household, state, and civil society. In particular, there is a need to address the implications of the increased formal political representation of women in government.

There is an ongoing transition in the gender regime in many Western countries. Notions of the path dependency and the specificity of gender relations in particular countries have been overstated. There are significant similarities in the increase in women's employment and the increased political voice of women in many Western countries, as well as differences between countries.

Conceptualizations of the U.K. as having a strong male-breadwinner logic (Lewis, 1992; O'Connor et al., 1999) are, at best, out of date. U.K. government policy in 2002 is oriented toward full employment for all. Work/life balance, or the reconciliation of care and employment, is assumed to include employment. The regulation of working time, support for child care, and the minimum wage are policies that are intended to ensure this.

The EU is an increasingly powerful polity in the context of globalization and has primary power to regulate the U.K. labor market. Globalization does not weaken all polities. Globalization is not an economic process that sweeps polities away. Rather, globalization restructures polities. The powers of the European Union have increased as a result of globalization. The global context does not inevitably reduce the likelihood of socially just policies for working women. Globalization should neither be equated with neoliberal versions of economic markets nor entail a move toward economic reductionism. Of course, increased global competition has been part of a process of restructuring the balance between capital and labor in which some workers, such as those with few educational qualifications who are working part-time, are increasingly vulnerable to low wages and job insecurity. However, politics still matter. The U.K. addresses the challenges of globalization in the context of the EU. The EU pursues a different strategy for capitalist development from that of the United States, one that involves full employment for women and regulation of labor markets so as to provide equal opportunities (though not equality). It is in this context that certain policies for women in employment are facilitated.

Globalization restructures in complex and contradictory ways. While there are downward pressures on the wages and conditions of some workers as a result of the enhanced power of global capital, these are not the only consequences of globalization. The implications of the increased power of global capital are significantly affected by political strategies. The political strategy of the EU towards globalization is significantly different from that of the U.S., especially in its concern for maintaining social cohesion. This modifies the regulation of markets, including labor markets, even of the more liberal member states of the EU, such as the U.K. Further, the modernization of the gender regime is creating a new political constituency of working women who are vocalizing their perceived interests in policies to assist combining home and work.

## NOTES

1. These tribunals, while procedurally less formal than courts, where decisions are reached by a panel including representatives from both employers and trade unions, nonetheless make legally binding decisions, although these can be appealed up to the highest levels of the court system.

2. UNISON organizes primarily, though not exclusively, low-paid workers in the public sector. For instance it is a major union in hospitals for cleaners, care assistants, and porters.

## REFERENCES

Berkovitch, Nitza. 1999. *From Motherhood to Citizenship: Women's Rights and International Organizations.* Baltimore, Md.: John Hopkins University Press.

Blackwell, Louisa. 2001. "Occupational Sex Segregation and Part-time Work in Modern Britain." *Gender, Work and Organization* 8, no. 2: 146–63.

Blundell, Richard, Lorraine Dearden, and Costas Meghir. 1996. *The Determinants and Effects of Work Related Training in Britain.* London: Institute for Fiscal Studies.

Bornschier, Volker, and Patrick Ziltener. 1999. "The Revitalization of Western Europe and the Politics of the 'Social Dimension.'" Pp. 33–52 in *European Societies: Fusion or Fission?* ed. Thomas Boje, Bart van Steenbergen, and Sylvia Walby. London: Routledge.

Callender, Claire, and Martin Kemp. 2000. *Changing Student Finances: Income, Expenditure and the Take-Up of Student Loans among Full- and Part-Time Higher Education Students in 1998/9.* Department for Education and Employment Research Brief no. 213. London: DfEE.

Castells, Manuel. 1997. *The Information Age: Economy, Society and Culture.* Vol. 2, *The Power of Identity.* Oxford: Blackwell.

Cerny, Philip G. 1996. "International Finance and the Erosion of State Policy Capacity." In *Globalization and Public Policy*, ed. Philip Gummett. Cheltenham: Edward Elgar.

Chase-Dunn, Christopher, Yukio Kawano, and Benjamin D. Brewer. 2000. "Trade Globalization since 1795: Waves of Integration in the World-System." *American Sociological Review* 65: 77–95.

Crouch, Colin, and Wolfgang Streeck, eds. 1997. *Political Economy of Modern Capitalism: Mapping Convergence and Diversity.* London: Sage.

Department for Education and Employment. 1999. *Learning to Succeed.* London: The Stationery Office.

———. 2000. "The Department's Aim and Objectives and Targets for 2002." At http://www.dfee.gov.uk/workplans/aims.htm.

Department of Trade and Industry. 2000a. *Part-Time Work: Public Consultation.* URN 99/1224. London: Department of Trade and Industry.

———. 2000b. *Work and Parents: Competitiveness and Choice: A Green Paper.* Cm 5005. London: The Stationery Office.

Dex, Shirley, Heather Joshi, Susan Macran, and Andrew McCulloch. 1998. "Women's Employment Transitions around Child Bearing." *Oxford Bulletin of Economics and Statistics* 60, no. 1: 79–98.

Dex, Shirley, and Andrew McCulloch. 1997. *Flexible Employment: The Future of Britain's Jobs.* Basingstoke: Macmillan.

Dolton, P., D. O'Neill, and O. Sweetman. 1996. "Gender Differences in the Changing Labor Market: The Role of Legislation and Inequality in Changing the Wage Gap for Qualified Workers in the UK." *The Journal of Human Resources* 31, no. 3: 549–65.

Ellis, Valerie, and Sue Ferns. 2000. "Equality Bargaining." In *Women, Diversity and Democracy in Trade Unions*, ed. Suzanne Gagnon and Sue Ledwith. Oxford: Oxford Brookes University.

Esping-Andersen, Gøsta. 1990. *The Three Worlds of Welfare Capitalism*. Cambridge, U.K.: Polity.

European Commission. 1999. "Gender Mainstreaming in the European Employment Strategy." Doc EQOP 61-99 DG EMPL/D/5, 1 October 1999. Brussels: European Commission.

European Parliament. Directorate General for Research. 1994. *Measures to Combat Sexual Harassment at the Workplace: Action Taken in the Member States of the European Community*. Working paper in the Women's Rights Series, European Parliament, Strasbourg, France.

Fawcett Society. 2000. *The Gender/Generation Gap*. London: Fawcett Society.

Fraser, Nancy. 1997. *Justice Interruptus: Critical Reflections on the "Postsocialist" Condition*. London: Routledge.

Gagnon, Suzanne, and Sue Ledwith, eds. 2000. *Women, Diversity and Democracy in Trade Unions*. Oxford: Oxford Brookes University.

Gottfried, Heidi, and Jacqueline O'Reilly. 2000. *The Weakness of a Strong Breadwinner Model: Part-Time Work and Female Labour Force Participation in Germany and Japan*. Wayne State Occasional Paper no. 3.

Gregg, Paul. 1998. "The Impact of Unemployment and Job Loss on Future Earnings." In HM Treasury, *Persistent Poverty and Lifetime Inequality: The Evidence*. Occasional Paper no. 10 (also CASE Report 5, LSE March 1999), 89–96.

Gregory, Jeanne. 1987. *Sex, Race and the Law: Legislating for Equality*. London: Sage.

Hakim, Catherine. 1992. "Explaining Trends in Occupational Segregation: The Measurement, Causes, and Consequences of the Sexual Division of Labour," *European Sociological Review* 8, no. 2: 127–52.

———. 1996. *Key Issues in Women's Work: Female Heterogeneity and the Polarisation of Women's Employment*. London: Athlone.

Hantrais, Linda. 1995. *Social Policy in the European Union*. Basingstoke: Macmillan.

Harkness, Susan. 1996. "The Gender Earnings Gap: Evidence from the UK." *Fiscal Studies* 17: 1–36.

Hay, Colin. 1997. "Anticipating Accommodations, Accommodating Anticipations: The Appeasement of Capital in the 'Modernization' of the British Labour Party, 1987–1992." *Politics and Society* 25, no. 2: 234–56.

Held, David. 1995. *Democracy and the Global Order: From the Modern State to Cosmopolitan Governance*. Cambridge, U.K.: Polity Press.

Hettne, Bjorn, Andras Inotai, and Osvaldo Sunkel, eds. 1999. *Globalism and the New Regionalism*. Vol. 1. Basingstoke: Macmillan.

HM Treasury. 1998. *The Working Families Tax Credit and Work Incentives*. The Modernisation of Britain's Tax and Benefits System No. 3. London: The Stationery Office.

———. 1999. *Supporting Children through the Tax and Benefit System*. The Modernisation of Britain's Tax and Benefits System No 5. London: The Stationery Office.

———. 2000. *Tackling Poverty and Making Work Pay—Tax Credits for the 21st Century*. The Modernisation of Britain's Tax and Benefits System No. 6. London: The Stationery Office.

———. 2001a. *The Budget: March 2001*. London: The Stationery Office.

———. 2001b. *Pre-Budget Report*. London: The Stationery Office.

Hicks, Stephen. 2000. "Trade Union Membership 1998–99: An Analysis of Data from the Certification Officer and Labour Force Survey." *Labour Market Trends* (July): 329–40.

Hirst, Paul, and Grahame Thompson. 1996. *Globalization in Question: The International Economy and the Possibilities of Governance.* Cambridge, U.K.: Polity.

Hobson, Barbara, ed. 2000. *Gender and Citizenship in Transition.* London: Macmillan.

Hoskyns, Catherine. 1996. *Integrating Gender: Women, Law and Politics in the European Union.* London: Verso.

Inter-Parliamentary Union. 1995. *Women in Parliaments: 1945–1995.* Geneva: Inter-Parliamentary Union.

———. 1999. *Women in National Parliaments: World Average; Regional Averages.* At http://www.ipu.org/wmn-e/world.htm.

———. 2000. *Women in National Parliaments.* At http://www.ipu.org/wmn-e/world.htm.

Jenson, Jane. 1997. "Who Cares? Gender and Welfare Regimes." *Social Politics* 4, no. 2: 182–87.

Jones, David R., and Gerald H. Makepeace. 1996. "Equal Worth, Equal Opportunities: Pay and Promotion in an Internal Labour Market." *The Economic Journal* 106: 401–9.

Joshi, Heather, Shirley Dex, and Susan Macran. 1996. "Employment after Childbearing and Women's Subsequent Labour Force Participation: Evidence for the 1958 Birth Cohort." *Journal of Population Economics* 9: 325–48.

Joshi, Heather, and Pierella Paci. 1998. *Unequal Pay for Women and Men: Evidence from the British Birth Cohort Studies.* Cambridge, Mass.: MIT Press.

Joshi, Heather, Pierella Paci, and Jane Waldfogel. 1999. "The Wages of Motherhood: Better or Worse?" *Cambridge Journal of Economics* 23: 543–64.

Klein, Naomi. 1999. *No Logo: Taking Aim at the Brand Bullies.* New York: Picador.

*Labour Market Trends.* 2001.

Ledworth, Sue and Fiona Colgan, eds. 1996. *Women in Organisations: Challenging Gender Politics.* Basingstoke: Macmillan.

———. 2000. "Women, Democracy and Diversity and the New Trade Unionism." In *Women, Diversity and Democracy in Trade Unions,* ed. Suzanne Gagnon and Sue Ledwith. Oxford: Oxford Brookes University.

Lewis, Jane. 1992. "Gender and the Development of Welfare Regimes." *Journal of European Social Policy* 3: 159–73.

———. 1997. "Gender and Welfare Regimes: Further Thoughts." *Social Politics* 4, no. 2: 160–77.

Liebert, Ulrike. 1999. "Gender Politics in the European Union: The Return of the Public." *European Societies* 1, no. 2: 191–232.

Low Pay Commission. 1998. *The National Minimum Wage: First Report of the Low Pay Commission.* Cm 3976. London: The Stationery Office.

Macpherson, David, and Barry Hirsch. 1995. "Wages and Gender Composition: Why Do Women's Jobs Pay Less?" *Journal of Labor Economics* 13: 426–71.

Manza, Jeff, and Clem Brooks. 1999. *Social Cleavages and Political Change: Voting Alignments and U.S. Party Coalitions.* Oxford: Oxford University Press.

Martin, H-P., and Schumann, H. 1997. *The Global Trap: Globalization and the Assault on Democracy and Prosperity.* London: Zed Press.

McRae, Susan. 1993. "Returning to Work after Childbirth: Opportunities and Inequalities." *European Sociological Review* 9, no. 2: 125–38.

Mitchell, Brian Redman. 1981. *European Historical Statistics 1750–1975.* London: Macmillan.

New Earnings Survey. 2000. Office of National Statistics, "New Earnings Survey." London: TSO.

Norris, Pippa, and Joni Lovenduski. 1995. *Political Recruitment: Gender, Race and Class in the British Parliament.* Cambridge: Cambridge University Press.

O'Connor, Julia, Ann Shola Orloff, and Sheila Shaver. 1999. *States, Markets, Families: Gender, Liberalism and Social Policy in Australia, Canada, Great Britain and the United States.* Cambridge: Cambridge University Press.

OECD. 1968, 1974. Organisation for Economic Co-operation and Development, "Labour Force Statistics: 1956–1966." Paris: OECD.

———. 2000. Organisation for Economic Co-operation and Development, "Labour Force Statistics: 1976–1999." Paris: OECD.

Ohmae, Kenichi. 1995. *The End of the Nation State: The Rise of Regional Economics.* London: HarperCollins.

Office for National Statistics. 1998. *Living In Britain: Results from the 1996 General Household Survey.* London: The Stationery Office.

———. 2001. *New Earnings Survey 2000.* London: The Stationery Office.

Ostner, Ilona, and Jane Lewis. 1995. "Gender and the Evolution of European Social Policies." Pp. 159–93 in *European Social Policy: Between Fragmentation and Integration,* ed. Stephan Leibfried and Paul Pierson. Washington, D.C.: Brookings.

Owens, Jane. 2001. *Evaluation of Individual Learning Accounts—Early Views of Customers and Providers: England.* Department for Education and Employment Research Brief no. 294. London: Department for Education and Employment.

Papworth, Jill. 2000. "An Uphill Struggle on the Nursery Slopes." *Guardian,* 20 May, Jobs and Money section, p. 2.

Pascual, Amparo Serrano, and Ute Behning, eds. 2000. *Gender Mainstreaming in the European Employment Strategy.* Brussels: European Trade Union Institute.

Peters, Julie, and Andrea Wolper, eds. 1995. *Women's Rights, Human Rights: International Feminist Perspectives.* London: Routledge.

Pillinger, Jane. 1992. *Feminising the Market: Women's Pay and Employment in the European Community.* Basingstoke: Macmillan.

Policy and Innovation Unit. 2001. *In Demand: Adult Skills in the 21st Century.* London: Cabinet Office Policy and Innovation Unit.

Rees, Teresa. 1998. *Mainstreaming Equality in the European Union: Education, Training and Labour Market Policies.* London: Routledge.

Reskin, Barbara, and Patricia Roos. 1990. *Job Queues, Gender Queues.* Philadelphia, Pa.: Temple University Press.

Riley, Rebecca, and Garry Young. 2000. *The New Deal for Young People: Implications for Employment and the Public Finances.* Employment Service Research and Development Report 62. London: Employment Service.

Rix, Andrew, Kyle Davies, Richard Gaunt, Amanda Hare, and Sarah Cobbold. 1999. "The Training and Development of Flexible Workers." *Labour Market Trends,* October 1999: 55–56.

Robinson, William I. 2001. "Social Theory and Globalization: The Rise of a Transnational State." *Theory and Society* 30: 157–200.

Rossilli, Mariagrazia. 1997. "The European Community's Policy on the Equality of Women: From the Treaty of Rome to the Present." *The European Journal of Women's Studies* 4, no. 1: 63–82.

Rubery, Jill, Mark Smith, and Colette Fagan. 1999. *Women's Employment in Europe: Trends and Prospects*. London: Routledge.

Ruggie, John Gerard. 1998. *Constructing the World Polity: Essays on International Institutionalization*. London: Routledge.

Sainsbury, Diane. 1996. *Gender, Equality and Welfare States*. Cambridge: Cambridge University Press.

Sassen, Saskia. 1999. "Embedding the Global in the National: Implications for the Role of the State." Pp. 158–71 in *States and Sovereignty in the Global Economy*, ed. David A. Smith, Dorothy Solinger, and Steven Topik. London: Routledge.

Scholte, Jan Aarte. 2000. *Globalisation: A Critical Introduction*. Basingstoke: Macmillan.

Shaw, Jenny, and Diane Perrons, eds. 1995. *Making Gender Work: Managing Equal Opportunities*. Buckingham: Open University Press.

Siltanen, Janet. 1990. "Social Change and the Measurement of Occupational Segregation by Sex." *Work, Employment and Society* 4, no. 1: 1–29.

Standing, Guy. 1999. *Global Labour Flexibility: Seeking Distributive Justice*. London: Macmillan.

Taylor-Gooby, Peter. 1997. "In Defence of Second-Best Theory: State, Class and Capital in Social Policy." *Journal of Social Policy* 26, no. 2: 171–92.

Walby, Sylvia. 1986. *Patriarchy at Work*. Cambridge: Polity.

———. 1990. *Theorizing Patriarchy*. Oxford: Blackwell.

———. 1997. *Gender Transformations*. London: Routledge.

———. 1999a. "The New Regulatory State: The Social Powers of the European Union." *British Journal of Sociology* 50, no. 1: 118–40.

———. 1999b. "The European Union and Equal Opportunities Policies." *European Societies* 1, no. 1: 59–80.

———. 2004. *Globalisation, Modernity and Difference*. London: Sage.

Waldfogel, Jane. 1995. "The Price of Motherhood: Family Status and Women's Pay in a Young British Cohort." *Oxford Economic Papers* 47: 584–610.

———. 1997. "The Effect of Children on Women's Wages." *American Sociological Review* 62: 209–17.

Wickham-Jones, Mark. 1995. "Anticipating Social Democracy, Preempting Anticipations: Economic Policy-Making in the British Labour Party, 1987–1992." *Politics and Society* 23, no. 4: 465–94.

Wild, Sheila. 2001. "The Work of the EOC." Presentation at conference, Progressing Gender Relations in Europe, 7 September, University of Salford.

Women and Equality Unit. 2002. *What the Government is Doing to Reduce the Gender Pay Gap*. London: Cabinet Office Women and Equality Unit and Department of Trade and Industry.

Women's National Commission. 1991. *Women Returners Employment Potential: An Agenda for Action*. London: Cabinet Office.

Women's Unit. 1999. *Voices*. London: Cabinet Office Women's Unit.

———. 2000. *Women's Incomes over the Lifetime*. London: The Stationery Office.

Wright, R. E., and Ermisch, J. 1991. "Gender Discrimination in the British Labour Market: A Reassessment." *Economic Journal* 101: 508–52.

Zabalza, A., and Z. Tzannatos. 1985. *Women and Equal Pay: The Effects of Legislation on Female Employment and Wages in Britain*. Cambridge: Cambridge University Press.

# 3

# European Gender Mainstreaming: Promises and Pitfalls of Transformative Policy[1]

*Alison Woodward*

Gender mainstreaming is innovative and its global spread is extraordinary. As True and Mintrom write about the spread of women's policy machinery internationally, "This rapid diffusion of a state-level bureaucratic innovation is unprecedented in the postwar era" (2001: 30). Gender mainstreaming is one widely adapted approach, which was developed in transnational networks and goes beyond women's policy machinery. As a policy strategy for change, it utilizes the language of efficiency and the instruments of public bureaucracy, yet demands that the vertical walls between policy sectors be broken down in favor of crosscutting governance. It requires no less than a radical redefinition of policy values and the insertion of gender equality as a fundamental goal in all policy. But what are the necessary conditions for this radical transformation to occur?

This chapter provides an initial discussion of the ways in which the mainstreaming approach aims to change the definitions of the situation as applied in government to include gender relations as a point of departure. It suggests factors that may affect whether the approach can become an institutional innovation that leads to gender being included in policy making as a given. The factors include the commitment to a gender mission, the level of sophistication in terms of gender/policy issues, the environmental context of resistance to gender initiatives, and the role of gender experts. It explores the role of these contextual factors as related to early experiences in the European Commission and in northern Europe.

## WHAT IS MAINSTREAMING?

Gender mainstreaming aims to enable the state to deliver gender-sensitive policy and transform gender relations. Its point of departure is an acknowledgement of the differences between men and women. It claims that the sources of policy injustice are found in the fact that existing structures are not gender neutral (Rees, 1998a: 172). Mainstreaming suggests that equal-opportunities for women and men should no longer be achieved solely through equal-opportunity-earmarked policies. A multi-stranded and total approach is necessary. The various policy-making fields should be imbued with gender awareness in order to incorporate equality goals into traditional policy areas (European Commission, 1996; Sensi, 1996).

Most national and international organizations trace a debt for the conceptualization of mainstreaming to the United Nations Beijing Platform for Action. Governments adopting the Beijing Platform for Action have undertaken a commitment to a strategy of mainstreaming gender perspectives throughout policy processes. The major component of the mainstreaming paragraph included in each major section of the Platform for Action is as follows:

> . . . governments and other actors should promote an active and visible policy of mainstreaming a gender perspective in all policies and programs so that, before decisions are taken, analysis is made of the effects on women and men, respectively.[2]

Mainstreaming can be regarded as a kind of "institutional innovation" in the sense used by Nedelmann (1995) or Inhetveen (1998), for ultimately it is hoped that mainstreaming will lead to a virtually reflexive consideration of the impact of policy on gender relations.

To what extent is it possible to merely insert gender concerns in an organizational setting designed with man in mind? When activists move inside, in the guise of bureaucrats with a feminist agenda (femocrats), politicians, or consultants, there are necessary compromises. Heikkinen (1999) is not alone in remembering that "mainstream" in Anglo-Saxon feminist terms used to mean "malestream" or dominant culture. Thus mainstreaming implicitly means accepting that there is a dominant culture. However, any review of the definitions of gender mainstreaming[3] indicates that compromises in the language of gender have been necessitated. The further one gets from an environment that has taken gender on board through a sophisticated and broadly based recognition of the problem, the more compromises in the tools which are meant to challenge and transform gender perception. In practice it seems that organizations adapt definitions of mainstreaming that are amenable to their institutional cultures, but these are actually sometimes far from the original UN ambitions. The amount of change seems to depend on how mainstreaming is introduced, by whom, the historical context, and the presence of opposition.

At a conference of the OECD in late 2000 (OECD, 2000), the Irish Minister of Equality noted that gender mainstreaming is fraught with difficulties. It does not promise quick wins, and requires disaggregated statistics, and a commitment of resources. However, the minister realized mainstreaming's ultimately transformative nature. It promises gains impossible with either legislative reform or affirmative action. At the same conference, demonstrating the wide misuse of the idea of mainstreaming, Heinz Fischer from Deutsche Bank claimed that business had been doing gender mainstreaming for years. Business seems to understand gender mainstreaming as simple equal opportunity in employment. It is easy to conclude with Mackay and Bilton that "There is widespread misunderstanding and confusion over the meaning of mainstreaming and related concepts . . . mainstreaming is sometimes referred to as a tool, sometimes a process or method, and sometimes a strategy." (2000: 2)

One of the main elements of confusion is that between equal opportunity, affirmative action, and gender mainstreaming. As the OECD's Development Assistance Committee Sourcebook explains, equal opportunities is more of a human-resource approach aimed at providing equal opportunities for women and men in the workplace (Schalkwyck and Woroniuk, 1998). When the European Commission attempted to adopt mainstreaming in 1996, they needed to couple the idea to the labor market. At that time they lacked the legal foundation of the Treaty of Amsterdam. However, the misconception that mainstreaming is simply "equal opportunities" is widespread and can be seen in a number of the projects that are now being called "mainstreaming." This problem is exacerbated by the fact that many European women's policy or emancipation offices are linked to employment issues. Gender mainstreaming is different than equal opportunity and should be transformative: "a deliberate and systematic approach to integrating a gender perspective into analysis, procedures and policies" (Schalkwyck and Woroniuk, 1998).

Gender mainstreaming and equal opportunities policy are thus complementary terms, not equivalents. Nelen and Hondeghem suggest that gender policy can be looked at using an analogy to a house (2000). I will expand a little on their gender equality house. The gender equality house in European countries was first built as a row house, floor by floor, but well separated from its neighbors. It was a vertical policy area, inhabited solely by women. The gender equality house can be envisioned as having three floors and a foundation—closely related to the chronology of developing equal opportunities approaches. To be able to stand it needs a solid foundation. This is the commitment of leading and powerful decision makers, who have been necessary for every stage in its construction. The first floor of the house focused on changing the legislative framework by eliminating discriminatory regulations and creating a level playing field. T. Rees (1999) calls this "tinkering." This in itself did not result in equal opportunities. The second story began to redress the consequences of past discriminations through affirmative actions, Rees's "tailoring." Both of these floors used the man as the measure of success. Women were to have opportunities equal to those available to men.

Mainstreaming indicates the thinking of a new architect, who sees gender equality or inequality as a product of gendered relations and institutions and wants to totally transform the house, breaking out of the row-house ghetto and changing the entire neighborhood.[4] Initially, gender mainstreamers occupy this penthouse, but they aim to break down the retaining walls of the policy ghetto of women's policy and change the entire street.[5]

## WHAT'S SO INNOVATIVE ABOUT MAINSTREAMING?

Mainstreaming can be an innovation. It is attractive to social movements for at least three reasons. First of all, it allows social issues to escape from marginal-policy ghettos. It transforms the woman question from a vertical special issue to horizontal general concern. Second, mainstreaming is innovative as it spurs the development of new policy instruments. Mainstreaming simply means doing policy with varied citizens in mind, yet as it is framed in a rational public-management language, the ambitions are tested and evaluated.

Continuous evaluation is one of the key demands of the mainstreamers, which requires new policy tools such as gender equality indicators, and gender-proofing instruments. This aspect is already materializing. By the beginning of 2002, the European Commission–funded data bank, DIGMA (Database for Instruments for Gender Mainstreaming)[6], included more than 200 different policy instruments and approaches to doing mainstreaming. Third, gender mainstreaming links a revolutionary goal: that is, the end of sexual inequality, to rational public administrative tools. Mainstreaming and its implementation would denote using bureaucratic tools to gain power over the definitions of women and men.

## THE DANGERS OF MAINSTREAMING?

Unfortunately there are many reasons to mistrust those who claim to be "mainstreaming." There is substantial scope for misunderstanding, indicated in the wide variety of European approaches to mainstreaming and in attempts to eliminate special women's policy machinery. A first problem is the term "mainstreaming" itself. It can be appropriated and given a new meaning. The further away from the femocrat center, the more frequent the misunderstanding of the term and its specific connotations. Some interpret the approach as meaning that vertical institutions for equal opportunity and women's policy machinery will necessarily disappear.

In European policy, the issue becomes even more complicated as all language groups are forced to adopt the English term, which leads to yet other uncontrollable currents of resistance unrelated to gender. For instance in France, the partners carrying out the inventory for the DIGMA index ended up using the term *approche intégrée*, and discovered that most social actors were still stuck with the goal of the seventies, "Equal pay for Equal work," and that there was a large gap in terms of information and knowledge about equality policy in general and mainstreaming in particular (Bastos, 2002: 35).

A second issue is the fact that gender issues have usually been the responsibility of a special women's policy machinery in government; it is not self-evident that other policy sectors take over gender monitoring. Some claim that gender awareness needs expertise and should be left to professionals (who are certified in women's studies, for example). The instruments developed thus far promote an expert rational-technocratic approach, with separate jargon and measurement criteria.

Institutional innovation best occurs in a context where values are present that can be mobilized in service of the new institution. Inhetveen discusses this in the context of quota regulations for women, but mainstreaming can also be seen in this framework (Inhetveen, 1998). Not only is training necessary for the institutionalization of gender awareness in policy making, but also a high level of cultural acceptance. A procedure will only become an institution if it is taken for granted.

The strategic problem is to develop something that circumvents the personalization of gender issues by bureaucrats and makes doing a gender analysis of a policy proposal as automatic as making a budget, an administrative ritual (Stark, 1998). It should be something that can be learned and carried out by the Weberian typical androgynous servant of the state. But mainstreaming gender is not quite like doing a budget in that the language of gender is still not the general language of society. A procedure not firmly based on common values will have a much more difficult job in becoming effective and in being continued.

Mainstreaming needs to be hard, and measurable, and will in this way be authoritative. The risk is that in finding the common language and routines, the transformative potential of asking the gender questions and questioning structures of power may be lost. Close analysis of national reports submitted in fulfillment of Beijing +5 suggests that administrators in sectors where gender awareness is only minimally present grasp at any straw to claim that they have already mainstreamed.

## MAINSTREAMING AS RATIONAL AND INNOVATIVE PRACTICE

In practice, governments attempting to bring gender into their policy process across the board through mainstreaming have used various approaches. They begin with a toolbox for doing mainstreaming—one tool or a mix with options ranging from analysis, awareness, and training to measurement. The question is what factors have been important in leading to a watered-down approach to mainstreaming as opposed to realizing the transformative potential. Judging from early experience, as well as evidence from case studies done on the European Union (Pollack and Hafner-Burton, 2000; Braithwaite, 2001; Bretherton, 1999, 2001; Mazey, 2000, 2001; Engstrom, 2000), when gender issues escape the women's policy ghetto, there is variance in the degree to which they take root in other policy areas. This is not solely due to the relative affinity or lack of clear-cut affinity to women's issues. These authors have begun to develop predictive frameworks for the degree to which mainstreaming is taken on board by an organization. Bouvret (2001) points out that the predictive framework of Hafner-Burton and Pollack suggests that the sympathetic policy frames of, for example, Directorate General (DG) for Development, would lead to great strides in mainstreaming. In fact, DG for Development has been left behind by the DG research due to institutional factors. Much of the success of mainstreaming will depend on the institutional and organizational setting and the methods used to carry out the project. Schalkwyk and Woroniuk (1998, 21–23), writing about the potential for development projects to mainstream, are among those[7] who set out some of the critical factors for predicting success. They identify the institution's mandate and area of work, its organizational history and culture, the current personnel, organizational routines and procedures, and external environment and pressures. On a case-to-case basis, such variables can be evaluated within a comparative framework and offer both predictions for success as well as handles for organizational change.

Schalkwyk and Woroniuk share in many ways the perspective of the Web of Institutionalization developed by Caren Levy (1996, 1998) for Gender in Development projects. She identifies thirteen interdependent elements that are considered as essential for gender institutionalization, including institutional culture, political commitment, the location of gender responsibilities, political responsibilities, the dominant frame of culture, resources, procedures and instruments, the quality of data, and the knowledge level of the staff.

An analysis of UN budgeting projects (Hannan, 2000) indicated the importance of similar factors. "Clear policy statements on gender equality and the work of the organization; clarity on gender mainstreaming in planning and budget instructions; explicit management support for gender mainstreaming; strong oversight and accountability functions; and increased dialogue between program staff, budget staff and gender specialists" were all seen as essential for successful mainstreaming. Some of the constraints identified were not directly related to gender perspectives but concerned technical and political capacity to produce clear statements on objectives and indicators.

Combining these insights but simplifying the list of factors for the purpose of estimating the transformative potential of gender mainstreaming, the following factors can all be expected to play a role in the depth of transformation of public-policy discourse and its gender sensitivity: commitment to a gender mission, the level of sophistication in terms of gender/policy issues, the environmental context of resistance to gender initiatives, and the role of gender experts. This group of factors is especially important for identifying the potential for institutional transformation, as it focuses in part on the actors and their belief cultures.

(1) *Commitment to a gender mission—dedicated actors and historical context*: How all-encompassing is the commitment to changing gender relations and how well anchored is it in the administration? Is it a policy managed by an ad-hoc group of cabinet members corralled by the prime minister in a symbolic political effort or does it come from a framework of a national commitment to equal opportunities or gender emancipation that predates the commitments made in the Beijing treaties? There can be varying degrees of consensus about the goals of a gender policy and different sorts of emphases. A particular government may emphasize economic autonomy for women, equal opportunities, or equal rights. They may have a widespread network of femocrats bearing this vision into various divisions of the public bureaucracy. On the opposite side of the continuum are the numerous governments who have isolated the woman question to a group of transitory employees in a special office. They work on policy developed by, for example, one particular minister, rather than a policy taken by the government as a whole. Accountability is a special issue going back to measurement—can managers be held accountable for their achievements, and are there indicators for success in achieving a gender-sensitive policy approach? A subvariable here may be the importance of a gender hero. All analysis schemes include the importance of real commitment from top figures in the organization, but case studies frequently identify one top power holder as being essential in convincing other top managers. In Nelen and Hondeghem's metaphorical gender equality house (2000), this commitment forms the roof, but actual examples of successful mainstreaming indicate that political and mission commitment may be the fundament, as I suggest above.

Policy entrepreneurs and heroes in alliances are as important, as is the degree of policy access.

(2) *Level of gender sophistication*: How well versed are actors in the administration on gender issues? Are research, gender-sensitive data sources, and training available to develop gender expertise? Some administrations have already developed a vision about how gender inequality arises and have ideas about the tools necessary for change. They may have a gender vocabulary that is shared by people working in various fields and anchored in a shared understanding. The establishment of specialized gender studies at advanced levels influences the availability in the public forum of sophisticated understandings of the workings of gender. An example of this situation is found in the Netherlands, where the instruments to do gender testing were anchored in a sophisticated theoretical understanding of gender relations. Aspects of policy to be examined then included issues such as an analysis of problems of organization of intimacy, the gendered division of labor, and the identification of processes of resources and gender rules (Verloo and Roggeband, 1996). This can be contrasted with the case in Flanders, where the first minister of equal opportunities had yet to develop an analysis of the reasons for gendered inequality, and was faced with inadequate data on gender relations. Here efforts to analyze the gender impacts of policy were inserted in a policy framework and state machinery with no gender vocabulary (Woodward and Meier, 1998).

(3) *Environmental context of resistance to gender initiatives*: To what extent are there vested interests that would be opposed to the transformation of gender relations or a reallocation of resources to enhance opportunities for women? If, for example, an analysis of European Union science policy indicates that women are substantially underprivileged and recommends monitoring for better apportionment of resources including new scientific terrain, this will be unpopular with those expecting a piece of the traditional scientific pie. The stronger the resistance to serious questioning of the fundamentals of gender in policy and in the administration itself, the more likely that the new questions of mainstreaming will be misinterpreted to mean that specific earmarked equal opportunities policies should be discontinued and replaced by empty motions.

(4) *The role of gender experts*: Who is given the task of carrying out mainstreaming? The Council of Europe definition indicates that "actors normally involved in policy making" (1998: 15) should be the ones responsible. This would mean the use of in-house personnel, coming perhaps from the women's policy machinery. Of course governments can choose between having their own personnel attempt to make previously gender-insensitive policy better or using external consultants with special gender competency. The use of an expert consultant fits in well with the technocrat approach to rational administration. Gender awareness can be marketed as a technical

expertise; to be able to calculate gender effects can become a specialization much like that of consultants working on environmental effects. Further, much of the rhetoric of mainstreaming is rather hermetic. It is transparent only to the initiated. As Bastos writes, the mainstream experts in France act as an aggressive avant-garde as if they are running a semantic revolution (2002: 35). However, if the goal of mainstreaming is transformation of the perception of the average bureaucrat and institutional transformation, then external experts need to be coupled to a training and evaluation process to create learning carryover. Otherwise the departure of the expert will mean the departure of awareness.

We see in the mainstreaming instruments and approaches thus far developed[8] a range of intrusiveness and sophistication. Here is where the demands of policy transformation reveal contradictions. More rationally inclined bureaucracies, less infiltrated with gender awareness, will be resistant to mainstreaming in its transformative sense of empowerment, and develop responses that are symbolic waves at gender awareness.

The question of the variation in sophistication and thoroughness becomes clearer when we look at the state of the prime European promoter of gender mainstreaming, the European Commission. Given its central role as an example, the European institution's experience with equal opportunities and mainstreaming has already formed the object of several studies. (Pollack and Hafner-Burton, 2000; Schmidt, 2001; Bretherton, 2001; Rees, 1998b, 2000; Schunter-Kleemann, 1999, 2000; Mazey, 2000; Bouvret, 2001; Braithwaite, 2001). A brief consideration of the case here can help us develop hypotheses to predict success of evolving programs.

## MOVING FROM THEORY TO PRACTICE IN EUROPE

Mainstreaming has been globally discussed, but is an explicit goal for the countries in the European Union, anchored in the Treaty of Amsterdam and supported by resolutions. The approach of the Commission is defined in "Incorporating equal opportunities for women and men into all Community policies and Activities" (European Commission, 1996: 67 final 21.2.1996). This formulation has a focus on equality rather than difference, but informal formulations after the Treaty of Amsterdam increasingly make space for a policy that recognizes difference and diversity (the European Commission, *Gender Equality Magazine*, for example). Officially the EU called for the development of methodological guidelines to build an equal opportunities dimension into all policies of the European Union (Hoskyns, 1997, 1999; Sensi, 1996, 1997). The most recent framework strategy (2001–2005) requires that mainstreaming occur in all policy areas and be anchored in the official work program of all the departments of the Commission. There is a required yearly monitoring.

## The European Commission: A Preliminary Discussion

### 1. *Commitment to a Gender Mission— Dedicated Actors and Historical Context*

The European Union bases its gender mainstreaming engagement on a number of statements of formal commitment (see summary, European Parliament, 1999, resolution preamble and points A–F), and has been strengthened in the foundation of its claims by the commencement of the terms of the Treaty of Amsterdam in May 1999. A high-level group of commissioners was appointed in 1995 to follow gender issues, which symbolizes commitment from the top to the gender mission. However, informants are critical about the engagement of many of the members of this group. Given the recent scandal and resignation of the Santer Commission it could perhaps be just as well that the Commission did not too wholeheartedly engage itself. The European Parliament noted the lack of knowledge about gender issues at the highest level of decision making and resolved to give this the highest priority (1999: point 7).

Formally, there is commitment to a gender mission, but informally there is no really widespread network of femocrat policy entrepreneurs. They are instead located in pockets of gender awareness and commitment close to policy areas of traditional female concern (gender, development, education to some extent, and recently research and science policy). Many would agree with Swiebel, who states that there is "for a longer time an apparently growing disorientation in which the emancipation policy at the European level has fallen. A clear vision is lacking. . . . What is European emancipation policy really all about?" (1999: 6).

### 2. *Level of Gender Sophistication*

Nonetheless, the work of the Equal Opportunities Cell and its network of contracted academic feminists and former and present national experts is a rich and fairly sophisticated source of ideas. The very spread of the idea of mainstreaming through a variety of projects with EU support (EU local-government initiative, European Structural Funds, NOW efforts, EQUAL) is an indication that the institutions of the European Union provide a kind of a benchmark level of sophistication in gender issues for some countries. The problem is that this sophistication remains in a feminist ghetto. Further, the sophistication is watered down when it comes to influencing the gender mission, which is related to the previous point. The European Parliament's review of mainstreaming progress indicates that the parliament "is disappointed that the measures that have thus far been taken have had little visible influence on the commission policy, with the exception of policy areas where there was already a long tradition and knowledge present on the promotion of equal opportunities for men and women" (1999). While the experts of the Commission recommend sophisticated state-of-the-art policy for others, their own internal testing seems very rudimentary, stopping at the question level, and never proceeding to transformation. Policy makers in the Commission are asked only two questions in the SMART instrument (Simple Method to Assess the Relevance of Policies): "Is gender relevant to your policy area?" and, if so, "How do you integrate gender concerns in the policy area?" (Council of Europe, 1998: 62).

### 3. *Environmental Context of Resistance to Gender Initiatives*

From all quarters (informants in EU and lobby groups such as the European Women's Lobby and European Parliament) there is a uniform criticism that mainstreaming and gender concerns do not touch the core areas of European Union policy and spending, such as agriculture, foreign policy, competition, environment, and transport. While these bastions may be traditionally hard to breach, even more disturbing is the fact that despite consistent lobbying "the great ambitions [of gender mainstreaming] do not stand up in relation to the tangible realities" (Swiebel, 1999: 5). The big new policy questions such as Agenda 2000 and the expansion to eastern Europe (Bretherton, 1999, 2001) hardly mentioned the notion of women or gender, although this has been rectified to some extent with the ambitions of the new Community Strategy on Gender Equality 2001–2005 (European Commission Employment & Social Affairs, 2001b).

There is substantial resistance in the core cultures of the institutions of the European Union to allowing gender to escape from the equal opportunities ghetto. This is symbolized by the extremely slow movement in appointments of women to higher decision-making posts in the bureaucracy, but even more dangerously by the way that mainstreaming is being utilized by some forces in the institutions. The special sector of the European Social Funds for women's employment (NOW) will in the future lose its earmarked "women's money" status to see the issue mainstreamed across employment policy. The European Parliament's own Committee on the Rights of Women narrowly escaped being disbanded at the end of the 1998 legislature, as allied men blithely claimed that with mainstreaming, they no longer had a function (Women of Europe Newsletter, 1999). The multinational nature of the European Commission, as I argue elsewhere (Woodward, 1996), may also lead to strengthening of gender boundaries in the organization. It may be that the stronger masculine rationality is in a public administrative setting, the more likely that initiatives to mainstream will stand as symbolic efforts. These factors will make the success of gender mainstreaming as transformative policy innovation quite difficult in the European Union setting, despite the presence of strong voices to move forward and external pressure from lobby groups such as the European Women's Lobby.

## 4. *The Role of Gender Experts*

The European Commission has made a relatively limited use of experts in the implementation of mainstreaming, primarily to author a small guide for gender impact assessment to be used by DG-level bureaucrats and provide specialized advice (the national experts delegated to DG V, now called Directorate General for Employment and Social Affairs). These experts come disproportionately from northern Europe, even outside the EU. There was an expert from Norway from 1996 to 1999 with substantial experience in Norwegian gender policy. Thus, the Commission only partially follows the recommendation of the Council of Europe that it use actors normally involved in policy making. Bureaucrats who have been appointed as responsible for equal opportunity policy within their units are to control policy emanating from their units. However, one of the showpieces of mainstreaming, the integration of gender thinking in the European Structural Funds and the European Funds for Regional Development, was assisted by an external expert who notes that the success was primarily due to "active support in terms of financial and human resources" (Lausberg, 1999: 2). Further, the internal bureaucrats in most divisions only use about 10 percent of their time for gender issues.

The substantial variation in approaches to mainstreaming present in the various divisions of the European Commission can be somewhat organized using an identification of important dimensions such as the above (Pollack and Hafner-Burton, 2000; Braithwaite, 2001; Bouvret, 2001). The research on the European Union indicates that mainstreaming does not proceed apace in all areas of policy at equal speed. This suggests the need for comparative research on the inroads of mainstreaming into normal policy making cross-nationally.

The Commission plays a strong role in stimulating action in the member states. Especially important has been the explicit coupling of a requirement to demonstrate gender awareness in applications for support under the European Social Fund European Commission [E-LINDA] (2001), which mentions a 10 percent quota for gender-earmarked money and implications of engaging in mainstreaming.

European national activity has also been stimulated by the initiatives of the Council of Europe to constitute an expert group on mainstreaming (Council of Europe, 1998). Finally European Union countries have agreed to implement the Platform for Action resulting from the 1995 UN Conference on Women in Beijing, which mandates an engagement in promoting gender equality across all policy areas for the empowerment of women. The reports from governments on progress since the Platform of Action, the Beijing +5 reports, indicate a varying level of awareness of the implications of mainstreaming (Council of Europe, 2000). Many governments seem not to have taken any concrete actions. However moving the goalposts further may have stimulated governments to make more work of more traditional equal opportunities efforts.

To give an indication of what insights further comparison may provide and to explore the utility of the variables indicated above, I have grouped a few of the cataloged examples of good practice in development of instruments in projects of mainstreaming from the Council of Europe 1998 report as well as several Belgian cases along just two dimensions suggested by the above discussion:

1. the context of gender sophistication and commitment evinced in official policy and length of experience with gender questions. This includes an evaluation of the level of commitment of power holders to seeing actual results of mainstreaming, including some measurement of financial and human-capital resources invested. As a bare minimum, a policy statement from the chief executive going beyond the acceptance of the Beijing Action Platform seems necessary, but as noted above in the case of the EU up until 1999, even the creation of a government cabinet-level working group is not always a reliable indicator of level of commitment.

2. the level of expertise called in to develop a mainstreaming instrument (do administrations work with their own untrained or semitrained bureaucrats or with certified experts?).

The projects included here were selected from the Council of Europe report of 1998 and were ones where available documentation and personal interviews helped in providing background information (see table 3.1) They crystallize the issue of the role of the gender expert from outside or inside the bureaucracy, and the issue of simplification, which holds the danger of deception rather than transformation in mainstreaming. "Gender expertise" in the table refers to the level of gender sophistication necessary to carry out the required analysis, while the implementers are those who carry out the analysis.

### High Gender Expertise Context/Expert Analyst

#### (1) *Sweden: The "Flying Expert"*

The "flying expert" was one of the approaches used by the Swedish government to carry out gender analyses in the various ministries of the Swedish national government, whereby an expert with gender competence would analyze a department in consultation with that administration to develop a comprehensive program for allowing the administration to carry out gender mainstreaming on its own (Stark, 1998).

**Table 3.1.  Gender Expertise in the State and Mainstream Implementers: The Results for Complexity of Mainstreaming Efforts**

| | Implementers | |
| --- | --- | --- |
| *Gender Expertise* | *Outside Experts* | *Internal Bureaucrats* |
| HIGH | 1) Sweden—Flying expert<br><br>2) The Netherlands—National Gender Impact Assessment consulting | 3) Sweden—Local authorities self-examination-3R approach<br><br>4) Denmark—Legislative review |
| LOW | 5) The Netherlands—Local Gender Impact Assessment (EET)<br><br>6) Flanders—Gender in Balance | 7) Flanders—Local Gender Impact Assessment (LEER)<br><br>8) Flanders—Regional Emancipation Effect Reporting (GIA)<br><br>9) Denmark—Local Authorities<br><br>10) European Commission—SMART initiative |

(2) *The Netherlands: National Gender Impact Assessment*

In the Netherlands, National Gender Impact Assessment (or Emancipation Effect Reporting) used professional consultancies. The Netherlands was one of the first to develop an instrument for testing policy, coupling it firmly to a sophisticated understanding of the sources and expressions of gender inequality. The GIA developed there involved a lengthy process and the analysis has been carried out primarily on policies that are already developed, rather than during the process itself. Experts have been necessary to do the analysis from the outside in the first years of its use, and thus it has only been done a few times (Verloo and Roggeband, 1996).

**High Gender Expertise Context/Bureaucratic Implementation**

(3) *Sweden: Local Authority Self-Examination 3-R Approach*

For many years, in its association of municipalities, Sweden has had large-scale projects on gender equality in local authorities. In connection with mainstreaming, a program called 3-Rs was launched, and carried out by municipalities themselves. The initial focus was, however, primarily on issues of representation in decision making (JÄMKO website, Council of Europe, 1998: 68).

(4) *Denmark: Legislative Review*

From 1995 on, Denmark has been experimenting with evaluating national legislative proposals from a gender perspective, beginning with labor-market legislation. The evaluation looks at whether the proposal promotes equality and what the consequences are for the relation between women and men. A help group from the equality minister provides expert advice to the actors (Council of Europe, 1998: 66–67).

## Lower Gender Expertise Context/External Expert

(5) *The Netherlands: Local Gender Impact Assessment (EET)*
(Kornalijnslijper, N. E. et al., 1998)

The situation in local townships is generally much less gender sophisticated than at the Dutch national level. The Dutch national instrument was adapted for local use by external experts. The sophisticated analysis of the relational aspect of gender inequality was all but eliminated. There was a substantial reduction of the ambitions of mainstreaming limiting it primarily to improving the social position of women and increasing choices for men and women in fields where they have had fewer opportunities, thus an equal opportunities approach. While the approach is perhaps a realistic reflection of what nontrained townships may be able to consider, it is very far from the institutional innovation implied by mainstreaming, and without substantive training effort, may strand as a shiny external model.

(6) *Flanders: "Gender in Balance"*

Outside experts were brought in to integrate gender sensibility into human-resource policy in the Flemish administration. The experts characterize the experience as one of both roses and thorns, with the thorns primarily to deal with the fact of the different points of departure in terms of gender understanding between the administrators and the outside experts. The project is continuing in four other divisions of the administration (Benschop and Verloo, 2000), also under the guidance of external experts.

## Lower Gender Expertise Context/Bureaucratic Implementation

(7) *Flanders: Local Gender Impact Assessment (LEER)*
(Vander Steene et al., 1999)

A simplified checklist was developed and accompanied by an intensive training process organized by the League of Cities and Municipalities to enable towns to understand the instrument. Use of the LEER (Local Emancipation

Effect Report) for analysis of policy is not required, but available as an alternative. Although target publics were involved in development of the instrument, the training process is still going on (Wildiers and Lobijn, 2001; Franken, 2001: 35). The routine itself will not be sufficient to serve for transformation. Municipalities are required to file reports on gender equality with the federal government, but there is no information available on compliance.

### (8) *Flanders: Emancipation Effect Reporting* (Gender Impact Assessment) (Woodward and Meier, 1997, 1998)

This instrument was developed by academic experts as a variation on the Dutch national instrument, and tested on potential policies to demonstrate their level of gender sensitivity. The intention was to develop an instrument that could be applied early in the policy process and lead to policy changes to limit negative effects on gender relations. The administration feels that the "instrument is too theoretical, and there was a lack of an implementation plan and the necessary political will to gain wide acceptance." Again the instrument will be further simplified, which on the one hand may allow normal policy actors to carry it out, but will necessarily on the other hand be coupled to a loss in sophistication and ability to identify more complex aspects of gender inequality.

### (9) *Denmark: Local Authorities*

Ringstead in Denmark was one of the experimental projects sponsored by the Nordic Council of Ministers in their pilot projects to spread mainstreaming in the Nordic countries. In this project, Denmark attempted in a local municipality to achieve greater gender balance in segregated jobs, which is more of an equal opportunities project than a mainstreaming project. The experience in the municipality with the need for a longer time frame to do transformation of expectations led to the decision to implement mainstreaming within national government using pilot projects in only a few ministries, rather than attempt to mainstream across the board (OECD, 2000: OECD mainstream website, speech Jytte Anderssen Danish Minister of Gender Equality, 24 November 2000).

### (10) *European Commission: SMART Initiative*

The gender impact assessment instrument for the European Commission was known as the SMART initiative. Given that the level of gender awareness and competence varies dramatically, a commission was given to an outside expert to develop a checklist for seeing whether policies needed to be gender-proofed or not. The SMART (Simple Method to Assess Relevance of Policies to Gender) instrument is undoubtedly one of the simplest developed, but also characterizes the enormous distance between the ambitions of mainstreaming and what organizations may make of it. It consists of two questions: is the policy proposal directed at one or more target groups? And, are there differences between women and men in the field of the policy proposal (with regard to rights, resources, positions, representation, values, and norms) (Council of Europe, 1998: 62)?

## Discussion and Conclusions

It is early to conclude much about the final impact of these efforts. New efforts and instruments are being developed constantly in Europe. Perhaps most importantly, there is substantial work being done on the "basement floor" of the gender equality house, as many governments took stock after Beijing +5 and filed national action plans for mainstreaming (e.g., the Netherlands Interdepartmental Plan of Action on Gender Mainstreaming, 1999–2002, Ministry of Social Affairs and Employment: Department for the Coordination of Emancipation Policy, 2000).

Generally, the most sophisticated, tailor-made, and time-consuming approaches involve the use of certified gender expertise and a detailed analysis of the policy process, as exemplified by national efforts in Sweden and the Netherlands. These countries can be said to be in the relatively luxurious situation of knowing what gender mainstreaming is, having sufficient gender data, and having developed a broad concept of gender equality (TECENA, 2000; Outshoorn, 1995, 1997). Yet they suffer from their very excellence, as they challenge policy makers with transformative issues. The costs of mainstreaming with this approach are quite substantial and will remain high until gender is taken to be a matter of course. It is probably not random that this approach was chosen by two countries with substantial sophistication in gender equality. But even with relative sophistication, mainstreaming can be difficult. Symptomatic is that the Nordic Council of Ministers launched its efforts in mainstreaming with pilot projects within the terrain of labor-market and youth policies. Yet even in these policy areas, which share frames that should be sympathetic to gender, many projects never get further than the level focusing on women's representation and other equal opportunity issues (OECD, 2000).

It was difficult to find cases fitting in the second cell, which could be characterized as the ideal situation envisioned by mainstreamers, in which the entire context is highly gender sensitive and bureaucrats are able to carry out mainstreaming. Swedish municipalities through their central organization and through more than a decade of project competitions are working in a highly gender sensitive context, and thus their project seems to have transformative potential over the long term. The Danes will rely on the expertise developed in the equality policy ghetto to begin to transform the mindsets of civil servants in other policy areas, and this may be a method of reaching transformation as well.

The fundamental commitment to improvement in gender relations is extremely important. The cases in less gender-committed settings carried out by external experts are the most vulnerable to the disappearing act. This is the case for both the Flemish administrative effort and the checklist for Dutch local authorities, where shared ownership of the project between the bureaucrats and the experts is more unclear. Only with continued resources and commitment from top agents can one expect real improvement beyond cosmetics in such cases.

In the fourth cell are the efforts carried out by in-house bureaucrats in environments of relatively low gender awareness, as in Flanders, the local example from Denmark, and the first European Commission SMART instrument. While all of these projects recommend continual training and awareness development, the instruments themselves are less intrusive. They involve a watchdog approach and can be carried out by civil servants with a low level of gender expertise. Both the broader European Commission and the Flemish case can be characterized as settings that are relatively resistant to gender equality issues. This can be seen in, for example, the gender segregation of top-level staffing, and the late adoption of gender equality statements. For different reasons, neither setting has a high degree of gender expertise present among its own staff members. Gender expertise is present primarily among employees of the gender equality machinery and specially recruited experts. There is relatively high mobility among staff in the European Commission, as promotion often entails transfer to another unit. Thus for example, in DG Development, staff members responsible for mainstreaming have been replaced frequently, and long vacancies have hamstrung progress, despite the presence of good gender impact instruments (Bouvret, 2001; Braithwaite, 2001).

For all of these settings it is essential that gender mainstreamers find a niche in the policy process that is routine and coupled with resources. Otherwise the risk is great that policy makers will talk about gender mainstreaming but not do it. In the ideal mainstreaming world, the fourth cell of the table will gradually become empty, as more sophisticated instruments are learned by bureaucrats who have become gender aware in the process of mainstreaming. Nonetheless, even the weaker instruments of Flanders; Ringstead, Denmark; or the local checklists to be used in the Netherlands have a great potential. By requiring their application, and thereby requiring that policy makers learn how to use them, gender tools become part of an institutional learning process. The necessity is to design an adaptable system that will keep doing gender even as different political winds blow. In some ways the simple model may be a better strategy than susceptible one-off reform packages with expensive external experts. The challenge is to expand this analysis using one or a combination of the predictive schemes identifying critical factors for success that have thus far been developed to carry out comparative research of mainstreaming efforts, successes and failures within different sorts of institutions at the international, national, regional, and local levels.

However, the "time when we don't need to speak this language because the languages will have changed" is going to be a long way off. Policy tools can perhaps speed up learning, and this is what mainstreaming is potentially well placed to do. It is to be hoped that the policy of mainstreaming will not entirely adapt the language of power, but will retain a strong accent of its own. In any critical understanding of the mainstreaming approach, the symbolic use of politics should not be ignored (Edelman, 1967; Harrop, 1992: 278). In its first applications, where external experts are called in to do showy projects, the risk is that it remains only a show, and that mainstreaming may not lead to a dramatically more sensitive policy process that no longer proceeds from male as the norm. Yet by moving beyond the walls of state feminism, mainstreaming efforts may create an "aha" effect in unsuspecting quarters, and serve as a mode of public learning.

The question posed was whether mainstreaming offered a promise or only pitfalls for women in European policy. The answer is a little of both, as mainstreaming is now being talked about and applied at all levels of government, with widely varying approaches. That women may disappear in the policy pit remains a risk thanks to blurring of affirmative action and equal opportunities with mainstreaming. However, gender mainstreaming and equal opportunity are not unrelated. As the OECD emphasizes,

> Greater equality between women and men can only be based on an understanding of their relative roles and needs as revealed through gender analysis. Conversely, enhancing the role of women through equal opportunity is helpful to implementing gender mainstreaming. But affirmative action alone does not necessarily build the capacities, systems and institutions needed to fully achieve the implementation and promise of gender mainstreaming (OECD webpage: http://www.oecd.org/subject/gender_mainstreaming/about/).

By agreeing to the terms of the Beijing Platform for Action (UN, 1995), governments have taken on an obligation to do something. It is to be hoped that the goals set by the international forum will lead to more than simply symbolic actions. The case of mainstreaming is a demonstration of how gender issues can spur creativity and can potentially transform policy making.

Mainstreaming began initially by speaking the language of modern management, which is results driven, requiring instrumental and rational measurement. This may ultimately bring about a heightened ability for policy makers to deal with the crosscutting problems of inequality that breach rational models. However, the mission to mainstream gender concerns into all areas of policy will ultimately require a fundamental commitment from those in power. Settings where political groups hope to reverse the progress of equality can use mainstreaming in dangerous ways, dismantling women's policy machinery and committing no resources in their place. Public organizations are at root political. Without a consideration of power relationships, the transformative potential of mainstreaming will come to naught. Speaking "truth" to power, as Wildavsky (1979) taught, requires using the language, but also recognizing that power is there.

Gender mainstreaming has the potential to permanently transform the language and images of policy making to become more inclusive and sensitive to diversity beginning with sex. Reaching this place ironically requires a strategic usage of the practices and existing language of politics and government, including building alliances to create contexts where gender awareness is a given and equality is a constant goal.

## NOTES

1. This chapter is an updated and condensed version of Woodward, 2001. Many thanks to discussion and comments from Florence Bouvret, Monica Goldmann, Hedwig Rudolf, Hildegard Theobald, Verena Schmidt, Ilse Lenz, and Heidi Gottfried, who provided many new insights during my stay at the Ruhr University in Bochum in 2001.

2. Schalkwyk and Woroniuk (1998: 27). The Development Assistance Committee Sourcebook of the OECD summarizes the number of paragraphs in the Platform where the mainstreaming ambition appears: 79 (education), 105 (health), 123 (violence), 141 (conflict), 164 (economic activity), 189 (power and decision making), 202 (institutional mechanisms for women's advancement), 229 (human rights), 238 (media), 252 (management of natural resources and the environment), 273 (children and youth).

3. A discussion of issues in definition can be found in Woodward, 2001.

4. The Swedish Minister for Emancipation Policy is quoted as saying at the end of 1996, "The challenge is to move the work for equality out of the annex into the main building" (Ministry of Social Affairs and Employment, 2000: 3).

5. Rees (1999) also uses metaphor, speaking of "Tinkering" for legislative reform, "Tailoring" for women-suited remedial strategies in a woman's policy ghetto, and "Transformation" for the third stage of mainstreaming. Mainstreaming builds on the presence of the first two stages, but goes further.

6. Can be found using the following gateway: http://www.destin.be/cgibin/amit/cgint.exe/7738-111?1=1&tmpl=top&GLB_BASE=digm through the Belgian women's documentation center Amazone.

7. See also OECD Conference in November 2000 on mainstreaming where many Nordic countries outline limiting factors on success—Main Messages, http://www.oecd.org/subject/gender_mainstreaming/main_messages.htm.

8. An in-depth review is beyond the confines of this chapter, but can be found in Behning and Pascual, 2001; Council of Europe, 1998, 2000; Mackay and Bilton, 2000; or Beveridge et al., 2000.

# REFERENCES

Bastos, Jean-Luc. 2002. "De uitwisseling van ervaringen en know-how voor de opbouw van een rechtvaardige maatschappij." Pp. 34–36 in *Gender mainstreaming: een concept, instrumenten, de praktijk: Akten van de studiedag 13 december 2001*. Brussels: Amazone.

Behning, U., and A. S. Pascual, eds. 2001. *Gender Mainstreaming in the European Employment Strategy*. Brussels: European Trade Union Institute.

Benschop, Yvonne, and Mieke Verloo. 2000. "Geen roos zonder doornen: Reflekties op gender mainstreaming." *Tijdschrift voor Genderstudies* 3, no. 4: 22–32.

Beveridge, Fiona, Sue Nott, and Kylie Stephen. 2000. "Mainstreaming and the Engendering of Policy Making: A Means to an End?" *Journal of European Public Policy* 7, no. 3: 385–405.

Bouvret, Florence. 2001. "Towards Sustainable Development? Gender Mainstreaming and Environmental Integration in the European Commission." Master's thesis, Department of Human Ecology, Vrije Universiteit, Brussels.

Braithwaite, Mary. 2001."Gender Mainstreaming in the European Commission: Explaining the Roller Coaster of Progress and Regression." Unpublished paper. Brussels: Engender/DUP.

Bretherton, Charlotte. 1999. "Preparing for the EU's Eastern Enlargement: A Strong Need for Gender Mainstreaming?" Unpublished paper. Personal communication, 1999. John Moores University of Liverpool.

———. 2001. "Gender Mainstreaming and EU Enlargement: Swimming against the Tide?" *Journal of European Public Policy* 8, no. 1: 60–81.

Council of Europe. 1998. *Gender Mainstreaming: Conceptual Framework, Methodology and Presentation of Good Practices*. Strasbourg: Council of Europe, EG-S-MS (98) 2.

———. 2000. *National Machinery, Action Plans and Gender Mainstreaming in the Council of Europe Member States since the 4th World Conference on Women*. Strasbourg: Council of Europe, EG (99) 12.

Edelman, Murray. 1967. *The Symbolic Uses of Politics*. London: University of Illinois Press.

Engstrom, Ole. 2000. "Norm Negotiations: The Construction of New Norms Regarding Gender and Development in EU Foreign Aid Policy." *Journal of European Public Policy* 7, no. 3: 457–76.

European Commission. 1996. *Incorporating Equal Opportunities for Women and Men into All Community Policies and Activities*. COM 96, 67.

———. 2000. *Gender Equality in the European Union: Examples of Good Practices (1996–2000)*. Brussels: European Commission, Directorate General for Employment and Social Affairs.

European Commission Directorate General Employment and Social Affairs, E-LINDA. 2001. *Equal Opportunities Governance: Making the Structural Funds a Project Financing Tool for Gender Mainstreaming: Compendium in English for the Dissemination of the LINDA II Project*. Turin: Abaco Editori s.r.l.

European Commission Employment & Social Affairs. 2001a. *Directory of Projects: Medium Term Action Programme on Equal Opportunities for Women and Men*. Vol. KE-37-01-348-EN-C. Luxembourg: European Commission Directorate General for Employment and Social Affairs Unit EMPL,G.1. Office for Official Publications of the European Communities.

———. 2001b. *Towards a Community Strategy on Gender Equality.* Vol. COM, 2000, 335. Luxembourg: Office for Official Publications of the European Communities.

European Commission (European Technology Assessment Network). 2000. *Science Policies in the European Union: Promoting Excellence through Gender Equality.* Brussels: European Commission EUR 19319-EN.

European Parliament. 1999. *Resolution A4-0072/99. Verslag over het voortgangsrapport van de Commissie inzake de follow-up van de mededeling Integratie van de gelijke kansen voor vrouwen en mannen in alle communautaire beleidsvormen en acties.* COM (98)0122-C4-0234/98.

Franken, Martha. 2001. "Mainstreamen in Vlaanderen. een stand van zaken." Pp. 31–38 in *Mainstreaming: na de theorie de praktijk! Studiedag 28 November 2000,* ed. Gelijke Kansen. Brussels: Ministerie van de Vlaamse Gemeenschap.

Gender Equality Magazine. 2000. Dossier: Anti Discrimination Measures Proposed. *Gender Equality Magazine* 8:17–19.

Hannan, Carolyn. 2000. *Gender Mainstreaming in Economic Development in the United Nations.* Paper presented at Gender Mainstreaming Competitiveness and Growth Conference, November, Paris, France.

Harrop, Martin, ed. 1992. *Power and Policy in Liberal Democracies.* Cambridge: Cambridge University Press.

Heikkinen, Mia. 1999. *Mainstreaming within Industrial Relations—Does It Exist?* Paper presented at European Sociological Association 4th Conference, Amsterdam, Netherlands.

Hoskyns, Catherine. 1997. "What Future for European Union Woman's Policy? A Study of Four Action Programs." *Europa Europe,* published in Italian.

———. 1999. "Gender and Transnational Democracy: The Case of the European Union." Pp. 72–87 in *Gender Politics in Global Governance,* ed. Mary K. Meyer and Elisabeth Prügl. Oxford: Rowman & Littlefield.

Inhetveen, Katharina. 1998. *Can Gender Equality Be Institutionalized* ? Paper presented at the 14th International Sociological Association World Congress RC 16-7, Montreal, Canada.

Kornalijnslijper, N. E., H. J. Lensink, and H. J. Hof. 1998. *Emancipatie Effectrapportage door gemeenten: Model en praktijkvoorbeelden.* Den Haag: VNG.

Lausberg, Sylvie. 1999. "Gelijke kansen bevorderen door een globale aanpak." *De Draad van Ariadne* 9: 2–3.

Levy, Caren. 1996. "The Process of Institutionalizing Gender in Policy and Planning: The Web of Institutionalisation." DPU Working Paper no. 74.

———. 1998. "Institutionalization of Gender through Participatory Practice." In *The Myth of Community: Gender Issues in a Participatory Development,* ed. Irene Guijt and Meera Kaul Shah. London: ITDG Publishing.

Mackay, Fiona, and Kate Bilton. 2000. *Learning from Experience: Lessons in Mainstreaming Equal Opportunities,* Governance of Scotland Forum. Edinburgh: University of Edinburgh.

Mazey, Sonia. 2000. "Introduction: Integrating Gender—Intellectual and Real World Mainstreaming." *Journal of European Public Policy* 7, no. 3: 333–45.

———. 2001. *Gender Mainstreaming in the EU.* London: Kogan Page.

Mazur, Amy, and Dorothy McBride Stetson, eds. 1995. *Comparative State Feminism*. London: Sage.

Ministry of Social Affairs and Employment: Department for the coordination of emancipation policy. 2000. *Netherlands Interdepartmental Plan of Action on Gender Mainstreaming 1999–2002*. Den Haag: Ministry of Social Affairs and Employment of the Netherlands.

Nedelmann, Birgitta. 1995. "Gegensätze und Dynamik politischer Institutionen." Pp. 14–40 in *Politisiche Institutionen im Wandel*, ed. Birgitta Nedemann. Opladen: Westdeutscher Verlag.

Nelen, Sara, and Annie Hondeghem, eds. 2000. *Equality Oriented Personnel Policy in the Public Sector*. Amsterdam: International Institute of Administrative Sciences: IOS Press.

Organisation for Economic Cooperation and Development. 2000. "Main Messages." Gender Mainstreaming, Competitiveness and Growth Conference, 23–24 November, OECD, Paris, France. At http://www.oecd.org/subject/gender_maistreaming/main_messages.htm.

Outshoorn, Joyce. 1995. "Administrative Accommodation in the Netherlands. The Department for the Coordination of Equality Policy." Pp. 168–85 in *Comparative State Feminism*, ed. Amy Mazur and Dorothy McBride Stetson. London: Sage.

———. 1997. "Incorporating Feminism." Pp. 109–26 in *Sex Equality Policy in Western Europe*, ed. Frances Gardiner. London: Routledge.

Pollack, Mark, and Emilie Hafner-Burton. 2000. "Mainstreaming Gender in the European Union." *Journal of European Public Policy* 7, no. 3: 432–57.

Rees, Teresa. 1998a. "Mainstreaming Equality." Pp. 165–83 in *Engendering Social Policy*, ed. Sophie Watson and Lesley Doyal. Buckingham: Open University Press.

———. 1998b. *Mainstreaming Equality in the European Union*. London: Routledge.

———. 1999. *Tinkering, Tailoring, Transforming: Principles and Tools of Gender Mainstreaming*. Paper presented at Gender Mainstreaming: A Step into the 21st Century Conference, Athens, Greece.

———. 2000. "The Learning Region! Integrating Gender Equality into Regional Economic Development." *Policy and Politics* 28, no. 2: 179–91.

Schalkwyk, Johanna, and Beth Woroniuk. 1998. *DAC Source Book on Concepts and Approaches Linked to Gender Equality*. At http://www.oecd.org/dac/Gender/htm/sourcebook.htm. Paris, France: Organisation for Economic Cooperation and Development, Development Assistance Committee.

Schmidt, Verena. 2001. "Gender Mainstreaming als Leitbild für Geschlechtergerechtigkeit in Organisatiesstrukturen." *Zeitschrift für Frauenforschung und Geschlechterstudien* 19, nos. 1 and 2: 45–62.

Schunter-Kleemann, Susanne. 1999. *Mainstreaming as an Innovative Approach of the EU Policy of Equal Opportunities*. Vol. 3. Bremen: Discussion papers, Wissenschaftliche Einheit Frauenstudien und Frauenforschung, Hochschule Bremen.

———. 2000. "Eurpaische Einigung und Geschlechterkultur- Transformationen der politischer Kultur der EU." *Zeitschrift fur Marxistische Erneuerung*. Presented as congress paper at network meeting "Arbeitsmarkt, Wohlfahrtsstaat und Geschlecht im internationalen Vergleich," 3–4 February, FHZ Berlin 2000.

Sensi, Dina. 1996. "L'Evaluation du Quatrième Programme 'Egalité des Chances.' Etude préparatoire." Unpublished. Liège: SEDEP.

———. 1997. Mechanismes et indicateurs de suivi du mainstreaming. Brussels: European Commission Equal Opportunities Unit. At http://europa.eu.int.dgo5/equ_opp/index_en.htm.

Stark, Agneta. 1998. *Gender Mainstreaming—Targeting Management.* Speech read at the Congress of "Equality is the Future," European Union Commission DG-V, September, Brussels, Belgium.

Status of Women Canada. 1996. *Gender-Based Analysis: A Guide for Policy Making.* Ottawa: Status of Women Canada.

Swiebel, Joke. 1999. "Mainstreaming als verdwijntruk." *Lover* 26, no. 2: 4–8.

TECENA (Tijdelijke expertiescommissie emancipatie in het nieuwe adviesstelsel). 2000. *Een wereld te winner: Tecenta's eindrapportage over het adviesstelsel met conclusies en aanbevelingen.* Den Haag: Tecena.

True, J., and M. Mintrom. 2001. "Transnational Networks and Policy Diffusion: The Case of Gender Mainstreaming." *International Studies Quarterly* 45: 27–57.

UN Fourth World Conference on Women. 1995. *Global Platform for Action—Beijing.* New York: United Nations Publishing.

Vander Steene, Annick, Mips Meyntjes, and Bie Hinnekint. 1999. *LEER, een instrument voor lokaal beleid op maat van mannen en vrouwen.* Brussels: Vlaamse Vereniging voor Steden en Gemeenten.

Verloo, Mieke, and Conny Roggeband. 1994. *Emancipatie-effectenrapportage: Theoretisch kader, methodiek en voorbeeldrapportages.* Den Haag: Vuga.

———. 1996. "Gender Impact Assessment: The Development of a New Instrument in the Netherlands." *Impact Assessment* 14, no. 1: 3–20.

Wildavsky, Aaron. 1979. *Speaking Truth to Power: The Art and Craft of Policy Analysis.* Boston: Little, Brown & Co.

Wildiers, Kristel, and Ann Lobijn. 2001. *Lokaal gelijkekansenbeleid: een uitdaging voor gemeente en OCMW.* Brussel: Politeia.

Women of Europe Newsletter. 1999. "The Deneutralisation of the European Parliament's Committee on Women's Rights." At http://europa.eu.int/comm/employment_social/equ_opp/infofem/infofem86_en.pdf.

Woodward, Alison. 1996."Multi-national Masculinities and European Bureaucracy." Pp. 167–85 in *Men as Managers, Managers as Men*, ed. D. Collinson and J. Hearn. London: Sage.

———. 2001. *Gender Mainstreaming in European Policy: Innovation or Deception?* Discussion Paper no. FS101-103. Berlin: Wissenschaftszentrum Berlin für Sozialforschung.

Woodward, Alison, and Petra Meier. 1997. *Handboek bij de Emancipatie-Effect Rapportage.* Brussel: Vlaamse Minister belast met het Geiljke Kansen Beleid en Brusselse Aangelegenheden, Ministerie van de Vlaamse Gemeenschap.

———. 1998. "Gender Impact Assessment: A New Approach to Changing Policies and Contents of Citizenship?" Pp. 95–106 in *Shifting Bonds, Shifting Bounds: Women, Mobility and Citizenship in Europe*, ed. Virginia Ferreira, Teresa Tavares, and Silvia Portugal. Oeiras: Celta Editora.

# II

## IMPLICATIONS OF GENDER
## IN THE WORKPLACE

# 4

# Institutionally Embedded Gender Models: Re-regulating Breadwinner Models in Germany and Japan[1]

*Heidi Gottfried and Jacqueline O'Reilly*

The differential economic performance of leading industrialized countries in the recent postwar period has stimulated interest in debates concerned with "varieties of capitalism" and their effects (Soskice, 2000). Comparative research in this area emphasizes the institutional complementarities and maps the relative strengths of the Japanese and German employment models, in comparison to the relative inequalities generated by "free-market" Anglo-Saxon economies (Crouch and Streeck, 1997). Through an anatomy of capitalism it uncovers a grid of dense institutional relationships as pillars that had supported the economic success of the German and Japanese models. A new focus on the interactions between industrial relations and social-welfare systems casts new light on these "economic miracles" of the past (Streeck, 2001). The continued neglect of gender, however, has prevented researchers from seeing the particular pressures on conservative welfare states in a period of restructuring, which are becoming more apparent in light of changing economic fortunes. We utilize the strengths of this body of work, while going beyond it by integrating a concern for systematic gendered differences.

Comparative welfare-state approaches increasingly integrate the institution of the family (Esping-Andersen, 1999) and/or gender (Korpi, 2000) as salient features to explain restructuring. Feminist approaches show how gender is consequential for mapping both boundaries within and between welfare regimes (O'Connor et al., 1999; Daly and Lewis, 2000; Bergqvist et al., 1999). But these welfare-state approaches pay less attention to the negotiation of gender as embodied in industrial-relations institutions and employment relations. There seems to be significant scope for the development of cross-national comparisons of gender relations, focusing not only on labor markets, but also on family/household relations and shifts in the gendered character of welfare regimes and regulations, and the effects these have on social change, specifically, on gender and work.

Incorporating theoretical insights inspired by the varieties-of-capitalism approach coupled with revised welfare-state approaches, we elaborate a framework for comparing institutionally embedded male-breadwinner models. The breadwinner model identifies the historical forms of the tacit gender bargain as embodied in laws and institutions regulating mutual obligations, rights, and relations between women and men within and between the areas of production and reproduction. In this chapter, we suggest that the legacy of the strong male-breadwinner model creates particular pressures on socially conservative welfare states in a period of restructuring. As Kathleen Thelen (1999, 397) conjectures,

> changes in gender relations and family structures are likely to reinforce elements of the universalistic and liberal welfare states (which both, though in different ways, support a high level of labor force participation by women) but these changes create new frictions and contradictions for conservative welfare states, which are premised on the single bread-winner model of the family. In other words we might as well expect a (politically consequential) collision between changing gender roles and welfare state development, but only in the conservative welfare states.

Through a paired comparison between Japan and Germany, we assess the contradictory pressures generated by socially conservative states. In Japan and Germany, trends such as growing unemployment, declining fertility, and increasing care needed by the aging population are invoked to support the call to further reinforce the male-breadwinner model. At the same time, contrary trends, including women's rising education and qualifications and growing labor shortages, contribute to eroding this model. Just as Julia O'Connor et al. (1999) examined the fine differences between liberal welfare states, we do the same for the two socially conservative countries. We show how Germany and Japan—both similar with respect to their conservative welfare systems—under the pressure of accumulating employment weaknesses, are being re-regulated in different ways. Differences between Germany and Japan are related to contrasting state–society relations: specifically the role of the Japanese state in trying to stem both economic and demographic decline on the one hand and the role of the social partners in Germany in stimulating employment growth and reducing unemployment on the other. The European Union (EU), as an emergent polity with legal authority over national governments in many matters of labor-market and equality regulations, will be a key aspect of our analysis of Germany.

# A COMPARATIVE FRAMEWORK:
## INSTITUTIONALLY EMBEDDED GENDER MODELS

Gosta Esping-Andersen was one of the first theorists to bring Japan into the orbit of comparative welfare analysis. Revisiting the three worlds of welfare capitalism, Esping-Andersen (1997, 21) cast east Asian welfare states, most notably Japan, as a "hybrid of existing welfare state characteristics" (1997, 21).[2] Japan combines liberal and conservative welfare regimes as a result of its occupationally divided social-insurance schemes and the emphasis on family and labor-market solutions to social welfare. Esping-Andersen correctly associates Japan with Germany as a socially conservative welfare regime. However, despite the introduction of the family between state and society, his analysis of relative degrees of familialism does not go far enough.[3] He treats the household as a unitary decision maker (Mahon, 2001, 27), because, in his analysis, gender relations lack a power dimension. It is not surprising that his new model lines up with earlier clusters, since class forces remain the primary determinant of welfare-state categories.

Feminist approaches recast welfare-state theory in ways that alter the lines of demarcation between and within regimes (Bergqvist et al., 1999; O'Connor et al., 1999), arguing that the "form and nature of contemporary welfare states" (Daly and Lewis, 2000, 282) cannot be understood unless gender or some allied concept (such as social care, maternalist discourse, (in)dependence, gender regime, or a family/gender model) is integrated into the analysis. Jane Lewis (1992) clusters countries in terms of shared institutional and cultural characteristics which, she argues, define a gender order. Ilona Ostner and Jane Lewis (1995) further develop this line of analysis, directing attention to the impact of particular social policies on either dismantling or reinforcing the male-breadwinner family model. Lewis has since reworked the theoretical armature of gender orders and, in collaboration with Mary Daly (2000, 282), reframes welfare-state analysis in terms of the concept of "social care," which "lies at the intersection of public and private." This focus on the social organization and relations of care broadens the analytical framework to encompass the gendered labor activity of everyday care at the microlevel and responsibilities for and costs of care among institutional domains at the macrolevel. As an overarching concept, the emphasis on social care allows them to explain both current developments and change over time by recognizing the historical shift in which, as they note, care has moved to the center of welfare-state concerns and issues of gender have assumed a more direct and prominent place in welfare-state policy (Daly and Lewis, 2000, 290).

There is little disagreement over the grouping of the Nordic countries, since all these societies socialize the care of both children and the elderly, but, Daly and Lewis show, not all privatized systems are the same. There are consequential distinctions between privatizing care as a family affair (through women's unpaid labor) or as a part of the voluntary service sector in between public and private spheres. The role of this "third sector" in delivering care services with public support, as in Germany and Japan, differentiates privatization in these societies from family-based care found in southern European countries (with the exception of Italy). Thus privatization is not simply a matter of marketizing or familializing care. Specifying the nature of privatization, like the boundaries between public and private, has practical implications for the gender division of labor.[4]

Despite these useful distinctions, an important linkage between work and family life is missing from this model, making it less than useful as a total explanation. For example, as Jill Rubery et al. (1998, 251) conclude, women's strategies of reconciliation of working and family life are limited to the options of either part-time working or withdrawal from the workforce, yet there are significant differences among European countries. Although part-time employment is common among older women and expanding among younger women, a part-time job in Japan is actually more comparable to a full-time, low-wage job in Europe (Houseman and Osawa, 2000). Rubery et al. not only link women's working strategies to social-care options, but also to gender biases in labor-market institutions and employment relationships.

Ellen Mutari and Deborah Figart (2001, 38–39) offer one of the few approaches that take work-time practices into account, showing how they serve as a means of harmonization between work and family life by relating the degree of flexibility in working hours to gender equity in work schedules and economic roles. Within their typology, gender equity ranges from the ideal-typical universal-caregiver model based on men and women's participation in both paid employment and caring labor, as envisioned by Nancy Fraser (1997), to the male-breadwinner model. The male-breadwinner work-time regime is reserved for countries in the Mediterranean where few options for flexible working time are available to mothers and households that depend on the income from men's traditional forty-hour workweek (Mutari and Figart, 2001, 43).

Mapping other member states of the EU, Mutari and Figart group the vast majority in an omnibus category of "transition work-time regimes." This category comprises seemingly disparate cases, such as Germany, Sweden, the Netherlands, Luxembourg, and Austria, that vary in the promise of gender equity and flexibility of working time. We believe that Mutari and Figart exaggerate the potential for innovative flexible arrangements to erode the male-breadwinner model in Germany. Since they are less concerned with the role of the state, their empirical indicators fail to fully capture the gender biases in the design of entitlements and how these affect women's strategies and facility for reconciling working and family life. Nonetheless, we agree that work-time practices are expressions of tacit gender negotiations within markets and "embody assumptions about alternative family structures" (Mutari and Figart, 2001, 38).[5]

Our comparative framework integrates the above perspectives on social care and work-time practices. More specifically, following Lewis's (1992, 162) original classification, figure 4.1 presents a diagram of strong to weak male-breadwinner models in terms of the tacit gender bargain that informs the division of caring responsibilities across institutional domains (family, state, and market), the division of gendered labor within the household (from female caregiver to shared care), and between the household and the labor market (from single earner to dual earner). Each model contours power in gender relations through the boundaries of public and private responsibilities (Shaver, 2000, 218). In strong male-breadwinner models, public responsibility upholds private, traditional male authority and responsibility for care is relegated to the private sphere of the family. In the dual-earner model, all adults participate in

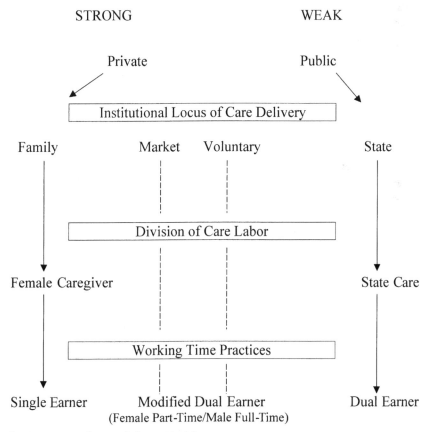

**Figure 4.1.   Male-Breadwinner Models**

the labor market (Lewis 2001, 154). The dual-earner model does not necessarily alter the division of care labor in the household. Liberal welfare systems tend to leave the provision of care to the private sector whereas social democratic systems publicly support care services.

Maternal employment reveals the nature of this tacit gender bargain, that is, the extent to which and under what conditions (work-time practices) women with children participate in the public sphere of employment. Lower rates of maternal employment, as a result of mothers dropping out of paid labor to care for children, have been associated with the male-breadwinner/female-caregiver model. Mothers' reduction of work-time schedules to rear children and/or care for elderly parents reflects a modification of the male-breadwinner model. In this model, women do not "freely" exchange their labor power in the same way that men do because of the prior demands families make on their labor time. A transition to the dual-earner model occurs as more women enter the workforce and remain employed full-time regardless of marital status and the presence of young children.

The earnings gap serves as a traditional measure of gender inequality in the labor market. We also include the percentage of employed population in low-wage work. The relative gender composition of low-wage work measures the extent to which wage-setting institutions privilege male breadwinners over female earners. Institutional mechanisms, such as trade union models and regulations, mediate market effects. Gender differences in rates of union membership reflect bias in the industrial-relations institutions.

Finally, fertility rates underscore how intimate body decisions are affected by the nature of the gender model. The adjustment of fertility, that is, having fewer children, may indicate one strategy for combining work and family life.

## EMPLOYMENT TRENDS AND CONTRACTUAL ADJUSTMENT: COMPARING GENDER MODELS

A review of employment and fertility trends makes visible the existence of different gender models and the persistence of the male-breadwinner model in Germany and Japan. In both societies, the male-breadwinner model has persisted, though the details of the two models differ.

In most of western Europe from the late 1960s onward, a more individualistic family/gender model has modified and, in some cases, weakened the male-breadwinner model. As Bosch (2002) shows, the percentage of households in which men alone contribute to household income has declined to less than one-third in most of these societies. Women's employment rate significantly increases with the rise in educational levels. In western Germany, slightly less than half the women with low educational levels are employed, but the rate jumps to 80.7 percent for women with high educational levels.[6] In Japan, this correlation is not consistent. Approximately 84 percent of university-educated women are employed, compared to 63 percent of high-school-educated women age 25–29; the level drops precipitously to 62 percent among the former and falls off less dramatically to 54.9 percent among the latter for those 30–34 years old (Ministry of Labour, 2000). These trends indicate the growth of labor-force participation among younger cohorts of married women, especially those with high educational attainment, but they also underscore divergence between Germany and Japan.

In both countries, maternal employment, while increasing over time, remains noticeably low at around 40 percent,[7] which is fairly evenly divided between part-time, full-time, and family work (see table 4.1).[8] Dual-earner couples in eastern Germany are more common than in western Germany (Anxo and O'Reilly, 2000). This pattern stems from different attitudes toward women's employment and overall lower levels of household income: eastern German women often cannot afford to take part-time jobs and are more likely

**Table 4.1. Modified Male-Breadwinner/Female-Caregiver Model**

| Case | Japan | Germany |
|------|-------|---------|
| Fertility rates[a] | | |
| 1960 | 2.01 | 2.37 |
| 1990 | 1.50 | 1.39 |
| Married/Cohabiting Mothers[b] | | |
| % Total Employed | 54[c] | 41 |
| % Working Full-Time | 17 | 21 |
| % Working Part-Time | 20 | 20 |
| Ratio of Female to Male Hourly | | |
| Earnings (Full-Time)[d] | 60.6 | 84.9 |
| Ratio of Part-Time to Full-Time Hourly | | |
| Earnings (Females) | 70.0 | 90.0 |
| % Low-Wage Work[e] | | |
| Overall | 16.0 | 13.0 |
| Male | 5.9 | 7.6 |
| Female | 37.2 | 25.4 |
| Union Density[f] | | |
| Male | 32.0 | 47.0 |
| Female | 22.0 | 22.0 |

[a] Source: Crouch, 1999, 460–61.
[b] Source: OECD, 1997, 83, table 3.1.
[c] Includes all married/cohabiting women with or without children (1992).
[d] Ministry of Labour, Basic Statistical Survey on Wage Structure 1999 (*Kimatte Shikyuusareru Gennkin Kyuuyo*). Other country data: ILO Yearbook of Labour Statistics, 1998, 849, table 5A.
[e] Low-paid work is defined as less than two-thirds of median earnings for all full-time employees (OECD, 1996, 4).
[f] Source: Union Density by Sex, 1985, by Western (1997, 27).

to remain unemployed looking for full-time work (Quack and Maier, 1994; O'Reilly, 1995). In the former East Germany, employed women contributed a larger proportion to household income than in the former West Germany: in 1988, 40 percent of household income in the east came from women's earnings, compared to 18 percent in the west (Einhorn, 1993). After reunification, western German women steadily increased their labor-force participation, although it has not reached the levels achieved by eastern German women. As a consequence, a more traditional but gradually modified male-breadwinner model, with mothers working part-time, is more common in western Germany than in eastern Germany.

Part-time employment has grown significantly in Japan and to a lesser extent in Germany. Part-time work is not simply a matter of working fewer hours than a full-timer, but is clearly linked to a different employment status. The designation of part-time workers in Japanese law is not based on working time but on status within the firm; thus part-timers can and often do work more than thirty-five hours a week (Gottfried and Hayashi-Kato, 1998; Osawa, 2001). In Germany, the growth of part-time employment has proceeded more slowly than in other industrialized countries alongside comparatively lower levels of female participation in paid employment overall. During the 1970s, West German trade unions played an important role in supporting the growth of part-time work for women, and later negotiated part-time work as a means of retaining jobs among the core male workforce when faced with rising unemployment and industrial restructuring. Initially conceived as a distinct employment status for women, part-time work was only partially secured through the social-welfare system. More recently, in 1997, the number of workers in marginal part-time employment (those working less than fifteen to eighteen hours a week or earning less than 630 DM per month) grew from 4.5 million in 1992 to 5.6 million. Women dominated in marginal part-time employment, which was constructed with a distinct dependent status and contractual conditions differentiating them from those working longer hours. Until April 1, 1999, those in marginal employment (*geringfugige Beschaftigung*) made no social contributions. As a result, there was a sharp division in the entitlements and risks associated with standard and nonstandard employment relationships in both countries.

On an hourly basis, female part-time employees are still likely to earn less than women working full-time (Dex et al., 1999, 504). Even though the gender wage gap in Germany is smaller than in Japan, more than one-third of German women employed part-time are in low-paid jobs. A higher proportion of the overall working population earns low wages and foregoes benefits in the Japanese economy than in Germany. Cross-national wage differences appear to be highly associated with the presence or lack of trade unions and generalized wage-setting agreements. German women benefit from more centralized industrial-bargaining structures (Gottfried, 2000), which is what we might expect from earlier research on income distribution and industrial wage setting in these countries (Western, 1997).

Recent research on Germany and Japan finds that female part-timers are more likely to encounter disadvantages than male part-timers, who experience short episodes of part-time employment usually at the point of entry into the labor market or in lieu of layoffs when they near retirement (Delsen, 1998). For women, disadvantages stem from the sequencing of part-time work during prime working ages. In Japan, regular employment declines from 73.3 percent for 25–29-year-old women to 49.8 percent for 35–39-year-old women, and part-time employment rises to nearly 40 percent for 34-year-old women until they reach retirement age (Ministry of Labour, 2000). Japanese women suffer high penalties for dropping out of full-time career tracks, since firm-specific labor markets contain few portals for reentry. Like Japanese women, German women, regardless of the hours worked prior to childbirth, are likely to withdraw from the labor market and reenter later, often in part-time employment (Bothfeld and O'Reilly, 2000). Part-time work has become an increasingly important adjustment strategy for firms and families. It represents a modification of the male-breadwinner model, but one that continues to reinforce female dependency on the employed husband in terms of income and benefit entitlements.

Despite institutional incentives for mothers to remain out of paid work or take up a part-time job, these measures have not sustained fertility levels comparable with those in countries where women exhibit higher rates of labor-force participation. In Japan fertility rates fell from 2.01 in 1960 to 1.50 in 1990, and in Germany from 2.37 to 1.39 over the same period (Crouch 1999, 460–61). Fertility rates have continued to drop in both Japan and Germany (table 4.1).

These patterns reveal common outcomes of institutionally embedded male-breadwinner models. In Japan and Germany, standard employment rights and conditions were based on a strong male-breadwinner model, resulting in similar fertility patterns and labor-market trends despite the significantly different historical origins of their welfare systems. While increasing differentiation and individualization have eroded the traditional bases of male authority, the legacy of the male-breadwinner model biases the design of entitlements to fit with a male-standard employment biography. The institutionally embedded nature of this model in the worlds of work and welfare constrain options for reform and renewal.

## RENEGOTIATING GENDER MODELS IN JAPAN AND GERMANY

We now turn to an examination of the policy legacies that shaped and perpetuated these male-breadwinner arrangements before examining how conservative welfare systems are undergoing pressure for change. During the postwar boom, conservative blending of social and Christian democracy in Germany (Pontusson, 1997) and Confucianism in Japan (Goodman and Peng, 1997; Esping-Andersen, 1999) have narrowly formulated the repertoire of care and labor regulations on the basis of an institutionally embedded male-breadwinner/female-caregiver model. Policies familialized caring services and defined benefits according to a male-standard employment relationship. The reliance on unpaid privatized care has led to the underdevelopment of social-care infrastructures and forced a trade-off for women between family formation and full-time continuous participation in the labor market.

Through a chronology of labor and care regulations, a noticeable discursive shift becomes evident during the 1980s as the state responded to the economic downturn and renewed political activism among feminist and women's groups. Yet we find that re-regulation in conservative welfare states remains rooted in the legacy of the male-breadwinner model. However, the trajectory of regulation cannot be understood in terms of a single impulse toward entrenching the nuclear family structure premised on the male-breadwinner/full-time housewife arrangement. Rather, we agree with Ito Peng (2000), who characterizes postwar policy as following a zigzag path with increasing lack of coherence.[9]

## Balancing Economy and Demography in Japan

In the political ferment that followed World War II, the Japanese state embarked on an ambitious project to modernize the war-torn economy. Along with rebuilding the physical infrastructure, the state codified basic employment rights governing employment relations. One core piece of legislation, the Labor Standards Law of 1947, set standards for regulation over embryonic industrial-relations institutions. This law also gave expression to and reinforced different labor-market experiences of and expectations for married women as compared to men. Several provisions sought to protect women's reproductive functions, granting six weeks of leave both prior to and after childbirth, permitting lighter workloads for pregnant workers, and allowing mothers of infants under one year to take two thirty-minute breaks for breast-feeding per day. At the same time, the Child Welfare Law of 1947 extended the principle of universal welfare to all children, thereby making available increased child-care services. But the impact of these measures was ambiguous; as Barbara Moloney (1995, 280–81) suggests, the "law emphasized a mother's ability to give birth, not her having time to rear [a child]," and had the effect of excluding women from some employment areas (see also Buckley, 1993, 349).

By the end of the 1950s, the corporate family-welfare system became a defining feature of the social contract between capital, labor, and the state, with implications for the division of caring labor across institutional domains between private and public sectors. Large companies in core economic sectors agreed to provide a family wage in exchange for cooperative relationships with enterprise-based trade unions. The family wage consisted of family, housing, and transportation allowances, low-interest loans, and large lump-sum retirement allowances. As a corporate family-welfare system, it encouraged "family formation and personal home ownership, discouraged married women's labor force participation, increased workers' dependence on the company . . . and served to rationalize low wages and the company practice of forced retirement after marriage or child birth" (Peng, 2002).[10] Most unions concentrated collective bargaining on achieving job security and improving company-based welfare benefits for their core male membership, although some unions demanded time off, for women only, to take care of babies. Even though the corporate family-welfare system supported the "alliance between corporate warriors and full-time housewives" (Kaku, 2001, 35), public child care expanded to accommodate women's increased regular employment in modernized sectors over the decade of the 1960s (Peng, 2002).

In the context of the sustained economic boom and social change, a significant shift occurred in the early 1970s when various state agencies called for the extension of welfare particularly for the elderly, and began to recognize women both as unpaid caregivers and as paid employees. As early as 1963, a report of the Economic Deliberative Council, later formulated into the Working Women's Welfare Law of 1972, encouraged married women to reenter the labor force through part-time employment without reducing their responsibility for household maintenance and dependent care (Uno, 1993, 305).[11] Some unions pushed to improve benefits for working mothers, and negotiated the first instance of child-care leave for female members in the professions (Buckley, 1993, 281).

It took the first oil shock in 1973–75 to shake the welfare system in this oil-dependent nation. In its aftermath, both the state and large corporations sought to foster labor-market flexibility and to downgrade welfare responsibility in order to lower labor costs without disruption to the male lifetime-employment system. Toward this end, the state mobilized the image of "Japanese-style welfare," which rooted policy objectives in an imagined cultural tradition to contrast with Western welfare systems (Kono, 2000). The state designated the family as the centerpiece of welfare delivery and looked to women as the means of flexible adjustment to changing market conditions. As a result, a new welfare mix concentrated on increasing marketized activities and informal voluntary support (Thränhardt, 1992,13).[12] The Japanese-style welfare approach signalled a noticeable discursive shift in which women were no longer portrayed principally as professional housewives, but rather as both unpaid caregivers and part-time workers.

Increasing regulation created a patchwork of reforms in the mid-1980s. Pressure from women's groups led to passage of the landmark Equal Employment Opportunities Law (EEOL) on the tenth anniversary of the United

Nations (UN) International Women's Year. The 1985 Nairobi Summit profoundly affected the push for a regulatory response to gender inequality in Japan. Japan's lack of progress on gender equality became more noticeable when viewed in relation to legal norms in other industrialized countries. The summit also reinvigorated feminist and women's groups' social activism on gender equality issues (Peng, 2002). A weak EEOL merely encouraged employers "to endeavor" to offer equal opportunities for women. A study of the impact of the EEOL more than a decade after its passage found that many large companies interpreted this conditional language by opening dual tracks for women only: a management track offering career opportunities and a kind of "mommy track" that destined many women to dead-end general office jobs (Hanami, 2000, 9; Roberts, 1994, 184).

The limits of the EEOL were nowhere more apparent than in the failure to extend principles of equal treatment to the growing number of women hired in nonregular employment (including both temporaries and part-timers). The Worker Dispatching Law (*Rodosha Haken Jigyo Ho*), which was passed a month after the EEOL, regulated temporary employment by adopting a "positive list" system that lifted the ban on agency temporary work for sixteen allowable jobs. The positive list excluded jobs in core manufacturing associated with men's work and allowed jobs in administrative functions associated with women's work. This regulation facilitated the use of temporary employment as a flexible staffing arrangement. In so doing, the state implicitly recognized the male-breadwinner model through which many highly qualified women, by virtue of their exclusion from the lifetime-employment system, would be available for nonregular employment in sex-typed jobs (Gottfried, 2002).

The 1986 introduction of a special tax exemption for married women's part-time income played a pivotal role in sustaining but modifying the male-breadwinner model.[13] This measure, like the 1961 tax reform, effectively subsidized stay-at-home wives, and the latter encouraged women to take up part-time employment by exempting from taxes the secondary earner's income (i.e., usually the wife's) if it fell below a stipulated threshold.[14] A study by Yukiko Abe and Fumio Ohtake (1997) found that two-thirds of married female part-timers adjusted their working hours in order to derive full benefits from the taxation system, and firms willingly facilitated this adaptation of hours. Tax reform not only rationalized lower wages of part-time work but also made it economically rational for some women to reduce their working hours to earn just enough to qualify for the exemption (Wakisaka and Bae, 1998).[15]

The economic crisis of the 1990s sharpened tensions, leading the state to revise the policy agenda toward what Sugimoto (1998, cited in Peng, 2000) calls a "new Japanese-style welfare Society." Most urgently, declining fertility rates precipitated this "new" emphasis, in which the pronatalist state sought to "balance" decreased fertility and increased female labor-force participation. An important initiative came under the Child Care Law (1992), which established a national standard of paid leave at 60 percent of wages for a fourteen-week period. It also entitled mothers or fathers to take a one-year leave, securing their job. Another state initiative culminated in the 1994 Ministry of Health and Welfare's Angel Plan, which promoted a set of comprehensive child and family policies directed at improving the environment to raise healthy children, as well as supporting efforts to make child rearing and employment compatible. Due to the observed gap in the fertility rate between nonemployed women (2.96) and employed women (0.60), a government committee surmised that women would depress their fertility as long as dependent care was experienced as a burden. The report resolved that the government should promote measures to remove the causes for low fertility. To support families (i.e., women) in balancing employment and child rearing, the state committed itself to the promotion of diversified child-care services, including extended hours, infant care, and private child-care facilities at companies as well as expansion of after-school programs (Roberts, 2001).

The new emphasis was carried through into labor-law reform. Most notably, the Part-Time Labor Law, passed in 1993, was designed to ease mothers' entry into and longevity in part-time (*paato-taimu*) work by encouraging more and better child-care services. The law was premised on the assumption that women would continue to perform unpaid caring labor. As with the EEOL, the moral language of "duty," when combined with the conditional verb "to endeavour," gave employers a high degree of discretion over compliance. The Part-Time Labor Law and the child-care initiatives introduced a new key word of "balance" into political discourse.[16] In using the term in relating part-time to full-time employment, the Part-Time Labor Law "[did] not reject the idea of reasonable differences between part-time and full-time regular employees" (Kezuka, 2000), and subsequent changes accepted unequal treatment for all those classified as part-timers, regardless of the number of hours worked (Osawa, 2001). In allowing unequal treatment, the Part-Time Labor Law was at odds with the EEOL. More ambivalently, the phrase "maintain balance" in reference to the linkage between family and employment recognized but provided insufficient relief for lifting the burdens of both child and elder care.

By the late 1990s, the deepening economic crisis, the looming demographic crisis (declining fertility and aging of the population), and the diminishing political hegemony of the Liberal Democratic Party opened new policy areas to gender-specific concerns and widened the scope of input by political agents for change. The twin issues of labor flexibility and care were taken up in the legislative agenda of 1999–2000. In their 1999 proposal for the Economic and Industrial Policy Vision for the Twenty-First Century, even the Ministry of Trade and Industry (MITI), the powerful economic agency whose authoritative guidance seemed far removed from gender issues, acknowledged the need to utilize the labor power of women and the elderly, largely in part-time work, in order to address the predicted labor shortage.

Policies addressing care took multiple and sometimes contradictory forms. The amended Child Care Law mandated employer contributions to offset the expense of child-care projects and entitled fathers to take leave to care for a sick child (Araki, 1998).[17] At the same time, other policies assumed and sought to shore up the modified breadwinner model: cash benefits were improved to encourage increased childbirth, and the dependent allowance for each additional child was increased and extended to children up to age six, as applied to low- and medium-income families (Sims, 2000, A8). Taking effect in April 1999, a seemingly gender-neutral approach granted family-care leave to either partner, who could receive 25 percent of his or her wages (Sato, 2000); this amount rose to 40 percent in 2001.[18] The Basic Law for a Gender-Equal Society took effect in June 1999, establishing an Office for Gender Equality in the Prime Minister's Office. Issued on December 17, 1999, the Basic Guidelines for Promoting Policies Dealing with Low Fertility Rates enacted a more ambivalent approach that addressed women as potential or actual mothers as well as employees.

While these initiatives modified the effects of the strong male-breadwinner model, revisions of the Employment Security Law and the Worker Dispatching Law attempted to further the goal of flexible adjustment through deregulation of capital–labor relations (Araki, 1999). The same laws that sought to relieve burdens and provide support in combining work and family for some working women also led to more precarious employment situations for women who filled in for those on leave. For example, the 1996 amendment of the Child Care and Family Care Leave Law liberalized agency temporary work for those who take child or family leave, except for those working in prohibited areas, on the condition that the work period does not exceed more than one year. In 1999, a compromise between the labor movement, which was formally opposed to deregulation, and employers led to an amendment to the Worker Dispatching Law that removed restrictions on the use of temporary employment, but limited the contract period to one year for the newly included production jobs (Weathers, 2000). In effect, the labor regulation covered men and women under different contractual terms.

The Japanese state's orientation toward regulation has increasingly centered on "balancing" demographics and developmental economics. This linguistic turn to "maintain balance" has not easily translated into policy making. Functional divisions defined different policy domains for each ministry, leading to reforms that reflected a lack of coherence and a piecemeal, patchwork approach to welfare. For example, the Ministry of Health and Welfare's concern with demography extended regulation in the form of support for both child care and elder care beyond what might be expected in a socially conservative welfare system. In contrast, however, the Ministry of Labour sponsored reforms that deregulated employment relations to the advantage of employers and a shrinking core of male workers. These measures actively encouraged part-time employment and allowed unequal treatment for non-core categories of the workforce (such as married women, older workers, and students).

### The Fatherland: Conservative Social Democracy in Germany

In West Germany during the postwar era, despite the formal establishment of equal legal rights, the implementation proved disappointing. In the 1950s and 1960s, formal equality distinguished between biological and later "functional" differences (i.e., over the domestic division of labor) between men and women. So although the official definition of housewife was dropped in 1977, in practice the organization of the social and tax system served to perpetuate this "special" status. In the German Democratic Republic, women enjoyed formal equality but shouldered responsibility for child care in addition to working full-time in the labor market.

In West Germany tax splitting and a progressive income tax encouraged labor-market withdrawal for married women and the use of parental leave (Quack and Maier, 1994, 79). It also discouraged wives from moving from part-time into full-time employment (Dingeldey, 1999; Bothfeld and O'Reilly, 2000). Anxo and O'Reilly (2000) point out that household income in Germany actually fell when wives moved from part-time to full-time jobs, because tax splitting reduced tax payments for the main earner in the household while supplementary earners were charged proportionately high rates of marginal tax. This contrasts with the situation in most other European countries, where taxation has shifted from a household to an individual basis.

During the 1980s and 1990s a combination of labor regulations removed restrictions on women's night work and equalized the age of retirement to sixty-five (applicable in 2001). Social policy related to working arrangements introduced maternity leave (*Mutterschaftsurlaub*) in 1979, providing women fourteen weeks of paid leave[19] and entitlement to 750 DM a month. Reforms to the maternity-leave law introduced in 1985 also entitled fathers to go on parental leave (*Erziehungsurlaub*). Those taking up parental leave were entitled to 600 DM a month for the first six months; after this date, those without any other source of income could continue to receive 600 DM a month until their children reached age two. As a protection against dismissal, the employment contract remained in force over the period of maternal leave. Attempts to reduce incentives to labor-market withdrawal were introduced in 1992 with a reform to the pension system that symbolically included a "baby year" as part of a woman's pension contributions. Nevertheless, only half of the women on parental leave return to work after three years, with only a quarter going back to their former posts (Ministry for the Family, the Elderly, Women and Young People, 1998, 110). Parental-leave provisions did not significantly alter the economic calculus that might have encouraged women either to work continuously or to reenter in full-time employment.

Moreover, the child-care allowance rewarded stay-at-home mothers, who qualified for extended benefits as long as they remained out of the labor force. After these reforms, still only 1.5 percent of fathers compared to 98.5 percent of mothers took up parental leave.

More recent reforms introduced in 2001 raised the maximum numbers of hours a parent on parental leave could work from nineteen to thirty per week, so as to raise the potential income of poorer families. It was also possible to choose to take parental leave for only one year at a rate of 900 DM a month, but receipt of this benefit depended on total household income.[20] According to the Ministry for the Family, the Elderly, Women and Young People (2000), these changes were coupled with attempts to encourage the extension of part-time employment and break the traditional gendered division of labor. It is, however, unlikely that these minor revisions will have the intended outcome on the gender division of labor, since the financial benefit is not high enough to offset the loss of income if the husband takes parental leave.

None of the above reforms sought to change either the institutional locus of care delivery or the availability of child-care services. Prior to reunification, the East German state had supported child-care facilities that enabled women to work full-time. Once the wall came down, child-care centers in the east lost funding. A recent reform introduced the right to a place in public child care for three- to six-year-olds, but a significant lack of provision remains, particularly in the former West Germany. Even more so, there are few child-care places for infants and young toddlers.

More proactive measures to facilitate women's advancement (*Frauenförderung*) were introduced in 1980 with the Equal Treatment Law (*Gleichbehandlungsgesetz*), which brought Germany into line with standards in other European countries. This allowed for compensation (*Schmerzengeld*) in cases of discrimination. In 1998 a reform to this law was enacted based on earlier developments at the Lände level. This initiative mandated quotas and laws to advance women (*Frauenfördergesetze*) for public-sector employers and made them voluntary for large private companies. One result has been the introduction of a women's representative (*Frauenbeauftragte*) to ensure a better working climate to promote women in public-sector organizations.[21] These representatives can support working women's claims and offer advice, but have no authority to change the rules for hiring and promotion (Weber, 2000, 20).

A new constellation of multilevel political and economic forces is shifting the playing field in Germany as part of the European Community. Sabine Berghahn (1999, 332) argues that the German case appears like a "ping-pong game" between the national and European levels over the improvement of equal opportunities. Since the 1970s, developments at the European level, particularly through the European Court of Justice (ECJ), have forced German law in a more progressive direction, though some cases have generated considerable ambiguity. For example, in the Kalanke case, taken to the European Court of Justice in 1995, a ruling was made to support the plaintiff's claim that a male candidate had been unfairly discriminated against in a recruitment process in Bremen. At the time, this was seen as a potential setback for women's advancement, but the ruling was subsequently overturned by the 1997 Marschall decision, which explicitly defined disadvantage to include its effects on women (see Berghahn, 1999, 322). Additional examples of the impact of ECJ rulings can be seen in the change of the German constitution, approved in 2000 by both chambers of the German parliament, lifting the ban on women bearing arms in the German army (*Bundeswehr*) (Liebert, 2000).

The EC Social Protocol agreement on part-time work is another example of the dynamic relationship between regional, national, and supranational levels of regulation. In Germany, concern with the rapid growth of marginal part-time employment led the Social Democratic–Green government in 2000 to enact legislation bringing this form of employment under the remit of the social security system, so that both employers and employees had to make social contributions (Bothfeld and O'Reilly, 2000). Further attempts to encourage work-time flexibility, as well as more general reductions in working hours, led to the enactment of a 2000 law entitling workers with at least six months' tenure to apply for a shorter workweek and also giving preferential treatment to part-time staff wishing to resume full-time employment. The absence of a directive on child care and caring work, however, leaves the question of reproductive work to be resolved in the mixed economy of privately and publicly provided care. The accumulation of EU case law has not signaled a single or coherent direction on equality measures.

## POLICY LEGACIES AND REFORM OF THE
## MALE-BREADWINNER MODEL: SIMILAR BUT DIFFERENT

In both Japan and Germany, we have tracked the conservative impulse behind the design of policies, including the tax and transfer system, family allowances, and limited support of child care for very young children. This array of policies contained disincentives to women's labor-force participation in full-time employment and created incentives for mothers to work part-time while taking care of children and elderly parents. As a consequence, women have tended to derive social benefits and rights as dependents of male breadwinners. Formal state regulation has moved toward encouraging female labor-force participation, to a greater or lesser extent on equal terms with men, but the fashioning of reforms, while addressing women as waged workers, continues to be cast in terms of the prevailing discourse on motherhood protection, which defines women's role primarily as unpaid caregivers (Moloney, 1995) and secondarily as paid workers. Policy shifts evident in Germany and Japan have failed to move far enough away from, and in fact have remained rooted in, socially conservative state ideologies.

On the basis of earlier research, we would argue that the persistence of the male-breadwinner model affecting the allocation of time within and between households in Germany and Japan is in part related to the design of the tax and transfer system (Abe and Ohtake, 1997; Wakisaka and Bae, 1998; Schettkat, 1989; Gustafsson, 1996). Rubery et al. (1998, 205) argue that in general

the tax and social security system and state child care and family policies either reinforce or modify the gender contract in two related ways. First, these policies shape female employment patterns through creating a range of labor supply incentives and disincentives. Second, women's employment patterns may be penalised in systems where benefit entitlements rest upon a record of full-time continuous involvement in the formal labor market.

Our analysis of Germany and Japan indicates that the structure of the tax systems reinforced married women's marginal employment through the use of the dependent-spouse tax allowance. In both cases, provisions not only privileged single breadwinners in the calculation of taxes but also penalized dual earners whose income exceeded a legal threshold. The tax code thus made it economically rational for households to limit the hours worked by women as long as their partners worked full-time. Based on the single-earner male breadwinner family, both the tax and social security systems have undermined measures aimed at gender equality in the labor market.

It is interesting that an almost synchronized timing of equal opportunity policy reflects the impact of transnational women's activity on national regulations in Germany and Japan. The removal of formal legal restrictions has not eradicated gender-based hierarchies. The implementation of official principles of equal treatment in these two countries has been weakened by lax legislation allowing voluntary compliance and the failure to include enforcement mechanisms, giving employers a high degree of discretion over recruitment, placement, and promotion. As sociologist Claudia Weber (2000, 21) has pointed out, at the enterprise level, both German and Japanese equal employment opportunity policies lack institutionalized support and incentives, which "would legally oblige the industrial relations partners . . . to 'fill' the abstract principles by implementing actual measures." There is evidence of uneven compliance by private-sector corporations in both countries. In the public sector, however, the stronger presence of unions and the influence of the social partners in Germany have produced a more far-ranging equal opportunity infrastructure than exists in Japan, where national organization of unions is relatively weak.

Legal traditions also help to explain different applications of equal-treatment principles. In Japan, equal employment opportunities law draws the concept of individual rights from liberal discourse, while much legal doctrine continues to stress the "one-main-income family model." One example is the formulation of the amended 1997 Equal Employment Opportunity Act. Morozumi (1998, 61) argues, "Under the recent recession when female students suffered many difficulties in getting regular employment, the government began to consider it an urgent issue to strengthen the anti-discrimination rules in employment. The revised act included a ban on sex discrimination in cases of hiring and promotion. But despite such moves the principle of equality at the individual level is not really rooted in the Japanese system." Morozumi (1998, 56–57) further contends, "Just distribution manifests itself in a family-related employment distribution, based on the idea that one family should be guaranteed one regular employment to support its living. Until recently, this model has not been challenged and there are little legal incentives for maintaining two regular employments in one family. This naturally entails greater difficulties to women than men in acquiring and keeping an established position in the labor market."

Of growing importance is the relationship of Germany vis-à-vis the region. Germany's membership in the EU has led to regulatory changes and a shifting terrain of multilevel governance institutions, which have modified the breadwinner model. The European Commission and European Court of Justice have promoted equal opportunity and, more recently, "gender mainstreaming" principles. There is, however, a dearth of literature on the record of national and subnational implementation of these directives and guidelines. Until recently, Germany has lagged behind other countries in implementing many of these directives (see Liebert, 2000). As a study of Spain by Celia Valiente shows, "national conceptual and practical equality differences led to varying implementation of the same EU equal pay directive" (cited in Cichowski, 2000, 111). This suggests continuation of uneven implementation even though many of the member states have adopted similar measures.

In both societies, more women are attaining qualifications that enable them to apply for core forms of employment, associated with more continuous patterns of labor-force participation and higher wages. Companies also have been willing to experiment with flexible working schedules, especially when they are part of a skill-retention strategy for highly qualified mothers. Ironically, concern with declining fertility rates has been greater in countries where women have lower, rather than higher, levels of labor-force participation. Added to this trend has been a growing concern with responsibility and payment for care of the aging population. Faced with different but significant labor-market problems, both Japan and Germany are modifying their male-breadwinner models. In Germany the issue has been reregulating marginal employment and trying to find alternative ways to reintegrate the unemployed, while in Japan concern with demographic trends has surfaced as a key policy area, resulting in a search for ways to encourage women to adjust work-time practices to accommodate increasing care needs.

The conservative underpinning of reform efforts may be exacerbating the crisis in institutions based on the male-breadwinner model of employment.

The appearance of weaknesses in the German and Japanese employment systems in the final decade of the twentieth century, as characterized by rising unemployment, restructuring of internal labor markets, and changing demographic trends, sheds new light on inadequacies of the traditional male-breadwinner model. These changes have resulted in contradictory pressures and demands on women's labor time and reflect the shifting but enduring dilemmas posed for women by socially conservative states.

## CONCLUSION

Our framework attempts to build a bridge between the varieties-of-capitalism and gendered-welfare-state approaches. The first approach suggests that shared institutional complementarities gave rise to phenomenal economic success in Germany and Japan. The failure of proponents of this approach to take note of gender biases implicit in industrial-relations institutions diverted attention from seeing that a strong and implicit male-breadwinner system has exacerbated current weaknesses in the labor market, especially with regard to the underutilization of married women in the labor market and inadequate provision of social care.

In this analysis we turned to welfare-state literatures specifying the institutional locus and division of social-care responsibilities that demonstrate the persistence of the male-breadwinner model in order to establish that the welfare state is gendered. The privatization of care has entailed withholding from the public sector resources needed for social-care infrastructures. While relatively low public support for caring services characterizes socially conservative welfare systems, Japan and Germany have pursued paths inconsistent with a singular impulse toward entrenching the male-breadwinner model. Social partners played a more significant role in promoting national standards in Germany. Thus, paid maternity leave is more generous in Germany than in Japan.[22] Alternatively, spurred by pronatalist concerns, the Japanese state has provided more public support for the expansion of child-care services than has Germany.

The drop in fertility rates in Japan and Germany reflects the dilemmas posed by an untenable relationship between unpaid reproductive responsibilities and paid employment requirements. A shrinking labor force resulting from a declining birthrate and a rapidly aging population raises demography to a paramount place on the political-economic agenda in both countries. Japan, even more than Germany, is experiencing what Daly and Lewis (2000, 289) call a "care crisis," namely, a decrease in the supply of unpaid caregiving labor due to its demographic profile and its financial and social factors, precisely at a time when the demand for caring services is rising. This demographic imperative may, however, "become a spur to gender equality in socially conservative or familialistic states" (Drew, 1999, 748).

The social-care perspective is a necessary but not sufficient component explaining the diversity of work-time practices. The higher incidence of nonstandard employment among Japanese women than among their German counterparts can also be attributed to gender biases in the industrial-relations systems and labor regulations. Japan has increasingly sought to "balance" demography and developmental economics by tinkering with labor regulations that would increase women's part-time work. While in both countries part-time work is a distinct employment status, Japanese women suffer higher penalties for working part-time and experience greater disadvantages in terms of compensation and promotion. In Japan labor regulations were designed to protect the core male workforce and left the peripheral female workforce outside the protected zone. The social partners in Germany fashioned strong regulations and collective norms in its industrial-relations system, but it too was geared toward the family wage. When faced with increasing unemployment, the German social partners negotiated innovative flexible work-time practices for the core male workforce and supported less secure part-time work for women.

Policies aimed at generating jobs and improving employment conditions for women and facilities for families are clearly undergoing change, but the process remains trapped within the policy legacy of a strong male-breadwinner model. Partial modifications aimed at balancing employment, pregnancy, child rearing, and elder care are still tied to that mode, with the result that they make contradictory demands on women as flexible workers and informal caregivers without sufficiently addressing unequal responsibilities for and undervaluation of caring labor. The lack of coherence has increased due to contradictory policy logics. For example, the extension of equality regulations aimed at removing barriers to equal opportunities has been undermined by labor and tax policies encouraging married women to work part-time. The latter are still premised on the outmoded male-breadwinner model.

By focusing our comparison of these two cases, which typify socially conservative welfare states, on the gender component of the labor market, we have been able to illuminate particular social and legislative initiatives and pressures and make the implicit gender bargain explicit. We have demonstrated that the economic success of these two countries during the post–World War II era has been due in large part to the array of gender policies pursued in each country, which pursue a family wage and protect a dominant male breadwinner. As political and demographic pressures alter the socioeconomic landscape and both societies grapple with a shortage of labor, however, these hidden gender dimensions of existing labor policies create significant problems and pose critical constraints on the welfare state's ability to respond to the emerging crisis.

## NOTES

1. We benefited enormously from suggestions by Karin Gottschall, Birgit Pfau-Effinger, Margarita Estevez-Abe, and David Fasenfest. Special thanks to Sonya Michel, Ann Shola Orloff, and Ito Peng, who pushed us to rethink our analysis.

2. Others view Japan in its own context rather than trying to fit the country into preexisting welfare-state models (Goodman and Peng, 1997, 193). Our approach tries to avoid this Western bias by offering a historically sensitive interpretation of Japanese developments.

3. When care is taken into consideration, France represents another anomaly in Esping-Andersen's tripartite welfare model. France's state-supported caring infrastructure resembles the social democratic Nordic countries more than the socially conservative continental countries (Letablier, 2001).

4. Marie-Therese Letablier has discussed the fascinating example of child minders whose care services are subsidized by the French state but are paid and used by individuals. She regards child minders as a compromise between public-provided care (e.g., crèches) and market-based care. This diversification of caring services suggests alternative resolutions that cannot be read fully as either public or private enterprises.

5. See Yeandle's (1999) synthesis of gender contracts, welfare systems, and nonstandard working schedules in her comparison between five European countries. She pays less attention to regulation shaping different gender models.

6. Data encompassing both former eastern and western zones of Germany are not readily available.

7. A 2000 labor-force survey conducted by the Japanese government indicates that just under 30 percent of mothers are employed when their children are below three, and that this number jumps to almost half of women in paid employment once their children reach four to six years of age.

8. A 1999 White Paper on Working Women released by the Ministry of Labour in March 2000 reports on women's perceptions of the existence of an age barrier in the Japanese labor market: 81.8 percent of those aged 35 to 39 and 72.4 percent of women aged forty and over claimed that they experience barriers to reemployment because of their age (General Survey, 2000).

9. Janneke Plantenga (2001) has made a persuasive argument for why child and elder care should be analytically separated. In the Dutch case, strong public support for elderly care, as a part of housing policy, diverges from private family-based child care.

10. According to a Japanese Ministry of Labour Survey on Employment and Management of Female Workers, the proportion of women workers who retired after either becoming pregnant or giving birth declined from 46.7 percent in 1971 to 31.2 percent in 1991 and 19 percent by 1997.

11. As Peng suggests (2000), the postwar Japanese state aided the development of a fairly comprehensive package of social security centered on the needs of the corporate sector that favored company-specific provisions for regular employees.

12. Thränhardt (1992, 14) notes that the state's "call [to women] to act as providers of cheap labor either in the 'voluntary movement' or in Confucian traditions as 'dutiful daughters-in-law' by shouldering the whole burden of taking care of the aging parents alone, was not answered in sufficient numbers."

13. A 1995 study cited by Kaku (2001, 37) shows that a wife's employment status is highly correlated to a husband's income. Husbands who report the highest income live in households where their wives are least likely to work. Family income is the lowest for those families where the wife works part-time. Tax policy appears to depress overall family income, especially among households with wives working part-time.

14. A residence tax levied on income over 99 million yen serves as another disincentive for women to work more than part-time (Kezuka, 2000).

15. Japanese employers offer fewer bonuses, annual pay raises, and retirement benefits to part-time employees than to regular employees (Kezuka, 2000). Those part-timers enjoying benefits saw their value decline during the 1990s (Osawa, 2001).

16. Article 3 of the law reads as follows: "employers shall endeavor to promote effective utilization of part-time workers' abilities in an effective manner, in due consideration of the actual work conditions of part-time workers concerned, and maintain balance with regular workers by securing proper working conditions, implement education and training, improving their welfare and improving employment management" (cited in Kezuka, 2000).

17. The Women's Bureau of the Ministry of Labour conducted a 1997 survey that found only 0.6 percent of male workers took child-care leave following the birth of a child (Sato, 2000).

18. We thank Ito Peng for her general comments and her specific reference to recent changes.

19. Women were entitled to take leave for six weeks before and eight weeks after birth.

20. It is reduced for couples earning more than 32,000 DM a year, or for single parents earning more than 26,400 DM annually.

21. On the Lände (state) level, over 1,200 equality agencies serve as mechanisms for consultation and grievance handling in the civil service (Weber, 2000, 19).

22. In his first policy speech on May 7, 2001, Prime Minister Junichiro Koizumi proposed a substantial increase in the number of day-care and after-school centers to ease women's entry into the labor force (Strom, 2001, W1).

## REFERENCES

Abe, Yukiko, and Fumio Ohtake. 1997. "The Effects of Income Tax and Social Security on Part-Time Labour Supply in Japan." *Review of Social Policy* 6: 45–64.

Anxo, Dominique, and Jacqueline O'Reilly. 2000. "Regulating Working Time Changes." Pp. 61–90 in *Working Time Changes: Social Integration through Working Time Transitions in Europe*, ed. Jacquline O'Reilly, Immaculada Cebrián, and Michel Lallement. Cheltenham: Edward Elgar.

Araki, Takashi. 1998. "Recent Legislative Developments in Equal Employment and Harmonization of Work and Family Life in Japan." *Japan Labour Bulletin* (April 1): 5–10.

———. 1999. "1999 Revisions of Employment Security Law and Worker Dispatching Law: Drastic Reforms of Japanese Labor Market Regulations." *Japan Labour Bulletin* (September 1): 5–10.

Berghahn, Sabine. 1999. "50 Jahre Gleichberechtigungsgebot: Erfolge und Ent-täuschungen bei der Gleichstellung der Geschlechter" ("Fifty Years of Equal Rights: Promises and Disappointments for Gender Equality.") In *Lernened Demokratie: 50 Jahre Bundesrepublik Deutschlands (Democray Learned: West Germany in the Past 50 Years)*, ed. Gunther Schmid and M. Kaase. Berlin: Editions Sigma.

Bergqvist, Christina, Anette Borchorst, Ann-Dorte Christensen, Nina Raaum, Viveca Ramstedt-Silen, and Auour Styrkarsdottir. 1999. *Equal Democracies: Gender and Politics in the Nordic Countries*. Oslo: Scandinavian University Press.

Bosch, Gerhard. Forthcoming. "Auf dem Weg zu einem Neuen Normalarbeitsverhält-nis? Veränderung von Erwerbsläufen und ihre Sozialstaatliche Absicherung" ("On the Way to a New Standard Employment Relationship? Change in Working Life and Social Security"). In *Zukunft der Arbeit und Geschlecht. Diskurse, Entwicklungsp-fade und Reformoptionen im Internationalen* Vergleich (*The Future of Work and Gender: Discourse, Path-Development, and Reforms in an International Perspec-tive*), ed. Karin Gottschall and Birgit Pfau-Effinger. Opladen: Leske + Budrich.

Bothfeld, Silke, and Jacqueline O'Reilly. 2000. "Moving Up or Moving Out? Transi-tions Through Part-Time Work in Germany and the UK." Pp. 137–72 in *Working Time Changes*, ed. Jacqueline O'Reilly, Immaculada Cebrián, and Michel Lalle-ment. Cheltenham: Edward Elgar.

Buckley, Sandra. 1993. "Altered States: The Body Politics of 'Being-woman.'" Pp. 347–72 in *Postwar Japan as History*, ed. Andrew Gordon. Berkeley: University of California Press.

Bundesministerium für Arbeit (Ministry of Labor). 1999. *Das 630-Mark-Gesetz: Die neuen Regeln zur geringfügigen Beschäftigung (The 630 German Mark Law: New Regulation of Marginal Employment)*. Available online at: http://www.bma .bund.de.

Bundesministerium für Familie, Senioren, Frauen und Jugend (Ministry for the Fam-ily, the Elderly, Women and Young People). 1998. *Die Familie im Spiegel der amtlichen Statistik (The Family Reflected in Official Statistics)*. 4 Aufl. Bonn: BMFSFJ

Cichowski, Rochelle. 2000. "Book Review Essay, Gender and Policy in Comparative Perspective." *Women & Politics* 21, no. 1: 107–15.

Crouch, Colin. 1999. *Social Change in Western Europe*. Oxford: Oxford University Press.

Crouch, Colin, and Wolfgang Streeck. 1997. *Political Economy of Modern Capitalism: Mapping Convergence and Diversity*. London: Sage.

Daly, Mary, and Jane Lewis. 2000. "The Concept of Social Care and the Analysis of Contemporary Welfare States." *British Journal of Sociology* 52, no. 2: 281–98.

Delsen, Lei. 1998. "Why Do Men Work Part-Time?" In *Part-Time Prospects*, ed. Jacqueline O'Reilly and Colette Fagan. London: Routledge.

Dex, Shirley, Paul Robson, and Frank Wilkinson. 1999. "The Characteristics of the Low Paid: A Cross-National Comparison." *Work, Employment & Society* 13, no. 2: 503–24.

Dingeldey, Irene. 1999. *Begünstigungen und Belastungen familialer Erwerbs- und Arbeitszeitmuster in Steuer- und Sozialversicherungssystem: Ein Vergleich zehn europäischer Länder. (The Promotion and Burden of Familial Employment and Work-Time Model in the Tax and Social Security Systems: A Comparison of Ten European Countries)*. IAT: Glesenkirchen.

Drew, Ellen. 1999. "Extended Review: Exploring Gender and Citizenship." *Work, Employment & Society* 13, no. 4: 745–48.

Einhorn, Barbara. 1993. *Cinderella Goes to Market: Citizenship, Gender and Women's Movements in East Central Europe.* London and New York: Verso.

Esping-Andersen, Gosta. 1997. "After the Golden Age?" Pp. 1–31 in *Welfare States in Transition: National Adaptations in Global Economies,* ed. Gosta Esping-Andersen. London: Sage.

———. 1999. *Social Foundations of Postindustrial Economies.* Oxford: Oxford University Press.

Fagan, Collette, and Jacqueline O'Reilly. 1998. "Conceptualising Part-Time Work: The Value of an Integrated Comparative Perspective," Pp. 1–31 in *Part-time Prospects: International Comparisons of Part-Time Work in Europe, North America and the Pacific Rim,* ed. Jacqueline O'Reilly and Colette Fagan. London: Routledge.

*Frankfurter Allgemeine.* 2000. "Germany's Female Troops to Carry Weapons." December 2, 1.

Fraser, Nancy. 1997. *Justice Interruptus: Critical Reflections on the "Postsocialist" Condition.* London: Routledge.

General Survey. 2000. "1999 White Paper on Working Women." *Japan Labour Bulletin* 39, no. 7: 1.

Goodman, Roger, and Ito Peng. 1997. "The East Asian Welfare States: Peripatetic Learning, Adaptive Change, and Nation-Building." Pp. 192–224 in *Welfare States in Transition: National Adaptations in Global Economies,* ed. Gosta Esping-Andersen. London: Sage.

Gottfried, Heidi. 2000. "Compromising Positions: Emergent Neo-Fordisms and Embedded Gender Contracts." *British Journal of Sociology* 52, no. 2: 235–59.

———. 2003. "Temp(t)ing Bodies: Shaping Gender at Work in Japan." *Sociology* 27, no. 2: 257–76.

Gottfried, Heidi, and Nagisa Hayashi-Kato. 1998. "Gendering Work: Deconstructing the Narrative of the Japanese Economic Miracle." *Work, Employment & Society* 12, no. 1: 25–46.

Gottfried, Heidi, and Jacqueline O'Reilly. 2001. "Die Schwäche eines starken Versorgermodells: Teilzeitarbeit und weibliche Erwerbsbeteiligung in Deutschland und Japan" ("The Weakness of a Strong Breadwinner Model: Part-Time Work and Female Employment in Germany and Japan"). Wissenschaftszentrum Berlin (Social Science Research Center Berlin), DP FSI 00-207.

Gustafsson, Siv. 1996. "Tax Regimes and Labour Market Performance." Pp. 811–39 in *International Handbook of Labour Market Policy and Evaluation,* ed. Gunter Schmid, Jacqueline O'Reilly, and Klaus Schömanns. Cheltenham: Edward Elgar.

Hanami, Tadashi. 2000. "Equal Employment Revisited." *Japan Labour Bulletin* (January 1): 6–10.

Houseman, Susan, and Machiko Osawa. 2000. "The Growth of Nonstandard Employment in Japan and the United States: A Comparison of Causes and Consequences." Unpublished paper prepared for Nonstandard Work Arrangements in Japan, Europe and the United States, W.E. Upjohn Institute, the Japan Foundation, and Japan Women's University, Kalamazoo, Mich.

ILO. 1998. *Yearbook of Labour Statistics.* Geneva: ILO.

Janneke Plantenga. 2001. Comments made at the Changing Work and Life Patterns in Western Industrial Societies sponsored by the Wissenschaftszentrum Berlin.

Kaku, Sechiyama. 2001. "Shifting Family Support from Wives to Children." *JAPANE-CHO* 28, no. 1: 35–42.

Kezuka, Katsutoshi. 2000. "Legal Problems Concerning Part-Time Work in Japan." *Japan Labour Bulletin* 39, no. 9: 5–10.

Kono, Makoto. 2000. "The Impact of Modernisation and Social Policy on Family Care for Older People in Japan." *Journal of Social Politics* 29, no. 2: 181–203.

Korpi, Walter. 2000. "Faces of Inequality: Gender, Class and Patterns of Inequalities in Different Types of Welfare States." *Social Politics* 7, no. 2: 127–91.

Letablier, Marie-Therese. 2001. "Work and Family Balance: New Trade Off in France." Paper presented at conference, Changing Work and Life Patterns in Western Industrial Societies, Berlin, September.

Lewis, Jane. 1992. "Gender and the Development of Welfare Regimes." *Journal of European Social Policy* 2: 159–73.

———. 2001. "The Decline of the Male Breadwinner Model: Implications for Work and Care." *Social Politics* 8, no. 2: 152–69.

Liebert, Ulrike. 2000. "Europeanizing the Military: The ECJ as a Catalyst in the Transformation of the Bundeswehr." Paper prepared for Joint Workshop on Europeanization in Transatlantic Perspective, Institute for European Studies, Cornell University and Jean Monnet Centre for European Studies, University of Bremen, Bremen.

Mahon, Rianne. 2001. "Theorizing Welfare Regimes: Toward a Dialogue." *Social Politics* 8, no. 1: 24–35.

Ministry of Labour. 1997. *Survey on Employment Trend, Japanese Working Life Profile, 1996–1997, Labour Statistics*. Tokyo: Japan Institute of Labour.

———. 1998. *Handbook of Labour Statistics*. Tokyo: Policy Planning and Research Department.

———. 2000. *White Paper on Female Labour (Josei Rodo Hakusho)*. Tokyo: Ministry of Labour.

Moloney, Barbara. 1995. "Japan's 1986 Equal Employment Opportunity Law and the Changing Discourse on Gender." *Signs* 20, no. 2: 268–302.

Morozumi, Michiyo. 1998. "Protection of the Established Position in Japanese Labour Law: Basic Normative Patterns under the Long-Term Employment System." *The International Journal of Comparative Labour Law and Industrial Relations* 14, no. 1: 41–63.

Mutari, Ellen, and Deborah Figart. 2001. "Europe at a Crossroads: Harmonization, Liberalization, and the Gender of Work Time." *Social Politics* 8, no. 1: 36–64.

O'Connor, Julia, Ann Shola Orloff, and Sheila Shaver. 1999. *States, Markets, Families: Gender, Liberalism and Social Policy in Australia, Canada, Great Britain and the United States*. Cambridge: Cambridge University Press.

O'Reilly, Jacqueline. 1995. "Le travail à temps partiel en Allemagne de l'Est et en Allemagne de l'Ouest: Vers un 'modèle sociétal sexué" ("Part-Time Work in East and West Germany: Towards a Social Gender Model"). *Cahiers du Mage* (Marché du Travail et Genre) 1, no. 2: 77–88.

OECD. 1991. *Employment Outlook 1991*. Paris: OECD.

———. 1994a. *Women and Structural Change: New Perspectives*. Paris: OECD.

———. 1994b. *The OECD Jobs Study: Taxation, Employment and Unemployment.* Paris: OECD.

———. 1996. *Employment Outlook June 1996.* Paris: OECD.

———. 1997. *Family, Market and Community: Equity and Efficiency in Social Policy.* Paris: OECD.

———. 1998a. *Employment Outlook June 1998.* Paris: OECD.

———. 1998b. *Labour Force Statistics 1977-1997.* Paris: OECD.

Osawa, Mari. 2001. "People in Irregular Modes of Employment: Are they Really Subject to Discrimination?" *Social Science Japan Journal* 4, no. 2: 183–99.

Ostner, Ilona, and Jane Lewis. 1995. "Gender and the Evolution of European Social Policies." In *European Social Policy: Between Fragmentation and Integration,* ed. Stephen Leibfried and Paul Pierson. Washington, D.C.: The Brookings Institution.

Peng, Ito. 2000. "Gender and Generation: Japanese Child Care and the Demographic Crisis." Unpublished paper from the School of Policy Studies, Kwansei Gakuin University.

———. 2002. "Gender and Generation: Japanese Child Care and the Demographic Crisis." In *Child Care and Welfare State Restructuring: Gender and Entitlement at Crossroads,* ed. Rianne Mahon and Sonya Michel. New York: Routledge.

Pontusson, Jonas. 1997. "Between Neo-Liberalism and the German Model: Swedish Capitalism in Transition." In *Political Economy of Modern Capitalism: Mapping Convergence and Diversity,* ed. Colin Crouch and Wolfgang Streeck. London: Sage.

Quack, Sigrid, and Friederike Maier. 1994. "From State Socialism to Market Economy—Women's Employment in East Germany." *Environment and Planning* 26, no. 8: 1171–1328.

Roberts, Glenda. 1994. *Staying on the Line: Blue-Collar Women in Contemporary Japan.* Honolulu: University of Hawaii Press.

———. 2001. "Globalization and Work/Life Balance: Gendered Implications of New Initiatives at a U.S. Multinational in Japan." Paper presented at the American Sociological Association, Anaheim, California, August.

Rubery, Jill, Mark Smith, Colette Fagan, and Damien Grimshaw. 1998. *Women and European Employment.* London and New York: Routledge.

Sainsbury, Diane. 2001. "Gender and the Making of Welfare States: Norway and Sweden." *Social Politics* 8, no. 1: 113–43.

Sato, Hiroki. 2000. "The Current Situation of 'Family-Friendly' Policies in Japan." *Japan Labour Bulletin* 39, no. 2: 7–10.

Schettkat, Richard. 1989. "The Impact of Taxes on Female Labor Supply." *International Review of Applied Economics* 3, no. 1: 1–24.

Shaver, Sheila. 2000. "Inequalities, Regimes and Typologies." *Social Politics* 7, no. 2: 215–19.

Sims, Calvin. 2000. "Japan's Employers Are Giving Bonuses for Having Babies." *New York Times,* May 20: A1.

Soskice, David. 2000. "Explaining Changes in Institutional Frameworks: Societal Patterns of Business Coordination." Pp. 167-183 in *Embedding Organizations,* ed. Marc Maurice and Arndt Sorge. Amsterdam and Philadelphia: John Benjamins.

Standing, Guy. 1999. *Global Labour Flexibility: Seeking Distributive Justice.* London: St. Martin's.

Streeck, Wolfgang. 2001. "High Equality, Low Activity: The Contribution of the Social Welfare System to the Stability of the German Collective Bargaining Regime." *Industrial and Labor Relations Review* 54, no. 3: 698–706.

Strom, Stephanie. 2001. "Japan's New Leader Hews to Austerity." *New York Times*, May 8: W1.

Thelen, Kathleen. 1999. "Historical Institutionalism in Comparative Politics." *Annual Review of Political Science* 2: 369–404.

Thränhardt, Anna Maria. 1992. "Dynamics of the Private Sector in the 'Japanese Model of the Welfare Society.'" Paper presented at the European Consortium for Political Research, Limerick.

Uno, Kathleen. 1993. "The Death of 'Good Wife, Wise Mother'?" Pp. 293–324 in *Postwar Japan as History*, ed. Andrew Gordon. Berkeley: University of California Press.

Wakisaka, Akira, and Haesun Bae. 1998. "Why is the Part-Time Rate Higher in Japan than in South Korea?" Pp. 252–64 in *Part-Time Prospects: International Comparisons of Part-Time Work in Europe, North America and the Pacific Rim*, ed. Jacqueline O'Reilly and Colette Fagan. London: Routledge.

Weathers, Charles. 2000. "Temp-to-Perm or Perm-to-Temp? Women Workers and Japan's Temporary Services Industry." Unpublished paper in authors' possession.

Weber, Claudia. 2000. "Does Flexibilization Enhance Women's Job Opportunities? A German-Japanese comparison." Paper presented at the IIRA World Congress, Tokyo, June.

Western, Bruce. 1997. *Between Class and Market: Postwar Unionization in the Capitalist Democracies*. Princeton, N.J.: Princeton University Press.

Yeandle, Sue. 1999. "Gender Contracts, Welfare Systems and Non-Standard Working: Diversity and Change in Denmark, France, Germany, Italy and the UK." Pp. 141–65 in *Global Trends in Flexible Labour*, ed. Alan Felstead and Nick Jenson. Houndsmill: Macmillan.

# 5

# Career Advancement Choices of Female Managers in U.S. Local Governments

*Wendy L. Hassett*

Over the last century, significant sociological and demographic changes in the U.S. workforce have increasingly focused attention on the participation of women at all levels of government. These changes have led to considerable academic interest in the extent of representation of women and minorities at various levels throughout political and administrative hierarchies. Most of the gender-related literature has concentrated on elected officials (e.g., Kelly and Boutilier, 1978; Sapiro, 1982; Thomas, 1994; Clark, 1998; Kathlene, 1998; Rosenthal, 1998; Deen and Little, 1999) and administrators at the state and federal level (e.g., Rehfuss, 1986; Guy and Duke, 1991; Kelly et al., 1991; Bullard and Wright, 1993; Newman, 1993; Naff, 1994; Daley, 1996; Olshfski and Caprio, 1996; Rusaw, 1996; Bowling and Wright, 1998; Mani, 2001; Saltzstein et al., 2001). But relatively little research has focused on gender-related issues in public administration at the local level. In this chapter, I pose a dialogue on this topic and develop some possible explanations for the lack of women in city manager positions today.

The chapter begins with a brief literature review addressing the broad topic of women in government and then focuses specifically on female city managers and those women in a position to become city managers, examining the unique organizational and personal challenges they face and the factors that impact their career advancement decisions in an attempt to suggest reasons why there are so few women employed as city managers. The chapter concludes by suggesting three findings that emerge from the literature to explain the lack of women in the city management profession, a domain of public administration that up to this point has not been adequately addressed and continues to need further exploration.

## REPRESENTATIVE-BUREAUCRACY ISSUES

The importance of having a bureaucracy that is representative of the populace has been a topic of discussion among public administration scholars for many years. Often this issue is framed as having two distinct facets: *passive* and *active* representation. *Passive* representation addresses the notion that the demographic mix inside the organization should mirror the demographic mix outside the organization symbolizing an equal access to power. *Active* representation means that individuals behave or "speak for" the group to which they belong (Rehfuss, 1986).

Carol Gilligan's (1982) book, *In a Different Voice,* set the stage for distinguishing gender differences in leadership, management styles, and political behaviors. Her documentation of the interaction of various personal issues that influence a woman's decisions, judgments, and perspectives supported her central assertion that men and women have different "voices." Gilligan advocates the idea that the female voice is one of caring and inclusion while the male voice is one of individualism and legalism (172–73). Although Gilligan's work has been criticized on methodological grounds, as being "essentialist" through its lack of the recognition of diversity among women by the use of overly broad and general categories of "women," and as being determinist (see, for example, Kerber, 1986; Spelman, 1988; Fraser and Nicholson, 1990), it nevertheless began a dialogue between and among men and women on the issues and the potential benefits of incorporating and embracing the positive aspects of feminine virtues and perspectives in leadership, whether private or public.

For a woman, a career decision is just one aspect of her life resulting from these influences. Unlike men who, regardless of marital status, achieve much of their identity and worth from their employment and expect full-time paid employment to be a large part of their lives, "women do not—necessarily" have the same experiences and expectations (Gustafson and Magnusson, 1991, 2; Daley, 1996). For women, quality of life may, but does not have to, rest solely on a career.

Fox and Schuhmann (1999) examined gender differences and similarities among city managers in their approaches to political leadership, the policy process, and decision making. Gender variations in these areas are of interest because policy decisions are based on an individual's experiences, beliefs, values, and attitudes. Similar to Gilligan's (1982) metaphor of a female voice, these authors concluded that female city managers were more likely to incorporate citizen feedback into their management style than were their male counterparts. If the findings of Fox and Schuhmann (1999) are true, should not these inherent strengths of female leaders in facilitation, inclusion, and citizen involvement be embraced? Certainly these qualities are too valuable to ignore in a democracy.

Although the differences between men and women in management should not be overstated (Lovrich and Jones, 1983), it is important to try to understand why so few women have risen to top management ranks in spite of affirmative action, equal opportunity, and other efforts to level the career playing field for women. Continuing this line of reasoning, since many of the barriers to career advancement have been removed through legislation, women should have been rapidly advancing to positions formerly dominated by men and should continue to do so. However, Fox and Schuhmann (1999) found that only approximately 11 percent of all chief city administrators were female. These results suggest influences at work other than legal ones.

## BRIEF HISTORY OF FEMALE PUBLIC-SECTOR EMPLOYEES

A brief review of the introduction of women working in government is appropriate. Soon after the invention of the typewriter and at about same time that the Pendleton Act[1] was approved, women began to fill public-sector clerical positions. The first federal law concerning "female clerks" was passed in 1864 and established their pay at about $600 per year, which was approximately half of what men earned for similar work (Van Riper, 1958, 159).

Ironically, one of the most significant hindrances to working women in the federal service was an 1870 statute that was actually intended to help women have more of an equal opportunity for employment. This statute stated that women "may, in the discretion of the head of any department" be hired to higher-level clerkships (Shafritz et al., 1992, 211). However, this law was construed to mean that appointing officers could exclude women for reasons unrelated to their ability to do the work. Subsequently, women were excluded from about 60 percent of the federal positions hired through the examination process. Unequal compensation continued until the Classification Act required "equal pay for equal work" in 1923. Marital status continued to be a legal reason for discrimination until 1937 (Shafritz et al., 1992). The numbers of working women increased, although in the clerical ranks only. In addition, it was quite common prior to World War II for women to leave the workforce permanently once they became pregnant (Van Riper, 1958).

Significant changes occurred during the years between the end of World War II and the 1960s. Working women began to be promoted to higher positions within governments. The Civil Rights Act of 1964 was landmark legislation for women's employment rights at the federal level because it prohibited discrimination on the basis of gender. Soon thereafter, the Equal Employment Opportunity Act of 1972, which amended the Civil Rights Act of 1964, brought the same requirements for nondiscrimination to state and local governments.

The Pregnancy Discrimination Act approved in 1978 amended Title VII of the Civil Rights Act of 1964. Under the provisions of this act, discrimination on the basis of pregnancy, childbirth, or related medical conditions constitutes unlawful sex discrimination under Title VII. Women affected by pregnancy or related conditions must be treated in the same manner as other applicants or employees with similar abilities or limitations.

Another piece of important federal legislation signed into law in 1993 that continues to impact working women is the Family and Medical Leave Act (FMLA). FMLA requires all levels of public-sector agencies and businesses with fifty or more employees to allow up to twelve weeks of unpaid leave for (1) the birth or adoption of a child; (2) the care of an immediate family member with a medical condition; or (3) a health-related condition of the employee including maternity leave (Nigro and Nigro, 2000). Although this legislation is not a "cure-all" for the issues women must deal with during their careers, it is an important first step that recognizes the importance of family and the roles women play outside the workplace as "mother" and "wife."

Collectively these laws opened doors for women to have access to and to retain jobs at all levels of government that had not been available in the past. In the following years, women have increased their numbers substantially in public-sector organizations. It is notable, though, that the increase has been largely horizontal rather than vertical and for the most part limited to jobs considered to be traditionally female (Guy, 1993; Stewart, 1990).

## THEORIES UNDERLYING CAREER ADVANCEMENT DECISIONS

The decision to seek career advancement has two components: a certain degree of dissatisfaction with one's current employment situation and a desire to advance. Without dissatisfaction, the desire to advance may be harbored for some time as simply a latent notion. Relative-deprivation theory may help explain some of the intricate aspects of the relationship between these variables. When and how feelings of deprivation or discontentment arise is a point of contention in the literature. Two ideas have developed from this theory, both having strong proponents. The "hope hypothesis" posits that when one's economic conditions improve, a hope for future improvements causes discontentment through a growing dissatisfaction with the present situation. On the other hand, "the futility hypothesis" argues that a long-term lack of economic improvement causes feelings of hopelessness and deprivation (Martin et al., 1987, 44). The latter has been cited as the reason for the need for legislation for equal opportunity.

Many researchers have shown that women who desire to pursue a career as well as to have a traditional family often face challenges not encountered by their colleagues. In reality, these two worlds often directly conflict, which may help to explain why women are still not equally represented in top public management positions. Several theories help to explain this complex decision process. Expectancy theory (Vroom, 1964) is based on the idea that individuals make decisions to maximize their rewards and minimize their costs. How women categorize and value various aspects of their lives (i.e., salary, career-related travel, after-hours work meetings, time with children and spouse, housework, vacations, etc.) will dictate the result of this calculation.

Similarly, rational-choice theories hold that individuals must anticipate the outcomes of alternative courses of action and calculate which will be best for them. Rational individuals choose the alternative that is likely to give them the greatest satisfaction (Heath, 1976, 3; Carling, 1992, 27; Coleman, 1973).

Festinger's (1957) dissonance theory provides an additional theoretical understanding of career decisions. It states that individuals need to have balance in their thoughts as well as their actions and will make the necessary life changes to achieve personal balance. If what an individual is getting from her life and what she wants out of her life are out of balance, she will search for ways to have the rewards match or exceed her desires. According to this theory, the greatest dissonance occurs when the incompatible alternatives are both equally attractive. This is often the case when women desire a traditional family as well as a full-time, professional career.

As an example of the influence dissonance may play in career choices, Sapiro (1982) finds in her study of the public and private lives of political activists that men and women handle family and career conflicts quite differently. Specifically, she reports that "women avoid some of this conflict by delaying pursuit of political office until their children are older and no longer, or at least less, dependent upon them. Men appear to create conflict for themselves by pursuing political commitments just when their family situations are most incompatible with additional obligations" (272). She goes on to say, "When conflicts arise, women appear to choose in favor of their families, men in favor of their political ambition" (274). Her research supports the contention that women seek to eliminate dissonance and arrive at a balance in their lives because women, more often than men, tend to relinquish career aspirations instead of facing the possibility of having to manage increased conflict.

Clearly, these theories converge in different ways for men and women to influence their career decisions that may explain why the typical career paths of men and women are so different, as are the career paths among women with different aspirations. Interestingly, women more often cite gender-specific issues that interfere with their careers than men do. In her nationwide survey of females in city management in spring 1994, Tracey Breen (1995) found that the women surveyed cited gender bias as the most significant barrier to their career advancement, closely followed by a lack of interest in aggressively pursuing their careers in municipal government.

## WHY ARE THERE SO FEW FEMALE CITY MANAGERS?

In examining the characteristics of male and female local-government managers, Renner (1990) noted that although a number of changes occurred in the prior two decades in such things as education levels, age, and geographic distribution, the rate of change of some characteristics had begun to level off. This is particularly true in the case of gender. According to Renner's data, 1 percent of all city managers were female in 1974, increasing to 5 percent by 1989. In 1999, approximately 11 percent of all chief city administrators were female (Fox and Schuhmann, 1999).

Although some increase in the number of women appointed to city management positions has been occurring quietly, the gender mix in the profession is far from representative of the population, suggesting underlying factors at work. A review of the literature and an examination of current trends suggests three factors that combine to influence the relatively low number of female city managers: (1) traditional "glass-ceiling" issues based on gender; (2) the council-manager form of government; and (3) career choices.

### Glass-Ceiling Issues

Every organization has a culture that is influenced by gender. There is a body of literature that strongly argues that this is especially true of public administration (see, for example, Ferguson, 1984; Stewart, 1990; Stivers, 1990, 1993; Guy, 1994; Naff, 1994; Lawn-Day and Ballard, 1996). Guy (1994) describes this influence as "gender ethos" defined as "the distinctive characteristics of an organization and the attitudes of people within it that affect relations between the sexes and women's ability to gain and use power" (85). The extent to which gender ethos impacts the organization will determine the expectations of women holding management positions in terms of balancing home and career, approaches to career advancement, and appropriate career paths.

Although women currently hold top-level positions in public organizations, many women still describe gender-related barriers as hindering their career advancement. The "glass ceiling" (Morrison et al., 1987) has been used to describe an organizational level which women have difficulty transcending "because of sociological restrictions which have the effect of limiting their opportunities for career development" (Carroll et al., 1995). The following discussion presents several of these types of organizational restrictions cited by women that influence their career advancement decisions.

Building on a discussion presented by Rosabeth Moss Kanter (1993) in *Men and Women of the Corporation*, Guy (1994) argues that "opportunity, power and numbers" are three "architectural elements" that push groups toward upward mobility or downward spirals (86). Individuals with opportunity work in a manner that generates more opportunity. Opportunity is associated with an increase in power. Guy stated that both opportunity and power "coincide with being a member of a group that constitutes a large enough proportion of the work force so that any one member of the group is not immediately noticeable as *different*" (87). These three elements combine to produce either support or a hindrance for career advancement and may help to explain why gender and the "differences" gender illuminates in organizations are such important concepts to understand.

Smith and Grenier (1982) also explore organizational power as it relates to women and offer a number of ways women can achieve power using the organizational structure. They recognize that power is seen in specific organizational circumstances. Power has historically been held in the line departments; at the top of the hierarchy; where there is a low degree of routine work; where there is a complex environment; where there is a high amount of responsibility over resources; where there is an increased span of control; and where there is a lack of formal rules to follow in making decisions. They argue that the larger and more centralized the organization is, the more organizational power can be achieved in positions at the top of the hierarchy, especially in positions that have the most latitude in decision making. Although their research does not specifically address city governments, the power positions they describe could easily apply to the city manager position and the top administrators that make up the management team.

The prevalence of, and policies surrounding, sexual harassment also play a role in how women view their opportunities or lack of opportunities for career advancement. Women in top management positions are more likely to perceive themselves as having been the subject of sexual harassment (Guy and Duke, 1991), resulting in a stronger view of gender bias, a stronger feeling of being "different," and a greater sensitivity to these issues in the workplace (Vertz, 1985). When present in an organization, sexual harassment magnifies the distinction between men and women because it "manifests the power differential between men and women" (Guy, 1994, 86). Guy (1994) argues how sexual harassment can dramatically affect the career of the rising female manager:

> Sexual harassment remains a career stopper. If women file a complaint, they are labeled a trouble maker and doomed. If they fail to complain, they continue to be intimidated and reminded of their second-class status. . . . A woman's response to sexual harassment will often harm her career more than she will imagine. To take any action is to place herself in the position of the messenger, accentuating her differentness from her male colleagues (86).

Workplace personnel policies and benefits are still other areas that may either help or hinder the potential career advancement of women. The more an organization views family demands as being "outside" and "unrelated" to the workplace, the more the organization will alienate women and hamper their advancement. "As one might expect, workplace policies that treat all workers as if they were men get the most support from men" (Guy, 1993, 290). Public employers that have policies and offer benefits that address the concerns particular to women such as pay equity and child care, coupled with a strong organizational culture opposed to discrimination and sexual harassment, will be work environments that will appeal to women and will be environments in which they are able to advance.

An organizational culture of support for female managers is also critical to counterbalance any employee or public resistance to women in management roles. Leanne Atwater et al. (2000) found a strong undercurrent of opposition by employees to having a female as a manager. They studied recipients' perceptions of discipline in the workplace. They found that when discipline was administered by a female, recipients were less likely to believe that the punishment was fair, were less likely to accept responsibility for their behavior, and were more likely to think the manager did not know how to deliver the discipline.

After studying reprimands from 163 workplace situations, these authors concluded that the average employee felt that the only thing worse than being reprimanded on the job was being reprimanded on the job by a female manager. Given that recipient reactions are a critical component of the success of discipline, the results of this study suggested women in the workplace might be at a disadvantage in this domain. Atwater et al. concluded that female managers might benefit from special training in how to deliver discipline and how gender expectations may impact supervisory effectiveness.

Naff (1994) presents yet another dynamic of the glass ceiling revealed by her study of women working at the federal level. The women in this study strongly felt that they must overcome deeply held stereotypes about women in order to advance their careers. She found that women perceived that they "faced an uphill battle in proving their competence" (513). This challenge was compounded by the perception that coworkers felt women received special consideration in their promotions based on their gender rather than on their ability to do the job, while women felt they were held to a higher standard. This author contends that "even perceptions of disparate treatment can have an adverse impact on women and the organizations for which they work" (507).

Although the subtle obstacles related to the "glass ceiling" affect the ability of women to advance, these barriers need to continue to be addressed in ways that will revive the likelihood of having a team of upper-level local-government managers that is truly representative. In spite of the fact that the "glass ceiling" has been touted as a major reason for the disparity between men and women holding upper management posts, it can only partially account for the discrepancy.

## Council-Manager Government

In the early years of the city management profession, cities offered fewer services and, therefore, spent less money than today. Prior to the New Deal and World War II, the business of city government was limited and focused on such things as public safety, water supply, roads and bridges, wastewater, and garbage disposal (Renner, 1990). Since the job requirements for a city manager during those years were largely technical, most of the city managers had a background in engineering. In the mid-1930s, 77 percent of city managers were engineers (Stillman, 1977) who were middle-aged white men (Ridley and Nolting, 1934).

As society became more complex, citizens demanded more services from their local governments. The expansion of municipal services was fueled by intergovernmental financial transfers from federal and state governments to localities and soon placed local governments in the position of implementing policies. The increased scope of service provision at the local level required a manager who was more of a management generalist than an engineer. During this era, the role of city managers was redefined and their individual characteristics and backgrounds began to slowly evolve (Renner, 1990).

Unlike many other public-sector organizations, the council-manager form of government is unique to localities. This local-government structure is based on the idea of cooperation and efficiency. All powers in the local government are concentrated in the city council. The mayor is generally elected at large by the voters in the city and has no administrative authority. The other members of the council, usually numbering from five to nine, are elected either by districts or at large. By centering all power in the city council headed by the mayor, council-manager government allows a majority on the council to make the decisions needed to provide direction and guidance to the municipality. The council appoints the city manager who serves at the pleasure of the council and is accountable to the council.

One of the principles of council-manager government is the separation between policy and administration. While the literature suggests that it is very difficult to have a perfect separation (or dichotomy) between policy and administration, the formal structure of the government promotes the separation of policy making and policy implementation. Clearly, the powers of the municipality are vested in the entire city council, including the power to hire and fire the city manager. The city council is the policy-making body of the municipal corporation and provides guidance and direction to the manager. The manager, in turn, plays a key role as policy advisor to the council (Montjoy and Watson, 1995).

Often the comparison of the corporate model is used to explain the roles and relationships among these individuals. Using this analogy, the city council plays the role similar to the board of directors of a private-sector corporation. The mayor acts as chairman of the board and serves as policy leader, and often as the spokesperson for the city with the media and the community. The city manager is the chief executive officer (CEO), who is responsible to the city council and runs the day-to-day operations of the city.

Although this form has been used very successfully throughout the country, the built-in structure of the council-manager form of government may work to discourage women from entering the city management profession. Since the city manager is hired by the city council and serves at its pleasure, he or she may be released from employment at any time with a majority vote of the council. This tends to contribute to the highly mobile lifestyle of most city managers. For city managers, mobility is not simply a "rite of passage" as in many private-sector organizations; it is a job requirement. In 1974, the average time in office for a city manager in any one city was 4.4 years and in 1965, it was only 3.5 years (Golembiewski and Gabris, 1995, 244). More recently, city managers in Florida were found to average 3.4 years in each city they served (Feiock and Stream, 1998). Other research reports the average time in office for a city manager in any one city is 6.9 years, an increase from 5.4 years the prior decade (Renner, 2001, 39). A nationwide survey of newly promoted city managers reports that they held their former positions for 5.1 years (Barber, 1988). A large majority of managers (86 percent) are hired from a city outside the city they serve (Barber, 1988).

This mobile lifestyle may be particularly uncomfortable for married women who, throughout their career, would be the cause of uprooting their children and husbands in order to attain either a career advancement or ongoing employment (Markham et al., 1983) as a city manager. In this scenario, a husband would have to subordinate his career to his wife's and follow her from city to city. Although this scenario is possible, it is atypical in our society and may prove to be difficult for a married couple to accept as a lifestyle since the social norm is for a woman to follow her husband's employment rather than for a man to follow his wife's employment.

While Barber (1988) found that most city managers are hired from outside the organization, Bremer and Howe (1988) suggest that one way that women may be able to avoid the mobility barrier temporarily is through stronger avenues for internal advancement. Certainly this is true for advancement within departments to the level of department head, but may also speak to the hiring of an individual to fill the top post of city manager. Since the gender distribution of assistant managers and assistant administrators is over one-third female according to *The 1990 Municipal Year Book* published by International City/County Management Association, this suggestion may have positive implications for women to move into the city manager position when it is vacated without having to relocate. Although they would represent the atypical career path identified by Barber, women holding assistant manager positions may break through the mobility barrier by pursuing city manager positions in their current cities when they become vacant, should they wish to pursue that career path. However, this would only be true for the first appointment. Subsequent city manager appointments would necessitate relocation.

Spousal employment is also explored in Barber's (1988) study. He found that close to half of the city managers sampled (97.2 percent of the sample were male) had spouses who were unemployed. Of the employed spouses, 19.2 percent had part-time employment and 31.1 percent had full-time employment. If the study had included female city managers only, the percentages for the employment status of husbands probably would have looked much different since it is more common for a female spouse to be unemployed or employed part-time than for a male spouse.

Still another atypical option would be separate living. Judy Kelsey, hired as city manager of Eureka, California, in 1978, is all too familiar with this option. She is quoted in a 1994 *Public Management* article as saying, "I felt I couldn't get married because I thought a council wouldn't hire me because I wouldn't be able to convince my husband to move." In lieu of marriage, she and her partner nurtured a seventeen-year relationship always living at least seventy-five miles apart (Wood, 1994).

Ms. Kelsey's comment raises another interesting aspect of the council-manager form of government: the city manager is appointed by an elected body. An examination of how this group arrives at a decision on whom to hire as the manager suggests an interesting and complex process. Hiring decisions made by elected officials throughout the country are central to this discussion since these officials compose the body that holds the responsibility for selecting who will serve their city in this important role.

Although often left unsaid during an executive search, city council members may withhold support for a female candidate strictly because of her gender. Although protections are in place to stifle this discrimination in the merit system, these protections are not in place in the selection of a city manager. Furthermore, council members most likely do not have training in the legal aspects of human-resource management and generally are not aware of the appropriate and effective ways to conduct a selection procedure.

In her study of female city managers in 1988, Bernadene Main obtained some surprising indications of verbalized gender bias during the interview process. Several respondents in her survey reported situations when they had been asked questions by members of city councils regarding "family planning methods," maternity leave, child-care arrangements, "getting dirty" while in the field, and possibly leaving the city one day to get married. Other women reported that councils had told them that they questioned whether the community was "ready" for a female city manager and whether a woman could be "tough enough" to handle the job (Main, 1988, 42–43).

Gender bias may be felt even if the council does not verbalize concerns. Wheeling, Illinois, Assistant Village Manager Joni Beaudry commented on her experiences: "When I interviewed for city manager positions, I was amazed by many councils' reluctance to hire a woman. It was evident in what they said and didn't say" (Szymborski, 1996).

Apparently some of the feelings expressed by council members in Main's study and in Beaudry's experiences are reflected by the history of the traditional male domination of the city management profession. Clearly, if few women hold or have held top administrative positions within the city government, and the position of city manager has always been held by a man, the position may be sex typed (Heilman, 1983) and perceived as being a "man's job." In this case, council members may have difficulty picturing a woman being successful in a top management role and supporting her selection.

Still another interesting aspect is the nature of a city manager's workload. In 1985, Newell and Ammons found that city managers reported working an average of 56.5 hours per week. This finding was later supported by Barber (1988) who found that over half of the newly promoted city managers in his study reported working 50 hours per week, over 20 percent reported working 60 hours per week, and slightly over 7 percent reported working over 60 hours per week. For women, this intense work schedule magnifies the difficulty balancing time spent on career priorities with family responsibilities.

Although the concept of the glass ceiling and the barriers caused by bureaucratic structures are not new to the literature, many researchers have neglected the trend of women *choosing* to leave local government or to remain stationary on their career ladders for reasons often related to their personal or domestic lives. Once these women choose not to advance their careers, they drop out of the already limited pool of female contenders for city manager positions.

## Career Choices

The culture of society has historically been one in which men attend to their work in the workplace and women attend to their families in the home. Typically, men have been free to be highly efficient in their work by relying on their wives "to act as shock absorbers and nurturers" (Nieva and Gutek, 1981, 136). In theory, the workplace and home are two separate and distinct categories. In reality, these two categories are interwoven in a complex pattern, especially for women (Camarena et al., 1990). The intersection of private and public lives is one that frequently presents problems for women who seek career advancement to top management positions.

The issue of domestic constraints for women in public-management positions is addressed in a 1985 *Public Administration Review* article by Laura

Vertz. She found that one of the most striking differences between men and women in top public-management posts was the extent of their responsibilities for domestic matters. Women clearly had the responsibility of running their homes, which she suggested restricted women more than men. As supported by Festinger's (1957) dissonance theory, Vertz found most women holding upper management positions made choices to bring a certain amount of balance to their lives by "more often remaining single or having fewer children" (417). Her data offered possible options available to women to achieve a certain degree of "balance" when faced with this kind of dissonance. She states:

> The available choices are: (1) to remain single and/or have fewer children, thereby lessening domestic constraints; (2) to develop personal relationships that include sharing domestic responsibilities; and/or (3) to put in the extra work required to perform two jobs—one at work and the other at home (417–18).

Guy and Duke (1991) build on this reasoning. They assert that women are in a "Catch-22" of the traditional versus nontraditional female role. In their research on Alabama public employees, these authors found that "only when women are non-traditional, i.e., when they do not have family obligations, are they more likely to rise in managerial ranks, while the opposite is true for men" (10). In discussing family obligations of men and women, Guy (1993) explains this paradox:

> The fact is that men in top-level positions tend to live traditional family lives, while women disproportionately live non-traditional lives. Women who lead traditional lives carry an extra burden of family obligations and are less likely to be promoted to managerial ranks. Women who do not lead traditional lives carry an extra burden of being "different" from most women (290).

Guy further states that 71 percent of women in top posts reported having no dependents while only 48 percent of male managers reported no dependents. In her study of high-ranking federal employees, Bayes (1991) found an analogous situation where 45 percent of the women had no children while this was true of only 7 percent of the top-ranking men.

Similarly, in their study of female integration into the managerial ranks in six state governments, Kelly et al. (1991) found:

> In all the states studied, women were much more likely to be living alone, never married or divorced, and living without dependents. Traditional sex roles did not interfere, because for women, they had been abandoned. The point is that the way women reconciled conflicting demands of work and home was to abandon one role for the other. To combine both relegates women to ranks lower in the hierarchy where the job does not consume as much time or energy (410).

Although not shown in her data, Vertz (1985) offers another option "for women to delay their careers, dealing first with raising a family" (418). Still another alternative that many women are choosing is to delay having a family so they can develop a career first (Furchtgott-Roth and Stolba, 1999, 16). Historically, the twenties have been viewed as the time in a woman's life to have children. However, this is changing. In light of both recent medical advancements and the option of adoption, introducing children into a family when the parents are thirty-five or older is no longer uncommon. (For a more detailed discussion on delaying childbrith in lieu of career advancement, see Hewlett, 2002.)

For those working women who also choose to have and raise children, the presence of children has an interesting interaction with their careers. Naff (1994) argues that a woman's decision to have children is perceived as being related to her commitment to her career and directly affects her career advancement. Her study found that while the careers of women lag behind the careers of men, women with and without children advanced at about the same rate for the first five years. After the first five years, however, childless women advanced at a much quicker rate than women with children, suggesting that "even women without children are assumed to be less committed to their careers until they have demonstrated their commitment by remaining in the work force for several years without having children" (512).

Several authors have found that children have a far different effect on the career advancement of men. Daley (1996) and Naff (1994) found that children have a positive effect on the career advancement of white men because as fathers they are seen as "stable, family men" (Daley, 1996, 159). Men are often viewed as being the breadwinner and, in that role, their financial and family responsibilities make them *more* committed to their careers while women are employed simply because they want to work (Naff, 1994).

Another interesting trend that is often left out of the discussion of the career advancement of women is that some women are choosing to cap their careers at a certain level, scale back their careers, or voluntarily leave the workforce permanently. The choice to self-select out of advancement by voluntarily "capping" one's career at a particular level and not attempting to advance is seen in the case of "career assistants." "Career assistants" is a term used to describe a fairly new phenomenon in which assistant city managers have no intention of advancing to the position of city manager. For them, their long-term career goals are to remain working as assistants (Rupp et al., 2000). This movement supports the finding of Fox and Schuhmann (1999) that the women in their national study of over 500 male and female city managers preferred "to be in the middle of a 'web' of interactions rather than to be on top of the hierarchy" (240).

This trend is not limited to municipalities. A recent Associated Press article addresses the concern of many state public-school officials about the lack of women applying for school superintendent positions. Stinson Stoup, who handled recruiting for the Pennsylvania School Board Association, stated: "We have been encouraging more women to apply, but it would appear that many women simply don't want to be superintendents." Some of the reasons cited for the unpopularity of the post include the fact that it is "highly political" and that the superintendent must deal with "multiple interest groups, a powerful school board, and unending turmoil" (Associated Press, 2000). These same descriptions could aptly apply to the post of city manager.

In other situations, women actually choose to scale back or permanently leave their careers possibly through early retirement once they have reached their goals of attaining a certain organizational level or when they are financially able to do so. Clearly, some women choose less pay and fewer job opportunities instead of a high salary and career advancement (Furchtgott-Roth and Stolba, 1999, 18). A recent article in a popular magazine addresses this growing trend:

> Among mothers 36–40, work schedules are changing. More are opting for part-time jobs. During those years, which often coincide with the birth of a second child, more are leaving the workforce altogether. The women most likely to go part time are those who earn the highest hourly pay. . . . Still, homemaking remains a luxury purchase. Among those mothers with lower hourly pay, rising numbers are taking full-time paying jobs. They can't afford to stay home (Quinn, 2000).

As it relates to domestic choices, the research seems to identify four distinct trends for working women. First, some women choose to alter their domestic goals so they better mesh with their career goals. This is evidenced by some women choosing to remain single, live alone, divorce, and/or have no or fewer dependents to minimize the potential of these issues interfering with their careers. A second trend is for other women to leave the workforce temporarily at various times in their lives to deal with domestic matters surrounding children. This withdrawal may occur early or late in a woman's career. A third trend is for women to "have it all" by attempting to advance their careers and also have and raise children. The final trend is for working women to decide not to seek career advancement. This decision encompasses several forms. Some women find a place near the top where they can still have a worthwhile career and at the same time achieve some balance with family responsibilities. In local governments, often this job is as an assistant city manager or department head. Other women choose to scale back their careers or choose to leave the workforce permanently after they reach a certain career goal. All of these trends combine to help to explain why there are relatively few female city managers in place today.

## RECOMMENDATIONS AND CONCLUSION

Career advancement involves a conscious decision. For each woman, this decision is complex and unique, usually based on an evaluation of the organizational culture, its structure, and domestic issues. This chapter has focused on how women make career choices and the motives for them to, or not to, pursue a career in city management. Three distinct findings emerge from the literature. First, traditional "glass-ceiling" issues are still found to exist and influence the career advancement of women. Second, the council-manager form of government has several inherent elements that may prove to be unappealing to qualified women evaluating a move into a city manager position. Finally, women make choices in domestic matters involving spouses, children, and domestic priorities that affect their desire to seek career advancement. Many women are simply choosing not to apply for city manager posts. All three of these factors help to explain why there are so few women holding city manager positions.

Although it is easy to say that women should strive to achieve the highest positions in local government, the choice to do so is multidimensional, involving personal and emotional decisions that have long-term implications. The theories discussed herein offer insight into the ways women make career choices. They support the assertion that when women develop personal career goals, they often thoughtfully weigh these goals against their obligations to family and home to be sure they will mesh in a way that will allow them to achieve what they desire from both worlds (Guy, 1994). How women prioritize their desires is as unique as they are.[2]

In their roles as leaders, city managers and members of upper-level management play critical roles in their localities as well as in their local governments. Because the most important and influential decisions are made at the top of an organization, the issue of representativeness and the influences gender has on city management is important to the field of public administration. While it is important not to overemphasize gender differences in public administration, local governments are clearly not immune to the gender issues that permeate public and private organizations.

## NOTES

1. The Pendleton Act of 1883 was a reaction to the general consensus that the increasingly important governmental functions should no longer be addressed through the use of a patronage system. The new system sought to establish an open, objective, and competitive hiring system based on examinations, prohibited terminations of civil-service employees for partisan reasons, enabled the establishment of a Civil Service Commission, and allowed the president to alter the coverage of civil-service protections.

2. Additional research is needed to explore further the reasons underlying the lack of female city managers throughout the country. Women in the position to become city managers who have the experience and education to do so hold many of the answers to these research questions. Those women who move into city manager posts as well as those who do not due to personal choice hold critical information for the furtherance of this body of research.

# REFERENCES

Associated Press. 2000. "Few Women in Education Become Superintendents." *Montgomery Advertiser*, October 26, p. 4A.

Atwater, Leanne E., David A. Waldman, and James A. Carey. 2000. "Gender and Discipline in the Workplace: Wait until Your Father Gets Home." Paper presented at the Academy of Management Annual Meeting, Toronto, Canada.

Barber, Daniel M. 1988. "Newly Promoted City Managers." *Public Administration Review* 48, no. 3: 694–99.

Bayes, Jane H. 1991. "Women in Public Administration in the United States." *Women & Politics* 11, no. 4: 85–109.

Bowling, Cynthia J., and Deil S. Wright. 1998. "Change and Continuity in State Administration: Administrative Leadership across Four Decades." *Public Administration Review* 58, no. 5: 429–44.

Breen, Tracey. 1995. "Survey Results: Women in City Management." *Michigan Municipal Review* (July): 208, 221.

Bremer, Kamala, and Deborah A. Howe. 1988. "Strategies Used to Advance Women's Careers in the Public Service: Examples from Oregon." *Public Administration Review* 48, no. 6: 957–61.

Bullard, Angela M., and Deil S. Wright. 1993. "Circumventing the Glass Ceiling: Women Executives in American State Governments." *Public Administration Review* 53, no. 3: 189–202.

Camarena, Phame, Rachel Seidensticker, and Anne C. Peterson. 1990. "Gender, Academic Achievement, and Emotional Well-Being as Predictors of Adolescent Career Paths." A paper presented at the biennial meeting of the Society for Research on Adolescence in Atlanta, Ga. Symposium chaired by J. Eccles.

Carling, A. 1992. *Social Divisions*. London: Verso.

Carroll, Franklin O., W. David Patton, and Leslie R. Alm. 1995. "The Glass Ceiling in the USDA Forest Service: Willing to Conform, Demanding Change." *Public Administration Quarterly* 18, no. 4: 457–77.

Clark, Janet, 1998. "Women at the National Level: An Update on Roll Call Voting Behavior." In *Women and Elective Office*, ed. Sue Thomas and Clyde Wilcox. New York: Oxford University Press.

Coleman, J. 1973. *The Mathematics of Collective Action*. London: Heinemann.

Daley, Dennis M. 1996. "Paths of Glory and the Glass Ceiling: Differing Patterns of Career Advancement among Women and Minority Federal Employees." *Public Administration Quarterly* 20, no. 2: 143–62.

Deen, Rebecca E., and Thomas H. Little. 1999. "Getting to the Top: Factors Influencing the Selection of Women to Positions of Leadership in State Legislatures." *State and Local Government Review* 31, no. 2: 123–34.

Feiock, Richard C., and Christopher Stream. 1998. "Explaining the Tenure of Local Government Managers." *Journal of Public Administration Research & Theory* 8, no. 1: 117–31.

Ferguson, Kathy E. 1984. *The Feminist Case Against Bureaucracy*. Philadelphia, Pa.: Temple University Press.

Festinger, Leon. 1957. *A Theory of Cognitive Dissonance*. Stanford, Calif.: Stanford University Press.

Fox, Richard L., and Robert A. Schuhmann. 1999. "Gender and Local Government: A Comparison of Women and Men City Managers." *Public Administration Review* 59, no. 3: 231–42.

Fraser, Nancy, and Linda Nicholson. 1990. "Social Criticism without Philosophy." In *Feminism/Postmodernism*, ed. Linda Nicholson. New York: Routledge.

Furchtgott-Roth, Diana, and Christine Stolba. 1999. *Women's Figures: An Illustrated Guide to the Economic Progress of Women in America*. Washington, D.C.: The AEI Press.

Gilligan, Carol. 1982. *In a Different Voice*. Cambridge, Mass.: Harvard University Press.

Golembiewski, Robert T., and Gerald Gabris. 1995. "Tomorrow's City Management: Guides for Avoiding Success-Becoming-Failure." *Public Administration Review* 55, no. 3: 240–46.

Gustafson, Sigrid B., and David Magnusson. 1991. *Female Life Careers: A Pattern Approach*. Hillsdale, N.J.: Lawrence Erlbaum Associates, Inc.

Guy, Mary E. 1993. "Three Steps Forward, Two Steps Backward: The Status of Women's Integration into Public Management." *Public Administration Review* 53, no. 4: 285–92.

———. 1994. "Organizational Architecture, Gender and Women's Careers." *Review of Public Personnel Administration* 14, no. 2: 77–90.

———. 1996. "Public Personnel and Gender." *Review of Public Personnel Administration* 16, no. 1: 5–6.

Guy, Mary E., and Lois L. Duke. 1991. "Career Advancement and Behavioral Style among Alabama's Public Managers: A Comparison by Sex." *Review of Public Personnel Administration* 11, no. 3: 1–16.

Hale, Mary. 1996. "Gender Equality in Organizations: Resolving the Dilemmas." *Review of Public Personnel Administration* 16, no. 1: 7–18.

———. 1999. "He Says, She Says: Gender and Worklife." *Public Administration Review* 59, no. 5: 410–24.

Hale, Mary, and Rita Mae Kelly, eds. 1989. *Gender, Bureaucracy, and Democracy: Careers and Equal Opportunity in the Public Sector*. Westport, Conn.: Greenwood Press, Inc.

Heath, A. 1976. *Rational Choice and Social Exchange*. Cambridge: Cambridge University Press.

Heilman, Madeline E. 1983. "Sex Bias in Work Settings: The Lack of Fit Model." *Research in Organizational Behavior* 5: 269–98.

Hewlett, Sylvia Ann. 2002. *Creating a Life: Professional Women and the Quest for Children*. New York: Talk Miramax.

Kanter, Rosabeth Moss. 1993. *Men and Women of the Corporation*. New York: Basic Books.

Kathlene, Lyn. 1998. "In a Different Voice: Women and the Policy Process." In *Women and Elective Office*, ed. Sue Thomas and Clyde Wilcox. New York: Oxford University Press.

Kelly, Rita Mae, and Mary Boutilier. 1978. *The Making of Political Women: A Study of Socialization and Role Conflict*. Chicago: Nelson-Hall, Inc.

Kelly, Rita Mae, Mary E. Guy, Jane Bayes, Georgia Duerst-Lahti, Lois L. Duke, Mary M. Hale, Cathy Johnson, Amal Kawar, and Jeanie R. Stanley. 1991. "Public Managers in the States: A Comparison of Career Advancement by Sex." *Public Administration Review* 51, no. 5: 402–12.

Kerber, Linda. 1986. "Some Cautionary Words for Historians." *Signs* 11, no. 2: 304–10.

Lawn-Day, Gayle A., and Steven Ballard. 1996. "Speaking Out: Perceptions of Women Managers in the Public Service." *Review of Public Personnel Administration* 16, no. 1: 41–58.

Lovrich, Nicholas P., Jr., and Charles E. Jones. 1983. "Affirmative Action, Women Managers and Performance Appraisal: Simultaneous Movement in Conflicting Directions?" *Review of Public Personnel Administration* 3, no. 3: 3–19.

Main, Bernadene. 1988. *Women as City Managers: A Portrait in 1988.* M.P.A. thesis, the Evergreen State College, Olympia, Wash.

Mani, Bonnie G. 2001. "Women in the Federal Civil Service: Career Advancement, Veterans' Preference, and Education." *American Review of Public Administration* 31, no. 3: 313–39.

Markham, William T., Patrick O. Macken, Charles M. Bonjean, and Judy Corder. 1983. "A Note on Sex, Geographic Mobility, and Career Advancement." *Social Forces* 61, no. 4: 1138–46.

Martin, Joanne, Raymond L. Price, Robert J. Bies, and Melanie E. Powers. 1987. "Now That I Can Have It, I'm Not So Sure I Want It: The Effects of Opportunity on Aspirations and Discontent." Pp. 42–65 in *Women's Career Development*, ed. Barbara A. Gutek and Laurie Larwood. Newbury Park, Calif: Sage.

Montjoy, Robert S., and Douglas J. Watson. 1995. "A Case for Reinterpreted Dichotomy of Politics and Administration as a Professional Standard in Council-Manager Government." *Public Administration Review* 55, no. 3: 231–39.

Morrison, Ann M., Randall P. White, and Ellen Van Velsor. 1987. *Breaking the Glass Ceiling.* Reading, Mass.: Addison-Wesley.

Naff, Katherine C. 1994. "Through the Glass Ceiling: Prospects for the Advancement of Women in the Federal Civil Service." *Public Administration Review* 54, no. 6: 507–14.

Newell, Charldean, and David N. Ammons. 1987. "Role Emphases of City Managers and Other Municipal Executives." *Public Administration Review*, May/June: 246–53.

Newman, Meredith Ann. 1993. "Career Advancement: Does Gender Make a Difference?" *American Review of Public Administration* 23, no. 4: 361–84.

Nieva, Veronica F., and Barbara A. Gutek. 1981. *Women and Work.* New York: Praeger Publishers.

Nigro, Lloyd G., and Felix A. Nigro. 2000. *The New Public Personnel Administration.* Itasca, Ill.: F.E. Peacock Publishers, Inc.

Olshfski, Dorothy, and Raphael Caprio. 1996. "Comparing Personal and Professional Characteristics of Men and Women State Executives: 1990 and 1993 Results." *Review of Public Personnel Administration* 16, no. 1: 31–40.

Quinn, Jane Bryant. 2000. "Revisiting the Mommy Track." *Newsweek*, July 17, p. 44.

Rehfuss, John A. 1986. "A Representative Bureaucracy? Women and Minority Executives in California Career Service." *Public Administration Review* 46, no. 5: 454–60.

Renner, Tari, 1990. "Appointed Local Government Managers: Stability and Change." Pp. 41–52 in *The Municipal Yearbook 1990.* Washington, D.C.: International City-County Management Association.

———. 2001. "The Local Government Profession at Century's End." Pp. 35–46 in *The Municipal Yearbook.* Washington, D.C.: International City-County Management Association.

Ridley, Clarence, and Orin F. Nolting. 1934. *The City Manager Profession.* Chicago: University of Chicago Press.

Rosenthal, Cindy Simon. 1998. "Getting Things Done: Women Committee Chairpersons in State Legislatures." In *Women and Elective Office*, ed. Sue Thomas and Clyde Wilcox. New York: Oxford University Press.

Rupp, Mary, Laura Huffman, and Terrence Moore. 2000. "Survey Says Role of *Assistant* Has Definitely Changed." *Public Management* 82, no. 6: 21–25.

Rusaw, A. Carol. 1996. "Achieving Credibility: An Analysis of Women's Experience." *Review of Public Personnel Administration* 16, no. 1: 19–30.

Salzstein, Alan L., Yuan Ting, and Grace Hall Salzstein. 2001. "Work-Family Balance and Job Satisfaction: The Impact of Family-Friendly Policies on Attitudes of Federal Government Employees." *Public Administration Review* 61, no. 4: 452–66.

Sapiro, Virginia. 1982. "Private Costs of Public Commitments or Public Costs of Private Commitments? Family Roles versus Political Ambition." *American Journal of Political Science* 26: 265–79

Shafritz, Jay M., Norma M. Riccucci, David H. Rosenbloom, and Albert C. Hyde. 1992. *Personnel Management in Government: Politics and Process*. New York: Marcel Dekker, Inc.

Smith, Howard L., and Mary Grenier. 1982. "Sources of Organizational Power for Women Overcoming Structural Obstacles." *Sex Roles* 8, no. 7: 733–46.

Spelman, Elizabeth V. 1988. *Inessential Woman: Problems of Exclusion in Feminist Thought*. Boston: Beacon Press.

Stewart, Debra W. 1990. "Women in Public Administration." Pp. 203–27 in *Public Administration: The State of Discipline*, ed. Naomi B. Lynn and Aaron Wildavski. Chatham, N.J.: Chatham House Publishers.

Stillman, Richard J., II. 1977. "The City Manager: Professional Helping Hand, or Political Hired Hand?" *Public Administration Review* 37, no. 6: 659–70.

Stivers, Camilla. 1990. "Toward a Feminist Perspective in Public Administration Theory." *Women and Politics* 10, no. 4: 49–65.

———. 1993. *Gender Images in Public Administration*. Newbury Park, Calif.: Sage.

Szymborski, Lee. 1996. "Why Are There So Few Women Managers?" *Public Management* 78, no. 12: 11–16.

Thomas, Sue. 1994. *How Women Legislate*. New York: Oxford University Press.

Van Riper, Paul P. 1958. *History of the United States Civil Service*. Westport, Conn.: Greenwood Press.

Vertz, Laura L. 1985. "Women, Occupational Advancement, and Mentoring: An Analysis of One Public Organization." *Public Administration Review* 45, no. 3: 415–23.

Vroom, V. H. 1964. *Work and Motivation*. New York: John Wiley.

Wood, Barbara. 1994. "Profile: A Woman's Place—in City Hall." *PM* 76, no. 5: 26.

# 6

# An Assessment of Women's Acceptance as Breadwinners in the United States

*Heidi M. Berggren*

One of the most significant economic and social trends over the last half century is the large-scale entry of women, particularly mothers, into the paid labor force. In 1940, women made up under 25 percent of the labor force, while today this proportion has increased to nearly half (U.S. Department of Labor, 2000). Furthermore, 20 percent of mothers with children under 6 were working in 1960, rising to 64 percent by 1999 (U.S. Census Bureau, 1999). These increases strained against society's approach to regulating work and family life. Historically, as a matter of social convention as well as public policy, work and family were treated as distinct, complementary, and gendered domains, with men serving as breadwinners and women presiding over family concerns (Coontz, 1988, 1997; Ferree, 1983; Gerstel and Gross, 1987; Gordon, 1994; Jacobs and Davies, 1994; Staggenborg, 1998). The growing presence of women in the workforce thus gives rise to the question of their treatment, relative to men, as workers and providers. Has the increase in working women been accompanied by a parallel trend of increased recognition of a breadwinning status, or have traditional role conceptions persisted in spite of altered circumstances?

This is an important question both from the normative standpoint of gender equity and the standpoint of evaluating current U.S. work-family policy, which in its evolution and present form has been heavily influenced by the interests of the private labor market (Kaitin, 1994; Wisensale, 2001.) It makes sense to consider what role historical patterns in recognition of women as breadwinners—a process occurring in the workplace and in the making of public policy aimed at regulating the labor market—have played in shaping this policy, since its goal is to help parents balance work and family. To assess whether growth in women's acceptance as breadwinners tracks their increased labor-force participation over the last half century, I first compare working women's and men's access to employer-provided benefits, which help working parents address family concerns. I use a research design that compares access to benefits from 1940 to 1990 in professional nurses, a modal women's occupation, and automobile mechanics and repairmen, a modal men's occupation. My findings of an advantage for men through most of the time period, which nonetheless diminishes and then reverses slightly at the end, suggest that society is slowly accepting women as breadwinners. In the second part of this chapter, I examine U.S. congressional hearings, over the same time period, on proposals aimed at regulating employers' provision of benefits. While overall testimony indicates increased acceptance of equal breadwinning roles for men and women, traditional gender-role conceptions are still quite prevalent. This suggests a somewhat weaker acceptance of an equal breadwinner role for women than women's improved access to benefits would suggest.

## EMPLOYER-PROVIDED BENEFITS

The literature attempting to explain the persistent pay gap between women and men has implications for the question of whether women have been progressing towards a breadwinner status. In 1992, the ratio of women's to men's wages was still only .65 (Skocpol, 2000, 126), which many explain as a function of "occupational segregation" or the concentration of women in low-paying occupations (Baker and Fortin, 1999; Bergmann, 1986; Bielby and Baron, 1986; Kessler-Harris, 1982; King, 1992; Mason, 1992; Oppenheimer, 1970; Reskin and Hartmann, 1986; Roos and Reskin, 1992; Sorensen, 1986). Women have been consistently paid less than men, so to the extent that higher levels of income enhance women's breadwinning capacity, these findings suggest a lack of progress in this regard. This literature clearly contributes to our understanding of women's treatment as workers. However, I argue that inequality in pay level is only a rough guide to determining the extent of acceptance of a breadwinner status for women. Employers' decisions about pay level are "how much" decisions that are often rationalized as mapping onto length of job tenure, level of expertise, extent of supervisory authority, and other evaluative criteria. The use of such criteria thus can mask the disproportionate accrual of compensation to men.

Employer-provided benefits are a less explored but potentially more revealing component of compensation, in terms of what patterns in access to—and themes in public debate over—these benefits may reveal about progress in gender equity and the extent of women's acceptance as breadwinners. As they emerged after World War II, these benefits—including insurance, health, pension, vacation, and others—help employees to address family concerns (Perman and Stevens, 1989), and as such require employers to make decisions not only about "how much" to compensate employees, but also "with what." Decisions about how much of which benefits to offer to employees and dependents are likely to bring employers' values and prejudices about gender roles to the forefront, with quite pointed implications for employees in their roles as breadwinners. As employer-provided benefits have constituted a growing portion of employee-compensation packages in the course of the last half century (Regalia et. al., 1997, 43)—the period corresponding with women's increased labor-force participation—assessing the extent of equality both in access and in political debate allows for a good test of society's acceptance of a worker and breadwinner role for women. I thus first build on existing cross-sectional studies, which have generally found that at recent points in time women have had restricted access to employer-provided benefits (DeViney, 1995; Hardy and Shuey, 2000; Nelson, 1994; Pearce, 1987; Perman and Stevens, 1989), by comparing women's and men's access to benefits over the last half century. To assess how the political sphere frames these patterns I then examine the treatment of gender in public-policy debates, as reflected in U.S. congressional hearings, over the regulation of employer's provision of benefits to employees.

## METHODOLOGY

### Access to Benefits in "Women's" vs. "Men's" Occupations

I compare access to employer-provided benefits from 1940 to 1990 in a numerically representative "women's" occupation with that in a numerically representative "men's" occupation. Essentially, this design serves as a quasi laboratory in which to acquire a general picture of women's and men's access to employer-provided benefits. I compare the largest—in terms of the total numbers of workers—majority women's and majority men's occupations that are generally comparable in size, pay level, and extent of unionization. I am thus able to control pay level and extent of unionization, important possible alternatives explaining why some workers have better access to benefits than others. The point is to see if the process of women's acceptance as breadwinners requires further explanation beyond that provided by studies of the pay gap. Controlling for pay level enables me to examine whether there is a deeper gender dynamic associated with benefits, as I theorize, that may be masked in studies that focus only on pay level. Unionization is another significant factor explaining access to employer-provided benefits—as unions typically use benefits as an incentive for joining. Historically, unions have been overwhelmingly male and often actively hostile toward women; thus low levels of unionization clearly would contribute to an explanation for why women have lesser access to benefits. This explanation implies that where women are unionized, they should have access on a relatively equal basis with men. However, the unique gender dynamic that I propose informs employers' decisions about benefits and implies that discrimination exists in the distribution of benefits independent of the more external organizational and political advantages associated with unionization. I thus control for extent of unionization by selecting women's and men's occupations that are similarly (though roughly so) unionized.

## Occupations

Professional nurses and automobile mechanics and repairmen are the largest—in terms of the total numbers of workers—majority women's and majority men's occupations that are roughly comparable on size, pay level, and extent of unionization. While I will detail the selection process below, the rationale for comparing these particular occupations—obviously involving qualitatively different types of work—warrants some explanation. Justification is found in the well-established literature on occupational segregation and comparable worth (Baker and Fortin, 1999; Baron and Newman, 1990; Bergmann, 1986, 1989; Bielby and Baron, 1986; Greig, Orazem, and Mattila, 1989; Kessler-Harris, 1982; King, 1992; Mason, 1992; Mount and Ellis, 1989; Oppenheimer, 1970; Reskin and Hartmann, 1986; Roos and Reskin, 1992; Sorensen, 1986; Taylor, 1989; Wittig and Lowe, 1989). This body of research generally suggests that while the nature of work may differ significantly between women's and men's occupations—in this case attending to people's health needs versus fixing cars—the work nonetheless may be quite similar in terms of the required amount of knowledge, level of skill, and amount of independent decision-making authority. While comparable worth concerns the equalization of pay between men and women, I draw attention to this literature only because it shows that while there may be qualitative differences between occupations there are also significant quantitative similarities that can justify their comparison.

I began by creating an aggregated file from Census Bureau data, consisting of the numbers of women and men working full-time in each occupation from census years 1940–1990.[1] The cases are year-occupations, and the counts and percentages are variables. To create this file, I extracted data from the University of Minnesota's online *Integrated Public Use Microdata Series*, or IPUMS (Ruggles and Sobek et al., 1997). IPUMS covers the time period 1890–1990, and contains variables that facilitate historical occupational research. For occupational delineations, I used the "Occ 1950" variable, which is based on a recoding of all occupations in all census years to 1950's categories. This recoding is important in the context of my study, as I need to be confident that a certain occupation involves the same work from census year to census year (Blau and Hendricks, 1979; King, 1992; Ruggles and Sobek et al., 1997).

Starting with the total counts of women and men in each year-occupation, in order to select a reduced set of potentially comparable representative women's and men's occupations (table 6.1), I first followed the "70 percent rule" (Sorensen, 1986, 365; Figart and Lapidus, 1996, 302) to reduce the file to year-occupations consisting of at least 70 percent women or 70 percent men, respectively. While this standard is used in studies of occupational segregation, many of which characterize occupations as involving distinctly "female" or "male" work (Baker and Fortin, 1999; Bergmann, 1986; Bielby and Baron, 1986; Kessler-Harris, 1982; King, 1992; Mason, 1992; Oppenheimer, 1970; Reskin and Hartmann, 1986; Roos and Reskin, 1992; Sorensen, 1986), I use it because it serves as an accepted quantitative criterion for determining modal women's and men's occupations. In the interests of ensuring that the occupations are as widely representative of the labor force as possible, I then reduced the file further by eliminating all but the largest occupations. I used the cutoff point of 1,000,000, or an average of 166,667 workers per occupation per census year. Studies of occupational segregation generally look at occupations with at least 40,000 individual workers per year, suggesting that this number can be used as a base-line indicator of significance in the labor market (Sorensen, 1989; England et al., 1994). Since my goal is maximum numerical representativeness, I selected a significantly higher minimum threshold.

This reduced set of potentially comparable women's and men's occupations also controls for pay. The IPUMS variable "occupational income score" rates each occupation in each census year on a 100-point income scale (Ruggles and Sobek et al., 1997),[2] thus allowing for assessment of the relative economic standing of each occupation in each census year. The original file included all occupations with full-time workers (see note 1), amounting to between 216 and 268 occupations for each census year. This set, however, contains only those women's and men's occupations within six points of each other in each census year. Given the range of the scale, there is extensive variability in the scores attached to each occupation, thus conferring confidence that a six-point spread between women's and men's occupations is sufficient to establish control on pay level.

The set of potentially comparable women's and men's occupations is presented in table 6.1. The data in table 6.1 are sorted by entries in the "total" column, presented separately for women and men to facilitate comparison. As explained, these are the occupations that remained after eliminating all that failed to include at least 1,000,000, and after controlling for pay level. In addition to maximum size, comparability in size was a selection criterion. Occupations with different numbers of workers are likely related to different organizational and political dynamics that could affect benefit levels. Thus, to control for occupation size, I have highlighted the largest women's and men's occupations that are also comparable in size. Professional nurses

**Table 6.1. Occupations, Overall Occupational Totals, and Occupational Totals by Census Year**

| Occupations | Total | 1940 | 1950 | 1960 | 1970 | 1980 | 1990 |
|---|---|---|---|---|---|---|---|
| Women's | | | | | | | |
| Stenographers, typists, and secretaries | 11,069,000 | 822,700 | 366,400 | 1,516,500 | 2,368,400 | 2,988,000 | 3,007,000 |
| Nurses, professional | 3,317,800 | 199,200 | 69,000 | 334,500 | 526,900 | 869,900 | 1,318,300 |
| Telephone operators | 1,086,700 | 151,400 | 81,300 | 240,700 | 235,800 | 247,000 | 130,500 |
| Men's | | | | | | | |
| Farmers (owners and tenants) | 8,643,800 | 3,750,600 | 809,400 | 1,685,900 | 946,600 | 766,300 | 685,000 |
| Truck and tractor drivers | 6,657,400 | 775,400 | 293,200 | 1,207,700 | 1,091,400 | 1,281,000 | 2,008,700 |
| Automobile mechanics and repairmen | 3,860,400 | 289,200 | 165,800 | 564,100 | 740,200 | 974,400 | 1,126,700 |
| Janitors and sextons | 3,766,400 | 220,000 | 74,100 | 343,300 | 715,400 | 1,115,000 | 1,298,600 |
| Carpenters | 3,009,800 | 252,300 | 140,800 | 513,900 | 567,900 | 685,600 | 849,300 |
| Farm laborers, wage workers | 2,921,800 | 1,008,400 | 215,300 | 500,000 | 383,500 | 389,900 | 424,700 |
| Shipping and receiving clerks | 1,867,900 | 169,300 | 65,600 | 219,900 | 312,800 | 504,200 | 596,100 |
| Deliverymen and routemen | 1,663,800 | 270,900 | 49,900 | 305,600 | 443,200 | 489,900 | 104,300 |
| Guards, watchmen, and doorkeepers | 1,585,500 | 126,900 | 45,600 | 176,700 | 220,500 | 396,300 | 619,500 |
| Painters, construction and maintenance | 1,199,400 | 130,200 | 59,700 | 208,500 | 222,800 | 246,100 | 332,100 |

Source: Ruggles and Sobek et al., 1997.

is the largest of the women's occupations that justifiably can be compared to any of the three highlighted men's occupations. The growth pattern of the highlighted occupations throughout the time span, which basically tracks population growth, constitutes another indicator of representativeness. Occupations that are growing at a similar rate to the population indicate a persistent economy-wide relevance. For all of these reasons, the set of highlighted occupations includes the final potential candidates for comparison.

The occupations selected for comparison of access to employer-provided benefits are professional nurses, the modal women's occupation, and automobile mechanics and repairmen, the modal men's occupation. According to the comparability-in-size standard, either janitors and sextons or carpenters would be a closer match to professional nurses, which has an occupational total falling between these two men's occupations. However, at this point the selection process was constrained by lack of data on extent of unionization and access to benefits.[3] Limited data for janitors and sextons and carpenters on both of these variables do exist, but the data sources are not comparable to those for professional nurses and the available data do not cover the whole time span. As detailed below, both unionization and benefits data on professional nurses and automobile mechanics and repairmen exist for most of the time period, and come from the same Industry Wage Survey, Department of Labor, series. I thus selected professional nurses and automobile mechanics and repairmen for comparison of access to employer-provided benefits.

Table 6.2 demonstrates that these occupations are comparable, in accordance with all of the appropriate criteria except for unionization, which I will discuss next.

Finally, as explained, extent of unionization is an important control variable in the context of this study. To this effect, it would be ideal to compare occupations with similar levels of unionization. Table 6.3 shows the percentages of workers in each occupation for each survey year working in establishments with collective-bargaining agreements covering the majority of workers.

The occupation of professional nurses is less unionized than automobile mechanics and repairmen for most of the period, but catches up to mechanics towards the end, finally surpassing it. The overall pattern for mechanics is the reverse of the pattern for nurses, but the decline is gradual. Based on this table, then, the degree of control appears a little low. However, it will become apparent in the analyses of the benefits data that the percentages of workers in both occupations with access to benefits are generally vastly higher than the percentages that are unionized. This would suggest that unionization only goes so far as an alternative explanation for access to benefits.

**Table 6.2. Comparability of Professional Nurses and Automobile Mechanics and Repairmen**

| | | Professional Nurses | Automobile Mechanics and Repairmen |
|---|---|---|---|
| 1940 | Percentage of women / % men | 95.08 | 99.83 |
| | Pay level (av. occ. score) / Pay level | 21 | 27 |
| | Total number of workers / Total | 199,200 | 289,200 |
| 1950 | Percentage of women / % men | 97.54 | 99.16 |
| | Pay level (av. occ. score) / Pay level | 21 | 27 |
| | Total number of workers / Total | 69,000 | 165,800 |
| 1960 | Percentage of women / % men | 96.95 | 99.73 |
| | Pay level (av. occ. score) / Pay level | 21 | 27 |
| | Total number of workers / Total | 334,500 | 564,100 |
| 1970 | Percentage of women / % men | 88.71 | 98.70 |
| | Pay level (av. occ. score) / Pay level | 22.06 | 27 |
| | Total number of workers / Total | 526,900 | 740,200 |
| 1980 | Percentage of women / % men | 88.17 | 99.16 |
| | Pay level (av. occ. score) / Pay level | 21.02 | 26.12 |
| | Total number of workers / Total | 869,900 | 974,400 |
| 1990 | Percentage of women / % men | 88.19 | 98.47 |
| | Pay level (av. occ. score) / Pay level | 21.43 | 26.20 |
| | Total number of workers / Total | 1,318,300 | 1,126,700 |

Source: Ruggles and Sobek et al., 1997.

**Table 6.3. Yearly Percentages of Workers in Each Occupation Working in Establishments with Collective-Bargaining Agreements Covering the Majority of Workers**

| Survey Years | Professional Nurses | Automobile Mechanics and Repairmen |
|---|---|---|
| 1956–58 | 0 | 26.1 |
| 1963–64 | 0 | 30 |
| 1969 | 10 | 30 |
| 1972–73 | 17.3 | 30 |
| 1978 | 15.4 | 25 |
| 1982–84 | 18.1 | 20 |
| 1988–89 | 24.6 | 20 |

Sources: U.S. Department of Labor Hospital and Auto Dealer Repair Shop *Industry Wage Surveys*, 1957 to 1990. (For 1957, the data on nurses is from the U.S. Department of Labor, Bureau of Labor Statistics' *Earnings and Supplementary Benefits in Hospitals* surveys of various cities throughout the country.)
Note: These are national-level data derived from U.S. Department of Labor hospital and auto dealer repair shop industry wage surveys published from 1957 to 1990 (see section, "Benefits," for details on these data sources; and see reference list, "Data Sources" section, subsections 2 and 3, for bibliographic details.)

## Benefits

I used U.S. Department of Labor surveys taken at numerous points throughout the 1940–1990 time span as sources for data on employer-provided benefits (see reference list, "Data Sources" section, subsections 2 and 3). These surveys measure the availability of benefits in establishments within large industry categories, but they also break down the data by detailed occupation.[4] Within the hospital industry, percentages of professional nurses employed by hospitals offering various types of benefits are presented.[5] Likewise, within the automobile dealer and repair industry, the surveys present percentages of mechanics and repairmen employed by establishments offering benefits. These percentages are either national averages or city averages given for a large number of cities across the country—I calculated national averages from the city averages when this was the case.[6] The identities and definitions of the specific benefits included are presented in table 6.4.[7]

Starting with national-level percentages in each occupation working at establishments offering the insurance, health, and vacation benefits defined in table 6.4, I then calculated an average across all types of insurance and health benefits for each occupation for each of the following survey years: 1945–47, 1956–58, 1963–64, 1969, 1972–73, 1978, 1982–84, and 1988–89[8] (see reference list, "Data Sources" section, subsections 2 and 3, for bibliographic details). Both occupations saw large, steady increases in access to all categories of benefits throughout the time span. In 1945–47, over 35 percent of automobile mechanics and repairmen were employed by establishments offering benefits, while just over 20 percent of professional nurses worked at hospitals offering benefits. By 1988–89, these figures increased to over 70 percent for both occupations (U.S. Department of Labor, 1947, 1948, 1989,

**Table 6.4. Benefit Plans Covered by U.S. Department of Labor Hospital and Auto Dealer Repair Shop Industry Surveys. Includes Plans Paid for in Whole or in Part by Employer, and Underwritten by a Commercial Insurance Company, or Paid Directly by the Employer from Current Operating Funds.**

*Life Insurance:*
  Provides indemnity in case of death of the covered worker and payment to beneficiaries.
*Accidental Death and Dismemberment Insurance:*
  Provides payments in case of death or loss of limb or sight as a direct result of an accident.
*Sickness and Accident Insurance:*
  Predetermined cash payments made to the insured on a weekly or monthly basis during illness or accident disability.
*Sick Leave, Full Pay, No Wait:*
  Provides full pay to the employee, without requiring a waiting period, during absence from work due to an illness (covers shorter period of absence than sickness and accident insurance benefits).
*Hospitalization Insurance:*
  Provides at least partial payment for hospital room charges (covers employee and usually dependents).
*Surgical Insurance:*
  Provides at least partial payment for in-patient surgery (covers employee and usually dependents).
*Medical Insurance:*
  Provides at least partial payment for doctors' fees for hospital, office, or home visits (covers employee and usually dependents).
*Catastrophe Insurance:*
  Provides coverage in case of sickness or injury involving an expense that goes beyond the normal coverage of hospitalization, surgical, and medical plans.
*Paid Vacation:*
  Excused leave of absence with full pay. Graduated by length of service.

1990). The next step was to calculate an "insurance and health benefits gap": the percentages of automobile mechanics and repairmen working at establishments offering benefits minus the percentages of professional nurses working at hospitals offering benefits.[9] I also calculated two "paid vacation gaps," in this case subtracting the percentages of automobile mechanics from the percentages of nurses[10] (see reference list, "Data Sources" section, subsections 2 and 3, for bibliographic details). The first gap reflects the difference in access to paid vacations of two weeks or more after five years of service (survey years 1956–58 through 1969), and the second, the difference in access to vacations of more than two weeks after five years (survey years 1972–73 through 1988–89). I will discuss all of these data and their significance in the results section later.

## WOMEN'S AND MEN'S ACCESS TO
## EMPLOYER-PROVIDED BENEFITS:
## ASSESSING WOMEN'S ACCEPTANCE AS BREADWINNERS

As explained above, starting with national-level percentages of employees in each occupation working at establishments offering the insurance, health, and vacation benefits defined in table 6.4, I calculated an average across all types of insurance and health benefits for each occupation for each of the available survey years. Figure 6.1 presents the results.

The basic pattern is a large advantage for auto mechanics in the earlier years, which diminishes in the later years and finally becomes a small disadvantage in the last two survey years. Is this pattern explicable on the basis of parallel patterns in unionization? Figure 6.2, representing the data in table 6.3 in chart form, shows the percentages in each occupation working at establishments with labor-management agreements.

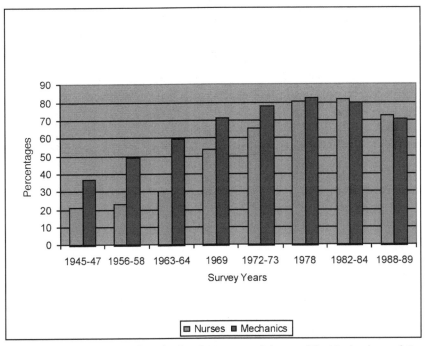

**Figure 6.1.** **Percentages of Professional Nurses and Automobile Mechanics and Repairmen Employed by Establishments Offering Insurance and Health Benefits (All Types)**

Sources: U.S. Department of Labor hospital and auto dealer repair shop industry surveys, 1947–1990 (see reference list, "Data Sources" section, subsections 2 and 3, for bibliographic details.)

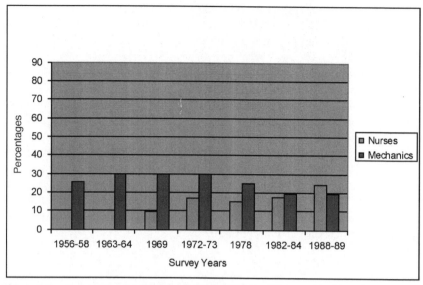

**Figure 6.2.    Percentages of Workers Employed by Establishments with Labor-Management Agreements Covering the Majority of Workers**

Sources: U.S. Department of Labor hospital and auto dealer repair shop industry surveys, 1947–1990 (see reference list, "Data Sources" section, subsections 2 and 3, for bibliographic details.)

Comparing figure 6.1, which presents average national-level percentages in each occupation working at establishments offering insurance and health benefits, to figure 6.2 allows me to address this question of the role of unionization in the distribution of benefits. While the patterns in the two figures mirror each other to a certain extent, the percentages of workers in both occupations with access to benefits are generally much higher in each survey year than the percentages that are unionized. This indicates that unionization only goes so far as an alternative explanation for discriminatory access to employer-provided benefits in the earlier survey years, and diminishing discrimination in the later years.

As such, it now makes sense to consider the possibility that the disparities in access shown in figure 6.1 are a function of additional factors. Figure 6.3 depicts the "insurance and health benefits gap" (calculation described earlier), which clarifies the patterns present in figure 6.1. Figures 6.4 and 6.5 show the "paid vacation gaps" (also calculated earlier), which highlight patterns in access to paid vacation benefits.

The significant advantage for auto mechanics on insurance and health benefits apparent in figure 6.3 diminishes over time and finally disappears. This pattern could indicate the influence of tradition-bound employer decision-making processes in the earlier survey years that transform in the later years into growing acceptance of a breadwinner status for women. As well, the large but diminishing advantage for nurses in access to vacation benefits (fig-

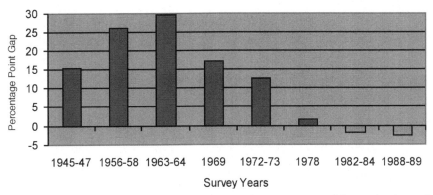

**Figure 6.3.   Insurance and Health Benefits Gap between Automobile Mechanics and Repairmen and Professional Nurses**

Sources: U.S. Department of Labor hospital and auto dealer repair shop industry surveys, 1947–1990 (see reference list, "Data Sources" section, subsections 2 and 3, for bibliographic details.)

ures 6.4 and 6.5) seems to reflect a nondiscriminatory perspective throughout the time period.

However, patterns of access to several notable categories of insurance benefits were masked by the calculations of averages used in figures 6.1 and 6.3. Throughout the time span, automobile mechanics and repairmen maintained an advantage in access to hospitalization, surgical, medical, and major medical

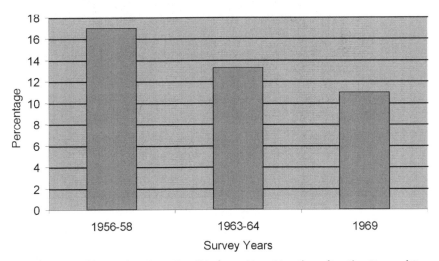

**Figure 6.4.   Paid Vacation Gap (Two Weeks or More Vacation after Five Years of Service) between Professional Nurses and Automobile Mechanics and Repairmen**

Sources: U.S. Department of Labor hospital and auto dealer repair shop industry surveys, 1957–1990 (see reference list, "Data Sources" section, subsections 2 and 3, for bibliographic details.)

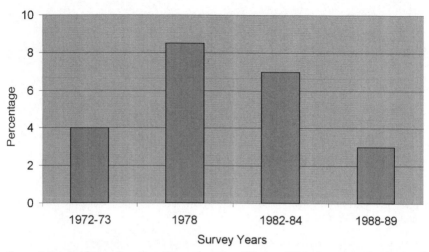

**Figure 6.5.   Paid Vacation Gap (More than Two Weeks of Vacation after Five Years of Service) between Professional Nurses and Automobile Mechanics and Repairmen**
Sources: U.S. Department of Labor hospital and auto dealer repair shop industry surveys, 1957–1990 (see reference list, "Data Sources" section, subsections 2 and 3, for bibliographic details.)

(or "catastrophe") insurance benefits while professional nurses maintained a significant advantage in access to "sick leave, full pay, no wait." By covering family members as well as the employee, hospitalization, surgical, medical, and major medical insurance benefits are the most comprehensive, family-supportive, and expensive categories of employer-provided insurance benefits. These benefits help employees to address potential life-and-death family concerns, including not only maintenance of good health for family members, but also substantial protection against health and financial disasters. Thus, while the professional nurses' advantage in sick leave and vacation benefits is certainly meaningful—paid vacations help families by enabling employees to take time off from work without loss of income—the advantage of automobile mechanics and repairmen in insurance and health benefits is more significant. These results thus could well indicate that men are still viewed as breadwinners to a greater extent than are women.

## POLITICALLY SALIENT VIEWS OF WOMEN AND MEN: BEYOND TRADITIONAL GENDER ROLES?

Overall, the trends in access to benefits suggest a rather lagged pattern of rising acceptance of women as breadwinners. The labor-force participation rate of women reached 50 percent in about 1965 and has steadily risen in recent decades (U.S. Census Bureau, 1999). However, as suggested in the analysis above, only in the 1980s does the male advantage in access to benefits disappear. While findings thus far draw the outlines of a pattern of slowly rising acceptance of female breadwinning, determining the existence of an actual pattern requires more than identification of correlations among general economic and social trends. Accepting (or not accepting) a bread-winning status for women is a complex ideological process, requiring critical examination of one's views of the economic and social status quo. Employers' decisions about providing benefits that help workers support their families, more so than decisions about pay level, are likely to bring to the forefront values regarding work, family, and gender. Given the importance of ideas and values in the process of accepting a breadwinning status for women, it makes sense to look at what employers and other influential participants in this process actually say about women and men and their relation to the spheres of work and family. The U.S. federal government, by way of its role as regulator of the labor market and its provision of an authoritative public forum in the form of the U.S. Congress, is highly relevant to this process of accepting women as breadwinners. I thus examine images of women and men in their work and family capacities as expressed in U.S. congressional-hearing testimony on proposals to regulate employer-provided benefits. Corresponding to the time period in the analyses above, I cover hearings from the 1940s to 1990.

## CONGRESSIONAL-HEARING TESTIMONY

I first gathered summaries of House and Senate hearings held from 1940 to 1990 on the following types of private employer-provided benefits: health insurance, disability insurance, life insurance, retirement, paid vacations, pregnancy disability leave, maternity leave, child care, and combinations of the foregoing.[11] This resulted in an initial total of 207 hearings. I then narrowed this set to hearings including actual discussion of workers receiving benefits aimed at helping family members, which left 166 hearings. Approximately 80 percent of the hearings thus potentially allow me to assess—both qualitatively and quantitatively—how gender figures into the discussion. Are these workers generally characterized in a nongendered manner as "parents," or "working men and women," or are they assumed to be male? Are women seen as dependent wives who receive benefits as a function of marriage, or as breadwinners providing benefits for their families? How often do these and other characterizations of workers receiving family-related benefits occur and what are the over-time patterns? While there are 166 hearings that should allow for such assessment, I examine the 84 hearings containing testimony provided by lawmakers and witnesses who were a significant presence in the benefits policy area at the federal level through most of the 1940–1990 time span.[12]

## GENDERED AND NONGENDERED STATEMENTS

I used the software "Non-numerical Unstructured Data: Indexing, Searching, Theorizing" (QSR N6)[13] to identify and chart the role played by gender in discussions of workers receiving benefits aimed at helping family members. As just explained, I expect a basic distinction between gendered and nongendered characterizations to emerge from these discussions, which would facilitate assessment of the extent to which women have been accepted as breadwinners over the time span. Since workers' access to and reception of family-oriented benefits is the topic of testimony being examined here, it is likely that witnesses will refer to actual workers and actual family members in terms that are generally either gender specific or gender neutral. Mothers, wives, fathers, husbands, parents, dependents, and heads of household are examples of both types of terms, the use of which can be very revealing of witnesses' views on women, men, and their relationships to work and family. To assess such usage, I searched for paragraphs containing the words "family" or "families" or "breadwinner" or "breadwinners," expecting the surrounding context to indicate which views are being expressed.

The 84 documents with hearing testimony related to workers receiving benefits aimed at helping family members contained a total of 369 paragraphs, covering the whole time period. Of these paragraphs, 194 contained both explicitly gendered and nongendered characterizations of such workers, as identified in the manner described above. Table 6.5 contains statements, from testimony on a variety of employer-provided benefits, which typify both characterizations. The cells in column 1, arranged in chronological order from the beginning of the time span to the end, display statements illustrating gendered views; while those in column 2 express nongendered views. One gendered statement and one nongendered statement are drawn from the testimony of each category of player in the benefits policy area.

The statements suggest some common themes concerning men and women in their work and family roles. In the "gendered" column, there are descriptive and vivid images of men as heads of families and breadwinners as well as indications that breadwinners are assumed to be male. There are no depictions of men taking care of children or other family members. Likewise, women appear either as passive and dependent on men for a variety of family benefits, or as mostly and elementally responsible for child rearing and homemaking even as they become responsible for breadwinning. However, in the "nongendered" column, either men and women are presented as fulfilling equal breadwinning roles, or gender-neutral "parents" and "workers" receive certain benefits that help their families. Notably underrepresented in this column, as in the gendered column, are characterizations of men as actual caretakers of children and other family members.

**Table 6.5. Sample Statements from Congressional-Hearing Testimony on Workers and Family-Oriented Employer-Provided Benefits**

| Gendered | Nongendered |
|---|---|
| "Senator, perhaps I do not accept that authority any more than do you. But that statement was made at a time when there was no widespread means of meeting that cost through insurance. I will agree with you right now that without insurance, anyone, the head of a family, the family income of which does not exceed $5,000 a year, is not ordinarily financially able to meet the cost of serious illness out of his own savings and money at hand. I agree thoroughly with that."<br>—Paul R. Hawley, Chief Executive Officer, Blue Cross Commission. NATIONAL HEALTH PROGRAM, 1949, PART 1. May 23–June 1, 1949. | "It is the Department of Labor's conviction that discrimination based on pregnancy is discrimination based on sex. To deny equal rights and equal benefits because of pregnancy could clearly work to the economic and employment disadvantage of many of this Nation's employed and employable women and their families."<br>—Alexis M. Herman, Director, Women's Bureau, DOL. LEGISLATION TO PROHIBIT SEX DISCRIMINATION ON THE BASIS OF PREGNANCY. April 6, 1977. |
| "The growth of health, welfare, and pension programs of various types in industry, largely as a result of trade-union action, has brought great benefits to the American worker and his family. These programs have provided him a greater measure of security, dignity, and independence in old age. They have given him access to better medical care, and have diminished the threat of indebtedness or pauperdom that too often accompanies the loss of health in the absence of any public program for the fair distribution of its heavy costs."<br>—George Meany, President, AFL-CIO. WELFARE AND PENSION PLANS LEGISLATION. May 27–July 1, 1957. | "We who are involved in multi-employer plans feel that their continued existence and health must be an important goal for everyone concerned about providing pension benefits for the working men and women in this country and their families."<br>—Robert A. Georgine, President, Building Trade Department, AFL-CIO. PENSION PLAN TERMINATION INSURANCE FOR MULTIEMPLOYER PENSION PLANS. March 18, 1980. |
| "This hearing is concerned with a specific proposal to enact such a system of insurance. It is aimed at providing protection for | "The discrimination standards also should be responsive to differences among the employees of a given employer. There may be |

continued

**Table 6.5.** *(continued)*

| Gendered | Nongendered |
|---|---|
| beneficiaries in the event the pension plan is terminated without sufficient funds to meet accumulated pension obligations. To the breadwinner who has planned his retirement in the expectation of regular pension payments, the failure to fulfill these payments is obviously a crushing blow to his hopes, his plans, and his aspirations. I would like to commend this committee for these hearings, for inquiring into a matter which is at once highly complex and highly charged with the public interest."<br>—Willard W. Wirtz, Secretary, DOL. FEDERAL REINSURANCE OF PRIVATE PENSION PLANS. August 15, 1966. | legitimate disparities in election of nontaxable benefits, between those who have children or other dependents and those who do not."<br>—Sally F. Goldfarb, National Organization for Women Legal Defense and Education Fund. FRINGE BENEFITS, PART I. July 26, 27, and 30, 1984. |
| "There are some 26 million housewives in the United States who are not otherwise covered by an employer's or employee's pension plan. These are women who do work, who raise their families and who do our cooking and cleaning and yet when they get into the retirement era there is no provision made for their own personal income. There is no provision made so that they are entirely dependent upon their husband's retirement plan or upon social security. This gives them that little additional feeling of security."<br>—Bertram L. Podell, Representative (D), New York. TAX PROPOSALS AFFECTING PRIVATE PLANS, PART 3. May 15 and 16, 1972. | "AARP believes that we must now seriously consider expanding coverage, lowering vesting, reducing the impact of integration, building in inflation protection, and establishing a system of portability so that future retirees can look forward to a decent standard of living throughout their lives. Without necessary changes, the private pension system will continue to be an empty promise for most American workers and their families."<br>—Judy Schub, Legislative Representative, AARP. THE PENSION GAMBLE: WHO WINS? WHO LOSES? June 14, 1985. |
| "Private pensions are generally not satisfactory as a source of retirement income for older women, either as dependents or as retired wage earners. Private pension plans tend to be associated | "First of all, I would like to deal very briefly with what we know. In terms of the problem, the chairman detailed it in his opening remarks. Roughly 17 percent of the population in this country today |

with higher paying positions, while women are generally employed in the lower paying jobs. Thus, many women who work are not covered by private pension plans. Even when a woman's work is covered by a pension plan, vesting provisions favor the individual who stays with the same firm for a relatively long period of time. The woman who moves in and out of the labor force to move with her husband, to raise children, or to fulfill other family obligations is at a serious disadvantage. She may fail to qualify for benefits under any pension plan because, in a lifetime of work, she has never worked long enough in one place to earn a vested right to benefits. Part-time work is seldom covered by private pension plans, yet many women spend a significant portion of their working lives in part-time employment and approximately 20 percent of the women in the work force at any given time are engaged in part-time work."

—Harriet Miller, Associate Director, AARP. ECONOMIC PROBLEMS OF AGING WOMEN. July 15, 1975.

"A great majority of life insurance is bought with the intention of protecting unsalaried homemakers against the loss of their husband's income through death. Higher payment for this protection comes from family budgets and so affects both women and men."

—Judy Goldsmith, President, National Organization for Women. NONDISCRIMINATION IN INSURANCE ACT OF 1983. February 22 and 24, 1983.

is not covered by insurance. The reason that you are looking at it and the reason that we are here, is that two-thirds of those people who are not covered are full-time workers and their families, and another two-thirds of that group work for firms with 100 or fewer employees."

—John J. Motley III, Director, Federal Government Relations, National Association of Manufacturers. THE HEALTH INSURANCE PROBLEM. May 6, and June 16 and 18, 1987.

"We are not talking just about women. We are also talking about men. In two-parent families where both parents work, men have much more serious parenting responsibilities than, frankly, my husband did when we were raising our family, and I was home full time. We have to look at the issue of empowering employees to respond to children's needs. That is not just a matter of day care, that is also a matter of attending parent conferences. If our business community wants people who stay in school, wants graduates who can read, write, and calculate, then they have an interest in allowing parents release time to go to parent conferences. In other words, we have to begin to face up to the systemic challenge that employees with significant parenting responsibilities pose to our society if we

continued

**Table 6.5.** (*continued*)

| Gendered | Nongendered |
| --- | --- |
| | want to have the work force and the vital economy that our way of life demands."<br>—Nancy L. Johnson, Representative (R), Connecticut. DAY CARE: ITS IMPORTANCE TO SMALL BUSINESS. June 8, 1988. |
| "Women continue to shoulder primary responsibility for the care dependents whether they be children, grandchildren, disabled family members, elderly parents, or other relatives. Most women work outside the home out of economic necessity, and the availability of quality, affordable dependent care services is therefore essential if they are to enter and remain in the work force."<br>—Olympia J. Snowe, Representative (R), Maine. ECONOMIC EQUITY ACT AND RELATED TAX AND PENSION REFORM. October 25, 1983. | "Eleven percent of the uninsured are the self-employed and their families, 13 percent are half-time employees and their families and 51 percent are full time employees or dependents of full-time workers. All of these factors make any single solution difficult."<br>—Carl J. Schramm, President, Health Insurance Association. EMPLOYEE HEALTH BENEFITS IMPROVEMENT ACT OF 1988. August 9 and September 22, 1988. |
| "We heard from one gentleman who says his ability to work past age 70 allows him to earn a third of his income, keeps him off of welfare, allows him to buy health insurance and maintain a car, keeps him the proud head of the family."<br>—Mark A. DeBernardo, Special Counsel for Domestic Policy, U.S. Chamber of Commerce. WORKING AMERICANS: EQUALITY AT ANY AGE. June 19, 1986. | "First, the job-based system of health insurance that has served the Nation well and provides good coverage for most workers and their families should be extended to the millions of other workers who have been left out of the present system. This simple step alone will provide coverage for 23 million workers and their dependents, two-thirds of the uninsured."<br>—Edward M. Kennedy, Senator (D), Massachusetts. BASIC HEALTH BENEFITS FOR ALL AMERICANS ACT. May 1 and June 23, 1989. |

There is only one statement of this sort (Nancy L. Johnson's statement, June 8, 1988).

While each type of characterization occurs throughout most of the time span, there are distinctive trends illustrated in figure 6.6. The overall pattern is one of a sharply rising incidence of both gendered and nongendered statements from the 1950s through the 1980s. Out of a total of 194 statements containing both types, 124 appeared in hearings held in the 1980s alone. Turning to a consideration of instances of each type of statement, of the 194 total statements, 89 fit the gendered and 105 the nongendered categories. Gendered statements are more prevalent through the 1970s, and while still rising in the 1980s, are significantly overtaken in this decade.

These findings bolster the judgment—based on the previous analysis of women's and men's access to benefits—that society, while slowly and grudgingly, is moving towards acceptance of equal breadwinning roles for women and men. Overall, there are more nongendered than gendered statements appearing in congressional testimony on workers and family-oriented employer-provided benefits, and the incidence of nongendered statements has risen over recent decades. This process is likely rooted in a variety of progressive social and political developments. Recent research (Katzenstein, 1998) implies that the extremely high level of commitment and determination

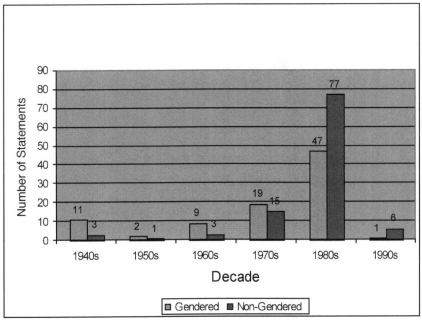

**Figure 6.6. Number of Statements from Congressional-Hearing Testimony on Workers and Family-Oriented Employer-Provided Benefits**

required for women to make significant inroads into the most "male" of occupations, religious and military work, could well indicate rising levels of
these qualities among women in all occupations—including nursing. Additional research (Gertzog, 1995) suggests that rising numbers of women at all
levels of political office over recent decades have resulted in better representation for women, including in their work lives. However, it is quite notable
that instances of gendered statements also rose at a fairly high rate. The rate
of increase was furthermore basically constant across hearing witnesses in all
categories (see note 12). It appears that traditional gender-role conceptions
are still quite prevalent at the end of the time period, perhaps more so than
findings from the first part of this study would suggest.

## CONCLUSION

In this chapter, I have asked whether the increase in the number of working
women over the last half century has been accompanied by a parallel trend
of increased recognition of a breadwinning status for women, or instead if
traditional role conceptions have persisted in spite of such altered circumstances. The findings in the first part of this chapter, of a disadvantage for
nurses relative to auto mechanics through most of the time period, diminishing and then reversing slightly at the end, were somewhat unexpected.
On the one hand, nurses experienced steadily rising access to benefits cul-
minating in a slight advantage over auto mechanics. On the other hand,
nurses remained at a significant disadvantage through most of the period, on
the whole suggesting a rather slow rate of acceptance of a breadwinning status. In general, these results suggest that society has slowly begun to accept
women as breadwinners.

The second part of this study, with some qualification, generally supports
this interpretation. While overall the results indicate increased acceptance of
equal breadwinning roles for men and women, traditional gender-role conceptions are still a prominent theme in the debate. This suggests a somewhat
weaker acceptance of an equal breadwinner role for women than women's
improved access to benefits would suggest.

Regarding future research, the slow rate of acceptance indicated both by
the patterns in women's and men's access to employer-provided benefits
and by the continued prevalence of traditional gender-role conceptions in
congressional testimony on employee benefits might well help explain re-
gressive characteristics of family-leave, child-care, and other benefits com-
prising present U.S. work-family policy. Many parents are effectively unable
to take advantage of such benefits as these are restricted and limited in numerous ways, suggesting persistence of traditional assumptions about work
and family and men's and women's roles in these areas (Bernstein, 1997;

Blank, 1997 and 1994; Burstein, Bricher, and Einwohner, 1995; *Congressional Quarterly*, 1993, 390; Coontz, 1997; Elison, 1997, 39; Kaitin, 1994; Marks, 1997, p. 57; Michel, 1999; Skocpol, 2000; Wisensale, 1997 and 2001). As the evolution and present form of current U.S. work-family policy has been heavily influenced by the interests of the private labor market (Kaitin, 1994; Wisensale, 2001), it makes sense to consider the roles historical patterns in women's and men's access to employer-provided benefits and the making of public policy aimed at regulating the labor market might have played in shaping this policy.

## NOTES

1. Census Bureau data sets are generally considered large enough to produce reliable national-level estimates of the proportion of women and men in each occupation (Blau and Hendricks, 1979; England et al., 1994; Figart and Lapidus, 1996; King, 1992; Roos and Reskin, 1992; Sorensen, 1989). I used the 1-in-100 national samples for 1940, 1950, 1960, 1970, 1980, and 1990.

Individuals were included in the initial file if they participated in the labor force, if they were between 18 and 64 years of age, if they worked 40 or more weeks during the year before the survey was taken, and if they worked 35 or more hours during the week before the survey. The last two conditions are intended to establish full-time status. I am ultimately interested in tracking access to employer-provided benefits. Historically, benefits have been available primarily to full-time workers only.

This selection process resulted in the following yearly total numbers of *occupations*: 1940: 216; 1950: 268; 1960: 267; 1970: 258; 1980: 220; 1990: 219.

2. For details on how this variable was constructed, see chapter 4, "Occupation and Income Scores," *IPUMS Design*, at http://www.ipums.umn.edu/usa/chapter4.

3. The benefits and unionization data will be discussed below.

4. I am confident that these industry-wide surveys are broadly representative of the extent of access to benefits in both occupations. In all survey years, the hospital and automobile mechanic and repairmen industries are the largest employers of professional nurses and mechanics and repairmen, respectively.

5. I also decided to focus on professional nurses employed by private hospitals, first because I am interested ultimately in assessing the role played by traditional views of men and women throughout society, not in a relatively small and unique segment of the labor force. The private-sector labor force, including nurses, is significantly bigger than the public sector. The type of hospital employing the large majority of all hospital workers, including nurses, is the private hospital. I also need the nursing data to be comparable to the automobile mechanics data, which only cover private-sector workers.

Benefits data are broken down by precise occupational categories in all survey years but two. For the hospitals *Industry Wage Survey* published in August 1984 and the *Industry Wage Survey: Hospitals and Nursing Homes* published in November 1980, the category "professional nurses" is not included. However, the category "full-time professional and technical" employees (which excludes physicians, managers, and executives) includes "general duty nurse," the largest occupation surveyed. General-duty nurses comprised one-fifth of the total employment covered by the survey.

6. The specific cities for which benefits data were presented differed slightly between the surveys for the two occupations, as well as from survey year to survey year. Therefore, in aggregating to the national level for each survey year, I included only those cities presenting data for both occupations.

7. I did not include pension benefits, because the data for the two sets of surveys were not comparable.

8. Figure 6.1, which will be discussed in the results section.

9. Figure 6.3, which will be discussed in the results section.

10. Figures 6.4 and 6.5, which will be discussed in the results section.

11. I focus on private- rather than public-sector benefits because I am interested in assessing acceptance of a breadwinner status for women throughout society, not in a relatively small and unique segment of the labor force. I thus searched Congressional Information Service indices for hearings on benefits in these private-sector categories, excluding hearings on Social Security, Medicare, Medicaid, Workmen's Compensation, and Military, Veterans' and Civil Servants' benefits.

12. These include: Republican and Democratic members of Congress, U.S. Department of Labor officials, employer interest groups (U.S. Chamber of Commerce, National Association of Manufacturers, and the National Federation of Independent Business), insurance interest groups (Blue Cross and Blue Shield associations, Health Insurance Association, and the Association of Private Pension and Welfare Plans), union interest groups (American Federation of Labor, Congress of Industrial Organizations, and the American Federation of Labor-Congress of Industrial Organizations), women's interest groups (National Organization for Women and the Older Women's League), and the American Association of Retired Persons.

13. In addition to other functions, NUD*IST searches plain-text documents for word patterns, keeping track of their occurrences in lines, sentences, paragraphs, sections, or entire documents.

# REFERENCES

## Articles, Books, and Software

Baker, M., and Fortin, N. M. 1999. "Women's Wages in Women's Work: A U.S./Canada Comparison of the Roles of Unions and 'Public Goods' Sector Jobs." *American Economic Review* 89: 198–203.

Baron, J. N., and Newman, A. E. 1990. "For What It's Worth: Organizations, Occupations, and the Value of Work Done by Women and Nonwhites." *American Sociological Review* 55 (April): 155–75.

Bergmann, B. R. 1986. *The Economic Emergence of Women*. New York: Basic Books, Inc.

———. 1989. "What the Common Economic Arguments against Comparable Worth are Worth." *Journal of Social Issues* 45, no. 4: 67–80.

Bernstein, A. E. 1997. *The Moderation Dilemma: Legislative Coalitions and the Politics of Family and Medical Leave.* Ph.D. diss., the Department of Government, Harvard University, Cambridge, Massachusetts.

Bielby, W. T., and Baron, J. N. 1986. "Sex Segregation within Occupations." *American Economic Review* 76: 43–47.

Blank, R. M. 1994. "The Employment Strategy: Public Policies to Increase Work and Earnings." In *Confronting Poverty: Prescriptions for Change,* ed. S. Danziger and D. H. Weinberg. Cambridge, Mass.: Harvard University Press.

———. 1997. *It Takes a Nation: A New Agenda for Fighting Poverty.* Princeton, N.J.: Princeton University Press.

Blau, F. D., and Hendricks, W. E. 1979. "Occupational Segregation by Sex: Trends and Prospects." *Journal of Human Resources,* 197–210.

Burstein, P., Bricher, M., and Einwohner, R. L. 1995. "Policy Alternatives and Political Change: Work, Family, and Gender on the Congressional Agenda, 1945–1990." *American Sociological Review* 60: 67–83.

*Congressional Quarterly.* 1993. "Provisions of the Family Leave Law." *Congressional Quarterly Almanac, 103rd Congress, 1st Session.*

Coontz, S. 1988. *The Social Origins of Private Life: A History of American Families 1600–1900.* London: Verso.

———. 1997. *The Way We Really Are: Coming to Terms with America's Changing Families.* New York: Basic Books.

DeViney, S. 1995. "Life Course, Private Pension, and Financial Well-Being." *The American Behavioral Scientist* 39 (November/December 1995): 172–85.

Elison, S. K. 1997. "Policy Innovation in a Cold Climate: The Family and Medical Leave Act of 1993." *Journal of Family Issues* 18.

England, P., et al. 1988. "Explaining Occupational Sex Segregation and Wages: Findings from a Model with Fixed Effects." *American Sociological Review* 53: 544–58.

———. 1994. "The Gendered Valuation of Occupations and Skills: Earnings in 1980 Census Occupations." *Social Forces* 73: 65–99.

Ferree, M. M. 1983. "Housework: Rethinking the Costs and Benefits." In *Families, Politics, and Public Policy,* ed. I. Diamond. New York: Longman.

Figart, D. M., and Lapidus, J. 1996. "The Impact of Comparable Worth on Earnings Inequality." *Work and Occupations* 23: 297–318.

Gerstel, N., and Gross, H. E. 1987. *Families and Work.* Philadelphia, Pa.: Temple University Press.

Gertzog, I. N. 1995. *Congressional Women: Their Recruitment, Integration, and Behavior.* 2d ed. Westport, Conn.: Praeger.

Gordon, L. 1994. *Pitied but Not Entitled: Single Mothers and the History of Welfare, 1890–1935.* New York: Free Press.

Greig, J. J., Orazem, P. F., and Mattila, J. P. 1989. "Measurement Error in Comparable Worth Pay Analysis: Causes, Consequences, and Corrections." *Journal of Social Issues* 45, no. 4: 135–51.

Hardy, M. A., and Shuey, K. 2000. "Pension Decisions in a Changing Economy: Gender, Structure, and Choice." *Journals of Gerontology, Series B: Psychological Sciences and Social Sciences,* 55B, no. 5: S271–S277.

Jacobs, F. H., and Davies, M. W. 1994. *More than Kissing Babies? Current Child and Family Policy in the United States.* Westport, Conn.: Auburn House.

Johnson, G., and Solon, G. 1986. "Estimates of the Direct Effects of Comparable Worth Policy." *American Economic Review* 76: 1117–25.

Kaitin, K. 1994. "Congressional Responses to Families in the Workplace: The Family and Medical Leave Act of 1987–1988." Pp. 9–35 in *More than Kissing Babies? Current Child and Family Policy in the United States,* ed. F. H. Jacobs and M. W. Davies. Westport, Conn.: Auburn House.

Katzenstein, M. F. 1998. *Faithful and Fearless: Moving Feminist Protest inside the Church and Military.* Princeton, N.J.: Princeton University Press.

Kessler-Harris, A. 1982. *Out to Work.* Oxford: Oxford University Press.

King, M. C. 1992. "Occupational Segregation by Race and Sex, 1940–88." *Monthly Labor Review* 115: 30–36.

Marks, M. R. 1997. "Party Politics and Family Policy: The Case of the Family and Medical Leave Act." *Journal of Family Issues* 18, no. 1.

Mason, M. A. 1992. "Standing Still in the Workplace: Women in Social Work and Other Female-Dominated Occupations." *Affilia* 7: 23–43.

Michel, S. 1999. *Children's Interests/Mothers' Rights.* New Haven, Conn.: Yale University Press.

Mount, M. K., and Ellis, R. A. 1989. "Sources of Bias in Job Evaluation: A Review and Critique of Research." *Journal of Social Issues* 45, no. 4: 153–67.

Nelson, J. I. 1994. "Work and Benefits: The Multiple Problems of Service Sector Employment." *Social Problems* 41 (May): 240–56.

Oppenheimer, V. K. 1970. *The Female Labor Force in the United States.* Berkeley: Institute of International Studies, University of California.

Pearce, D. M. 1987. "On the Edge: Marginal Women Workers and Employment Policy." Pp. 197–210 in *Ingredients for Women's Employment Policy,* ed. C. Bose and G. Spitze. Albany: SUNY Press.

Perman, L., and Stevens, B. 1989. "Industrial Segregation and the Gender Distribution of Fringe Benefits." *Gender and Society* 3, no. 3: 388–404.

QSR N6. Full Version. QSR International Pty Ltd.

Regalia, M., Lefkowitz, M., Hawkins, D., and Lee, P. 1997. *Employee Benefits, 1997 Edition, 50th Anniversary: Survey Data from Benefit Year 1996.* Washington, D.C.: U.S. Chamber of Commerce.

Reskin, B. F., and Hartmann, H. I. 1986. *Women's Work, Men's Work.* Washington, D.C.: National Academy Press.

Roos, P. A., and Reskin, B. F. 1992. "Occupational Desegregation in the 1970s: Integration and Economic Equity?" *Sociological Perspectives* 35: 69–91.

Skocpol, T. 1995. *Social Policy in the United States: Future Possibilities in Historical Perspective.* Princeton, N.J.: Princeton University Press.

———. 2000. *The Missing Middle.* New York: W.W. Norton and Company.

Sorensen, E. 1986. "Implementing Comparable Worth: A Survey of Recent Job Evaluation Studies." *American Economic Review* 76: 364–67.

———. 1989. "The Crowding Hypothesis and Comparable Worth." *Journal of Human Resources* 25: 55–89.

Staggenborg, S. 1998. *Gender, Family and Social Movements.* Thousand Oaks, Calif.: Pine Forge Press.

Steinberg, R. J. 1990. "Social Construction of Skill." *Work and Occupations* 17: 449–82.

Taylor, S. H. 1989. "The Case for Comparable Worth." *Journal of Social Issues* 45, no. 4: 23–37.

U.S. Census Bureau. 1999. *Statistical Abstract of the United States.*

U.S. Department of Labor, Women's Bureau. 2000. "Facts on Working Women." March. At http://www.dol.gov/dol/wb/public/wb_pubs/millennium52000.htm (accessed November 15, 2001).

Wisensale, S. K. 1997. "The White House and Congress on Child Care and Family Leave Policy: From Carter to Clinton." *Policy Studies Journal* 25, no. 1.

———. 2001. *Family Leave Policy: The Political Economy of Work and Family in America.* Armonk, N.Y.: M. E. Sharpe.

Wittig, M. A., and Lowe, R. H. 1989. "Comparable Worth Theory and Policy." *Journal of Social Issues* 45, no. 4: 1–21.

## Data Sources

### (1) Occupations

Ruggles, S., and Sobek, M. et al. 1997. *Integrated Public Use Microdata Series: Version 2.0.* Minneapolis: Historical Census Projects, University of Minnesota. At http://www.ipums.umn.edu/.

### (2) Employer-Provided Benefits: Professional Nurses

U.S. Department of Labor, Bureau of Labor Statistics. 1947. *The Economic Status of Registered Professional Nurses, 1946–47.* Bulletin 931.

U.S. Department of Labor, Bureau of Labor Statistics. 1957a. *Earnings and Supplementary Benefits in Hospitals: St. Louis, Missouri, June 1956.* Bulletin 1210-1. March.

U.S. Department of Labor, Bureau of Labor Statistics. 1957b. *Earnings and Supplementary Benefits in Hospitals: Portland, Oregon, May and July 1956.* Bulletin 1210-2. May.

U.S. Department of Labor, Bureau of Labor Statistics. 1957c. *Earnings and Supplementary Benefits in Hospitals: Buffalo, New York, June 1956.* Bulletin 1210-3. May.

U.S. Department of Labor, Bureau of Labor Statistics. 1957d. *Earnings and Supplementary Benefits in Hospitals: Baltimore, Maryland, June 1956.* Bulletin 1210-4. May.

U.S. Department of Labor, Bureau of Labor Statistics. 1957e. *Earnings and Supplementary Benefits in Hospitals: Chicago, Illinois, August 1956.* Bulletin 1210-5. May.

U.S. Department of Labor, Bureau of Labor Statistics. 1957f. *Earnings and Supplementary Benefits in Hospitals: Boston, Massachusetts, August 1956.* Bulletin 1210-6. May.

U.S. Department of Labor, Bureau of Labor Statistics. 1957g. *Earnings and Supplementary Benefits in Hospitals: Cleveland, Ohio, November 1956.* Bulletin 1210-7. May.

U.S. Department of Labor, Bureau of Labor Statistics. 1957h. *Earnings and Supplementary Benefits in Hospitals: Dallas, Texas, November 1956.* Bulletin 1210-8. June.

U.S. Department of Labor, Bureau of Labor Statistics. 1957i. *Earnings and Supplementary Benefits in Hospitals: Cincinnati, Ohio, September 1956.* Bulletin 1210-9. July.

U.S. Department of Labor, Bureau of Labor Statistics. 1957j. *Earnings and Supplementary Benefits in Hospitals: Philadelphia, Pennsylvania, July 1956.* Bulletin 1210-10. August.

U.S. Department of Labor, Bureau of Labor Statistics. 1957k. *Earnings and Supplementary Benefits in Hospitals: Atlanta, Georgia, September 1956.* Bulletin 1210-11. August.

U.S. Department of Labor, Bureau of Labor Statistics. 1957l. *Earnings and Supplementary Benefits in Hospitals: Memphis, Tennessee, December 1956.* Bulletin 1210-12. August.

U.S. Department of Labor, Bureau of Labor Statistics. 1957m. *Earnings and Supplementary Benefits in Hospitals: San Francisco-Oakland, California, November 1956.* Bulletin 1210-13. August.

U.S. Department of Labor, Bureau of Labor Statistics. 1957n. *Earnings and Supplementary Benefits in Hospitals: Los Angeles-Long Beach, California, January 1957.* Bulletin 1210-14. August.

U.S. Department of Labor, Bureau of Labor Statistics. 1957o. *Earnings and Supplementary Benefits in Hospitals: Minneapolis-St. Paul, Minnesota, March 1957.* Bulletin 1210-15. August.

U.S. Department of Labor, Bureau of Labor Statistics. 1957p. *Earnings and Supplementary Benefits in Hospitals: New York, New York, February 1957.* Bulletin 1210-16. August.

U.S. Department of Labor, Bureau of Labor Statistics. 1964. *Industry Wage Survey: Hospitals, Mid-1963.* Bulletin 1409. June.

U.S. Department of Labor, Bureau of Labor Statistics. 1971a. *Industry Wage Survey: Hospitals, March 1969.* Bulletin 1688.

U.S. Department of Labor, Bureau of Labor Statistics. 1974. *Industry Wage Survey: Hospitals, August 1972.* Bulletin 1829.

U.S. Department of Labor, Bureau of Labor Statistics. 1980a. *Industry Wage Survey: Hospitals and Nursing Homes, September 1978.* Bulletin 2069. November.

U.S. Department of Labor, Bureau of Labor Statistics. 1984a. *Industry Wage Survey: Hospitals.* Bulletin 2204. August.

U.S. Department of Labor, Bureau of Labor Statistics. 1990. *Industry Wage Survey: Hospitals, March 1989.* Bulletin 2364. August.

## (3) Employer-Provided Benefits: Automobile Mechanics and Repairmen

U.S. Department of Labor, Bureau of Labor Statistics. 1948. *Supplementary Wage Practices in American Industry. 1945–46.* Bulletin 939.

U.S. Department of Labor, Bureau of Labor Statistics. 1959. *Wage Structure: Auto Dealer Repair Shops, Summer 1958.* Report 141. January.

U.S. Department of Labor, Bureau of Labor Statistics. 1965. *Industry Wage Survey: Auto Dealer Repair Shops, August–October 1964.* Bulletin 1452. June.

U.S. Department of Labor, Bureau of Labor Statistics. 1971b. *Industry Wage Survey: Auto Dealer Repair Shops, August 1969*. Bulletin 1689.

U.S. Department of Labor, Bureau of Labor Statistics. 1975. *Industry Wage Survey: Auto Dealer Repair Shops, June 1973*. Bulletin 1876.

U.S. Department of Labor, Bureau of Labor Statistics. 1980b. *Industry Wage Survey: Auto Dealer Repair Shops, June 1978*. Bulletin 2060. April.

U.S. Department of Labor, Bureau of Labor Statistics. 1984b. *Industry Wage Survey: Auto Dealer Repair Shops, November 1982*. Bulletin 2198. August.

U.S. Department of Labor, Bureau of Labor Statistics. 1989. *Industry Wage Survey: Auto Dealer Repair Shops, July 1988*. Bulletin 2337. July.

# III

## RECONCILIATION OF WORK AND FAMILY LIFE: MATERNITY, PARENTAL, AND FAMILY LEAVE

# 7

# Parental Leave and Gender Equality: What Can the United States Learn from the European Union?[1]

*Linda Haas*

By the beginning of the twenty-first century, over half (54 percent) of all women ages 15–64 who lived in the fifteen societies affiliated with the European Union were employed for pay, a dramatic increase from a quarter of a century earlier (Commission of the European Communities [CEC], 2001a). The increase in women's labor-force participation is related to several social and economic developments common throughout industrialized societies, including women's ability to control their own fertility, expansion of opportunities for women in education and employment, and an increase in demand for labor in the service sector (United Nations, 2000).

The treaty that binds EU members clearly states: "The Community shall . . . promote throughout the Community equality between women and men." While women are at least 40 percent of the labor force in each EU member state, their status is still quite different from men's. In 2000, one-third of employed women in the EU worked part-time (in contrast to 6 percent of employed men). There existed a persistent gender gap in pay, with women's hourly wages averaging 86 percent of men's. Like women in other industrialized societies, EU women find it difficult to break through glass ceilings to take positions of authority in work organizations (CEC, 2001a). Women's traditional responsibility for children remains a significant barrier to employment opportunities. As long as women are the ones who reduce their work commitment and hours to accommodate young children's needs, it is easy for employers to offer women less lucrative and responsible employment positions (Selmi, 2000). American women who have access to parental leave work longer into their pregnancies and return to the labor market sooner, thus increasing their average pay over time (Hofferth, 1996; Selmi, 2000; Waldfogel, 1997)

Government policy could help reconcile employees' work and family obligations. According to van Doorne-Huiskes, den Dulk, and Schippers (1999a, 172), "In countries with a more extensive government policy regarding work-family arrangements, women have higher labour participation rates and the gender gap in wages is smaller." Two types of government policy could help mothers combine employment with child rearing and redistribute care responsibilities between women and men, while keeping "children's interests at the heart of public policy" (Wilkinson, 1997, 20). The first is government-mandated paid parental leave from employment, so fathers and mothers can take time off from work to care for young children without jeopardizing their positions in the labor market. The second is government-guaranteed day-care places for children of employed parents ages 0–6, along with substantial support in helping parents pay for high quality child care (Kamerman, 2000).

Government-mandated paid parental leave and subsidized child care are policies that require a fundamental change in attitudes about gender, parenting, and work in industrialized societies, whereby both mothers and fathers are assumed to be responsible for the care of young children, and government and employers are held responsible for assisting parents in this extremely important task. Both changes provide parents substantial practical assistance in balancing work and family roles and at the same time represent a significant ideological shift, whereby the demands of "social reproduction" are given at least equal weight as the demands of "production" (Leira, 1998).

Parental leave and child care are public policies widely discussed in countries in the European Union as effective strategies for increasing women's labor-market involvement, facilitating work-family reconciliation, and encouraging couples to have children (since the present low fertility rate threatens future economic productivity) (van Doorne-Huiskes et al., 1999a). The European Union's treaty guideline (no. 18) for work-family reconciliation sets the stage for the EU to promote parental leave and child care: "Member states . . . will design, implement and promote family-friendly policies, including affordable, accessible and high quality care services for children and other dependents, as well as parental and other leave schemes" (CEC, 2001b). So far, parental leave has received more legislative attention than child care in nations associated with the European Union. This chapter describes the development of EU parental-leave policy and its effects on individual countries within the Union. It discusses how cross-national variations in parental-leave policy both reflect and contribute to societal attitudes toward gender equality, in particular, equal employment opportunity for women and men's active participation in child care. Swedish parental-leave policy receives extended attention, since Sweden has the oldest and most generous and flexible parental-leave program, aimed at both parents, and designed to promote equal sharing of breadwinning and child-care responsibilities (Haas, 1992). EU policy on parental leave is compared to American policy, and the successes and problems associated with parental leave in the EU and U.S. are considered for what we can learn about the development and effectiveness of parental-leave policy.

## DEFINITIONS AND SOURCES

*Parental leave* is gender-neutral, job-protected leave from employment, designed to facilitate employed parents' care of small children at home. In this chapter, the focus is on parental-leave benefits guaranteed by international and national law. Parental-leave benefits can also be granted by state and regional laws, collective bargaining agreements, and contractual agreements between employees and employers. Parental leave is distinct from other types of leave that working parents might take. *Maternity leave* grants women job-protected time off before and after childbirth; *paternity leave* offers new fathers a few days or weeks to be with the family after childbirth or adoption with job protection; *family leave* offers individuals some days off per year to deal with illnesses or accidents involving a close family member; *child-rearing leaves* are job-protected leaves that typically last several years until a child is four or older, usually unpaid or paid at a low level.

Government-mandated parental leave has the potential of bringing about substantial change in employers' treatment of working parents. Such legislation restricts the rights of the employer to dictate employment conditions by granting workers the privilege of remaining at home to care for children. Compulsory regulations can also affect working arrangements more indirectly, through helping to create a new normative climate within work organizations (den Dulk, 1999). As organizations become more aware of parents' needs, learn how to adapt to mandated leave, and discover the benefits leave taking can have for employees' personal development, the family responsibilities of all workers may receive more attention and organizations may choose to supplement the benefits offered by national legislation (den Dulk, 2001).

Information on the development of parental-leave policy in the European Union comes from recently published studies on social policy in Europe, unpublished research conducted by New Ways to Work (a nonprofit organization committed to changing British parental-leave policy), personal experience observing and providing advice to groups developing parental policy in Sweden and the U.K., and European Union reports and official statistics.

## DEVELOPMENT OF EUROPEAN UNION POLICY REGARDING PARENTAL LEAVE

The Treaty of Rome in 1957 established the European Economic Community (EEC). This treaty concerned six nations: Belgium, France, Germany, Italy, Luxembourg, and Netherlands. From the beginning, the EEC's main goal was the creation of a common market, achieved by increasing the mobility of goods, labor, capital, and services across national lines, without harming member states' economic competitiveness (Ostner, 2000). The 1957 Treaty mandated some workers' rights, including equal pay for men and women doing equal work. At the time of the Treaty's signing, one-third of women in EEC countries worked for pay and their wages averaged 45 percent of men's (Murray, Neij, and Lindblom, 2000). According to Rees (1998, 52), labor-market concerns "took precedence over any particular gender equality agenda."

In 1973, three more nations joined the European Community—Denmark, Ireland, and the United Kingdom. Equal employment opportunity for women became a more serious objective for EEC social policy in the 1970s, after a substantial increase in the numbers of women in the paid labor force (Hantrais, 2000). EEC directives prohibited sex discrimination in workers' pay and treatment and encouraged member states to develop affirmative action initiatives to improve women's situation in the labor market. According to Rossilli (2000), directives gave ideological support to women's movements in member states, especially those in southern Europe, to pressure national governments for guarantees against sex discrimination. An Equal Opportunities Unit was established in 1976 under the office of Employment, Industrial Relations and Social Affairs to study how equality legislation was enforced and to recommend new policies in EEC nations (Rees, 1998).

Greece, Portugal, and Spain joined the EEC in the 1980s, bringing the total number of member states to twelve. In 1982, the Community set up an Advisory Committee on Equal Opportunities for Men and Women, made up of national experts, to work with the Equal Opportunities Unit (Rees, 1998). Subsequently, the Community developed two action programs "intended to redress the weak EC record of equality legislation" (Rossilli, 2000, 6). These programs focused on strengthening individual women's rights in the labor market through increasing women's representation in specific occupations and training programs (Rees, 1998).

The first EEC proposal to mandate parental leave was introduced in 1983, to ensure that diverse national policies would not hinder European economic integration. At this point, the Community still was not interested in developing social policy, so equality concerns were not high on the legislative agenda (Ostner, 2000). The first parental-leave proposal did not progress very far because it was seen as too radical, proposing leave rights to men as well as women (Lohkamp-Himmighofen and Dienel, 2000). The United Kingdom is typically credited with blocking this first parental-leave proposal (Rubery et al., 1998).

The European Women's Lobby was founded in 1990 by the EEC and the Committee on Women's Rights of the European Parliament to maintain the momentum of legislative activity on behalf of women workers. This Lobby helped facilitate two new action programs, including a 1990 resolution to combat sexual harassment in the workplace and a 1992 recommendation on child care, neither binding on member states, but designed to encourage them to take the status of women workers more seriously (Rossilli, 2000).

In response to the dramatic increase in the numbers of mothers in European labor forces, a new proposal for parental leave was drafted to help employed mothers and fathers reconcile work and family responsibilities. The parental-leave directive (part of the first Social Policy Agreement) mandated leave for all male and female workers who had an employment contract or relationship as defined by law (Ostner, 2000). In late 1991, this agreement was included in the Maastricht Treaty, signed by eleven of the twelve member governments. The U.K. refused to sign because it disapproved of policy that would support married mothers' employment (Stratigaki, 2000). Since the U.K. did not sign the agreement, it was not bound by EU law to adopt a parental-leave policy.

The Maastricht Treaty's directive covering parental leave broke new ground by being "the first binding EC-instrument primarily aimed at the reconciliation of occupational and family life" (Schmidt, 1997, 113). It is recognized more for being the first agreement on any social-policy issue under the new treaty than it is for its impact on member states' national parental-leave provisions (Hall, 1998). The directive lacked specifics, so it was followed by a 1994 "white paper," directing member states to adopt a minimum of three months of unpaid parental leave, available up to the child's second birthday, with guaranteed job reinstatement and continuous insurance coverage (Stratigaki, 2000).

In 1995, with the admission of Austria, Finland, and Sweden, the European Economic Community became the European Community (the EC), made up of fifteen nations under an umbrella body, the European Union (EU). During the same year, the EU established an Advisory Committee on Equality. According to Bergqvist and Jungar (2000), the committee was established because of pressure from Anita Gradin, the first EU commissioner from Sweden. Two of the six committee members were from the new member states of Sweden and Finland, which already had legislation granting fathers' rights to paid parental leave (Stratigaki, 2000).

In 1997, all fifteen EU member states signed the Amsterdam Treaty on European Union, which included a social-policy agreement with a specific directive on parental leave developed by the Advisory Committee on Equality. This agreement obligated all EU members (including the U.K.) to grant three months of unpaid parental leave to both men and women workers (with at least one year's tenure with an employer) as an individual "nontransferable right," available until biological or adopted children were eight years old (Lohkamp-Himmighofen and Dienel, 2000). Parental-leave rights are gender neutral so that "men should be encouraged to assume an equal share of family responsibilities" (Stratigaki, 2000, 43). The directive requires member states to take necessary measures to protect workers against dismissal on the ground of an application for, or the taking of, parental leave and to guarantee workers the right to return to the same job or to an equivalent or similar contract on their return from parental leave. Member states should provide for the maintenance of entitlements to benefits during leave, such as sickness insurance.

It was left up to individual governments to decide if parental leave would be transferable from one parent to the other, if it could be taken part-time, and whether it should be paid. Individual nations also decide the length of notice to be given employers, the circumstances under which parental leave may be postponed by the employer, whether employees of small businesses may be exempt from leave rights, and whether to grant parents on leave entitlement to social security benefits. All member states except the U.K. were obligated to follow the parental directive by changing their national legislation within one year of the signing of the Amsterdam Treaty, i.e., by the end of 1998. The U.K. was granted a two-year compliance period (until the end of 1999), since it had not earlier developed parental-leave legislation in response to EU directive.

Rossilli (2000) maintains that the parental-leave directive in the Amsterdam Treaty did not challenge laws already in place in most member states or substantially improve EC parents' access to parental leave. However, at the end of 1998, the European Community began "infringement proceedings" against Italy, Luxembourg, and Portugal for failing to comply with the parental-leave directive deadline (CEC, 1999). By 1999, these nations had parental legislation in place.

Since 1998, the European Union has established new employment guidelines for its member states, which include equal opportunities for women and men. All states are required to undertake "gender mainstreaming," which involves analyzing the effects of any proposed new employment policy or program on women and men (CEC, 1999). Member states have agreed to increase women's labor-force participation rate to 60 percent by 2010. By the end of 2000, six states had already met this goal (including Denmark, Finland, the Netherlands, Portugal, Sweden, and the U.K.) and another was very close (Austria) (Eurostat, 2001). National development of family-friendly policies such as parental leave is seen as an important way "equal opportunities" can be achieved (CEC, 2001b).

## VARIATIONS IN EU MEMBER
## STATES' PARENTAL-LEAVE POLICY

While the European Union has become a formidable international organization, with a strong commitment to maximizing member states' economic well-being, it has not eliminated national sovereignty. Member states can react to

EU directives "with ingenious strategies for evading and delaying," or take steps to establish themselves as worthy exceptions (Schunter-Kleemann, 1995, 84). The European Union is said to have influence "largely through reliance on soft law rather than binding legislation" (Hantrais, 2000, 3). "European directives . . . tend to represent minimum standards and to provide only a broad framework within which each member state is required to implement national measures" (Lohkamp-Himmighofen and Dienel, 2000, 66). By 2000, this minimum standard involved thirteen weeks of unpaid parental leave for male and female workers (distinct from paid maternity leave, paternity leave, and family-care leave offered to workers to care for sick family members). In 2001, fourteen of the fifteen states offered at least thirteen weeks of full-time leave; Netherlands, however, offered only part-time leave (for six months). (See table 7.1 for specifics about each country's current parental-leave benefit.)

Going beyond the minimum standard, nine of fifteen EU nations have arranged for parents to take *paid* parental leave for the first child (although this pay can be at a low flat rate, e.g., in Austria). Paid-leave lengths vary from three to thirty-six months. In five EU countries (Austria, Belgium, Denmark, Italy, and Sweden), there are special incentives for fathers to take leave, usually in the form of granting parental leave as an individual nontransferable entitlement or providing extra leave days to families where the father takes some leave.

Parental-leave policies in EU nations can be analyzed from the perspective of "the caring dimension of welfare states" (Knijn and Kremer, 1997). According to Knijn and Kremer (1997, 330), "modern welfare states have shaped the needs and rights of caregivers and care receivers . . . in ways that contribute to gender inequality in citizenship rights." They describe four "dilemmas" of care in modern societies, which can be addressed by social policy: whether care is regarded as a private or public responsibility, whether care should be unpaid or paid, whether care contributes to dependence or independence of caregivers and care receivers, and the rights of care receivers and caregivers. Daly and Lewis (2000, 285) maintain that care should be considered as a form of labor, taking place within a "normative framework of obligation and responsibility," with emotional and financial costs. They identify "certain tendencies around care in particular welfare states" (2000, 289), but do not present a typology of welfare states based on the caring dimension of government policy. One tendency is to collectivize care by providing tax-funded care programs (e.g., paid parental leave, subsidized public child care). Another tendency is to privatize care, encouraging family members to take on care responsibilities without compensation or supporting and regulating care given by volunteers. Regardless of whether care is collectivized or privatized, so far women have been much more involved in giving care than men (Daly and Lewis, 2000).

**Table 7.1. Parental-Leave Entitlements in the European Union**

| | Entitlement (Effective Date) | Leave Length | Father Incentive | Payment | Flexibility | Limits |
|---|---|---|---|---|---|---|
| Austria[a] | Family (1997) | 18 months for parents to share until child is 2 | Additional 6 months if father takes 6 months' leave | Paid at flat daily level of $15 | Part-time leave can be taken | Can be transferred once between parents |
| Belgium | Individual (nontransferable) (1998) | 3 months for each parent until child is 4 | Family loses 3 months if father doesn't take it | Paid at flat monthly rate of $435 | Part-time leave can be taken | |
| Denmark | Family "parental leave" | 14 weeks for parents to share until child is 1 | Father gets extra two weeks | Paid weekly at $327 | Both can be taken part-time | |
| | Individual "child care leave" (1998) | 26 weeks for each parent until child is 8 | Family loses 26 weeks if father doesn't take it | Paid weekly at $208 | | Employer can postpone |
| Finland | Family "parental leave" (1985) Family "care leave" (1998) | 26 weeks for parents to share 10 weeks for parents to share until child is 3 | Averages 66% of pay | Paid at flat monthly rate of $217 | Both can be taken only full-time | Each leave can only be split into two blocks |
| France | Family (1994) | 36 months for parents to share until child is 3 | | Unpaid for first child; flat monthly rate of $397 if 2 or more children | May be taken part-time; parents can take simultaneously | |

| Country | Type (year) | Duration | | Payment | Flexibility | Other |
|---|---|---|---|---|---|---|
| Germany | Family (2001) | 2 years for parents to share until child is 3, plus 1 year until child is 8 | | Means-tested maximum monthly rate of $413 | May be taken part-time & at same time by both parents | Can be transferred between parents only three times |
| Greece | Individual (nontransferable) (1999) | 3 months for each parent until child is 3.5 | | Unpaid | | Denied in businesses with fewer than 50 workers |
| Ireland | Individual (nontransferable) (1998) | 14 weeks for each parent until child is 5 | | Unpaid | Can be taken part-time with consent of employer | Employer can postpone for "business reasons" |
| Italy | Family (2000) | 10 months for parents to share until child is 8 | Family has 1 additional month if father takes at least 3 months' leave | 30% of earnings | | |
| Luxembourg | Individual (1999) | 6 months for each parent until child is 5 | | Paid at flat rate of $1336 per month tax free | May be taken part-time | Must take in one block; employer can postpone if work would be disrupted |
| Netherlands | Individual (nontransferable) (1997) | 6 months for each parent of reduced hours | | Unpaid | No full-time leave | Employer can postpone if replacement worker cannot be found |

continued

**Table 7.1.** *(continued)*

| | Entitlement (Effective Date) | Leave Length | Father Incentive | Payment | Flexibility | Limits |
|---|---|---|---|---|---|---|
| Portugal | Individual (nontransferable) (1999) | 3 months for each parent until child is 6 | | Unpaid | Can be taken part-time or full-time | No job protection after one year |
| Spain | Individual (1999) | Each parent can take up to 36 months until child is 4 | | Parental leave is unpaid | | |
| | Maternity leave (can transfer to father) | Mother can transfer 10 weeks to father | | Maternity leave paid at 100% of earnings | | |
| Sweden | Family (2002) | 450 days for parents to share until child is 8 | 60 days reserved for each parent, lost if not taken | 360 days paid at 80% wages; 90 days at flat daily rate of $6 | May be taken part-time | |
| U.K. | Individual (2000) | 13 weeks for each parent until child is 5 | | Unpaid | | |

Sources: New Ways to Work, 1998; Moss and Deven, 1999; and research reports provided to the European Industrial Observatory (Cristovam, 1999; Feyereisen, 1999, 2001; Gaechter, 1999; Hall, 1999; Jorgersen, 2001; Schulten, 2000; Trentini, 1999).
[a]Schattovits (2001) reports parental leave is being replaced by a child-care benefit January 2002, whereby parents have $488 a month to spend on child care or to pay themselves to stay home until child is four.

A gender-neutral ideology of care has recently been developed by the American Economic Policy Institute (Appelbaum et al., 2002). If "valued care" were the norm, employees would have control over their work schedules so they could take paid time off to care for family members and taking leave would not jeopardize job security, career opportunities, or long-term income. Valued care implies that care is a joint private–public responsibility, offering families financial compensation for parental leave and access to affordable, high-quality dependent-care services provided by individuals in well-paying jobs.

Government policy can influence the development of policy and ideology in support of valued care. The fifteen nations in the European Union can be divided into groups based on the extent to which government parental-leave policy is likely to contribute to the ideal of valued care. Specifically, we can look at the extent to which government policy (1) gives parents the opportunity to be released from work to care for young children, (2) gives parents reasonable financial compensation while on leave along with job security and benefits, and (3) strongly encourages fathers to take parental leave, to help redistribute care responsibilities between women and men. This approach seems congruent with the work of Lewis (1997, 170), who recommends evaluating "gender regimes" in terms of the "two main questions for feminists concerning the provision of unpaid work: how to value it and how to share it more equally between men and women."

Several welfare-state typologies have previously been developed, examining variations in government support for economic equality, family support, and patriarchy (e.g., Anttonen and Sipila, 1996; Duncan, 1996; Fraser, 1994; Gauthier, 1996; Korpi, 2000; Mosesdottir, 2000; Pfau-Effinger, 1999b; Rantalaiho, 1997). None appear to be a good fit for classifying European parental-leave policies, because none focuses squarely on the caring dimension of welfare states. Consequently, a new typology of care policy models is piloted here.

### Privatized (Non-interventionist) Care Model

Four EU states fall in this category—Greece, Italy, Portugal, and Spain. Governments do not recognize or value "harmonization of paid work and care" (Knijn and Kremer, 1997, 348). Care of young children is a privatized, not collectivized, responsibility, done primarily by mothers or extended family members. Social expectations call for men to be strongly oriented toward the labor market as family breadwinners, while women (even if they work for pay) are held responsible for home and caregiving (Duncan, 2000). Cultural ideology strongly differentiates between private and public spheres; women and men are regarded as competent in only one sphere (family or work), complementing one another (Pfau-Effinger, 1999a).

Parental leave has been available only since 1998 in response to EU directives (see table 7.1). Greece and Portugal offer the EU minimum—three months for each parent, unpaid. Greece allows employers of small businesses with fewer than fifty employees to deny leave to workers. Spain offers both parents a longer period of unpaid parental leave with a return to their jobs guaranteed (up to three years). But this leave is still unpaid, signifying that this time is not socially valued. Italy offers parents some financial compensation for taking leave (30 percent of earnings), but this amount is too low to be regarded as adequate compensation for giving care. There is some incentive for Italian fathers to take leave since families receive an extra month if the father takes a minimum of three months' leave (see table 7.1). In general, governments following this care model do not promote or encourage fathers' use of leave benefits. Virtually no fathers take leave under normal circumstances, partly because the leave is unpaid (Spain), not guaranteed in all types of companies (Greece), or not an individual nontransferable right of fathers (Italy) (den Dulk, 1999; Fagnani, 1999; Valiente, 2000). Policy makers assume that an employee who takes leave has an employed spouse or other means of financial support. Since women on average earn less than men, this creates a financial incentive for leaves to be taken by mothers, reinforcing the idea that women are secondary earners (Rubery et al., 1998).

Three of these states (Greece, Italy, and Spain) have the lowest women's overall labor-force participation in the European Union (40 percent) and women's unemployment rates double that of men's (CEC, 2001b; Eurostat, 2001). These three nations also score the lowest of all EU states on a composite index measuring women's equal employment opportunities (based on gender differences in employment rates, women's share of higher job positions, the gender wage gap, the proportion of women with low incomes, and the male-female gap in unpaid time spent caring for children and other persons—Plantenga and Hansen, 2001). Women in Portugal have a much higher employment rate (60 percent), apparently because of a fast developing economy. In all four countries, the state has limited involvement in encouraging mothers' labor-force participation and does not accept responsibility for providing supports for working parents. The proportion of children under age three attending places in publicly funded services for children is very low (under 12 percent) (CEC, 2001b; Plantenga and Hansen, 2001). Working mothers rely on extended family members for child-care assistance (van Doorne-Huiskes et al., 1999a).

## Family-Centered Care Model

Societies in this group include Austria, Belgium, France, Germany, and Luxembourg. Policy making is shaped by a traditional religious heritage and/or a strong public commitment to the preservation of the traditional family (Rantalaiho, 1997). Women's contribution to the economy is much more recognized than it is in the first group of states, but men are still held more responsible for family income provision (Lewis, 1992). According to Plantenga and Hansen (2001), these societies fall in the middle of EU states in terms of ensuring women's equal employment opportunities. Women's labor-force participation rates are also in the middle range for the EU—between 50 percent and 59 percent (CEC, 2001b).

Governments are actively concerned about family support, with an interest in raising birthrates back up above replacement levels. To promote fertility, the model for work-family reconciliation emphasizes making it possible for women to combine multiple roles, by sequencing care work and paid employment or by working part-time (van Doorne-Huiskes et al., 1999a). Public support for caregiving is in line with the sequencing concept. It is assumed that mothers will stay home with children during their first few years of life. Parental leaves could be classified as "child-rearing leaves" (see table 7.1). Four of the five nations (Austria, Belgium, France, and Germany) offer long job-protected leaves, around three years in length per child. Leave takers receive a low flat rate of compensation ($400 to $500 per month), far from the equivalent of lost earnings, representing caregiving's low status. Luxembourg offers a shorter leave (six months), with high compensation for parents on leave ($1336 per month), made possible by the Fund for Employment, whose coffers have been swelled by a new "social contribution" tax on fuel oils (Feyereisen, 1999).

Theoretically, leaves can be taken by either parent, but restrictions often apply (e.g., in Austria it can be transferred between parents only once; in Luxembourg, the employer can deny leave if it will seriously disrupt work). Each state provides fathers with some incentive to take leave, either by offering more days of leave to families where the father takes some of the leave (an extra sixty days in Austria, and ninety days in Belgium), or by allowing fathers to take leave part-time simultaneously with mothers (as happens in France, Germany, and Luxembourg). In reality, few fathers take leave, with estimates ranging about 2 percent. This low take-up rate is partly blamed on the low level of financial compensation offered parents in most of these states (Devan and Nuelant, 1999; European Commission, 1998; Pettinger, 1999; Rost, 1999; Thenner, 1999). Almost one-third of Luxembourg men in the Eurobarometer study reported themselves willing to take parental leave (European Commission, 1998). But legislation is written so that a parent must take leave in a single block of time, which is often hard for male workers to arrange.

France is often mentioned as a European country that stands out in terms of support for mothers who wish to work outside the home and for children's well-being (e.g., Fagnani, 1996). French mothers have had a high rate of participation in the labor market, in comparison to mothers in the nearby countries. Following World War II, France set up an impressive network of child-care facilities focusing on children ages three and over, to encourage women to enter the labor market and reduce the labor shortage. France had parental-leave in place before the EU directive, unlike other countries in this category. By 2001, however, the French parental-leave system seems to fit the family-centered care model. In her study of the French parental-leave system, Fagnani (1999, 80) discovered that mothers' dominance of long parental leave contributed to "a return to the traditional gender division of domestic work within the family . . . , mothers' occupational downgrading upon return to work . . . , [and] gender discrimination in the labor force by reinforcing employers' prejudices toward female workers."

## Market-Oriented Care Model

Ireland, Netherlands, and the United Kingdom are EU nations that have held strong traditional values concerning the role of women and men and the importance of mothers devoting themselves to home and children (Duncan, 2000; Lewis, 1992; Pfau-Effinger, 1999a). None of these societies had parental leave before the European Union imposed its directive, and none offered paid leave by 2001. Parental-leave policies remain limited in scope— in Ireland and the U.K. parents have the right to only fourteen weeks, while Netherlands allows only part-time leave. In Ireland and Netherlands, employers can postpone leave if employee absence is judged to seriously disrupt work. None of these societies have established any special incentives for fathers to take unpaid parental leave and take-up by fathers is reported to be low (CEC, 2001b).

Lack of support for working parents is well established; less than 8 percent of children under age three are in publicly funded day-care places (Plantenga and Hansen, 2001). On an index evaluating women's "equal opportunities," Netherland's and Ireland's scores are close to those of the most traditional societies (Greece, Italy, and Spain). The U.K. does somewhat better, falling in the middle third of EU nations (Plantenga and Hansen, 2001).

What is distinctive about this group of nations is that their governments have recently come to value women's labor-market contributions, and instead of developing government policies to financially support working parents, each nation is intent on convincing *employers* to become more actively involved in helping employees combine work and family roles.

Ireland historically has been a society with a strong emphasis on separate roles for men and women. Until recently, it also had mass unemployment and a poor economy. As recently as 1997, only 43 percent of women with children under age sixteen were employed (Moss and Deven, 1999). The Irish economy is now rapidly moving toward full employment and suddenly there is concern about how to recruit and retain women workers and help employees manage work-life balance. Instead of developing state policies, the Irish government is looking for the private sector to become more involved in work-life reconciliation. In 1999, a program for "prosperity and fairness" was agreed upon, calling for companies to develop family-friendly policies such as flextime, job sharing, telecommuting, and parental leave. So far, family-friendly companies are mostly in the public sector or employ large workforces. Many medium- and small-sized firms still regard work-family benefits as unnecessary costs on business (Dobbins, 2000). To supply day care, the Irish government is looking toward nonprofits and private-sector institutions in local communities.

The Dutch government intends to reconcile work and family life by convincing mothers and fathers to work part-time. Netherlands already has the highest proportion of women working part-time in the EU (60 percent in 2000), as well as the highest portion of men (15 percent) (Grunnell, 2000b). In 2000, the lower house of Parliament passed the Part-Time Employment Act, giving employees the right to request a reduction in work hours (Dobbins, 2000). The Dutch government has been less interested than most EU societies in providing state-organized child care (van Doorne-Huiskes et al., 1999a) and only 3 percent of children used any formal child-care arrangements (public or private) in 2001 (CEC, 2001b). A government proposal would make it a legal requirement for employers to subsidize one-third of employees' child-care costs. Half of all collective bargaining agreements presently provide for this (Grunnell, 2000a).

Until the early 1990s, only 40 percent of mothers of preschool-age children in the U.K. were in the paid labor force (Korpi, 2000). This has now changed, with maternal employment rates steadily increasing to the same level of many other European societies (presently 61 percent) (Moss and Deven, 1999). According to Lewis (1999, 45), "the emphasis on individual responsibility for family, a neo-liberal approach to employment policy and reliance on market forces have . . . led to an emphasis on the business case for work-family arrangements." Businesses are concerned about the costs of recruitment and retention of workers, and this concern has been used to coax companies to become more family friendly. One-third of children under age three are cared for in private and public child-care settings, and the government has set a goal of 1.6 million more private and public places by 2004 (CEC, 2001b). This has led so far to only modest development of on-site child care, paid maternity leave, and paid paternity leave. In 2001, the government announced its intention to develop legislation to require employers to consider parents' requests for flexible working arrangements (Hall, 2001).

Although the U.K. was the last EU member state to incorporate the EU parental-leave directive in national legislation in 1999, some groups (e.g., Trades Union Congress) would like to catch up for lost time by pushing for paid leave, while others (e.g., Fathers Direct) would like to see special incentives for fathers to take parental leave. According to a 1996 European

Commission survey, one-third of British men expressed willingness to take parental leave three years before the entitlement existed.

Portugal may soon fit the model of market-oriented care. Women's high labor-force participation has been facilitated by plentiful informal caregivers, involving domestic servants, grandparents, and other family members (Plantenga and Hansen, 2001). As these informal resources decline, the government has declared: "a better balance between work and family life is a right and a duty for both male and female workers, as well as a responsibility that society must undertake" (Cristovam, 2001). But the focus is on drawing *employers'* attention to work-family issues and fathers' right to take parental leave (CEC, 2001b; Cristovam, 1999).

## Valued-Care Model

Three EU nations in Scandinavia (Denmark, Finland, and Sweden) have come a long way toward the goal of integrating women in the labor market, and in providing comprehensive support systems for working parents (Wilkinson, 1997). There are, however, important differences between Scandinavian countries in attitudes toward men's participation in unpaid work and political support for gender equality (Ellingsaeter, 1998; Rantalaiho, 1997). Accordingly, Denmark and Finland will be discussed first, as nations on a trajectory of slow progress toward developing parental leave as an instrument to promote the valued-care norm. Since Sweden has set a somewhat more radical course, it will be discussed in detail below.

Denmark's rating for equal employment opportunities for women ties for first with Sweden's (Plantenga and Hansen, 2001). Public funding of child care is also well developed, with 48 percent of children ages 0–3 attending publicly funded services (Plantenga and Hansen, 2001). A high proportion of mothers of children ages 0–15 are in the labor force (80 percent) (Moss and Deven, 1999). Working parents have access to two types of subsidized leaves—parental leave (a family entitlement of fourteen weeks, sixteen weeks if father takes at least two weeks) and child-care leave (an individual entitlement of twenty-six weeks). Both leaves are paid, at about 60 percent of usual wages (Rostgaard, Christoffersen, and Weise, 1999). After fifteen years of discussion, in 1999 Denmark gave fathers an incentive to take parental leave by offering families two extra weeks if couples shared leave. This has so far had little effect on fathers' taking parental leave. Only 4 percent of Danish fathers take leave. Parents' reasons for fathers' little use of leave include economic costs (since compensation is low and fathers usually earn more income than mothers) and employer resistance. Fathers feel they would risk dismissal if they asked to take leave and sense it would be difficult for employers to find suitable substitute workers. Mothers' lower attachment to paid work and lower status in the labor market, as well as fathers' lack of interest in taking leave, have also been named as contributing factors for mothers' dominance of leave (Rostgaard et al., 1999). According to a 1996 survey, only 28 percent of Danish fathers would consider using parental leave (European Commission, 1998). In 2001, the government announced plans to launch a new educational campaign to convince men to take advantage of parental leave (CEC, 2001b).

Finland's gender arrangement has been described as more traditional than Denmark's. According to Bradley (1998, 211), "the weaker strain of social democracy and strength of the agrarian center in Finland has resulted in a more traditional system of regulation of family relationships and is reflected in an antipathy to social engineering." Women have been acknowledged as having the right to combine work and family, but there is little interest in a redistribution of responsibility between men and women for child care (Rantalaiho, 1997). In comparison to Denmark, women's labor-force participation rate is lower (72 percent), mothers' employment rate is lower (70 percent), and a smaller proportion of children under age three are in publicly funded child care (22 percent) (CEC, 2001b; Moss and Deven, 1999). The compensation level for Finnish parental leave is higher than for all other EU nations except Sweden (averaging 66 percent of earnings), and a relatively high proportion of men (over 40 percent) in a 1996 survey said they would consider taking leave to look after a child (European Commission, 1998). But by 1997, only 4 percent of Finnish fathers took leave, possibly because it is available only on a full-time basis, which can be difficult for men to arrange (Salmi and Lammi-Taskula, 1999). Salmi and Lammi-Taskula (1999, 105) state: "In present conditions, the net effect of parental and care leaves is to maintain the traditional gender pattern in families and in the labour market."

## SWEDEN

In societies modeling valued care, work-family reconciliation would be reflected in an equal sharing by men and women of paid and unpaid work. The social importance of giving care would be officially recognized; and the division between private and public spheres of social life would be blurred. Both women and men would feel entitled to government support for reconciling work and family roles (Lewis and Smithson, 2001). Because men's involvement in child care would be promoted, parental leave would be adequately paid, it would not be transferable to mothers, and there would be financial incentives for fathers to take leave. Maximum flexibility in taking leave would be offered (e.g., it could be taken part-time, parents can take turns several times, taken anytime until the child reached school-age), to encourage parents to negotiate a shared division of labor for child care. High-quality publicly subsidized day care would complement the parental-leave program. Only one of the EU countries aspires to develop this radical model of gender relations, although it has not yet succeeded in reaching it—Sweden.

As early as 1968, Sweden set itself apart from other nations when policy makers began advocating a new gender model, where "Equality means that women and men have the same rights, obligations and opportunities to have a job which gives them economic independence, to care for home and children, and to participate in political, union and other activities in society" (Statistiska Centralbyrån, 1990, my translation). Sweden is recognized as being the first society where the "dual-breadwinner" family is the norm (Bergqvist and Jungar, 2000; Mosesdottir, 2000). Alongside Sweden's goal of gender equality is the value placed on children as a precious resource. According to Leira (1994, 102), the Swedish government has "made considerable efforts to bridge the gap between the demands of the market for labour and the demands of children for care."

To support gender equality and children's well-being, several significant policy developments have occurred. The first was the establishment in the early 1970s of an individualized taxation system, so that women's income earning doesn't drive household tax rates higher. (Within the EU, Denmark, Finland, and the U.K. also have this type of tax system—Plantenga and Hansen, 2001.) The second significant development was equal employment opportunity legislation in the 1980s, which supported women's entry into nontraditional occupations and equal pay for comparable work. (EU nations are increasingly involved in equal employment opportunity efforts because of EU directives, many developed by Swedes.) The third significant development was the increase in supply of heavily subsidized and high-quality public child care throughout the 1980s and 1990s, to the point that waiting lists have disappeared and the vast majority of all children ages 1–6 (74 percent) are in publicly subsidized child care (Statistiska Centralbyrån, 2001). (The supply of day care for children under twelve months is small; policy makers want parents home during a child's first year.) In 2001, day-care fees were lowered to facilitate women's employment and to encourage couples to have larger families. The maximum *monthly* fee is $137 for the first child, $92 for the second child, and $46 for a third (Swedish Institute, 1999).

The fourth important development in Sweden's campaign to bring about gender equality concerns parental leave. Sweden was the first country to mandate paid parental leave for both mothers and fathers, in 1974. In contrast to other EU countries, the Swedish parental-leave program at the outset encouraged fathers' use of benefits through educational campaigns directed at prenatal centers, social-insurance offices, and workplaces. Fathers were encouraged to take leave to develop relationships with young children and the nurturing aspects of their personalities (Haas, 1992).

Swedish feminists expressed concern that joining the EU would negatively impact Sweden's efforts to bring about equality between women and men in the public spheres of employment and politics and in the private sphere of the home (Bergqvist and Jungar, 2000). By 1995, Sweden had progressed further than other EU states in developing policies and programs designed to increase women's opportunities in the labor market and politics and men's opportunities to participate actively in child care. This was reflected in the high labor-force-participation rate of Swedish mothers (75 percent of mothers with preschool-aged children) and greater involvement of men in family life (Haas and Hwang, 1999; Moss and Deven, 1999). The 1994 referendum on joining the EU barely passed, since 52 percent of Swedish women voted against (Bergqvist and Jungar, 2000). To ensure recognition for Sweden's perspective on gender equality, many Swedish female politicians became EU parliament members, to help Sweden "serve as a role model" (Bergqvist and Jungar, 2000, 161).

Currently, Sweden has the most generous and flexible parental-leave program in the EU. Parents are entitled to share 450 days of paid leave at the birth or adoption of a child. Twelve months of this leave are paid at 80 percent of salary up to a certain income level (now $45,000), with the remaining three months paid at a low flat rate ($6 a day). Leave can be taken out in quarter, half- or full-time days, anytime before the child completes the first year of school. There are no restrictions in how often parents can take turns taking leave. Employers' tax contributions pay for parental leave and all employers, regardless of company size or situation, must abide by the parental-leave mandate. Fathers are more likely than mothers to take advantage of the flexibility offered in the program, by taking leave on a part-time basis (Haas, 1992).

When it originated in 1974, the parental-leave benefit system in Sweden was based on a "family" entitlement—the leave basically came with the child and parents were expected to negotiate who would take leave, how, and when. According to Bergqvist and Jungar (2000, 167–68), "a completely individual and gender-neutral design would have given parents an independent right to a certain number of months of paid leave, which would not be transferable to the other party." Swedish policy makers are slowly moving toward the nontransferable model, despite popular opinion supporting parents' right to decide between themselves how the leave will be distributed. To encourage more fathers to take leave, in 1995 two months of the leave became nontransferable individual rights—one month for the father and one month for the mother. Nontransferable leave was extended to two months for each parent in 2002.

In a 1996 survey, 70 percent of Swedish men said they were willing to consider taking leave to stay home to care for a child. This was by far the highest proportion of any national group (European Commission, 1998). For children born in 1995, 70 percent of fathers actually have taken parental leave, for an average of two months (Näringsdepartementet, 1999). The shift to nontransferable (individual) rights to parental leave appears responsible for this increase.

Employers are now under more pressure to facilitate fathers' leave taking, since families lose a significant amount of benefits if fathers do not take advantage of months set aside for fathers. Fathers' routine absence from work while on parental leave has required companies to rethink the way work is organized, often to the benefit of the company (e.g., in encouraging cross training, telecommuting, and helping parents keep in touch with work while on leave). As more fathers take leave, some companies have begun to recognize the "business case" for fathers taking leave. Fathers who return from taking leave are now often viewed as having greater potential as workers, especially at the management level, because they are better able to handle stress, balance multiple responsibilities, develop interpersonal skills, and meet important new challenges. The benefits of fathers' leave taking have become so widely recognized by employers that many (e.g., Ericsson) now offer fathers additional economic incentives to take leave (Berg, 1999).

Parental leave has not resulted in the complete sharing of child care among mothers and fathers in Sweden. A large (but declining) proportion of mothers of small children work part-time in order to combine work and family roles. While the majority of fathers take leave, fathers still take much less leave overall, only 12 percent of all parental-leave days taken (Näringsdepartementet, 1999). Swedish parents attribute fathers' taking less leave to two main factors—economics and interpersonal politics. Parents report that men take less leave because of the gender gap in income; families suffer less economically if mothers rather than fathers stay home. In reality, fathers at all income levels take leave and the average family loses little income if the father takes leave because of tax breaks and the long-term economic benefits of mothers' continuous participation in the labor force (Riksförsäkringsverket, 2000). Another important reason for unequal sharing of leave offered by parents is that mothers want to monopolize the leave. As long as Swedish women are concentrated in a narrow range of occupations and experience difficulties breaking through the glass ceilings of work organizations, it seems likely that some women will find staying home with pay a more attractive alternative than going to work. Couples are more likely to share leave when mothers have high education and high-status positions in the labor force (Haas, 1992). Swedish policy makers continue to develop programs and strengthen legislation to guarantee women equal employment opportunity, although progress is slow. On the other hand, as long as women take parental leave more often and longer than men, gender-specific work conditions in the labor market will likely persist and gender differences within the labor market will be reinforced (Widerberg, 1991). Recently a Swedish parliamentary committee found that there was a need to strengthen employment protection for employees taking parental leave (Berg, 2001).

## LESSONS FOR THE UNITED STATES?

In some respects, the development of parental-leave policy in the United States is strikingly similar to the development of EU parental-leave policy. In other respects, the European Union has made more progress toward improving parents' opportunities to combine work and family roles and consequently toward equal employment opportunity for women. What could the U.S. learn from the EU?

### Development of Parental Leave in the United States

Like EU nations, the United States has experienced a rapid increase in employment rates for women, and parental-leave policy has evolved accordingly. By 1985, 54 percent of American married women were employed for pay, up from 32 percent in 1960 (Wisensale, 2001). While it became illegal for U.S. companies to discriminate against pregnant women in 1978, many mothers simply were forced to choose between keeping their jobs and staying home with their newborn children. By 1990, the U.S. Department of Labor estimated that 37 percent of female employees in firms with 100 or more employees could take unpaid maternity leave, averaging 20 weeks; 18 percent of male employees could take paternity leave, averaging 19 weeks, while paid parental-leave was extremely rare (Wiatrowski, 1990). Five states allowed women to collect "temporary disability insurance" at the time of childbirth, but these policies did not allow fathers to stay home with children (Wisensale, 2001). Four additional states passed parental-family-leave legislation by 1993, granting unpaid job-secured leave, varying from six weeks to twenty-four weeks in length (Wisensale, 2001).

In 1985, Representative Pat Schroeder introduced the Parental and Disability Leave Act in the U.S. House of Representatives, offering parents up to eighteen weeks of unpaid leave with guaranteed return to their jobs. Over the next eight years, the proposal was amended to attract more cosponsors, passing Congress for the first time in 1990. President George Bush vetoed the measure in 1990 and again in 1992. President Bill Clinton signed the Family and Medical Leave Act of 1993, the first piece of legislation he signed after taking office, granting twelve weeks of coverage to workers in businesses with fifty or more employees. Before 1993, the United States and South Africa were the only industrialized nations with no national maternity leave policy (Hyde, 1995). The U.S. law is broader than EU parental-leave policy; it can be used to care for a newborn or newly adopted child, or it can be used to care for a child, spouse, or parent with a serious health condition, or to treat one's own serious health condition.

U.S. development of family-leave policy coincided in time with development of EU parental-leave policy, since the first proposal to mandate parental-leave in the European Community was introduced around the same time, in 1983. In both settings, governments recognized that women's contributions to the economy would be limited unless a way could be found to provide women with job guarantees before and just after childbearing (Malin, 1994). In both settings, a concern for gender equity was considered to be an important backdrop for the law. The EU has an official policy of gender equity, granting equal opportunities for women and equal treatment under the law. The United States does not have a similarly broad declaration of gender equality (which the unsuccessful Equal Rights Amendment to the Constitution aimed to provide). Nevertheless, during the development of the U.S. proposal, it was clear that special treatment for women (i.e., giving maternity leave only to women) would be politically unacceptable (Wisensale, 2001). Feminists lobbied the U.S. government to recognize caring work as a legitimate break from paid employment, by providing job-protected, gender-neutral parental-leave (Hyde, 1995; Wexler, 1997).

In both the U.S. and EU, leave proposals did not get very far after they were first introduced because they were seen as too radical. Bernstein (1997) maintains that passage of national parental-leave policy in the U.S. depended heavily on the efforts of political "insiders," who were successful at framing family leave as a family issue rather than as a women's or feminist issue. In the European Union, passage of parental-leave minimum standards also depended on advocates' ability to frame the issue in a nonthreatening (nonfeminist) way, by emphasizing the development of fair and equitable labor standards across national lines, a prerequisite for economic cooperation involving EU members.

The U.S. and EU policies are similar in many ways, although the U.S. law allows leave for different reasons. Both offer about three months of leave during any twelve-month period, which is unpaid, and available only to full-time employees and workers with one year of tenure. As in the European Union, U.S. leave takers are guaranteed health benefits while on leave (if they had these benefits before taking leave) and the right to return to their former job or its equivalent. Neither policy offers fathers special incentives to participate in early child care. While both U.S. and EU laws are similarly modest in scope, especially in comparison to parental-leave policy in Sweden, passage of each law has been regarded as a very important symbolic first step in the development of government support for working parents (Vogel, 1995).

Some American states (seventeen in all) have family-leave policies that offer parents more benefits than the FMLA. For example, thirteen states extend coverage to employees in some small businesses, while six states provide for longer leave (fourteen weeks to two years). Debate on family leave in individual states before 1993 helped to keep the national debate on parental-leave going in the U.S., much as the development of parental-leave policies in individual EU member states helped to drive the development of EU policy on parental leave (Wisensale, 2001). The majority of states within the European Union, however, have gone much further than any American state in developing their own parental-leave programs in a direction more likely to bring about equal employment opportunity for women and increased sharing of child care by fathers, by offering wage compensation, flexibility in administration, and/or special incentives for fathers to take leave. Sweden has become the leader in developing parental-leave policy in the European Union. So far, no particular American state has pioneered reform of parental leave, although several have attempted to follow the 2000 recommendations of the U.S. Office of Personnel Management to develop at least six weeks of paid parental leave in connection with the birth or adoption of a child.

Passage of the FMLA appears to have encouraged some U.S. businesses to voluntarily offer leave to employees. In 2000, about one-fourth of businesses covered by the FMLA offered leave longer than twelve weeks and 29 percent covered employees who had worked for the same employer for less than twelve months. By 2000, one-third of companies not covered by the FMLA had voluntarily chosen to offer at least twelve weeks of family leave to employees (Waldfogel, 2001). By 2001, the U.S. Office of Personnel Management estimated that paid maternity leave was available for about half of the female workforce, mainly through disability insurance coverage provided by employers, while 7 percent of new fathers had access to some type of paid parental leave (U.S. Office of Personnel Management, 2001). A national survey of employees in 2000 found that two-thirds of leaves were compensated by employers, but the average length of leave taken was short, at ten days (Waldfogel, 2001).

### Limits of the U.S. Law

Despite its important symbolic value as a policy supporting working parents, the U.S. law appears to be severely limited in its ability to substantially enhance parents' opportunities to take care of young children, in comparison to EU policies. It appears that only about 60 percent of all U.S. employees are eligible to take leave under the Family and Medical Leave Act, primarily because only full-time, year-round workers are eligible and because of the high proportion of U.S. workers who are employed by small businesses that are exempt from coverage (Marks, 1997). The EU minimum standard allows governments to limit parental-leave coverage for business reasons, but covers the vast majority of employees. In contrast, the FMLA goes further to allow small businesses with fewer than fifty employees to be exempt from the law altogether and to allow employers to exclude "key employees" (those earning in the top 10 percent) from coverage. The exclusion of key employees is significant, because this sends the messages to employees that the company culture does not support high-level managers taking parental leave, which would have a dampening effect on others' decisions regarding leave taking. Small businesses were very active in opposing passage of the FMLA, which helps to explain why they are excluded from the mandate. Since 1993, several attempts have been made to extend the FMLA to workers in businesses with twenty-five to forty-nine employees, to lengthen the leave to twenty-four weeks, and to provide financial benefits to workers who use it, for example, through using surplus state unemployment compensation funds (Wisensale, 2001). These efforts have failed, mainly because of business opposition.

The proportion of employees in "covered establishments" (businesses with fifty or more employees) who knew whether or not they were covered by the act actually dropped from 60 percent in 1995 to 49 percent in 2000 (Waldfogel, 2001). National studies of employees conducted in 1995 and 2000 revealed that the same low proportion of workers (16 percent) had taken family or medical leave using this law in the eighteen months prior to the survey (Waldfogel, 2001). Men's usage of leave provisions for all reasons was about half that of women's, increasing slightly from 12.7 percent in 1995 to 13.5 percent in 2000. Women's usage actually declined slightly from 20.0 percent in 1995 to 19.8 percent in 2000. The average number of leave days taken (for all covered reasons) in the past eighteen months was low, only ten days, remaining the same in the two surveys (1995 and 2000) (Waldfogel, 2001). In 2000, most employees working for firms covered by the law felt they would have been able to take leave if they needed to do so (Waldfogel, 2001). However, those who experience difficulties tended to disproportionately be members of minority groups and/or occupants of low-status jobs (Gerstel and McGonagle, 1999; Wexler, 1997).

In 2000, there was an increase in employees' likelihood of using the leave to care for a newborn or newly adopted child, rising to 18 percent from 14 percent in 1995. But this was associated with an even bigger drop in the proportion of employees who took leave to care for their own health (61 percent to 47 percent) (Waldfogel, 2001). (This raises the question, are parents compromising their own health in order to save leave for child-care purposes?) Altogether, these usage rates suggest that less than 3 percent of employees use the FMLA within an eighteen-month period to care for a newborn or newly adopted child. This is the same percentage of employees estimated to use employer-provided leave before the Family and Medical Leave Act was in place (Selmi, 2000).

Employers' interest in the FMLA appears to be low. There was no increase in the proportion of covered employers who had heard of the law from 1995 to 2000, remaining at only 59 percent (seven years after the leave was established). A declining percentage of covered businesses reported themselves to be in compliance with the law (from 88 percent in 1995 to 84 percent in 2000). There was also evidence that businesses were beginning to feel more constrained by the legislation than earlier (perhaps as an economic recession loomed). The proportion of businesses that thought it was somewhat easy or very easy to comply with the law declined from 85 percent in 1995 to 64 percent in 2000, even though the proportion of workers taking leave and the amount of leave taken had not changed (Waldfogel, 2001).

Using the framework previously presented that examines the caring dimension of modern societies, the United States appears to fit best into the privatized (noninterventionist) care model, where care of young children is still regarded as a private responsibility of mothers, rather than a responsibility that society and fathers share. The family-centered care model does not fit the U.S. well, since the government remains unconcerned about the impact of work-family conflict on childbearing and since American women tend to return to the labor market within one year after childbirth, not sequencing child rearing and paid employment. It appears likely that the U.S. will join some EU nations in aiming for the market-oriented care model, where corporations are encouraged to offer leave policies that benefit working parents. One proposal along these lines, made by Selmi (2000, p. 712), advocates "creating a government contract set-aside program aimed at rewarding employers who succeed in encouraging their employees to take family leave."

Could the U.S. develop a paid-leave policy based on the valued-care model, now best represented by Sweden? American political values would need to dramatically shift. Higher social importance would need to be allocated to giving and receiving care, blurring lines between work and family responsibilities, improving women's employment opportunities, and facilitating men's equal sharing of early child care.


## CONCLUSION

The availability of paid and flexible parental leave for both mothers and fathers could set the stage for questioning gendered patterns of giving care and rendering less visible the dividing line between the public sphere of employment and the private sphere of family life (Liebert, 2001). According to Selmi (2000, 755), "one way of moving toward the goal of greater gender equality would be to find ways to encourage, or induce, men to take leave around the birth of their children and ultimately to spend more time caring for their children."

In 1999, the fifteen countries belonging to the European Union began to take seriously the needs of working parents to reconcile employment and family responsibilities by agreeing to a minimum standard for parental leave. Despite EU directives, parental-leave policies are still poorly developed in many member states, reflecting a low valuation of care and little interest in fathers' more active sharing of early child care. Parental-leave policy tends to reinforce the traditional division of labor whereby men are families' primary breadwinners and women are children's primary caregivers. While the European Union has set an ambitious course to bring about equal employment opportunity for women in its member states, it has been less interested in contesting the division of unpaid work in the home and in promoting fathers' care of young children (Rees, 1998; Schunter-Kleemann, 1999). According to Drew (2000, 108), "across the EU fifteen member states women's integration into the labor market is still hampered by their caring obligations and individual family circumstances." Further progress toward gender equality depends on EU challenging the traditional division of domestic labor prevalent in member states, which it could do by reforming parental leave. Selmi (2000, 760) states: "given the experience of other countries and states that offer more generous leave . . . drastic measures will be necessary in order to prompt men actually to take family leave. . . . [M]oving to a system of paid leave, by itself, would likely be a necessary but ultimately insufficient condition to achieve that goal."

There is little sign that the European Union will adopt drastic measures in the near future. While the Fourth Action Programme for gender equality for 1996–2000 stated: "The promotion of equality . . . is a question of promoting long-lasting changes in parental roles, family structures, institutional practices, the organization of work and time" (Sperling and Bretherton, 1999, 69–70), the newly adopted Fifth Action Programme for gender equality for 2001–2005 makes no mention of reforming parental leave or encouraging a redistribution of care responsibilities between women and men, although it does call for removing tax disincentives to women's employment, reducing the gender wage gap, and improving women's share of decision-making positions in government and companies (Broughton, 2000). The EU and member states publish annual updates on "gender perspectives," to report statistics and initiatives related to women's position in the labor force, but these updates do not discuss men's share of family work or take-up of parental leave (Carley, 2001).

Activist women within the EU continue to lobby for change. In its latest position statement, the European Women's Lobby (2001) calls for substantial reform in EU parent-leave policy:

> Parental leave regulations must ensure a generous and paid parental leave, reaching much further than the existing Community directive. A more lengthy and paid parental leave will stimulate parents to choose both labour market activity and a certain period of care for children. To promote a shared responsibility between women and men concerning the care for children, parental-leave regulations should include both maternity leave and paternity leave, reserving a mandatory part of the parental leave for each parent.

Parental leave must be widely used by men to reduce the stigma parenthood now has on women's employment opportunities. The experiences of EU countries and especially Sweden suggest some conditions under which parental leave would likely help to bring about a shared-work/valued-care model of gender relations, where men and women are both expected to be actively involved in breadwinning and child care (Appelbaum et al., 2002). To move toward a model of valued care, parental-leave policy needs to develop in the following ways, in the United States and in the European Union:

- Parental leave should be a universal, individual, nontransferable right of all working mothers and fathers, as a strong incentive for fathers to take leave and to force all employers (regardless of firm size) to accommodate men who want to take leave.
- Parental leave must offer job protection, full benefits, and substantial pay, both as a symbol of its social value and to facilitate both parents' taking it, regardless of income level.
- Parental leave should be flexibly administered, so that parents can take turns taking leave and so leaves can be taken part-time as well as full-time.
- To facilitate fathers' taking of parental-leave, their rights must be actively promoted by substantial educational campaigns through prenatal-care and social-benefits delivery systems as well as work organizations.
- To reduce the negative impact of taking leave on parents' employment opportunities, the "business case" for supporting parents' rights to paid leave should be studied, articulated, and disseminated (see Rapoport et al., 2002).
- To promote solidarity between working parents and the rest of society, and to ensure the public's support for parental-leave, the benefits to society of parental-leave programs should be studied and widely publicized. Parental leave shows promise of increasing fertility rates above replacement level, reducing troublesome low worker-retiree ratios. Children who are well cared for early in life and who have strong relationships with both parents are less likely to suffer problems that society will need to endure and pay for down the road. Parental-leave programs can reduce unemployment and encourage workplace cross training. They can also set a precedent for reduction in work hours for all workers, helping individuals at all stages of the life cycle manage work-life balance.

## NOTE

1. This is a revised version of a paper presented at the 2000 meetings of the National Council on Family Relations, Minneapolis, Minnesota. The author wishes to thank Carrie Farris and Elizabeth Henderson for helpful research assistance and Heidi Gottfried for helpful comments. June 2, 2002.

## REFERENCES

Aaronson, S. 1995. "Providing Paid Family Leave." Testimony to the Commission of Family and Medical Leave, San Francisco, June 26.

Anttonen, A., and Sipila, J. 1996. "European Social Care Services." *Journal of European Social Policy* 6: 87–100.

Appelbaum, E., Bailey, T., Berg, P., and Kalleberg, A. 2002. *Shared Work/Valued Care.* Washington, D.C.: Economic Policy Institute. Accessed February 23, 2002 at www.epinet.org.

Berg, A. 1999. "Ericsson Provides Extra Parental Leave Pay." *European Industrial Relations Observatory On-line.* Updated September 28, 1999. Accessed December 21, 2001 at www.eiro.eurfound.ie.

———. 2001. "Parental Leave Legislation to Be Reviewed." *European Industrial Relations Observatory On-line.* Updated November 7, 2001. Accessed December 31, 2001 at www.eiro.eurfound.ie.

Bergqvist, C., and Jungar, A. 2000. "Adaptation of Diffusion of the Swedish Gender Model?" Pp. 160–79 in *Gendered Policies in Europe,* ed. L. Hantrais. London: St. Martin's Press.

Bernstein, A. 1997. "Inside or Outside? The Politics of Family and Medical Leave." *Policy Studies Journal* 25: 87–99.

Bradley, D. 1998. "Equality and Patriarchy." *International Journal of the Sociology of Law* 26: 197–216.

Broughton, A. 2000. "European Commission Proposal for the 5th Gender Equality Action Programme." *European Industrial Relations Observatory On-line.* Updated July 28, 2000. Accessed January 1, 2002 at www.eiro.eurofound.ie.

Carley, M. 2001. "Gender Perspectives—Annual Update 2000." *European Industrial Relations Observatory On-line.* Updated March 28, 2001. Accessed December 31, 2001 at www.eiro.eurofound.ie.

Commission of the European Communities. 1999. *Equal Opportunities for Women and Men in the European Union—1999.* Annual report from the Commission, Brussels, March 5.

———. 2001a. *Joint Employment Report 2001.* Updated September 17, 2001. Accessed December 28, 2001 at http://europa.eu.int.

———. 2001b. *Assessment of the Implementation of the 2001 Employment Guidelines.* Brussels: Commission of the European Communities. Updated November 16, 2001. Accessed January 3, 2002 at http://europa.eu.int.

Cristovam, M. 1999. "Conference Highlights Equal Opportunities." *European Industrial Relations Observatory On-line.* Updated August 28, 1999. Accessed December 31, 2001 at www.eiro.eurofound.ie.

———. 2001. "New Initiatives on Gender Equality." *European Industrial Relations Observatory On-line.* Updated July 28, 2001. Accessed December 31, 2001 at www.eiro.eurofound.ie.

Daly, M., and Lewis, J. 2000. "The Concept of Social Care and the Analysis of Contemporary Welfare States." *British Journal of Sociology* 51: 281–98.

Deitch, C., and Huffman, M. 2001. "Family-Responsive Benefits and the Two-Tiered Labor Market." Pp. 103–30 in *Working Families,* ed. R. Hertz and N. Marshall. Berkeley: University of California Press.

den Dulk, L. 1999. "Employers and Parental Leave." Pp. 227–47 in *Parental Leave,* ed. P. Moss and F. Deven. The Hague/Brussels: NIDI/CBGS Publications.

———. 2001. "Work-Family Arrangement in Organizations." Pp. 59–84 in *Women's Employment in a Comparative Perspective,* ed. T. Van der Lippe and L. Van Dijk. New York: Aldine de Gruyter.

Deven, F., and Nuelant, T. 1999. "Parental Leave and Career Breaks in Belgium." Pp. 141–54 in *Parental Leave,* ed. P. Moss and F. Deven. The Hague/Brussels: NIKI/CBGS Publications.

Dobbins, T. 2000. "Managing the Work-Life Balance." *European Industrial Relations Observatory On-line.* Updated September 28, 2000. Accessed December 31, 2001 at www.eiro.eurofound.ie.

Drew, E. 2000. "Reconciling Divisions of Labour." In *Gender, Economy and Culture in the European Union,* ed. S. Duncan and B. Pfau-Effinger. New York: Routledge.

Duncan, S. 1996. "The Diverse Worlds of European Patriarchy." Pp. 74–110 in *Women of the European Union,* ed. M. Garcia-Ramon and J. Monk. London: Routledge.

———. 2000. "Introduction." In *Gender, Economy and Culture in the European Union,* ed. S. Duncan and B. Pfau-Effinger. New York: Routledge.

Ellingsaeter, A. 1998. "Dual Breadwinner Societies." *Acta Sociologica* 41: 59–73.

European Commission. 1998. *Equal Opportunities for Women and Men in Europe?* Vienna, Austria: European Commission.

European Women's Lobby. 2001. "Contribution by the EWL for the Informal Ministerial Meeting on Gender Equality and Social Security." Updated January 15, 2001. Accessed December 30, 2001 at www.womenlobby.org.

Eurostat. 2001. "Community Labour Force Survey 2000." Updated June 21, 2001. Accessed December 30, 2001 at europa.eu.int/comm./eurostat.

Fagnani, J. 1996. "Family Policies and Working Mothers." Pp. 126–37 in *Women of the European Union,* ed. M. Garcia-Ramon and J. Monk. London: Routledge.

———. 1999. "Parental Leave in France." Pp. 69–84 in *Parental Leave,* ed. P. Moss & F. Deven. The Hague/Brussels: NIKI/CBGS Publications.

Feyereisen, M. 1999. "Parental Leave Introduced as National Action Plan is Implemented." *European Industrial Relations Observatory On-line.* Updated March 28, 1999. Accessed January 1, 2002 at www.eiro.eurofound.ie.

———. 2001. "Parental Leave Being Taken up, but Not By Men." *European Industrial Relations Observatory On-line.* Updated November 7, 2001. Accessed January 1, 2002 at www.eiro.eurofound.ie.

Fraser, N. 1994. "After the Family Wage." *Political Theory* 22: 591–618.

Fullerton, H. 1999. "Labor Force Participation." *Monthly Labor Review* 122: 3–13.

Gaechter, A. 1999. "Parental Leave Reform Slow to Come." *European Industrial Relations Observatory On-line.* Updated May 28, 1999. Accessed December 31, 2001 at www.eiro.eurofound.ie.

Gauthier, A. 1996. *The State and the Family.* Oxford, U.K.: Clarendon Press.

Gerstel, N., and McGonagle, K. 1999. "Job Leaves and the Limits of the Family and Medical Leave Act." *Work and Occupations* 26: 510–34.

Grunnell, M. 2000a. "Government Proposes to Make Employers Meet One-Third of Child Care Costs." *European Industrial Relations Observatory On-line.* Updated June 28, 2000. Accessed December 31, 2001 at www.eiro.eurofound.ie.

———. 2000b. "Part-Time Employment Act Seeks to Promote Combining Work and Care." *European Industrial Relations Observatory On-line.* Updated February 28, 2000. Accessed December 31, 2001 at www.eiro.eurofound.ie.

Haas, L. 1992. *Equal Parenthood and Social Policy.* Albany: State University of New York Press.

Haas, L., and Hwang, P. 1999. "Parental Leave in Sweden." Pp. 45–68 in *Parental Leave,* ed. P. Moss and F. Deven. The Hague/Brussels: NIKI/CBGS Publications.

Hall, M. 1998. "The EU Parental Leave Agreement and Directive." *European Industrial Relations Observatory On-Line*. Updated January 28, 1998. Accessed December 31, 2001 at www.eiro.eurofound.ie.

——. 1999. "UK Introduces New Rights to Time Off Work for Family and Domestic Reasons." *European Industrial Relations Observatory On-line*. Updated December 28, 1999. Accessed December 31, 2001 at www.eiro.eurofound.ie.

——. 2001. "Parents to Have Legal Right to Request Flexible Working." *European Industrial Relations Observatory On-line*. Updated November 12, 2001. Accessed January 1, 2002 at www.eiro/eurofound.ie.

Hantrais, L. 2000. "From Equal Pay to Reconciliation of Employment and Family Life." Pp. 1–26 in *Gendered Policies in Europe*, ed. L. Hantrais. London: St. Martin's Press.

Hofferth, S. 1996. "Effects of Public and Private Policies on Working after Childbirth." *Work and Occupations* 23: 378–404.

Hyde, J. 1995. "Women and Maternity Leave." *Psychology of Women Quarterly* 19: 299–313.

Joesch, J. 1997. "Paid Leave and the Timing of Women's Employment before and after Birth." *Journal of Marriage and the Family* 59: 1008–21.

Jorgensen, C. 2001. "Fathers Fail To Use Parental Leave Entitlement." *European Industrial Observatory On-line*. Updated February 28, 2001, asscessed January 1, 2002. Available at www.eiro.eurofound.ie.

Kamerman, S. 2000. "Parental Leave Policies." *Social Policy Report* 14: 3–25.

Knijn, T., and Kremer, M. 1997. "Gender and the Caring Dimension of Welfare States." *Social Politics* 4: 329–67.

Korpi, W. 2000. "Faces of Inequality." *Social Politics* 7: 127–91.

Leira, A. 1994. "Combining Work and Family." Pp. 86–106 in *Economic Restructuring and Social Exclusion*, ed. P. Brown and R. Crompton. London: University College Press.

——. 1998. "Caring as a Social Right." *Social Politics* 5: 362–78.

Lewis, J. 1992. "Gender and the Development of Welfare Regimes." *Journal of European Social Policy* 2: 159–73.

——. 1997. "Gender and Welfare Regimes." *Social Politics* 4: 160–77.

Lewis, S. 1999. "Work-Family Arrangements in the UK." Pp. 41–57 in *Work-Family Arrangements in Europe*, ed. L. van Dulk, A. van Doorne-Huiskes, and J. Schippers. Amsterdam: Thela-Thesis.

Lewis, S., and Smithson, J. 2001. "Sense of Entitlement to Support for the Reconciliation of Employment and Family Life." *Human Relations* 54: 1455–81.

Liebert, U. 2001. "Degendering Care and Engendering Freedom." Pp. 262–88 in *Women and Welfare*, ed. N. Hirschmann and U. Liebert. New Brunswick, N.J.: Rutgers University Press.

Lohkamp-Himmighofen, M., and Dienel, C. 2000. "Reconciliation Policies from a Comparative Perspective." Pp. 49–67 in *Gendered Policies in Europe*, ed. L. Hantrais. London: St. Martin's Press.

Malin, M. 1994. "Fathers and Parental Leave." *Texas Law Review* 72: 1047–95.

Marks, M. 1997. "Party Politics and Family Policy." *Journal of Family Issues* 18: 55–71.

Mosesdottir, L. 2000. "Pathways towards the Dual Breadwinner Model." *International Review of Sociology* 10: 189–205.

Moss, P., and Deven, F., eds. 1999. *Parental Leave*. The Hague/Brussels: NIKI/CBGS Publications.

Murray, J., Neij, J., and Lindblom, M. 2000. *Ett jämställt Europa* [A Gender Equitable Europe]. Stockholm: Utrikesdepartementet [Department of Foreign Affairs].

Näringsdepartementet (Department of Trade and Industry). 1999. *Jämställdhetspolitiken inför 2000-Talet* [Equality Policy for the 21st Century]. Regeringens Skrivelse [The National Government's Report Series], no. 24.

New Ways to Work. 1998. "Parental Leave in European Union Countries." Updated November 1998, accessed January 1, 2002. Available at www.europa.eu.int.

Ostner, I. 2000. "From Equal Pay to Equal Employability." Pp. 25–42 in *Gender Policies in the European Union*, ed. M. Rossilli. New York: Peter Lang.

Pettinger, R. 1999. "Parental Leave in Germany." Pp. 123–40 in *Parental Leave*, ed. P. Moss and F. Deven. The Hague/Brussels: NIKI/CBGS Publications.

Pfau-Effinger, B. 1999a. "Change of Family Policies in the Socio-Cultural Context of European Societies." *Comparative Social Research* 18: 135–59.

———. 1999b. "Welfare Regimes and the Gender Division of Labour." Pp. 69–96 in *Working Europe*, ed. J. Christiansen, P. Koistinen, and A. Kovalainen. Brookfield, Mass.: Ashgate.

Plantenga, J., and Hansen, J. 2001. "Assessing Equal Opportunities in the European Union." Pp. 273–204 in *Women, Gender and Work*, ed. M. Loutfi. Geneva: International Labour Office.

Rantalaiho, L. 1997. "Contextualising Gender." Pp. 16–32 in *Gendered Practices in Working Life*, ed. L. Rantalaiho and T. Heiskanen. New York: St. Martin's Press.

Rapoport, R., Bailyn, L., Fletcher, J., and Pruitt, B. 2002. *Beyond Work-Family Balance—Advancing Gender Equity and Workplace Performance*. San Francisco: Jossey-Bass.

Rees, T. 1998. *Mainstreaming Equality in the European Union*. London: Routledge.

Riksförsäkringsverket [National Social Insurance Office]. 2000. Båda blir bäst— Attityden till delad föräldraledighet [Both Are Best—Attitudes toward Shared Parental Leave]. Stockholm: Riksförsäkringsverket #1.

Rossilli, M. 2000. "Introduction: The European Union's Gender Policies." Pp. 1–23 in *Gender Policies in the European Union*, ed. M. Rossilli. New York: Peter Lang.

Rost, H. 1999. "Fathers and Parental Leave in Germany." Pp. 249–66 in *Parental Leave*, ed. P. Moss and F. Deven. The Hague/Brussels: NIKI/CBGS Publications.

Rostgaard, T., Christoffersen, M., and Weise, H. 1999. "Parental Leave in Denmark." Pp. 25–44 in *Parental Leave*, ed. P. Moss and F. Deven. The Hague/Brussels: NIKI/CBGS Publications.

Rubery, J., Smith, M., Fagan, C., and Grimshaw, D. 1998. *Women and European Employment*. London: Routledge.

Salmi, M., and Lammi-Taskula, J. 1999. "Parental Leave in Finland." Pp. 85–122 in *Parental Leave*, ed. P. Moss and F. Deven. The Hague/Brussels: NIKI/CBGS Publications.

Schattovits, H. 2001. "New Approaches to Public Part-Time Care Schemes for Pre-school Children." *Family Observer*, no. 3 (European Observatory on Family Matters): 12–13.

Schmidt, M. 1997. "Parental Leave." *The International Journal of Comparative Labour Law and Industrial Relations* 13: 113–26.

Schulten, T. 2000. "New Provisions on Parental Leave and Childcare Payments." *European Industrial Relations Observatory On-line*. Updated July 28, 2000. Accessed January 1, 2002 at www.eiro.eurofound.ie.

Schunter-Kleemann, S. 1995. "Welfare States and Family Policies in the EU Countries." *NORA —The Nordic Journal of Women's Studies*: 74–85.

——. 1999. "Gender Mainstream as a Strategy for Modernizing Gender Relations?" In *Family Issues between Gender and Generations*, ed. S. Trnka. Vienna, Austria: European Observatory on Family Matters.

Selmi, M. 2000. "Family Leave and the Gender Wage Gap." *North Carolina Law Review* 78: 707–82.

Sperling, L., and Bretherton, C. 1999. "Women and Policy." Pp. 69–110 in *Women and Public Policy*, ed. S. Baker and A. van Doorne-Huiskes. Brookfield, Mass.: Aldershot.

Statistiska Centralbyrån [Central Bureau of Statistics]. 1990. *På tal om kvinnor och män* [Talking about women and men]. Stockholm: Statistiska Centralbyrån.

——. 2001. *Jämställdhet* [Gender Equality]. Updated March 8, 2001. Accessed April 1, 2001 at www.scb.se.

Stratigaki, M. 2000. "The European Union and the Equal Opportunities Process." Pp. 27–48 in *Gendered Policies in Europe*, ed. L. Hantrais. London: St. Martin's Press.

Swedish Institute. 1999. "Child Care." *Fact Sheets on Sweden*. October. Stockholm: The Swedish Institute.

Thenner, M. 1999. "Parental Leave in Austria." Pp. 155–72 in *Parental Leave*, ed. P. Moss and F. Deven. The Hague/Brussels: NIKI/CBGS Publications.

Trentini, M. 1999. "New Law Adopted on Parental Leave." *European Industrial Relations Observatory On-line*. Updated October 28, 1999. Accessed January 1, 2002 at www.eiro.eurofound.ie.

United Nations. 2000. *Women and Men in Europe and North America*. New York: UN.

U.S. Office of Personnel Management. 2001. "Paid Parental Leave." Updated November 6, 2001. Accessed December 31, 2001 at www.opm.gov.

Valiente, C. 2000. "Reconciliation Policies in Spain." Pp. 143–59 in *Gendered Policies in Europe*, ed. L. Hantrais. London: St. Martin's Press.

van Doorne-Huiskes, A., den Dulk, L., and Schippers, J. 1999a. "Work-Family Arrangements in the Context of Welfare States." Pp. 1–19 in *Work-Family Arrangements in Europe*, ed. L. den Dulk, A. van Doorne-Huiskes, and J. Schippers. Amsterdam: Thela-Thesis.

——. 1999b. "Epilogue." Pp. 166–73 in *Work-Family Arrangements in Europe*, ed. L. den Dulk, A. van Doorne-Huiskes, and J. Schippers. Amsterdam: Thela-Thesis.

Vogel, L. 1995. "Considering Difference: The Case of the U.S. Family and Medical Leave Act of 1993." *Social Politics* 2: 111–20.

Waldfogel, J. 1997. "Working Mothers Then and Now." Pp. 92–123 in *Gender and Family Issues in the Workplace*, ed. F. Blau and R. Ehrenberg. New York: Russell Sage.

——. 2001. "Family and Medical Leave." *Monthly Labor Review* 124: 17–23.

Wexler, S. 1997. "Work/Family Policy Stratification." *Qualitative Sociology* 20: 311–22.

Wiatrowski, W. 1990. *Employee Benefits Focus on Family Concerns in 1989*. U.S. Department of Labor, Bureau of Labor Statistics, Report 90-160.

Widerberg, K. 1991. "Reforms for Women—on Male Terms." *International Journal of the Sociology of Law* 19: 27–44.

Wilkinson, H. 1997. *Time Out—The Costs and Benefits of Paid Parental Leave*. London: Demos.

Wisensale, S. 2001. *Family Leave Policy: The Political Economy of Work and Family in America*. Armonk, N.Y.: M. E. Sharpe.

# 8

## Solving a Problem or Tinkering at the Margins? Work, Family, and Caregiving

*Steven K. Wisensale*

Within the last few years the United States moved into the number one position in at least two categories: the percentage of women working full-time, and the hours worked per employee per year. With respect to the former category, the United States has the highest percentage (60 percent) of women working full-time in the world. Concerning the second category, in 2000 the United States became the number one country in the world in hours worked per employee each year (1,996), surpassing Japan, Canada, and Britain. On average, Americans work 350 hours more per year (almost nine full workweeks) than Europeans. Such trends have placed a major burden on the family and affected policies in the workplace. It is precisely this very busy (and sometimes blurred) intersection of work and family that former Labor Secretary Robert Reich (2001) has identified as *the* major social-policy flash point for the next twenty-five years.

This chapter is divided into five major parts. First, the historical roots of the conflict between work and family will be identified and discussed. In part 2 the response of the private sector will be explored and the recent emergence of the "family-friendly corporation" will be analyzed. Part 3 will be devoted to the response of the public sector with a special focus placed on the Family and Medical Leave Act. Part 4 will examine family care and its costs both in terms of providing such care and failing to do so. And finally, part 5 will concentrate on recent policy initiatives to address the issue of work and family. Specific weaknesses will be identified and policy recommendations will be put forth.

## PART I—HISTORICAL ROOTS OF
## THE WORK AND FAMILY CONFLICT

Both historians and sociologists alike have argued that the social roles often assumed by both men and women are determined to a great extent by society's production process (Clark, 1998). Early communal societies were sometimes matriarchal in structure but often vanished when technological advances produced surpluses beyond what was needed and men created the concept of private property to grant them rights to the surplus. "With the emergence of private property came male dominance over women, motivated partly by men's desire to control women's reproductive activities to assure transmission of property to legitimate heirs" (Clark, 1998, 224). Thus, during the developmental stages of capitalism, the sexual division of labor and the nuclear family were both fortified because they contributed to the growth of capital. Such a model performed two important tasks that had a positive effect on employers.

First, because women performed unpaid tasks such as childrearing and housekeeping, women provided a benefit to employers who, in essence, could hire two workers for the price of one. That is, because women performed unpaid tasks (Marx referred to it as "unproductive" and omitted such work by women from his value theory), the employer only had to pay the male worker a minimum amount. If, on the other hand, the male employee paid a person other than his wife to perform such tasks, he (the employee) would be likely to demand higher wages from his employer to cover such costs.

Second, women also benefited employers indirectly by providing emotional support and a happy home life that enabled their husbands to relax and prepare for another day of demanding factory work. For the men of the working class, both the home and the family served as peaceful enclaves far away from long hours of alienating work (Zaretsky, 1976). Put another way by Mutari, Boushey, and Fraher (1997), "the consumption of labor power takes place in the private sphere of the capitalist workplace, along with the 'productive' consumption of equipment and materials. The restoration of labor power takes place in the private household, facilitated by the consumption of home-produced use values and wage goods" (96).

But Marx pointed out in *Capital* that the role of women was not always confined to the private home. Capitalism infiltrated the family and did harm without remorse if given the opportunity. "Compulsory work for the capitalist usurped the place, not only of children's play, but also of free labor at home within moderate limits for the support of the family. . . . We see how capital, for the purposes of its self-expansion, has usurped the labor necessary in the home of the family" (Marx, 1967, 394–95). However, when viewed from a much broader perspective, women, and married women in particular, were excluded from the workplace.

Heidi Hartmann (1981), for example, concludes that patriarchy and capitalism have had a long-term partnership. "Men reserved union protection for men and argued for protective labor laws for women and children. Men sought to keep high wage jobs for themselves and to raise male wages generally . . . through a 'family wage' system that gradually came to be the norm for stable working class families" (Hartmann, 1981, 21). The family-wage system, which assumed that the male breadwinner could and should support his family on his paycheck, became the dominant "domestic ideal."

Such reasoning coincides with the work of Engels who argued a century and a half ago that the division of labor within the household between men and women not only benefited the capitalists, but also produced the gender inequities that became magnified by society as a whole. Under socialism, however, child care provided by the state would enable women to enter the workforce and male supremacy at home *and* at work would ultimately vanish. "The supremacy of the man in marriage is the simple consequence of his economic supremacy, and with the abolition of the latter will disappear of itself" (Engels, 1972, 145).

Although Engels's dream for a socialist society never came true in the United States, a combination of forces contributed to the increase of women entering the workforce and the gradual breakdown of the family-wage system and its replacement by the "living wage," a gender-neutral term to be sure. The massive shift from an agrarian to an industrial society, spurred on by World War II, brought many women into the labor force. The civil rights movement in the sixties, the rise of feminism in the seventies, and the decline of manual labor and the expansion of the service sector also contributed to the increase in women entering the job market.

Equally important, according to Rubin and Riney (1995), wives' labor-force participation expanded most rapidly from the early 1970s through the 1980s. "Rising prices combined with wage stagnation for male workers generated a period of transition for families. Many wives worked to implement desired lifestyles and to finance higher housing costs" (16). By the 1980s more women chose to attend college, postpone marriage, and have fewer children than their mothers. Simply put, by the 1980s better-educated women were entering the labor market and choosing to stay longer. This desire to remain attached to the job market, even after childbirth, eventually spawned a variety of advocacy groups that pressured government to provide state-sponsored child care and family-leave programs (Cohen and Katzenstein, 1998). These developments also challenged the private sector that eventually produced, in some cases, the emergence of what is commonly referred to as the "family-friendly corporation." An offshoot of traditional "welfare capitalism," this relatively new concept is the topic of discussion in the next section of this chapter.

## PART II—THE RESPONSE OF THE PRIVATE SECTOR

In 1993 Houston Oilers offensive tackle David Williams missed a football game against the New England Patriots when he decided to remain in Houston with his wife for the birth of their child. Despite endless pleas from his teammates and coaches, Williams stood by his decision because he was particularly concerned about his wife's health condition. "My family comes first," he stated. "That's the way I've always been, and that's the way I always will be, long after I'm finished being a football player" (Fried, 1998, 22). As a result of his actions, Williams was fined one week's salary ($111,111) and threatened with a suspension. Covered under the 1993 Family and Medical Leave Act, he challenged the Oilers' actions while his attorney threatened to file a grievance against the team if they did not withdraw their fine.

Similarly, several years later a Maryland state trooper requested from his superiors four to eight weeks' leave of absence to care for his wife who had just survived a complicated and life-threatening childbirth experience. When Mr. Knussman was denied his request and offered only two weeks instead, he sued the state of Maryland on the grounds of sex discrimination under the 1993 Family and Medical Leave Act. When Knussman won $375,000 in 1998, it marked the first time the FMLA had been employed in a sex discrimination case and it was also a first for a monetary award under that particular law.

Predictably, both cases received national media attention. But contrary to popular impressions that are often left with the public following such sensational news coverage, the challenge of balancing work and family is not new. On January 5, 1914, Henry Ford initiated what many consider the greatest experiment in welfare capitalism: the five-dollar daily wage and the eight-hour day (Foner, 1982). With it came a profit-sharing program and more leisure for workers, but not without strings attached. Also a part of Ford's initiative was the creation of a Sociology Department. Consisting of 100 employees hired by Ford himself, the department was responsible for overseeing the employees' spending patterns, their use of free time, and whether or not they were meeting their family obligations. Any smoking, drinking, and gambling habits were identified and monitored. Unacceptable behavior was not tolerated. The homes of all assembly line workers were visited regularly to "ensure conformity of workers' home life to company standards of order, cleanliness, and temperance" (Ferber and O'Farrell, 1991, 22).

Failure to comply with company rules could result in the withholding of an employee's wages until the deficiencies were corrected (Meyer, 1984). Furthermore, profit sharing, which represented a large portion of the five-dollar wage program, was not available to young men who had no dependents, family men living alone, or men who were divorcing (Foner, 1982). Therefore, to Henry Ford, efficiency "meant both the creation of a stable, disciplined labor force on the job and the reproduction of that work force through family life" (Foner, 1982, 10). While some described it as "benevolent paternalism," the Ford sociological program also helped to prevent, at least temporarily, the likelihood of his workers joining labor unions. That ended, however, with World War I, which brought with it inflation, the devaluation of the five-dollar day, the rise of unions, and the use of strikes more frequently.

Ford's Sociology Department was dismantled in 1921. However, the reasons for its creation and the functions it served should not be dismissed lightly. Despite being called a "traitor to his class" by his fellow industrialists and being denounced by the *Wall Street Journal* for committing an "economic crime," Ford still stands as an example of a corporate head who at least understood the importance of the relationship between work and family (Foner, 1982). While scholars continue to debate Ford's motives, be they humanitarian, paternalistic, or economic, the point to be emphasized here is that work and family constitute a very complex and dynamic relationship. At the very least, Henry Ford understood that.

A modern-day version of Henry Ford's welfare capitalism surfaced on February 3, 2000, when Ford Motor Company announced it was providing a free Hewlett-Packard computer and Internet access at $5 a month to all of its 350,000 global employees. One day later, Delta Airlines announced that its 72,000 employees worldwide would be given a computer and Internet access at $12 a month for 36 months. In official statements issued by both companies, a primary objective of both of these programs is to help employees become more comfortable with using technology in their daily lives and, therefore, more inclined to transfer their new and improved skills to the workplace. Critics, on the other hand, may wonder whether or not the primary reason for such actions is to encourage workers to take more work home, thus invading and disrupting the personal and family lives of the workers.

To complicate matters further, while Henry Ford's focus was on *men* during their hours of leisure, today's focus is on *both* men and women on the job and at home. For clearly, even conservative economist Gary Becker admits, the most dramatic development of the twentieth century has been the migration of women into the labor force. But contrary to what many may believe, the attachment of women to the workplace is not necessarily new. What is new, however, is the attachment of *mothers* to the workplace.

One of the most significant developments since the end of World War II has been the steady, if not dramatic, increase in the number of women entering the workforce. In 1940 nearly 86 percent of married women were full-time homemakers (Goldin, 1990). By 1996, however, 61 percent were in the paid labor force (Institute for Women's Policy Research, 1996). However, the most impressive period of growth for married female workers occurred between 1960 and 1996 when the rate practically doubled, climbing from 32 percent in 1960 to 61 percent in 1996.

Even more significant has been the rise in the number of mothers entering the labor market during this time period. For example, working mothers of children under six have increased from about 37 percent in 1975 to 63 percent in 1996 (Tauber, 1996). Today, mothers represent the fastest-growing sector of the entire U.S. workforce (Grundy and Firestein, 1997). Women with children have a higher employment rate than women overall (67.7 percent to 56.8 percent) and even women with children under age six are employed at a higher rate (59.7 percent) than women overall (56.8 percent) (Institute for Women's Policy Research, 1996). On one hand this is not surprising, as women's child-rearing years also tend to be the peak years of their earning potential. On the other hand, this phenomenon of working mothers is indeed remarkable in that many American women are working without the support system (child care and family leave) commonly available to women in other countries.

## THE EMERGENCE OF THE FAMILY-FRIENDLY CORPORATION: FACT OR FICTION?

According to researcher Lottie Bailyn (1996), the phrase "work and family" first appeared in the *Wall Street Journal* in 1980 with a report that the New England Merchants Bank had called upon a university professor to run lunchtime seminars for working parents called "Balancing Work and Family Life." The next mention of the phrase by the *Journal* was nine years later when it was reported that more corporate managers and their spouses were seeking counseling because of work and family conflicts. Two years later, in 1991, Sue Shellenbarger began her regular column in the *Journal* on "work and family" issues. However, when she elected to have children she found an unsympathetic employer that forced her to make too many compromises, prompting her to temporarily leave the newspaper to tend to her family's needs. Drawing attention to her own personal conflict with work and family when she returned to the paper, Shellenbarger's articles became so popular the *Journal* requested that her one short piece every three weeks be expanded to a weekly column. Other publications began to cover work and family issues as well.

Beyond receiving coverage in the mainstream press and serving as a focal point for academic researchers, the topic "work and family" also attracted the attention of practitioners who developed a specialty in the subject and served as consultants to businesses and labor unions. For example, in 1983 Work/Family Directions was created. The Boston-based consulting firm continues to provide a variety of work and family services to corporations nationwide. In 1988, a newsletter, *The National Report on Work and Family*, was begun and continues to be published twice a month. It covers legislation, litigation, and employee-employer issues. A year later Dana Friedman and Ellen Galinksy formed the Families and Work Institute, which has been extremely productive in preparing and disseminating reports on this topic. Other centers and institutes were created during this same time period and continue to specialize in work and family issues. These include Boston College's Center for Work and Family that was created by Brad Googins (1991), the Radcliffe Public Policy Institute at Harvard, and the Center for Working Families at the University of California at Berkeley. The Institute of Women's Policy Research and the National Partnership for Women and Families, both of which are based in Washington, D.C., also focus on work and family issues. Examples of for-profit organizations that specialize in work/life matters are Hewitt Associates and Great Place to Work Institute. Still lagging behind, however, on family and work issues are American business schools.

Meanwhile, throughout the 1980s in particular, there were stirrings in both the labor and management camps concerning the issue of work and family. In 1986, for example, the AFL-CIO Executive Council issued a resolution confirming its commitment to America's working families. "The family is the key to social stability, community progress, and national strength. To strengthen the family is at the heart of the labor movement's long struggle to raise wages and living standards" (AFL-CIO, 1992, 10). In 1988 the Coalition of Labor Union Women (CLUW), which was founded in 1974 for the sole purpose of moving work- and family-life issues to the top of collective-bargaining agendas, organized a national demonstration. "The American Family Celebration" brought together 40,000 union members and their families to lobby for the "American Family Bill of Rights," that included job security, health care, education, and equal opportunity (Grundy and Firestein, 1997). The CLUW also created a special guide, *Bargaining for Family Benefits* (Coalition of Labor Union Women, 1991), that was designed to help negotiate work and family benefits in union work sites.

For many years one of organized labor's pet causes was the "family wage," the concept that each worker should earn a sufficient amount of money to support a family. Although feminists in particular were suspicious of this goal of unions because it appeared to apply to men only and sent out echoes of the traditional homemaker/male-breadwinner household, this view changed over the years. Today the term "living wage," rather than "family wage," is used most frequently by labor unions and is directly linked to efforts to increase the minimum wage for workers. Living-wage regulations often require any employer receiving public funds to pay wages that provide a basic, decent standard of living for all workers and their families (Grundy and Firestein, 1997). Other pro-family causes taken up by labor include high-quality child care, family and medical leave, health-care insurance, free public education, and the 35-hour workweek, to name a few. By 1997, the Labor Project for Working Families compiled a database consisting of more than

450 examples of union contracts that include work and family benefits (U.S. Department of Labor, 1992, 10).

While labor unions and other organizations have been in the forefront on work and family issues, many businesses have been reluctant to join the march. Historically, the private sector has always shielded itself against unnecessary costs and excessive government regulations. To some, the work and family issue represents the latest version of the Trojan Horse that would allow big government to intervene in corporate personnel matters. However, this perception is not held by every component of the business community. A term that emerged fairly recently and is now quite common in both the research literature and the mainstream media is the "family-friendly corporation." It can be found in the works of Galinsky et al. (1993), Harker (1996), and Googins (1991), among others. It is also visible in such popular publications as *Business Week, Fortune,* and *Working Mother.* A number of organizations and publications have developed criteria for judging "family-friendliness" among corporations and have produced annual "best company" ratings.

Perhaps the most popular and well-known set of criteria that is used to identify family-friendly corporations is found in the annual survey conducted by *Working Mother* magazine. Using more than thirty different categories that include paid parental leave, adoption aid, lactation programs, flextime, child care, elder care, the percentage of female employees in management, the prevalence of resource and referral programs, and wage scales, the survey has been completed in each of the last fourteen years. In 1986, when the annual study began, only thirty companies were honored as "family friendly." By 1999 *Working Mother* was naming (not ranking) its top 100 companies for family-friendliness. While companies in 1986 were given special recognition for providing lactation programs, adoption assistance, and backup care, such policies are now common practices among the "top 100."

The methodology employed by *Working Mother* is multifaceted and is refined regularly. Eligible companies include private or public corporations of any size. Not included in the surveys are government agencies, divisions of larger companies, or firms in the work/life or child-care business. The comprehensive questionnaire that is used consists of queries about a company's culture, employee demographics, specific policies on work and family life, and women's advancement. Participating companies are also required to submit supporting documents, including written personnel policies, handbooks on employee benefit programs, results of employee surveys, and, if applicable, reports of special in-house task forces or advisory committees. The methodology has been designed and is monitored by some of the nation's leading experts on employer-employee relations. For example, Norman D. Costa is an industrial and research psychologist who is the president and founder of Expert Survey Systems (ESS) in Brewster, New York. Lynn Martin is the former secretary of labor and an expert on women's advancement in corporations. And John Pepper is a trailblazer on work and family issues and former CEO of Proctor & Gamble, a consistent "100 Best Company" (*Working Mother*, 1999).

The responses to the questionnaire are organized under six major categories, with each category consisting of eight to ten subcategories. First there is leave for new parents. This includes paid leave, lactation programs, paternity leave, and adoption aid. Second is the category of flexibility. Included is the availability of flextime, permission to work at home, and a compressed workweek (percentage of employees who put in 40-hour workweeks in under five days). The third category is child care, which includes on-site or near-site centers, a dependent-care fund, and a resource and referral service, among other benefits. Fourth is work/life. Is managers' pay tied to employee satisfaction? Are employee surveys and task forces used to gauge worker satisfaction or to generate new ideas related to work/life matters? And is there a resource and referral service for elder care? The fifth category concerns the advancement of women within the firm. Measures include the total percentage of female employees, the percentage of female senior executives, and the opportunity for women to advance internally. The sixth and final category is pay. Does the company offer average or high pay and is there at least one (preferably more than one) savings option, such as profit sharing, a stock-purchase plan, a company-paid pension, and so forth?

The responses to the questionnaire are compiled, analyzed, and verified. Companies are then written up and rated on a scale of one to five (five the highest, one the lowest) under each of the six categories described above. For those companies that applied but failed to make the top 100 list, *Working Mother* provides feedback that identifies specific areas of weakness that demand attention.

By 1999, survey results indicated that the most progressive companies on the list were dominating the work/life (*Working Mother* prefers this term rather than "work/family") movement in three distinct areas. First, they understand the importance of a flexible work schedule. Every company on the list of 100 offers flextime and 69 of them are training managers on how to implement alternative work schedules. Second, the "top 100" are willing to listen to their employees and even seek out their advice. No less than 95 percent have surveyed their employees on work/life issues and 88 percent have created work/life task forces. And third, the best companies communicate well with their employees. Rather than simply including obligatory family-friendly language in their employee manuals, good companies provide appropriate informational websites, high-tech bulletin boards, and chat rooms devoted to personnel issues.

Although *Working Mother* elects not to rank its top 100 companies, it does maintain a "top ten" list of corporations that have appeared on the magazine's list most frequently during the last fourteen years. Presented in

**Table 8.1. The 10 Companies That Appeared Most Frequently on *Working Mother*'s Annual List of "Top 100" Family-Friendly Companies (1986–1999)**

| Companies | Years on the List |
| --- | --- |
| IBM Corporation | 14 |
| Lincoln Financial | 13 |
| Bank of America | 11 |
| Prudential | 10 |
| Lotus Development | 9 |
| CIGNA Corporation | 8 |
| Fannie Mae | 6 |
| Ely Lilly and Company | 5 |
| First Tennessee | 5 |
| Deutsche Bank | 4 |

table 8.1 are the ten companies that were listed in the 1999 edition of the magazine.

IBM has made the top 100 list each of the 14 years the survey has been completed. Emphasizing its mission to become "the premier global employer for working mothers," the company remains unmatched for its policy on leave for childbirth, which gives parents (mothers *and* fathers) three years of job-guaranteed leave. If necessary, parents may be required to return to work after only one year. It maintains an $8.3 million dependent-care fund and supports 47 near-site centers, where IBM employees are given priority in placement, and 2,610 family child-care homes. In 1998 the firm initiated new programs in New York and North Carolina that screen nannies for those employees who prefer in-home care for their children. It also hosted its first-ever conference for Women in Technology, drawing 500 women from 29 different countries (*Working Mother*, 1999).

Besides IBM, other companies have moved forward on work/life issues as well. At Bristol-Meyers Squibb, employees can request that free baby formula be mailed to them in installments during their infant's first year. Chase Manhattan Bank provides backup child-care service as a safety net for working parents whose baby-sitter may fail to show up on time or calls in sick. Similarly, Eastman Kodak of Rochester, New York, offers backup elder care as well as free in-home assessments of elderly dependents. Rockwell added lactation rooms, Autodesk expanded eligibility requirements for its child-care subsidies, and American Express, in response to employee concerns, created a new flextime policy.

As was the case with Henry Ford's Sociology Department, the motivations of family-friendly companies are not solely altruistic. Bottom-line benefits are visible. For example, Prudential estimates that its resource and referral program, designed to assist workers in finding appropriate services to meet their personal and family needs, has saved the company $7 million in reduced absenteeism and turnover. CIGNA, one of the nation's largest insurance companies, contends that its lactation program has reduced new moms' absences by 27 percent. The Benjamin Group, a small company of only seventy-two employees headed by a female CEO, provides on-site child care and twenty-four-week maternity leave which helps reduce the employee turnover rate. According to company founder Sheri Benjamin, the money to fund its family-friendly policies is generated by avoiding the use of expensive headhunters to fill job vacancies—an average of $20,000 per position filled (*Working Mother*, 1999).

Other positive reports about the financial benefits generated by a family-friendly workplace also can be found in mainstream pro-corporate publications, including *Business Week* (1996). In a feature article entitled "Balancing Work and Family: Big Returns for Companies Willing to Give Family Strategies a Chance," readers learned about First Tennessee National Bank. Efforts to balance work and family resulted in an improved employee retention rate that converted to a $106 million profit gain over two years. Aetna Life and Casualty Company cut its resignations in half by extending its unpaid parental leave to six months, saving it $1 million a year in hiring and training expenses. Other companies, such as Dupont, Eddie Bauer, Marriott, Motorola, and Unum Life Insurance, offer comparable family-friendly benefits that produce similar results.

And, not to be overlooked when discussing cost issues, a daily visit to *Working Mother's* website reveals that the top 100 companies do as well or better on the stock market when compared to less family-friendly corporations. The performance of the top 100 companies are monitored and reported every day and graphs illustrating performances over the long term are provided as well. Each company's profile, based on the six major categories discussed above, is available at *Working Mother's* website at www.workingmother.com.

However, not everyone is in agreement with *Working Mother's* approach or the efforts by other organizations to classify certain companies "family friendly." In the April/May 2000 issue of *Ms. Magazine*, Betty Holcomb (2000) concludes that "family-friendly" policies are anchored to a strong class bias. That is, argues Holcomb, low-wage workers are half as likely as managers and professionals to have flextime, less likely to have on-site child care, more likely to lose a day's pay when they must stay home to care for a sick child, and three times less likely to get company-sponsored tax breaks to help pay for child care. Unfortunately, Holcomb contends, such practices take place within many of the companies that appear in the "top 100" of *Working Mother's* annual listing.

The Marriott Corporation, for example, which consistently makes the "best companies" lists, created a Department of Work and Family Life in 1989. Located at the company's headquarters in Bethesda, Maryland, the department oversees its 206,000 employees, half of whom are women. Among the company's offerings are a resource and referral program, a child-care discount program, a family-care spending account, and regularly scheduled work and family seminars. Each quarter it publishes *The Balance*, a quarterly newsletter on work and family issues. Marriott, however, also was the target of Betty Holcomb's criticism in her 2000 article in *Ms.* Holcomb contends that employees who work nontraditional shifts for Marriott do not have equal access to family-friendly services.

Similarly, Anita Garey also sees class bias in the manner in which *Working Mother* presents itself to the general public. Featured on the cover of almost every issue is a "mother-of-the-month." However, from 1993 through 1998 the mothers on the covers have held the following occupations: actor, astronaut, attorney, broadcast journalist, college administrator, concert violinist, corporate executive, engineer, entrepreneur, fitness expert, opera director, photographer, professor, and radio producer. "Waitresses, sales-clerks, secretaries, and nurses are still the invisible working mothers," writes Garey (Garey, 1999, 4).

But still, according to a study completed by the Families and Work Institute (Galinsky and Bond, 1998), the struggle to balance/integrate work and family life continues. This is despite the fact that at least 100 companies can be identified each year as family friendly and others seek to be included on the list. While surveys show that nearly 90 percent of companies permit employees to take time off to attend school events, and half let workers stay home with mildly ill children without using vacation or sick days, relatively few companies go beyond this stage. For example, a mere 9 percent of companies offer child care at or near the workplace, only 33 percent offer maternity leaves of more than 13 weeks, and less than a quarter (23 percent) of the nation's corporations offer elder-care resource and referral services. By the time the federal Family and Medical Leave Act was passed in 1993, less than 6 percent of the companies provided such a benefit for their employees.

## PART III—THE RESPONSE OF THE
## PUBLIC SECTOR: THE FAMILY AND MEDICAL LEAVE ACT

When President Clinton signed the FMLA in the White House Rose Garden on February 5, 1993, he may have temporarily muffled those critics who reminded policy makers that the United States was one of three industrialized nations without such a policy on the books. However, the law is quite limited in scope and does not apply to all family types, nor does it cover all caregiving scenarios. It only applies to about 6 percent of the nation's corporations and 60 percent of the workforce. Because it is unpaid, most single parents cannot afford to take time off from work even if given the opportunity. Also, although the law is touted as an example of intergenerational policy making, it does not cover grandchildren who care for grandparents, nor does it cover in-law care. That is, a wife may care for her elderly mother or father but she cannot provide such care to her mother-in-law or father-in-law and be covered under the act. And further, the FMLA is totally insensitive to same-sex partners. Despite the fact that more than a thousand communities, corporations, nonprofit organizations, and universities have adopted domestic-partnership policies that grant equal status to same-sex couples with respect to benefit coverage, the FMLA does not apply to this type of nontraditional family.

But nonetheless, the bill-signing ceremony in the Rose Garden marked the end of a long struggle to adopt a family-leave policy and represented the beginning of a new administration that promised change for America's families. "While the Republicans talk about family values, the Democrats show that they value families," proclaimed Clinton numerous times during the 1992 campaign. But beyond that, the adoption of the FMLA also symbolized the federal government's recognition that both the family and the American workplace have changed considerably over the years. Therefore, appropriate policies were needed to address these changes.

Because the FMLA is often discussed in terms of child care, little attention has been devoted to its potential for addressing major long-term care demands—particularly as the baby boom generation enters retirement and more families will be called upon to address the personal health-care needs of their elderly relatives. Between 2000 and 2001 more than twenty states introduced legislation to provide paid leave to family caregivers through the use of state unemployment insurance trust funds. However, almost all of the state initiatives limited the coverage to "baby care." In short, the original intergenerational structure of the law is slowly being dismantled by well-intentioned state legislators who are seeking to provide paid leave. This can be particularly problematic in light of future projections of the long-term care needs of an aging population.

That said, this chapter now addresses four research questions. First, who is using the FMLA and why? But more specifically, to what extent has the FMLA been used by family caregivers to provide assistance to the elderly? Second, if our past is our future, what do we know about the history of family caregiving and what role will adult children play in the future in addressing the needs of their elderly parents? Third, what are the costs of supporting or not supporting family care of the elderly and how should the FMLA be factored in to such cost assessments? And fourth, what are the major shortcomings in the existing FMLA with respect to care of the elderly and how should states address these weaknesses as they put forth initiatives to provide paid leave?

## Who is Using the FMLA and Why?

Since the FMLA was implemented on August 5, 1993, the Department of Labor has evaluated it twice—in 1995 and 2000. On April 30, 1996, the Commission on Leave issued its first report: *A Workable Balance: Report to Congress on Family and Medical Leave Policies.* The 314-page document concluded that the FMLA had a positive impact on employees overall and was not the burden on businesses that some had predicted. Ninety percent of companies covered by the law reported no negative impact. "For most employers, compliance is easy, the costs are non-existent or small and the effects are minimal," states the report. "Most periods of leave are short, most employees return to work, and reduced turnover seems to be a tangible effect" (Commission on Leave, 1996, xxii).

In more specific terms, between 1993 and 1995 nearly 15 million people used the Family and Medical Leave Act for either personal reasons or to care for a family member. The percentage of all leave takers and their reasons for taking leave are presented in table 8.2 in descending order as reported in the Department of Labor's 1995 and 2000 surveys.

It was also reported that 3.4 percent of employees who needed leave did not take it. And, of those, about 66 percent indicated that the reason they did not use the FMLA was because they could not afford it (Commission on Leave, 1996). Almost half of all employees who needed leave and did not take it because they could not afford it needed time off for their own health condition. The next most common reason workers needed leave was to care for an ill parent (20 percent). This issue of affordability would be raised again by President Clinton in May 1999 when he called for paid leave during a commencement address at Grambling State University in Louisiana.

The second major evaluation of the FMLA completed by the Department of Labor was published in 2000. In *Balancing the Needs of Families and Employers: Family and Medical Leave Surveys*, the Department of Labor reported that the total number of workers who took leave under the FMLA increased since the 1995 survey to 23.8 million, or 16.5 percent of all workers.

**Table 8.2.  Percentage of All Leave Takers Reporting Reasons**

|                                              | 1995 Survey | 2000 Survey |
|----------------------------------------------|-------------|-------------|
| Own health                                   | 60.0%       | 52.4%       |
| Care for newborn, adopted, or foster child   | 13.3%       | 18.5%       |
| Care for ill parent                          | 8.6%        | 13.0%       |
| Care for ill child                           | 7.6%        | 11.5%       |
| Maternity/disability                         | 3.8%        | 7.9%        |
| Care for ill spouse                          | 3.7%        | 6.4%        |
| Care for ill relative                        | 3.1%        | n/a         |

Note: Percentages do not add up to 100% because respondents could choose more than one category.

With respect to reasons for taking time off from work, there was a marked decrease in taking time off for one's own health from 60 percent to 52.4 percent. But, as illustrated in table 8.2, there were increases in all of the remaining categories. Most relevant to this discussion, however, was the conclusion that in 2000, as was the case in 1995, almost half of the workers who needed leave and did not take it needed leave for their own health condition. Equally significant, the second most common reason workers needed leave (but could not take it) was to care for an ill parent, rising from 20 percent in 1995 to 23 percent in 2000. And, as was the case in 1995, the major reason workers needed leave and did not take it was its cost. They simply could not afford to take time off (Department of Labor, 2000).

It was this concern over affordability that surfaced in the 1995 survey and was later confirmed by the 2000 study that prompted the Clinton administration to propose paid leave. When the president directed the Department of Labor to explore ways states may use surplus unemployment insurance (UI) funds to provide some sort of wage replacement for leave takers he limited his recommendation to the birth or care of a newborn or newly adopted child. Although the elderly in general and the AARP (American Association of Retired Persons) in particular played a crucial role in producing votes for the adoption of the FMLA in 1993, the states that followed Clinton's directive in 1999 apparently viewed the inclusion of elder care in their paid-leave initiatives as too expensive. In short, while a broad constituency produced votes at the federal level in 1993, a broad constituency at the state level would cost votes—or so it was believed. Consequently, the intergenerational structure of the FMLA was reduced to "Baby UI," despite the fact that demands of family care for the elderly have been steadily increasing.

## PART IV—THE ROLE OF THE FAMILY IN PROVIDING CARE TO YOUNG AND OLD

The number of persons aged sixty-five and older has increased substantially over the last thirty years (Manton and Stallard, 1994). Just in the ten-year period between 1980 and 1990, the number of persons sixty-five or older increased from 25.5 million (11.3 percent of the total U.S. population) to 31 million (12.5 percent of the total population). Equally significant is the trend within the trend. That is, during that same time period, the population of those over eighty-five grew considerably, from 2.2 million in 1980 (about 1 percent of the U.S. population) to 3.0 million in 1990 (about 1.2 percent of the U.S. population) [U.S. Bureau of the Census, 1996]). This growing age group in particular, with its multiple chronic illnesses, will place great demands on the health-care system in general and family caregivers in particular. And, in terms of future population projections, there appears to be no relief in sight.

According to existing census data, moderate projections indicate that the population of people sixty-five and over, who represented 12.5 percent of the total U.S. population in 1990, will increase to 13.3 percent by 2010 and reach as high as 20.4 percent by 2050. For the elderly minority the increase is even more rapid, rising from 13 percent of the elderly population in 1990 to 16 percent in 2000, to 22 percent in 2020, and to 33 percent by 2050 (U.S. Bureau of the Census, 1996). By mid-century, the elderly population, like the U.S. population as a whole, will be very heterogeneous in race, ethnicity, and socioeconomic status. Clearly, with the baby boom population aging, the demand for family care will increase and companies will be pressured by employees for release time to assist aging parents. Signs of this potential conflict are already quite visible on the horizon.

In a 1997 study of 1,509 people conducted for Metropolitan Life by the National Alliance for Caregivers and the American Association for Retired Persons (AARP), surveyors found that one in four families had at least one adult who had provided care for an elderly relative or friend in the previous twelve months. On average, the caregivers surveyed were forty-five years of age or older in 1996, and they provided about eight years of care (National Alliance for Caregivers and AARP, 1997). In a follow-up study two years later, it was learned that 62 percent of 55 individuals surveyed indicated that they had asked supervisors, coworkers, or management for some kind of help or support with their caregiving responsibilities at home (MetLife, 1999). However, only 23 percent of companies with 100 or more employees have programs in place to support elder care (Families and Work Institute, 1997). "Elder care is to the twenty-first century what child care has been the last few decades," contends Joyce Ruddock, head of the Long-Term Care Group at Metropolitan Life (*New York Times*, 1999, 1).

Viewed from another perspective, an aging population has continued to increase in size while families have undergone major changes during the past three decades: higher divorce rates, postponement of marriage, lower fertility, smaller families, and, particularly relevant to this discussion, the fact that there are more dual-earner couples than ever before in American history. Today about 65 percent of all married couples are dual earner. This is a significant development because families, and especially women within families, have played a key role in providing informal care and support for older, frail elderly relatives at virtually no cost to the taxpayers. After all, only 7 percent of families rely exclusively on formal care arrangements (Wolf, 1994; Soldo and Freedman, 1994) and nearly three out of four caregivers (72 percent) are female, with the median age of employed female caregivers currently hovering around 45 (American Association of Retired Persons, 1988).

Whether or not working women will be able to provide informal care to the elderly in the future remains an unknown, as does the role that government will play in addressing both the current and future needs of family caregivers. But paid leave would help. However, today policies geared to informal care either come in the form of relatively small tax breaks or as fairly limited in-home services reserved mostly for low-income elderly. But ultimately, social trends, such as more women entering the labor market, will affect the *supply* of caregivers, while the obvious demographic trend of population aging will increase the *demand*. It is at this intersection in particular that economist Shirley Burggraf, in *The Feminine Economy and Economic Man*, poses perhaps the two most haunting questions for policy makers to consider in addressing the role of the FMLA in long-term care policy. First, "How can society get women's work done when women no longer volunteer for their traditional jobs?" And second, "Now that the opportunity cost of women's productivity in alternative tasks is becoming increasingly and explicitly expensive, who is going to pay the costs?" (Burggraf, 1997, 26).

## The Issue of Cost in Family Care

Long-term care is extremely expensive for the elderly, their families, and American taxpayers. In order to understand this complex issue, at least four points should be emphasized. First, Medicare does not cover long-term care (other than for a short transition period), either in nursing homes or at home (Binstock, Cluff, and Von Mering, 1996). Medicaid, on the other hand, is available for such coverage but it is means-tested and, therefore, limited to low-income elderly. Still, between 60 and 80 percent of Medicaid funds are consumed by the elderly for long-term care services—either for institutional or home care (Weiner, 1996). Second, long-term care insurance, once viewed as a potential cure-all for the long-term care crisis, is not only expensive but also limited in scope. At least two studies report that only 20 percent of the aged population can afford private long-term care insurance and far fewer elect to purchase it (Crown, Capitman and Leutz, 1992; Weiner, Illston, and Hanley, 1994). Third, long-term care spending is biased toward institutional care, not home care. For example, in 1993 about 70 percent of the money was devoted to nursing care while only about 30 percent was directed toward home care (Feinberg, 1997). And fourth, out-of-pocket expenses are high. It is estimated that about 44 percent of the total costs of long-term care are covered by families (Weiner, Illston, and Hanley 1994). Similarly, out-of-pocket payments cover 51 percent of nursing-home costs and 26 percent of home-care expenditures (Feinberg, 1997).

Placed in aggregate terms, according to the National Academy on an Aging Society (2000), care provided by family members and friends was estimated to have an economic value of $196 billion in 1997. This amount far exceeds the amount spent that year on nursing-home care ($83 billion) and home health care ($32 billion) (Levine and Memmott, 1999). But coupled with these data is the fact that 76 percent of caregivers are unpaid, thus saving taxpayers

billions of dollars annually. Of those who are paid, however, 43 percent receive payments from Medicaid and about 37 percent of paid caregivers receive out-of-pocket payments from the elderly who employ them (National
Academy on an Aging Society, 2000).

But the money saved for taxpayers by the gallant efforts of family caregivers does not come without cost to someone. Nor should it be assumed
that such care will continue without disruption. That red flag was raised on
December 1, 1999, with the release of the "1999 MetLife Juggling Act Study,"
which was produced for the MetLife Mature Market Institute in conjunction
with the National Alliance for Caregivers and the National Center for Women
and Aging at Brandeis University. The report was a follow-up to MetLife's
1997 study that concluded that 25 percent of all U.S. households provide
care for an elderly person.

According to the 1999 study, caregiving costs individuals as much as
$659,000 over their lifetimes in wages lost and social security and pension
contributions not being made because they "take time off, leave their jobs
entirely, or experience compromised opportunities for training, promotions,
and 'plum' assignments" (MetLife, 1999, 1).

Broken down further, the caregivers studied reported $566,500 in lost
wages, $67,000 in lost retirement contributions, and $25,500 in lost social security benefits. Added to these figures was an additional $19,500 in food,
transportation, assistance with rents and mortgages, and the cost to retain
home-care professionals. Furthermore, nearly 30 percent stated they had
passed on promotions, training opportunities, and new assignments. About
84 percent of the caregivers made adjustments to their work schedules by
taking sick leave or vacation time if available, decreasing work hours and
thus reducing their income, taking an unpaid leave of absence, switching
from full- to part-time employment, or resigning or retiring. Equally important, it was learned that few of the respondents' employers offered programs,
resources, or services to assist their employees in meeting their caregiving
obligations (MetLife, 1999).

A similar research strategy that explored the cost of *not* providing caregivers support in general and family leave in particular was employed by the
Institute of Women's Policy Research (IWPR) eleven years earlier. In its special report, *Unnecessary Losses: Costs to Americans for the Lack of Family
and Medical Leave*, the IWPR concluded that dollars lost by female employees who have no maternity leave far exceed the costs of unpaid leave shouldered by corporations. Based on its study of 7,000 families, the IWPR found
that all women in the workforce who have babies lose earnings in the birth
year as well as subsequent years. But because women without maternity
leave also lose their jobs, they bear a total salary loss of $607 million annu-
ally (1988 figures). In addition, taxpayers must provide another $108 million
in federal income assistance in the form of public-welfare programs to cover

periods of unemployment for some workers. All told, according to the IWPR, because both the public and private sector fail to provide adequate leave policies, the annual cost to families and taxpayers in 1988 exceeded $715 million (Institute for Women's Policy Research, 1988).

Policy makers in Washington were not oblivious to the toll that caretaking responsibilities were taking on America's families, both emotionally and financially, nor were they unaware of the weaknesses of the original Family and Medical Leave Act. Between 1993 and 1999, almost twenty initiatives were put forth by members of Congress to expand the Family and Medical Leave Act. Some wanted the law to apply to smaller companies, others wanted to include additional hours to address basic family needs, such as taking children to dental appointments or attending parent-teacher meetings. Still others proposed that the coverage be expanded to include domestic partners, parents-in-law, and grandparents. Several proposals were extremely narrow in focus and specific in structure, such as allowing employees to take leave for literacy training, allowing leave to make living organ donations, and preventing employers from requiring employees to take FMLA disputes to arbitration instead of court. All legislative proposals failed, however (Gladstone, 1999; Jordan, 1999). In the meantime, a new White House strategy was slowly emerging.

## PART V—THE POLICY DEBATE

### Toward Paid Leave: The Devolution of the FMLA and State Strategies

When President Clinton celebrated the fourth anniversary of the Family and Medical Leave Act during his weekly radio address on February 1, 1997, he reminded listeners that the FMLA was the first piece of legislation he signed. He also took the opportunity to praise the bill's success and called upon Congress to expand the law. Workers should be permitted to take up to twenty-four hours of unpaid leave a year to attend parent-teacher conferences or take a child to dental or medical appointments, he argued. "By expanding family leave we can enable millions more of our fellow Americans to meet their responsibilities both at home and at work," he stated. "Our society can never be stronger than the children we raise or the families in which we raise them" (Office of the Press Secretary, 1997).

Congress did not respond to the president's proposal in 1997, nor did it respond two years later when he recommended that the law be expanded further. Beyond his recommendation that twenty-four hours be added to address family obligations, Clinton also urged Congress to cover more workers. In his State of the Union address on January 19, 1999, the president reminded Americans that the law was not only effective, but its impact on business was minimal. "I think it's time, with all the evidence that it has been so little burdensome to employers, to extend family leave to more Americans working for smaller companies" (Office of the Press Secretary, 1999). Although bills to amend the law were introduced in both houses of the 106th Congress, none moved beyond committee.

In the House, Representative William Clay (D-Mo.), sponsor of the original leave bill in 1985, introduced H.R. 91, the "Family and Medical Leave Improvement Act." The bill reduced the employee cutoff requirement from fifty workers to twenty-five and included elder care in the additional twenty-four-hour provision that Clinton had proposed two years earlier. The decision to include elder care should not be ignored. After all, once the original leave bill in the 1980s was expanded to include care of elderly parents, the FMLA picked up more support. A similar strategy was employed in 1999, at least in the House. In the Senate, a companion bill, the "Family and Medical Leave Fairness Act" (S. 201), was introduced by Chris Dodd (D-Conn.). However, unlike Clay's proposal, the Dodd bill did not include elder care, thus following a pattern from the 1980s. That is, Dodd was hesitant about including elder care in the original FMLA but eventually changed his mind when he needed more votes in the Senate.

Confronted with a Republican Congress in the second half of his first term, the lame duck and beleaguered president, who survived an impeachment trial in the Senate, realized that few of his legislative proposals would succeed. To overcome this obstacle, the president followed a path not unfamiliar to his predecessors. He deliberately bypassed Congress by issuing orders to his federal agencies. Frustrated over Congress's inability to expand the FMLA, Clinton chose to change the venue of the debate in the spring of 1999 from Capitol Hill to the Department of Labor.

In his commencement address at Grambling State University in Louisiana on May 23, 1999, the president announced two new initiatives aimed at the FMLA. First, he directed the Department of Labor to explore ways states may use surplus unemployment insurance funds to subsidize parents who use the FMLA to care for a newborn or newly adopted child (thus "Baby UI"). The second initiative recommended that federal employees be permitted to use up to twelve weeks of accrued sick leave to care for a seriously ill child, parent, or spouse. Prior to 1999, federal workers could only use up to thirteen days of accrued sick leave per year to care for seriously ill family members. "I believe it is imperative that your country give you the tools to succeed not only in the workplace but also at home. If you or any American has to choose between being a good parent and successful in your careers, you have paid a terrible price, and so has your country," he told the graduates (President's Commencement Address, 1999).

The following day, Clinton issued an Executive Memorandum entitled "New Tools to Help Parents Balance Work and Family." In the memo, the president ordered the secretary of labor, Alexis Herman, to propose regulations that would allow states to use unemployment insurance (UI) funds to support parents on leave following the birth or adoption of a child. He also called upon the secretary to develop model legislation that states could adopt in following these new regulations (Presidential Memorandum, 1999).

Under the president's proposal, states would be permitted to tap the surpluses of their unemployment insurance trust funds to cover twelve weeks of parental leave. In short, any employee leaving work under the FMLA for the birth or adoption of a child would be classified as temporarily laid off, and therefore declared eligible for unemployment compensation. The idea runs parallel to the use of temporary disability insurance (TDI), which provides a wage replacement for new mothers in five states (New York, New Jersey, Rhode Island, California, and Hawaii). Companies in TDI states are required to offer paid leave to new mothers, just as it would be offered to other employees who were ill or temporarily disabled (Meyers, 1995).

Spurred on by Clinton's initiative, thirteen states, between May 23, 1999, and July 2000, introduced legislation that included a provision for some type of paid family leave. These included California, Connecticut, Georgia, Illinois, Indiana, Maine, Massachusetts, Maryland, Minnesota, New Hampshire, New Jersey, Vermont, and Washington. No state succeeded in passing paid-leave legislation, and only three states (Connecticut, Massachusetts, and New Jersey) proposed coverage that extended beyond "baby care" (Baby UI) and included coverage for elder care. Connecticut's proposal, for example, was designed to use only UI funds to cover the birth or adoption of a child while other leaves, such as time off for elder care, would be funded through a new Medical Leave Insurance Fund. Both Massachusetts and New Jersey produced similar hybrid proposals that would allow UI to cover childbirth and adoption but care of other family members would be funded through separate mechanisms. Massachusetts referred to its elder-care component as a "family employment trust fund" while New Jersey named its version "family temporary disability" or FTD leave.

One year later, in 2001, the number of states proposing paid leave doubled from thirteen to twenty-six. A summary of the state initiatives is presented in table 8.3. Although there was much activity in the states, no state succeeded in passing paid-leave legislation.

As presented in table 8.3, only five of the twenty-six states included coverage of elder care in their legislative initiatives: Hawaii, Indiana, Massachusetts, New Hampshire, and New Jersey. All five states produced a variety of proposals that ranged from exclusive use of UI benefits (Indiana) to the use of UI and TDI hybrid models (Massachusetts and New Jersey), to the creation of trust funds independent of either TDI or UI models (Hawaii and New Hampshire). But the most important point to be emphasized here is that apparently relatively few states are willing to support caregivers of the elderly, despite

**Table 8.3.  State Paid-Leave Initiatives—2001**

| State | Proposal |
| --- | --- |
| Arizona | Up to 12 weeks of UI for care of newborn or newly adopted child |
| California * | Recommended expanding TDI to cover family care |
| Connecticut | Motion to permit public employees to use sick leave for child care |
| Florida | Up to 12 weeks of UI to care for a newborn or newly adopted child |
| Hawaii * | "Family Leave Insurance Fund" would cover family care |
| Illinois | 12 weeks of UI coverage for chidbirth or newly adopted child |
| Indiana * | 12 weeks of UI coverage to care for ill family member |
| Iowa | Accrued sick leave to be used for the adoption of a child |
| Kansas | 12 weeks of UI coverage to care for newborn or newly adopted child |
| Maryland | 12 weeks of UI to care for newborn or newly adopted child |
| Massachusetts * | UI coverage for parental leave, TDI coverage for family care |
| Minnesota | UI coverage for newborn/newly adopted child (state shares costs) |
| Mississippi | 12 weeks of UI coverage for birth or adoption of a child |
| Missouri | Tax credits for employers who provide paid maternity leave |
| Nebraska | 12 weeks of UI coverage for newborn or newly adopted child |
| New Hampshire * | Payroll tax to fund a "Family and Disability Trust Fund" |
| New Jersey * | TDI/UI hybrid to cover newborn, adoption, or family care |
| New Mexico | 12 weeks of UI coverage for newborn or newly adopted child |
| New York | Effort to expand TDI to cover family care (ongoing study) |
| Oregon | 12 weeks of UI coverage for newborn or newly adopted child |
| Pennsylvania | Revised 2000 bill that covered newborns and adoptees |
| Texas | 12 weeks of leave under UI for childbirth or newly adopted child |
| Vermont | Use of general funds to cover parental leave—not UI funded |
| Virginia | Study completed in 2000 recommended paid leave under FMLA |
| Washington | "Family Leave Insurance Fund" funded by workers and employers |
| Wisconsin | Several proposals designed to provide a wage replacement |

*Indicates coverage for elder care

demographic trends that reveal a growing elderly population and a rise in dual-earner couples. Where then, given the facts as we know them, do we go from here?

### Addressing Weaknesses and Making Policy Recommendations

There are at least four steps that can be taken to make the Family and Medical Leave Act more compatible with the demands associated with long-term care of the aged. First, let us make family leave paid leave and do it immediately! As discussed earlier, dual-earner couples and single parents are especially burdened financially—despite the recent economic boom. Of the three industrialized nations in the world without paid leave, the United States is the richest and the strongest of all. It has taken us much too long as a nation to recognize and respect housework and caregiving responsibilities as *work*. Therefore, particularly in light of a growing elderly population, it is time for such activities to be compensated. Caregivers will continue to provide services and save taxpayers money on institutional care while remaining attached to the labor force. Corporations, families, and society in general will be better for it.

Second, in pushing for paid leave, let us not sacrifice the family for the baby. That is, in 1985, when legislative strategists deliberately expanded the original bill to include family care, they did so for two reasons. First, they were fostering "equal treatment" (family care) over "special treatment" (maternity leave). And second, a broader-based bill that extended beyond maternity leave attracted more votes in the House and Senate, giving a shot in the arm to a fledgling coalition that was dividing its time between lobbying for child care (passed in 1990) and family leave (adopted in 1993). It does not necessarily follow that advocates should now shrink the benefit by confining it only to care of newborns in order to appease opponents and attract political support. But the "Baby UI" initiative does that very thing!

But even if the current political strategy is correct, the timing is off. Like it or not, the year 2000 has come and gone and we are about to witness the retirement of massive numbers of baby boomers. The state will depend on informal family care to help cushion the costs of what certainly will be an astronomically expensive long-term care system. Requests for intermittent leave to care for an elderly parent will increase substantially. Furthermore, by maintaining *family* in the policy and not specifically targeting childbirth, the growing backlash among childless workers is more likely to be defused. After all, it is quite likely that at some point they too will need time off to care for a spouse, a parent, or themselves. And besides, by offering paid leave only under circumstances associated with childbirth, are we not trading in "equal treatment" for "special treatment" and revisiting a familiar battleground from years past?

Third, family leave should apply to more companies and be available to more workers. The fifty-worker threshold should immediately be reduced to at least twenty-five, and lowered regularly over time so that more employees in smaller companies are covered under the law. As discussed previously, those in higher-income brackets who work for larger firms are more likely to take leave than are lower-income employees in smaller companies. Most of the potential caregivers are women (much more family care needs to be done by men), who tend to work for lower wages in smaller businesses. Not only do they deserve the same level of benefits as those who earn more in bigger companies, but it is also in society's best interest that they be rewarded. They will remain attached to the workforce and provide an important service (caregiving) at a very reasonable cost, while saving taxpayers a bundle in the process by either preventing or postponing formal institutional care.

And fourth, the law should be further expanded in another way. As currently written, grandparent care, in-law care, and the care provided by partners in a committed, domestic-partnership type of relationship are not covered. A few states have addressed several of these shortcomings, but other states and the federal government should follow. Clearly, the family has changed and continues to do so. Unfortunately, too many well-meaning policy makers continue to harbor nostalgic images of the family that are anchored in 1950s TV sitcoms. If we expect to address our future long-term care needs adequately, we need to recognize and value families more for the functions they perform than for the forms they take.

With respect to paid-leave policy, we are long overdue and so much more work still needs to be done. But we should at least rejoice over the fact that an important issue has been placed on the political agenda in at least twenty-six states and the debate has begun. Hopefully, this chapter provides one more informative point of reference in a continuing dialogue about an important issue.

# REFERENCES

AFL-CIO. 1992. *Putting Families First: AFL-CIO Working Family Resource*. Washington, D.C.: AFL-CIO.

American Association of Retired Persons. 1988. *A National Study of Caregivers: Final Report*. Washington, D.C.: American Association of Retired Persons and the Travelers Foundation.

Bailyn, L. 1996. *Beyond Work and Family: Adventures on the Fault Line*. Cambridge, Mass.: Radcliffe Public Policy Institute, Radcliffe College.

Binstock, R., L. Cluff, and O. von Mering. 1996. "Issues Affecting the Future of Long-Term Care." In *The Future of Long-Term Care: Social and Policy Issues*, ed. R. Binstock, L. Cluff, and O. von Mering. Baltimore, Md.: Johns Hopkins University Press.

Burggraf, B. 1997. *The Feminine Economy and Economic Man*. New York: Harper & Row.

*Business Week*. 1996. "Grading Family-Friendliness." *Business Week* (September 16, 1996): 18–23.

Clark, B. 1998. *Political Economy: A Comparative Approach*. 2d ed. Westport, Conn.: Praeger.

Coalition of Labor Union Women. 1991. *Bargaining for Family Benefits: A Union Member's Guide*. New York: Coalition for Labor Union Women.

Cohen, S., and M. F. Katzenstein. 1988. "The War over the Family is Not over the Family." In *Feminism, Children and the New Families*, ed. Sandford M. Dornbusch and Myra H. Strober. New York: The Guilford Press.

Collins, C., Chris Hartman, and Holly Sklar. 1999. *Economic Disparity at the Century's Turn*. Boston: United for a Fair Economy.

Commission on Leave. 1996. *A Workable Balance: Report to Congress on Family and Medical Leave Policies*. Washington, D.C.: U.S. Department of Labor.

Crown, W. J. Capitman, and W. Leutz. 1992. "Economic Rationality, the Affordability of Private Long-Term Care Insurance, and the Role for Public Policy." *Gerontologist* 32: 478–85.

Department of Labor. 2000. *Balancing the Needs of Families and Employers: Family and Medical Leave Surveys*. Washington, D.C.: U.S. Department of Labor.

Engels, F. 1972. *The Origin of Family, Private Property, and the State*. New York: International Publishers. Reprinted from original publication.

Families and Work Institute. 1997. *National Study of the Changing Workforce*. New York: Families and Work Institute.

Feinberg, L. 1997. *Options for Supporting Informal and Family Caregiving: A Policy Paper*. San Francisco: American Society on Aging.

Ferber, M, and B. O'Farrell. 1991. *Work and Family: Policies for a Changing Work Force*. Washington, D.C.: National Academy Press.

Foner, P. 1982. *History of the Labor Movement in the United States*. Vol. 6, *On the Eve of America's Entrance into World War I, 1915–1916*. New York: International Publishers.

Fried, Mindy. 1998. "Taking Time: Parental Leave Policy and Corporate Culture." Philadelphia, Pa.: Temple University Press.

Galinsky, E., and J. Bond. 1998. *The 1998 Business Work-Life Study: A Sourcebook*. New York: Families and Work Institute.

Galinsky, E., J. Bond, and D. Friedman. 1993. *Highlights: The National Study of the Changing Workforce*. New York: Families and Work Institute.

Garey, A. 1999. *Weaving Work and Motherhood*. Philadelphia, Pa.: Temple University Press.

Gladstone, L. 1999. *The Family and Medical Leave Act: Proposed Amendments*. Order code: 97017. Washington, D.C.: Congressional Research Services.

Goldin, C. 1990. *Understanding the Gender Gap: An Economic History of American Women*. New York: Oxford University Press.

Googins, B. 1991. *Work/Family Conflicts: Private Lives—Public Responses*. New York: Auburn House.

Grundy, L., and N. Firestein. 1997. *Work, Family, and the Labor Movement*. Cambridge, Mass.: Radcliffe Public Policy Institute, Radcliffe College.

Harker, Susan. 1996. "The Family-Friendly Employer in Europe." Pp. 48–62 in *The Work-Family Challenge: Rethinking Employment*, ed. Suzan Lewis and Jeremy Lewis. Newbury Park, Calif.: Sage.

Hartmann, H. 1981. "The Unhappy Marriage of Marxism and Feminism: Towards a More Progressive Union." In *Women and Revolution*, ed. L. Sargent. Boston: South End Press.

Holcomb, B. 2000. "Family Friendly for Whose Family?" *Ms. Magazine* (April/May 2000): 40–45.

Institute for Women's Policy Research. 1988. *Unnecessary Losses: Costs to Americans for the Lack of Family and Medical Leave*. Washington, D.C.: Institute for Women's Policy Research.

————. 1996. *The Status of Women in the States: Politics, Economics, Health, and Demographics*. Washington, D.C.: Institute for Women's Policy Research.

Jordan, L. 1999. *FMLA Proposals*. Office of Legislative Research. Hartford, Conn.: Connecticut General Assembly.

Levine, A., and M. Memmott. 1999. "The Economic Value of Informal Caregiving." *Health Affairs* 18, no. 2: 182–88.

Manton, K., and E. Stallard. 1994. "Interaction of Disability Dynamics and Mortality." Pp. 217–78 in *Demography of Aging*, ed. Linda G. Martin and Samuel H. Preston. Committee on Population, National Research Council. Washington, D.C.: National Academy Press.

Marx, K. (1967) 1867. *Capital*. Reprint, New York: International.

MetLife. 1997. *MetLife Study of Employer Costs for Working Caregivers*. Westport, Conn.: MetLife Mature Market Institute.

————. 1999. *MetLife Juggling Act Study*. Westport, Conn.: MetLife Mature Market Institute.

Meyers, M. 1995. "Taking Pregnancy Leaves." Minneapolis: *Star Tribune*, February 6, 1995: A1.

Meyer, S. 1984. *The Five-Dollar Day*. Albany: State University of New York Press.

Mutari, E., H. Boushey, and W. Fraher. 1997. *Gender and Political Economy: Incorporating Diversity into Theory and Policy*. Armonk, N.Y.: M.E. Sharpe.

National Academy on an Aging Society. 2000. *Caregiving: Helping the Elderly with Activity Limitations*. Washington, D.C.: National Academy on an Aging Society.

National Alliance for Caregiving and American Association for Retired Persons (AARP). 1997. "Family Caregiving in the U.S." Washington, D.C.: National Alliance for Caregiving.

*New York Times*. 1999. "What's the Problem?" "Week in Review," August 9, 1999.

Office of the Press Secretary. 1997. The President's Weekly Radio Address. February 1, 1997. Washington, D.C.: The White House.

————. 1999. The President of the United States, State of the Union Message, January 27, 1999. Washington, D.C.: The White House.

Presidential Memorandum. 1999. "Memorandum for the Heads of Executive Departments and Agencies: New Tools to Help Parents Balance Work and Family." May 24. Washington, D.C.: The White House.

President's Commencement Address. 1999. Grambling State University, Grambling, La., May 23. Washington, D.C.: The White House.

Reich, R. 2001. *The Future of Success: Working and Living in the New Economy*. New York: Random House.

Rubin, R., and B. Riney. 1995. *Working Wives and Dual-Earner Families*. Westport, Conn.: Praeger.

Soldo, B., and Vicki A. Freedman. 1994. "Care of the Elderly: Division of Labor Among the Family, Market, and State." In *Demography of Aging*, ed. Linda G. Martin and Samuel H. Preston. Committee on Population, National Research Council. Washington, D.C.: National Academy Press.

Tauber, C. 1996. *Statistical Handbook on Women in America*. Phoenix, Ariz.: The Oryx Press.

United States Bureau of the Census. 1996. *65+ in the United States*. Current Population Reports, Special Studies, P23-190. Washington, D.C.: United States Bureau of the Census.

United States Department of Labor. 1992. Bureau of Labor-Management Relations and Cooperative Programs. *Work and Family Provisions in Major Collective Bargaining Agreements*. Washington, D.C.: United States Department of Labor.

Wiener, J. 1996. *Can Medicaid Long-Term Care Expenditures for the Elderly Be Reduced?* New York: The Commonwealth Fund.

Wiener, J., L. Illston, and R. Hanley. 1994. *Sharing the Burden: Strategies for Public and Private Long-Term Care Insurance*. Washington, D.C.: Brookings Institution.

Wolf, D. 1994. "The Elderly and Their Kin." In *Demography of Aging*, ed. L. Martin and S. Preston. Committee on Population, National Research Council. Washington, D.C.: National Academy Press.

*Working Mother*. 1999. "*Working Mother*'s Top 100 Companies." *Working Mother*. September. At www.workingmother.com.

Zaretsky, E. 1976. *Capitalism, the Family and Personal Life*. New York: Harper & Row.

# 9

# The Employment Insurance Model: Maternity, Parental, and Sickness Benefits in Canada

*Eileen Trzcinski*

In Canada, maternity, parental, and sickness benefits are provided through a combination of public and private policies. These policies have developed through the interaction of federal legislation, judicial decisions, and private-sector initiatives. For maternity and parental benefits, the Canadian Employment Insurance program provides far more extensive coverage to employees than do private-sector policies. The Canadian Employment Insurance program, previously named the Unemployment Insurance program, provides on average up to fifty weeks of wage replacement for absences from work on account of sickness, pregnancy and childbirth, and care for newborn or newly adopted children. Under certain circumstances, workers are entitled to sixty-five weeks of wage replacement.

Despite the availability of fifteen weeks of sickness benefits under the Employment Insurance (EI) program, however, most workers rely on private-sector benefits, that is, employer-provided paid sick leave or disability insurance benefits, rather than EI benefits during absences from work on account of sickness. In comparison, however, the private sector is far less effective in providing for wage replacement during maternity and parental leaves. Wage replacement through the unemployment insurance program is much more prevalent than through private policies. In 2001, the Canadian EI program covered 12.79 million workers and provided regular unemployment benefits to 514,289 persons, sickness benefits to 44,762 persons, maternity benefits to 49,372 women, and parental benefits to 31,837 persons.

This chapter provides historical and current information on the Canadian employment insurance program. It also presents evidence that addresses two questions specific to the implementation of family and medical benefits in the United States. The first question concerns whether and to what extent government wage-replacement policies replace private-employer policies. The second question concerns whether parents automatically adjust their leave-taking behavior to match the maximum number of weeks covered by wage-replacement policies.

## I. WOMEN IN THE LABOR MARKET IN CANADA

The labor-market experience of women in Canada parallels that of women in other advanced industrial Western countries. Women tend to be concentrated in female-dominated occupations, to work part-time at higher rates than men, and to have average earnings beneath male earnings. According to Statistics Canada Labour Force Survey data for 2001, 70 percent of all employed women were concentrated in teaching, nursing or related health occupations, clerical or other administrative positions, or in sales and service occupations (Housing, Family and Social Statistics Division, Statistics Canada, 2002). In 2001, 27 percent of all employed women worked part-time compared with 10 percent of employed men. Among women who worked part-time, 20 percent reported they worked part-time on account of child-care or other responsibilities; however, a higher percentage, 25 percent, reported they worked part-time because they were unable to find suitable full-time employment (Housing, Family and Social Statistics Division, Statistics Canada, 2002).

### Wages and Fringe Benefits

Table 9.1, which presents hourly earnings by gender, indicates that women earned on average 82 percent of male hourly wages in 1999. Although men and women tended to be evenly distributed among middle earners ($12.00 to $19.99), 37.1 percent of all women earned less than $12.00 per hour compared with 23.0 percent of men, while 25.3 percent of all women earned more than $20.00 per hour compared with 41.4 percent of men. Lower earnings for women are not limited to wages alone, but also are reflected in lower percentages of women than men receiving different types of fringe benefits. In 1999, 37.2 percent of all female workers compared with 30.4 percent of male workers received no nonwage benefits (table 9.2).

### Employment and Unemployment Rates

Table 9.3 indicates that the employment rate of women with young children under the age of three increased by 34.3 percentage points between

**Table 9.1. Hourly Earnings, 1999**

| | % of Employees by Earning Categoary | | | |
|---|---|---|---|---|
| | Less than $12.00 | $12.00–$19.99 | $20.00 and above | Mean Hourly Wage |
| Overall | 30.4 | 36.6 | 33.0 | $19.04 |
| Gender | | | | |
| Men | 23.0 | 35.6 | 41.4 | $21.09 |
| Women | 37.1 | 37.5 | 25.3 | $17.16 |

Source: Statistics Canada, 2001, table 14, page 37.

**Table 9.2. Nonwage Benefits, 1999**

| | % of Employees Who Are Included in: | | | | | | |
|---|---|---|---|---|---|---|---|
| | Employer-Sponsored Pension | Group RRSP | Life/Disability Insurance Plan | Sup. Medical Insurance Plan | Dental Plan | Stock Purchase Plan | No Non-wage Benefits |
| Overall | 37.8 | 17.6 | 56.2 | 52.9 | 51.8 | 7.3 | 33.9 |
| Gender | | | | | | | |
| Men | 39.7 | 20.0 | 61.9 | 58.9 | 57.5 | 8.2 | 30.4 |
| Women | 36.0 | 15.4 | 51.0 | 47.3 | 46.6 | 6.4 | 37.2 |

Source: Statistics Canada, 2001, table 15, page 40.

| | Vacation Plan | Sick Leave |
|---|---|---|
| Overall | 76.7 | 54.3 |
| Gender | | |
| Men | 79.2 | 55.9 |
| Women | 73.1 | 52.0 |

Source: Drolet and Morissette, 1998, table 5, page 18.

1976 and 2001, from 27.7 percent in 1976 to 62.0 percent in 2001. For women aged 25–44, employment increased from 49.9 percent to 75.3 percent during the same period (table 9.4). At the beginning and middle of this period, women tended to have unemployment rates that were higher than unemployment rates for men. In the 1990s and early 2000s, however, this pattern had reversed, with women's unemployment rates dropping below men's in all years except 2000. During the same period, married mothers tended to have higher participation rates than single mothers (Housing, Family and Social Statistics Division, Statistics Canada, 2002).

Table 9.3.  Percentage of Women with Children Employed, by Age of Youngest Child, 1976–2001

| Year | Youngest Child Under Age 3 | Youngest Child Aged 3–5 | Total with Youngest Child Under Age 6 |
|---|---|---|---|
| 1976 | 27.7 | 36.9 | 31.5 |
| 1977 | 29.4 | 37.8 | 32.7 |
| 1978 | 32.1 | 40.7 | 35.5 |
| 1979 | 34.8 | 43.0 | 37.9 |
| 1980 | 37.1 | 45.3 | 40.2 |
| 1981 | 39.6 | 46.7 | 42.3 |
| 1982 | 39.7 | 46.6 | 42.3 |
| 1983 | 42.4 | 48.0 | 44.6 |
| 1984 | 44.4 | 49.2 | 46.2 |
| 1985 | 46.9 | 52.1 | 48.9 |
| 1986 | 49.7 | 54.5 | 51.6 |
| 1987 | 50.6 | 56.4 | 52.9 |
| 1988 | 52.3 | 58.5 | 54.7 |
| 1989 | 53.2 | 59.4 | 55.7 |
| 1990 | 53.8 | 59.8 | 56.1 |
| 1991 | 54.8 | 60.3 | 56.9 |
| 1992 | 54.5 | 59.7 | 56.5 |
| 1993 | 55.1 | 59.8 | 56.9 |
| 1994 | 56.2 | 59.4 | 57.5 |
| 1995 | 56.7 | 60.7 | 58.3 |
| 1996 | 58.4 | 60.8 | 59.4 |
| 1997 | 59.2 | 62.4 | 60.6 |
| 1998 | 59.9 | 64.2 | 61.7 |
| 1999 | 60.7 | 66.3 | 63.1 |
| 2000 | 60.9 | 67.8 | 63.8 |
| 2001 | 62.0 | 67.4 | 64.2 |

Source: Housing, Family and Social Statistics Division, Statistics Canada, 2002, table 5, page 12.

**Table 9.4. Percentage Employed and Unemployed, Age 25–44, by Sex, 1976–2001**

| | Percent Employed | | Percent Unemployed | |
|---|---|---|---|---|
| Year | Women | Men | Women | Men |
| 1976 | 49.9 | 90.9 | 7.4 | 4.7 |
| 1977 | 51.0 | 90.1 | 8.0 | 5.4 |
| 1978 | 53.4 | 90.0 | 8.6 | 5.7 |
| 1979 | 55.6 | 90.7 | 7.7 | 5.1 |
| 1980 | 57.8 | 90.1 | 7.0 | 5.4 |
| 1981 | 60.2 | 90.1 | 7.5 | 5.5 |
| 1982 | 59.7 | 85.5 | 9.6 | 9.3 |
| 1983 | 60.5 | 84.0 | 10.4 | 10.7 |
| 1984 | 62.0 | 84.5 | 10.5 | 10.1 |
| 1985 | 63.5 | 85.5 | 10.3 | 9.3 |
| 1986 | 66.2 | 86.2 | 9.2 | 8.6 |
| 1987 | 67.4 | 87.0 | 8.7 | 7.7 |
| 1988 | 69.3 | 87.8 | 7.9 | 6.7 |
| 1989 | 70.4 | 87.8 | 7.9 | 6.8 |
| 1990 | 71.4 | 86.6 | 7.9 | 7.7 |
| 1991 | 70.4 | 83.5 | 9.4 | 10.2 |
| 1992 | 69.4 | 81.3 | 9.6 | 11.6 |
| 1993 | 69.1 | 81.6 | 10.3 | 11.4 |
| 1994 | 69.6 | 82.4 | 9.5 | 10.2 |
| 1995 | 70.5 | 83.1 | 8.6 | 9.3 |
| 1996 | 70.9 | 82.9 | 8.9 | 9.5 |
| 1997 | 72.2 | 84.0 | 8.1 | 8.6 |
| 1998 | 73.3 | 85.1 | 7.2 | 7.6 |
| 1999 | 74.3 | 85.7 | 6.6 | 6.9 |
| 2000 | 75.2 | 86.5 | 6.0 | 6.0 |
| 2001 | 75.3 | 85.9 | 6.3 | 6.7 |

Source: Housing, Family and Social Statistics Division, Statistics Canada, 2002, table 13, page 19.

## II. LEGISLATIVE HISTORY OF THE CANADIAN EMPLOYMENT INSURANCE SYSTEM

Throughout its history, the Canadian unemployment insurance system has functioned as a dynamic system, frequently changing in response to economic, demographic, and labor-market pressures. Begun as a modest program in 1940, the Canadian Unemployment Insurance program ranked as one of the most generous and comprehensive unemployment insurance systems in the world in the 1970s and 1980s (Human Resources Development

Canada, 2002a). In the 1990s, Canada modified and dismantled many of the more generous provisions of its unemployment insurance system. The most dramatic statistic associated with these changes concerns the percentage of unemployed Canadians receiving unemployment benefits. In 1990, 86.85 percent of the unemployed received unemployment benefits, while less than 50 percent received such benefits in the late 1990s: 48.1 percent in 1996 (Picot, Myles, and Pyper, 2002) and 45 percent in 1998 (Human Resources Development Canada, 2000d). At its most generous level, the wage replacement rate was 75 percent. Over time the wage replacement rate was lowered to 55 percent for most workers. Chart 9.1 presents a chronology of the major legislative changes in the Canadian unemployment system.

These changes occurred as a result of (1) internal and external economic pressures, (2) the objections of the business community to the generosity of the unemployment insurance system, (3) Canada's geographical location as a neighbor to the United States with its far more limited unemployment and social-welfare policies, and (4) the stringent conditions negotiated in the North American Free Trade Agreement. Despite these changes, the current form of the Employment Insurance program in Canada represents a model

**Chart 9.1.  A Chronology of Unemployment (Employment) Insurance Legislation Since 1971**

**UI Act Effective June 27, 1971**
- Generously liberalized the pre-1971 system:
- Provided nearly universal coverage (commencing Feb. 2, 1972)
- Eased eligibility
- Added a series of special benefits—sickness, maternity, and retirement

**Bill C-69 Effective Jan. 1, 1976**
- Disqualification increased from three to six weeks for those who quit without just cause, were fired because of misconduct, refused to accept suitable employment, failed to attend a placement interview, or refused to follow instructions from personnel handling their claims
- Maximum age for coverage reduced from seventy to sixty-five
- Replacement rate reduced from 75 percent to 66.67 percent for claimants with dependents

**Bill C-14 Effective Jan. 1, 1979**
- Entrance requirement for new and reentrants set at twenty weeks of work (effective July 1, 1979)
- Replacement rate reduced to 60 percent
- Benefit claw-back introduced to retrieve benefits paid to high-income recipients

**Bill C-156 Effective Jan. 1, 1984**
- Seasonal fishermen benefits modified
- Maternity benefits modified
- Adoption benefits introduced

**Bill C-21 Effective Nov. 18, 1990**
- Repeat users no longer required 6 additional weeks
- Penalty increased from 6 to 7–12 weeks for quitting without just cause, dismissals because of misconduct, and refusal to accept suitable employment; and replacement rate dropped to 50 percent for these claimants

**Bill C-113 Effective April 4, 1993**
- Those who quit without just cause, were fired because of misconduct, or refused to accept suitable employment became ineligible for benefits
- Replacement rate dropped to 57 percent from 60 percent

**Bill C-17 Effective July 7, 1994**
- Replacement rate raised to 60 percent for low-earnings claimants and claimants with dependents; reduced to 55 percent for others

**Bill C-12 Effective July 1, 1996**
- System renamed Employment Insurance (EI)
- Replacement rate for repeat users dropped by one percentage point for each 20 weeks of use in the past 5 years, up to the maximum of 5 percentage points
- Repeat claimants faced a benefit claw-back of up to 100 percent, depending on earnings and the weeks of benefits in the last 5 years
- Weekly maximum insurable earnings (MIEs) revised to $750

**Bill C-12 Effective Jan. 1, 1997**
- Hours/earnings coverage requirement abolished, every hour of work insurable
- Entrance requirement and benefit entitlement based on hours of work instead of weeks
- Average earnings over the last 20 weeks used to calculate amount of benefits

Source: Lin, Zhengxi, 1998, Appendix, pp. 15–16.

of employment policy that simultaneously functions as labor-market policy, family policy, income distribution policy, and gender policy. In addition, as the federal government in Canada subjected its unemployment insurance program to many substantial reductions, it nevertheless continued to expand the availability of parental benefits, including adoption benefits.

## Unemployment Act of 1971

Fifteen weeks of maternity benefits were first provided under the unemployment insurance system in 1971; adoption benefits were added in 1984. Maternity benefits were added to the unemployment insurance system under the UI Act of 1971 as part of a set of special benefits that included sickness and retirement benefits as well as maternity benefits. In addition to creating special benefits, the UI Act of 1971 reduced eligibility requirements and increased benefits. Eligibility requirements for special benefits were more stringent than for regular unemployment insurance benefits. While workers could quality for regular benefits with a minimum of eight weeks of covered employment, they needed to accumulate twenty weeks for special benefits. Claims for maternity benefits also needed to satisfy the "Magic 10" rule, which stipulated that ten of the twenty weeks of covered employment needed to be accumulated in the first half of the qualifying period.

## Bill C-21

The next major change affecting caregiving benefits occurred in 1990, when parents of newborn children became eligible for ten weeks of wage replacement. On November 18, 1990, Bill C-21 became law in Canada. This bill, which dramatically altered the Unemployment Insurance Act, tightened entrance requirements, reduced the duration of benefits, and lowered the benefit rate. The Act contained one major amendment concerning parental and adoption benefits. Maternity benefits remained unchanged with fifteen weeks of benefits available to a biological mother. The adoption benefit was eliminated and replaced with parental benefits. These parental benefits were available up to a maximum of ten weeks and were available to both biological and adoptive parents, including biological mothers who could take the parental benefit in addition to maternity benefits. This change was in part a reaction to legal challenges to the provision of adoption benefits under the unemployment insurance system without the provision of benefits for biological parents. The rationale and outcomes of these legal challenges are discussed more fully in the following section.

The new ten-week benefit was allocated on a "per birth or adoptive placement" basis. The benefit could be shared by the parents as they saw fit, but needed to be taken within fifty-two weeks of the child arriving home. Both parents, if eligible, were able to receive benefits at the same or different times, but the total available benefit was ten weeks combined for mother and father. The same parent could also split his or her own benefit throughout the fifty-two-week period. As with maternity benefits, claimants needed to wait two weeks before receiving benefits. A biological mother did not, however, need to deal with another two-week waiting period if she claimed parental benefits after receiving her maternity benefits.

## Employment Insurance Act of 1996

In July 1996, Canada replaced its unemployment insurance system with the Employment Insurance system. Labeled as a fundamental restructuring of the unemployment insurance system, the new program was designed (1) to limit unemployment insurance benefits to unemployed workers with strong labor-market attachments and (2) to curtail benefits to workers in seasonal industries and to workers who made frequent claims for unemployment insurance benefits. At the same time, the program was designed (1) to place greater emphasis on re-employment initiatives and (2) to provide more targeted protection to low-income families with unemployed workers still covered under the new program. Chart 9.2 provides a listing of the major reforms introduced by the 1996 legislation.

### Chart 9.2. Elements of Reform under Employment Insurance Act of 1996

**Reduction in Maximum Insurable Earnings**
- The MIE was reduced to $750 a week (the equivalent of $39,000 per year) in 1996 and was frozen at this level until 2000. This reduced the maximum weekly benefit to $413 (55% of $750) from $448 in 1995 and $465 for first 6 months of 1996.

**Reduced Maximum Benefit Duration**
- Effective July 1996, the maximum length of a claim was reduced from 50 to 45 weeks.

**New Entrants and Reentrants**
- Effective July 1996, new entrants and reentrants to the labor force needed 26 rather than 20 weeks of work to qualify for EI. In January 1997, the 26 weeks were converted to 910 hours.
- Applies only to those who have had minimal or no labor-market attachment over the past 2 years. Workers who have at least 490 hours of work in the first year of employment need only 420 to 700 hours in the next year.

**Benefit Calculation**
- Weekly benefits are calculated as follows:
- Total earnings over the 26-week period preceding the establishment of the claim, divided by the greater of the number of weeks of work in this period or the minimum divisor of 14 to 22 (depending on the regional rate of unemployment). The result is multiplied by 55% to determine the weekly benefit.

**Intensity Rule**
- The intensity rule reduces the benefit rate by 1 percentage point for every 20 weeks of regular or fishing benefits collected in the past 5 years.
- The maximum reduction is 5 percentage points.
- Does not apply to special benefits.

**First-Dollar Coverage**
- Effective January 1997, all earnings, from the first dollar, are insurable, up to the annual MIE. There are no weekly minimums or maximums for determining earnings.

**Premium Refunds**
- Beginning in 1997, workers earning $2,000 or less per year have their premiums refunded.

**Increased Sanctions for Fraud**
- Effective July 1996, penalties for fraud by employers and claimants were increased.
- Effective January 1997, claimants who have committed fraud since June 1996 face higher entrance requirements.

Source: Human Resources Development Canada, 2000d, Appendix 1.1.

The changes have had differential effects on men and women beneficiaries. The more stringent entry and reentry requirements have had greater adverse effects on women; while a greater percentage of male beneficiaries have been affected by the intensity rule. Because men tend to have higher family incomes than women, men have been more frequently affected by changes in the benefit repayment provisions (Human Resources Development Canada, 2000d).

The most recent changes to the employment insurance system occurred in 2000 and 2002 and were implemented through budgetary changes. On December 31, 2000, workers with 600 hours of covered employment in the qualifying period became eligible for thirty-five weeks of parental benefits and a total of fifty weeks combined of maternity, sickness, and parental benefits. The government announced that these changes were intended to "increase the duration, accessibility and flexibility of parental benefits in order to support families in balancing the demands of work and family during a child's critical first year" (Human Resources Development Canada, 2000d, 5). In addition to extending adoption and parental benefits to thirty-five weeks, only one parent needed to serve a two-week waiting period, claimants needed to accumulate 600 instead of 700 hours of covered employment in the fifty-two-week period before the claim, and claimants were allowed to earn up to $50.00 a week or 25 percent of their weekly benefit (whichever was higher) without a reduction in EI benefits (Human Resources Development Canada, 2000b). On March 20, 2002, claimants were allowed to collect a maximum of sixty-five weeks of benefits, if certain conditions were met regarding the timing of claims for sickness, maternity, and parental benefits.

## III. SPECIAL CHARACTERISTICS
## OF THE CANADIAN UI/EI PROGRAM

Three special features of the Canadian employment insurance system affect the level of benefits received by claimants: the intensity rule, the benefit repayment feature for high earners (the claw-back), and the family supplement. Another feature includes the provision for employers to establish supplemental insurance plans.

### Intensity Rule

The intensity rule was designed to introduce an experience-rating component into the employment insurance system. According to the intensity rule, the wage replacement rate is reduced by 1 percentage point for every twenty weeks of unemployment insurance benefits received in the past five years. The intensity rule can result in a maximum reduction of the wage replacement rate from 55 percent to 50 percent of insurable earnings. The intensity rule is not applicable to claimants of special benefits, that is, maternity, sickness, and parental benefits, or to claimants who are receiving the family supplement (Human Resources Development Canada, 2000d).

### Family Supplement

The family supplement was introduced in 1996 to replace the low-income supplement, which had provided 60 percent wage replacement levels instead of the 55 percent to low-income individuals. The family supplement provides additional benefits to claimants in low-income families with children by increasing the maximum benefit rate from 55 percent to 80 percent of their insurable earnings (Human Resources Development Canada, 2000c). Claimants who receive the Canada Child Tax Benefit and whose net family income is beneath $25,921 per year are eligible for the family supplement. The total monthly benefit cannot exceed the maximum benefit amount, which equaled $413 per week in 2000. In 1999, 11.4 percent of all EI claimants received the family supplement: 16 percent of all female claimants and 7.3 of all male claimants received the family supplement (Human Resources Development Canada, 2000d).

### Claw-Back

The benefit replacement provision (referred to as the claw-back) is designed to ensure that high-income earners repay some of their benefits once their annual net income exceeds a certain threshold. The claw-back provision also functions in conjunction with the intensity rule in that frequent claimants are required to repay a higher percentage of their employment insurance benefits. Both the family supplement and the benefits replacement provisions apply to special benefits as well as to regular benefits.

### Supplemental Insurance Plans

The Employment Insurance program includes provisions that provide tax advantages to employers and to employees when employers establish a supplemental employment insurance plan. Such plans can provide wage replacement during the two-week waiting period prior to the eligibility for special benefits and can provide income top-ups to benefits received as long as the total wage replacement does not exceed the benefit recipient's usual wage (Human Resources Development Canada, 2000e, 2002b).

## IV. UNEMPLOYMENT INSURANCE, CANADIAN COURT DECISIONS, AND THE CHARTER OF RIGHTS

Within Canada, judicial decisions have played a critical role in clarifying and defining access to maternity, sickness, and parental benefits available both under the unemployment insurance program and under private-sector policies. The following discussion provides a summary of the major landmark decisions in Canada that affected the availability of maternity and parental leave and benefits. Trzcinski and Alpert (1994) provide a more detailed discussion of the legal decisions and the historical context and also present an extensive comparison of judicial and legal precedents in the United States and Canada.

### The "Difference Principle"

In *Bliss v. Attorney General of Canada* (1978), the Canadian Supreme Court addressed the issue of whether discrimination on the basis of pregnancy is sex discrimination. This case arose out of a claim by a woman for unemployment insurance benefits. The woman made the claim for ordinary benefits a few days after she gave birth to a child. She satisfied the requirements for these benefits in terms of weeks of insurable earnings, availability for work, and inability to locate employment. She was not, however, entitled to pregnancy benefits, which had more stringent eligibility requirements than did regular UI benefits. Her claim for ordinary benefits was rejected under section 46 of the UI Act, which denied all types of regular and nonmaternity special benefits to female claimants during a fourteen-week period surrounding a birth (eight weeks before birth and six weeks after birth).

The Supreme Court of Canada dismissed the appeal and affirmed the judgment of the Federal Court of Appeal, finding that section 46 of the UI Act did not contravene section 1(b) of the Canadian Bill of Rights. Specifically, the Supreme Court of Canada ruled that the denial of regular unemployment benefits to women during pregnancy and after childbirth did not contravene the equality provision of the Canadian Bill of Rights. In this decision, the Supreme Court (with Justice Ritchie delivering the judgment) argued that the pregnancy benefits provided by the UI program constituted a special set of benefits for a specific class of individuals: pregnant women. The provision of this special benefit, however, required compensation, which was restricted eligibility for "regular" unemployment insurance benefits. This restriction applied to all pregnant women, whether or not they were eligible for the maternity benefits. Ritchie held that the legislation could be viewed as "providing additional benefits to one class of women, specifying the conditions which entitle a claimant to such benefits and defining a period during which no benefits are available."

The validity of this decision rested upon the premise that pregnancy discrimination was not sex-based discrimination. Here Justice Ritchie invoked the "difference principle": that biological differences between women and men account for the inequities in this case. The argument that pregnancy discrimination was not sex-based discrimination rested on the premise that the relevant distinction was not between women and men, but instead between pregnant persons and nonpregnant persons.

## Section 15 of the Canadian Charter of Rights and Freedoms

The timing of the *Bliss* decision coincided with deliberations in Canada on language and other specific protections to be included in the Canadian Charter of Rights and Freedoms. According to Pal and Morton (1986), *Bliss* had broad political implications for feminist objectives. After *Bliss*, feminist organizations began to argue that since the Bill of Rights had proven ineffective to ensure equality of rights to women, a constitutionally entrenched charter of rights with stronger and more explicit guarantees was needed. Feminists groups effectively bargained their support for Prime Minister Trudeau's and the Liberal Party's efforts at developing a Canadian constitution. What resulted was section 15 of the Charter of Rights and Freedoms, which provides the most far-reaching constitutional guarantee of equality to be found in any liberal democracy in the world and which would ultimately be interpreted to preclude any further decisions like *Bliss* (Fudge, 1987):

> 15(1) Every individual is equal before and under the law and has the right to the equal protection and equal benefit of the law without discrimination, and, in particular, without discrimination, based on race, national or ethnic origin, colour, religion, sex, age or mental or physical disability.

## Removal of Unfair Disadvantages

In *Brooks, Allen, and Dixon et al. v. Canada Safeway Ltd.* (1989), three women filed discrimination complaints. Susan Brooks, Patricia Allen, and Patricia Dixon were part-time cashiers employed by Safeway. All three became pregnant during 1982. At the time each of the appellants became pregnant the plan provided maternity benefits that would not be payable on the same terms as benefits for other disabilities. It was not disputed in this case that the Safeway plan treated pregnancy differently from other health-related causes of inability to work. Justice Dickson, who delivered the judgment in this case, rejected this reasoning. Although he agreed that pregnancy is not characterized properly as a sickness or an accident, he argued that it is "a valid health-related reason for absence from the workplace and as such should not have been excluded from the Safeway plan." He further argued that the exclusion must be evaluated in light of the underlying rationale of the plan.

Justice Dickson then argued that the Safeway plan, which excluded coverage for pregnant employees, was discriminatory under the definition provided in *Andrews v. Law Society of British Columbia* (1989). According to the judgment in *Andrews*, one purpose of antidiscrimination legislation is the removal of unfair disadvantages which have been imposed on individuals or groups in society. In *Andrews*, it was also held that such an unfair disadvantage may result when the costs of an activity from which all of society benefits are placed upon a single group of persons. Dickson held that these criteria were satisfied in this case. Justice Dickson further emphasized that a refusal to find the Safeway plan discriminatory would undermine one of the purposes of antidiscrimination legislation. The Justice noted that laws and polities that embody pregnancy-based discrimination can create structural barriers to equality that have disadvantaged women in our society and that the removal of such unfair impositions upon women and other groups in society is a key purpose of antidiscrimination legislation.

## Parental-Leave Benefits

Prior to 1990, the UI Act also provided for adoption benefits for fifteen weeks. The same rules that applied for receiving maternity benefits applied for adoption benefits (Schwartz, 1988). In *Schachter v. Canada et al.* (1990), Schachter applied for a declaration that benefits should be payable under the UI Act to the natural fathers of babies on the same basis as benefits are payable to adoptive parents. The Federal Court of Canada, under Justice Heald, held that the failure of the UI Act to provide benefits to natural parents similar to those of adoptive parents was an inequality and amounted to discrimination contrary to section 15(1) of the Canadian Charter of Rights and Freedoms. The court declared that the natural mother and father of a newborn child should be entitled to benefits under the act in respect of periods taken off work to care for the child on the same terms as adoptive parents.

The finding that section 32 was discriminatory within the meaning of section 15(1) was straightforward. More complex were the arguments concerning the proper remedy, given the existence of discrimination. The Federal Court declined to declare section 32 invalid, but instead declared that natural parents of a newborn child were entitled to benefits on the same basis as adoptive parents.

In July 1992, the Supreme Court of Canada released its decision in the *Schachter* case. In *Schachter v. Canada et al.* (1992), discrimination was not the primary issue. The ruling of the lower court regarding the violation of section 15(1) of the Canadian Charter of Rights and Freedoms was not questioned. Instead the issue in the *Schachter* case at the Supreme Court of Canada was whether the courts have the power to remedy discriminatory laws by extending benefits to those who have been wrongfully denied. According to the Women's Legal Education and Action Fund (WLEAF), which intervened in the case, "the federal government argued that the courts should be limited to striking down the legislation in such circumstances" (Women's Legal Education and Action Fund, 1992a). The Supreme Court reached a unanimous decision, where it ruled that courts have three options when a law is found to be inconsistent with the Charter and set out guidelines on how a court should respond when a law is found to be in violation of the Charter of Rights and Freedoms. The three options are: (1) the courts can strike down the law; (2) the courts can strike down the law but suspend the effect of the decision so that the legislature has the opportunity to revise the law to be consistent with the Charter; or (3) the courts can rewrite the law so it is consistent with the Charter. In the *Schachter* case, the courts laid out the guidelines, but did not rule on the appropriate option, given that the legislature had previously rewritten the law to make it consistent with the Charter.

## V. HISTORICAL AND CURRENT ADMINISTRATIVE DATA ON USAGE AND COST OF THE UI/EI PROGRAM

Tables 9.5 through 9.10 provide background information on payments and usage of the Canadian Unemployment Insurance system. In 2001, the Employment Insurance system covered 12.79 million workers (table 9.5). Although the

Table 9.5. Employment Insurance Program (EI), Persons Covered by Employment Insurance Program, Computed Annual Average (Data in Thousands)

| Year | Persons Covered |
|------|-----------------|
| 1971 | 5,439 |
| 1990 | 11,260 |
| 1991 | 10,984 |
| 1992 | 10,857 |
| 1993 | 10,834 |
| 1994 | 11,092 |
| 1995 | 11,271 |
| 1996 | 11,302 |
| 1997 | 11,418 |
| 1998 | 11,717 |
| 1999 | 12,079 |
| 2000 | 12,502 |
| 2001 | 12,790 |

Source: Statistics Canada, 2002b.

numbers of workers covered by the UI/EI system increased steadily from 1971 to 2001, the number of persons receiving benefits per year fluctuated in response to economic conditions and to the parameters of the UI system. During the two periods 1982–1985 and 1991–1993, table 9.7 indicates that more than one million persons per year received regular benefits on account of unemployment. In 2000 and 2001, the sharp restrictions to the program introduced in the mid-1990s together with a strong economic performance resulted in the lowest number of regular beneficiaries during the entire period 1976–2001. Specifically, there were 486,380 beneficiaries of regular benefits in 2000 and 521,363 in 2001.

Prior to the implementation of extended parental and adoption benefits in 2000, the number of beneficiaries of maternity and parental benefits also peaked in 1992 with 57,918 claimants of maternity benefits and 33,513 of parental benefits. Table 9.6 indicates that the percentage of newborns whose parents received maternity or parental benefits increased steadily from 29.9 percent in 1976 to 51.9 percent in 1990 and then fluctuated between 45.7 percent and 52.8 percent during the period 1991 to 1998.

**Table 9.6. Employment Insurance Support to Newborns, 1976 to 1998**

| Year | Beneficiaries as a Percentage of Total Births (Coverage Rate) Beneficiaries/Births × 100 (%) |
|---|---|
| 1976 | 29.9 |
| 1977 | 32.0 |
| 1978 | 33.8 |
| 1979 | 35.1 |
| 1980 | 35.8 |
| 1981 | 37.1 |
| 1982 | 38.4 |
| 1983 | 38.7 |
| 1984 | 42.1 |
| 1985 | 43.1 |
| 1986 | 44.2 |
| 1987 | 46.5 |
| 1988 | 46.8 |
| 1989 | 49.1 |
| 1990 | 51.9 |
| 1991 | 48.5 |
| 1992 | 52.8 |
| 1993 | 51.7 |
| 1994 | 47.9 |
| 1995 | 45.7 |
| 1996 | 48.3 |
| 1997 | 51.1 |
| 1998 | 48.7 |

**Table 9.7.** Employment Insurance Program (EI), Income Beneficiaries by Type of Income Benefit, Annual Number of Persons, 1976–2000

| Year | Total Income Benefits[a] | Total Regular Benefits[b] | Regular Benefits | Sickness Benefits | Maternity Benefits | Adoption Benefits | Parental Benefits |
|---|---|---|---|---|---|---|---|
| 1976 | 701,448 | 0 | 595,820 | 24,760 | 23,257 | 0 | 0 |
| 1977 | 751,551 | 0 | 668,543 | 29,099 | 30,372 | 0 | 0 |
| 1978 | 802,607 | 0 | 615,219 | 25,272 | 31,830 | 0 | 0 |
| 1979 | 713,426 | 0 | 615,219 | 25,272 | 34,132 | 0 | 0 |
| 1980 | 702,716 | 0 | 603,941 | 24,498 | 34,717 | 0 | 0 |
| 1981 | 720,280 | 0 | 620,176 | 24,157 | 37,022 | 0 | 0 |
| 1982 | 1,137,707 | 0 | 1,031,435 | 23,428 | 39,122 | 0 | 0 |
| 1983 | 1,247,966 | 0 | 1,119,009 | 22,372 | 39,009 | 0 | 0 |
| 1984 | 1,194,426 | 0 | 1,066,221 | 24,320 | 42,175 | 0 | 0 |
| 1985 | 1,145,209 | 0 | 1,019,002 | 24,897 | 43,370 | 0 | 0 |
| 1986 | 1,095,471 | 0 | 972,139 | 25,802 | 44,294 | 0 | 0 |
| 1987 | 1,032,968 | 0 | 909,046 | 28,430 | 46,029 | 0 | 0 |
| 1988 | 1,104,652 | 0 | 883,919 | 31,092 | 49,399 | 0 | 0 |
| 1989 | 1,029,687 | 0 | 888,624 | 32,371 | 52,502 | 299 | 0 |
| 1990 | 1,120,812 | 0 | 962,734 | 32,728 | 55,820 | 368 | 1,387 |
| 1991 | 1,365,328 | 0 | 1,156,007 | 31,267 | 55,528 | 432 | 28,142 |
| 1992 | 1,388,278 | 0 | 1,148,108 | 32,116 | 57,918 | 312 | 33,513 |
| 1993 | 1,291,914 | 0 | 1,073,182 | 32,445 | 55,708 | 304 | 32,811 |
| 1994 | 1,114,807 | 0 | 895,968 | 34,522 | 54,263 | 294 | 32,584 |
| 1995 | 956,960 | 0 | 736,584 | 35,720 | 53,535 | 342 | 32,402 |
| 1996 | 911,469 | 0 | 707,049 | 34,796 | 51,618 | 359 | 32,043 |
| 1997 | 775,866 | 646,573 | 605,112 | 32,275 | 49,362 | 312 | 30,839 |
| 1998 | 754,194 | 613,880 | 577,226 | 37,750 | 48,766 | 351 | 30,165 |
| 1999 | 700,251 | 564,665 | 531,664 | 40,690 | 49,286 | 360 | 30,697 |
| 2000 | 654,389 | 514,528 | 486,380 | 44,762 | 49,372 | 361 | 31,837 |

Source: Statistics Canada, 2002b.
[a] The number of beneficiaries receiving total income benefits excludes employment insurance claimants receiving employment and support measures benefits.

Table 9.8, which presents nominal yearly payments under the UI/EI program, shows that nominal payments follow a similar pattern to number of beneficiaries: the highest dollar amounts of benefits were paid out in the early 1990s. Total nominal payments for regular benefits in the late 1990s and 2000 were lower than for other years in the period 1976–2000. During the same period, payments peaked for maternity benefits in 1992 and for parental benefits in 1993.

The Canadian Employment Insurance system is now financed exclusively through employer and employee contributions. As a result of reductions in annual maximum insurable earnings and the premium rate, annual maximum contributions declined from $1,245 in 1994 to $936 in 2000 for employees and from $1,745 to $1,310 for employers (table 9.9). Historical nominal amounts of average weekly benefits by benefit type are presented in table 9.10.

## VI. SOURCES OF WAGE REPLACEMENT DURING ABSENCES FROM WORK IN CANADA

This section presents analyses of wage replacement during absences from work in Canada based on data from Statistics Canada, Absence from Work Surveys, 1990–1993. The annual Survey of Absence from Work is conducted as a supplement to the Labour Force Survey and provides information on absences from work by paid employees due to illness, accident, and pregnancy. It includes number of hours worked, number of absences and duration, reasons for absence, and type of compensation received. The survey only provides information on absences that last two or more weeks. Sample size is 26,000 per year.

Table 9.11 presents the type of compensation received for the most recent absence from work of two or more consecutive weeks, by reason for absence. Absence from Work Survey data indicate that the type of compensation received varied by reason for absence. Absences that occurred as a result of pregnancy or childbirth or as a result of an accident had higher rates of compensation than did absences that occurred on account of illness. In 1992, 91.3 percent of the most recent absences on account of pregnancy and 92.2 percent of the most recent absences on account of accident received some form of financial compensation. In the same year, 82.4 percent of the most recent absences on account of illness received some form of financial compensation. Major differences occurred not only in whether any compensation was received for the most recent absence, but also in the source of compensation received for the three types of absences.

**Table 9.8. Employment Insurance Program (EI), Nominal Benefit Payments by Type of Benefit, Annual, 1971–2000**

| Year | Total Regular Benefit Payments | Sickness Benefits | Maternity Benefits | Adoption Benefits | Parental Benefits |
|---|---|---|---|---|---|
| 1971 | 25,010,142 | 788,728 | 1,005,271 | 0 | 0 |
| 1972 | 141,680,047 | 4,904,534 | 3,3035,917 | 0 | 0 |
| 1973 | 154,244,153 | 6,681,569 | 5,562,485 | 0 | 0 |
| 1974 | 160,378,553 | 8,193,388 | 6,809,010 | 0 | 0 |
| 1975 | 242,309,640 | 9,249,191 | 8,513,452 | 0 | 0 |
| 1976 | 251,640,514 | 10,816,969 | 11,635,398 | 0 | 0 |
| 1977 | 290,423,304 | 12,985,768 | 14,352,371 | 0 | 0 |
| 1978 | 333,905,788 | 13,117,086 | 16,274,851 | 0 | 0 |
| 1979 | 285,934,766 | 12,098,657 | 17,304,092 | 0 | 0 |
| 1980 | 312,379,350 | 12,889,160 | 19,562,126 | 0 | 0 |
| 1981 | 342,982,385 | 13,688,448 | 22,754,326 | 0 | 0 |
| 1982 | 637,168,745 | 14,534,628 | 26,331,011 | 0 | 0 |
| 1983 | 755,791,946 | 14,956,161 | 26,680,671 | 0 | 0 |
| 1984 | 735,427,193 | 17,046,595 | 32,993,201 | 255,909 | 0 |
| 1985 | 747,942,938 | 18,391,668 | 36,044,270 | 320,380 | 0 |
| 1986 | 767,490,188 | 20,172,105 | 39,378,938 | 345,495 | 0 |
| 1987 | 756,368,291 | 23,224,454 | 42,179,487 | 386,392 | 0 |
| 1988 | 775,781,732 | 27,096,585 | 47,221,920 | 393,372 | 0 |

(continued)

**Table 9.8.** (continued)

| Year | Total Regular Benefit Payments[a] | Sickness Benefits | Maternity Benefits | Adoption Benefits | Parental Benefits |
|------|------|------|------|------|------|
| 1989 | 820,560,409 | 29,708,430 | 52,690,175 | 402,246 | 0 |
| 1990 | 941,145,695 | 32,533,118 | 59,620,540 | 439,405 | 123,640 |
| 1991 | 1,231,941,178 | 34,138,555 | 64,879,656 | 585,802 | 29,270,452 |
| 1992 | 1,283,350,006 | 36,441,622 | 69,593,394 | 434,179 | 40,994,912 |
| 1993 | 1,214,123,178 | 36,418,065 | 67,222,352 | 420,584 | 41,099,858 |
| 1994 | 1,000,208,552 | 36,925,868 | 64,589,936 | 391,294 | 39,996,402 |
| 1995 | 819,853,013 | 37,964,087 | 64,713,893 | 483,158 | 39,979,080 |
| 1996 | 802,799,741 | 37,236,949 | 62,101,309 | 502,172 | 39,927,216 |
| 1997 | 713,464,168 | 35,717,242 | 59,587,917 | 453,470 | 38,000,368 |
| 1998 | 688,525,438 | 38,512,690 | 58,113,648 | 523,170 | 37,003,700 |
| 1999 | 649,547,294 | 42,339,002 | 60,101,319 | 566,511 | 38,333,678 |
| 2000 | 602,520,828 | 47,789,545 | 61,192,672 | 555,971 | 40,689,022 |

Source: Statistics Canada, 2002b.

[a] Total regular benefits are the sum of regular, training, job creation, and self-employment benefits provided under the income benefit program.

**Table 9.9.   Impact of Changes to the Employment Insurance (EI) Premium Rate, Maximum Insurable Earnings, 1994 to 2000**

| Year | Maximum Annual Insurable Earnings | Premium Rate per $100 of Insurable Earnings | | Annual Maximum Contribution ($) | |
|------|-----------------------------------|----------|----------|----------|----------|
| | | Employee | Employer | Employee | Employer |
| 1994 | $40,560 | 3.07 | 4.30 | 1,245 | 1,743 |
| 1995 | $42,380 | 3.00 | 4.20 | 1,271 | 1,780 |
| 1996 | $39,000 | 2.95 | 4.13 | 1,151 | 1,611 |
| 1997 | $39,000 | 2.90 | 4.06 | 1,131 | 1,583 |
| 1998 | $39,000 | 2.70 | 3.78 | 1,053 | 1,474 |
| 1999 | $39,000 | 2.55 | 3.57 | 994.50 | 1,392.30 |
| 2000 | $39,000 | 2.40 | 3.36 | 936 | 1,310 |

Source: Human Resources Development Canada, 2000a, www.hrdc-drhc.gc.ca/common/news/insur/9979. shtml.

Although absences on account of illness are covered under the Canadian Unemployment Insurance, only 19.0 percent of these absences received compensation under the UI program in 1992. A far greater percentage of the most recent absences on account of illness, 60.0 percent, received private compensation in the form of full or partial pay from the employer or through group insurance. These large differences suggest that administrative data concerning length of benefit periods cannot be applied to all absences that occur on account of illness. Specifically, administrative data indicate that annual average weeks of employment insurance benefits paid per beneficiary ranged from 4.0 to 4.8 weeks per year during the period 1988 to 1996 (table 9.12). Absence from Work Survey data, however, indicate that the average number of weeks of employment insurance received per absence for illness was less than two weeks per absence (table 9.13). These differences occur because UI/EI administrative data only cover absences with an employment insurance claim, while the Absence from Work Surveys cover all absences longer than two or more weeks, including those absences receiving no wage replacement under the UI/EI system.

Absences that occurred as a result of pregnancy or childbirth, on the other hand, were far more likely to be compensated under the UI program (86.8 percent in 1992) than through private compensation (16.5 percent in 1992). Another pattern that emerged across this time period centers on the extent to which employees received compensation from both public and private sources. For the most recent absences resulting from illness, 39.2 percent were compensated by a combination of public and private sources in 1992 compared with 14.7 percent of the most recent absences resulting from pregnancy or childbirth.

**Table 9.10. Employment Insurance Program (EI), Average Weekly Payments by Type of Benefit, Annual Averages, 1971–2001**

| Year | Regular Benefit Payments | Sickness Benefits | Maternity Benefits | Adoption Benefits | Parental Benefits |
|------|-------------------------|-------------------|--------------------|-------------------|-------------------|
| 1971 | 45.09 | 44.52 | 47.32 | 0.00 | 0.00 |
| 1972 | 62.11 | 61.99 | 59.47 | 0.00 | 0.00 |
| 1973 | 68.24 | 69.31 | 71.34 | 0.00 | 0.00 |
| 1974 | 74.62 | 74.67 | 78.76 | 0.00 | 0.00 |
| 1975 | 84.92 | 84.91 | 89.06 | 0.00 | 0.00 |
| 1976 | 93.16 | 96.37 | 104.04 | 0.00 | 0.00 |
| 1977 | 101.37 | 106.33 | 107.67 | 0.00 | 0.00 |
| 1978 | 109.43 | 115.95 | 117.60 | 0.00 | 0.00 |
| 1979 | 107.50 | 116.00 | 117.27 | 0.00 | 0.00 |
| 1980 | 119.90 | 128.00 | 129.88 | 0.00 | 0.00 |
| 1981 | 128.90 | 137.02 | 142.22 | 0.00 | 0.00 |
| 1982 | 143.68 | 149.44 | 154.64 | 0.00 | 0.00 |
| 1983 | 153.85 | 160.70 | 169.14 | 0.00 | 0.00 |
| 1984 | 160.04 | 171.64 | 178.35 | 199.01 | 0.00 |
| 1985 | 169.07 | 184.28 | 187.76 | 213.44 | 0.00 |
| 1986 | 178.74 | 196.04 | 197.07 | 230.35 | 0.00 |
| 1987 | 187.17 | 207.08 | 207.38 | 243.61 | 0.00 |
| 1988 | 199.02 | 217.05 | 218.55 | 259.65 | 0.00 |
| 1989 | 212.47 | 228.09 | 232.10 | 275.58 | 0.00 |
| 1990 | 230.00 | 239.42 | 245.98 | 293.41 | 179.45 |
| 1991 | 244.48 | 248.26 | 260.67 | 323.22 | 271.55 |
| 1992 | 252.81 | 255.13 | 272.66 | 331.00 | 275.49 |
| 1993 | 256.02 | 255.31 | 275.57 | 341.99 | 282.23 |
| 1994 | 251.80 | 245.52 | 273.53 | 340.80 | 278.93 |
| 1995 | 252.96 | 245.24 | 274.78 | 348.66 | 279.10 |
| 1996 | 255.32 | 246.81 | 274.70 | 346.50 | 380.58 |
| 1997 | 249.72 | 232.73 | 272.42 | 335.75 | 275.68 |
| 1998 | 255.30 | 236.40 | 274.35 | 343.23 | 280.09 |
| 1999 | 261.08 | 241.65 | 279.79 | 351.33 | 286.13 |
| 2000 | 265.15 | 247.53 | 285.30 | 351.96 | 293.23 |
| 2001 | 279.36 | 253.49 | 290.05 | 351.43 | 293.51 |

Source: Statistics Canada, 2002b.

**Table 9.11.** Percent of Leaves Receiving Compensation for the Most Recent Absence from Work of Two or More Consecutive Weeks, by Reason for Absence and Type of Compensation Received (1989–1992)

| Type of Compensation | Illness | Accident | Maternity or Parental |
|---|---|---|---|
| | | Reason for Absence | |
| Compensation, Any Source | | | |
| 1989 | 78.9 | 85.8 | 89.9 |
| 1990 | 80.4 | 86.0 | 85.0 |
| 1991 | 82.4 | 88.7 | 91.1 |
| 1992 | 82.4 | 92.2 | 91.3 |
| Unemployment Insurance | | | |
| 1989 | 16.8 | 7.7 | 84.4 |
| 1990 | 15.8 | 8.6 | 80.5 |
| 1991 | 14.9 | 7.6 | 83.2 |
| 1992 | 19.0 | 10.6 | 86.8 |
| Group Insurance | | | |
| 1989 | 23.9 | 12.9 | 1.4 |
| 1990 | 24.5 | 12.6 | 1.8 |
| 1991 | 24.1 | 12.6 | 1.0 |
| 1992 | 24.7 | 10.8 | 3.6 |
| Full Pay from Employer | | | |
| 1989 | 30.7 | 12.2 | 5.8 |
| 1990 | 32.2 | 15.4 | 5.2 |
| 1991 | 32.7 | 18.7 | 7.6 |
| 1992 | 32.4 | 15.8 | 6.0 |
| Partial Pay from Employer | | | |
| 1989 | 7.1 | 5.4 | 9.0 |
| 1990 | 6.0 | 4.6 | 8.3 |
| 1991 | 7.1 | 6.6 | 11.2 |
| 1992 | 7.0 | 4.5 | 8.1 |
| Unemployment Insurance & Wage Replacement from Employer or Group Insurance | | | |
| 1989 | 38.4 | 17.9 | 14.2 |
| 1990 | 39.1 | 20.4 | 14.1 |
| 1991 | 40.0 | 25.7 | 18.8 |
| 1992 | 39.2 | 20.5 | 14.7 |
| Wage Replacement from Employer or Group Insurance | | | |
| 1989 | 59.6 | 28.9 | 14.8 |
| 1990 | 61.4 | 31.3 | 14.6 |
| 1991 | 61.3 | 36.0 | 19.4 |
| 1992 | 60.0 | 29.5 | 16.5 |

Source: Statistics Canada, Absence from Work Surveys, 1990–1993, author's calculations.

Table 9.12. Number of Beneficiaries, Annual Weeks Paid, and Average Weeks per Beneficiary, Annual Data (1988–2000)

| Year | Sickness Beneficiaries | Weeks Paid | Weeks/ Ben.[a] | Maternity Beneficiaries | Weeks Paid | Weeks/ Ben.[a] | Parental Beneficiaries | Weeks Paid | Weeks/ Ben[a] |
|---|---|---|---|---|---|---|---|---|---|
| 1988 | 31,092 | 124,863 | 4.0 | 49,399 | 215,821 | 4.4 | 0 | 0 | |
| 1989 | 32,371 | 130,288 | 4.0 | 52,502 | 226,782 | 4.3 | 0 | 0 | |
| 1990 | 32,728 | 135,938 | 4.2 | 55,820 | 242,151 | 4.3 | 1,387 | 457 | 3.0 |
| 1991 | 31,267 | 137,404 | 4.4 | 55,528 | 248,728 | 4.5 | 28,142 | 107,442 | 3.8 |
| 1992 | 32,116 | 142,841 | 4.4 | 57,918 | 255,185 | 4.4 | 33,513 | 148,676 | 4.4 |
| 1993 | 32,445 | 142,673 | 4.4 | 55,708 | 243,930 | 4.4 | 32,811 | 145,562 | 4.4 |
| 1994 | 34,522 | 150,419 | 4.4 | 54,263 | 235,993 | 4.3 | 32,584 | 143,254 | 4.4 |
| 1995 | 35,720 | 154,833 | 4.3 | 53,535 | 235,347 | 4.4 | 32,402 | 143,101 | 4.4 |
| 1996 | 34,796 | 150,856 | 4.3 | 51,618 | 225,964 | 4.4 | 32,043 | 142,279 | 4.4 |
| 1997 | 32,275 | 153,464 | 4.8 | 49,362 | 218,600 | 4.4 | 30,839 | 137,648 | 4.5 |
| 1998 | 37,750 | 162,910 | 4.3 | 48,766 | 211,569 | 4.4 | 30,165 | 131,948 | 4.4 |
| 1999 | 40,690 | 175,219 | 4.3 | 49,286 | 214,584 | 4.4 | 30,697 | 133,791 | 4.4 |
| 2000 | 44,762 | 193,083 | 4.3 | 49,372 | 214,308 | 4.3 | 31,837 | 138,617 | 4.4 |

Source: Statistics Canada, 2002b.
[a] Author's calculations.

**Table 9.13. Mean Number of Weeks of Most Recent Absence from Work of Two or More Consecutive Weeks and Mean Number of Weeks of Unemployment Insurance Received (Standard Deviations in Parentheses)**

| | | *Illness or Accident* | *Pregnancy or Parental* |
|---|---|---|---|
| Mean Number of Weeks of Most Recent Absence | | | |
| | 1989 | 7.424 | 17.581 |
| | | (7.688) | (9.183) |
| | 1990 | 8.089 | 18.605 |
| | | (8.081) | (9.100) |
| | 1989–1990 | | 18.144 |
| | | | (9.146) |
| | 1991 | 8.229 | 21.266 |
| | | (8.388) | (11.044) |
| | 1992 | 8.141 | 22.009 |
| | | (8.436) | (10.950) |
| | 1991–1992 | | 21.656* |
| | | | (10.993) |
| Mean Number of Weeks of Unemployment Insurance Compensation Received | | | |
| | 1989 | 1.149 | 12.455 |
| | | (3.751) | (7.308) |
| | 1990 | 1.257 | 12.197 |
| | | (4.340) | (7.658) |
| | 1991 | 1.084 | 15.839 |
| | | (3.842) | (10.489) |
| | 1992 | 1.326 | 17.536 |
| | | (4.130) | (10.303) |

* Statistically significant at .10 level.
Source: Statistics Canada, Absence from Work Surveys, 1990–1993, author's calculations.

Table 9.14 examines the relationship between private-sector versus unemployment benefits and the duration of absences through the use of regression analyses. Based on pooled data from the 1990 to 1993 Absence from Work Surveys, these regressions indicate that the length of absences from work that occurred as a result of illness or accident were more strongly associated with private-sector policies than were absences that occurred as a result of pregnancy. Specifically, the *beta* correlation coefficient between number of weeks for most recent absence and weeks of unemployment insurance benefits received was 0.61 for maternity and parental absences, 0.48 for illness, and 0.30 for accidents. In comparison, the *beta* correlation coefficient between weeks for most recent absence and weeks of full pay from employer was 0.09 for maternity/parental absences, 0.35 for illness, and 0.25 for accidents.

These results have implications for the wage replacement debate within the United States. First, the evidence from Canada suggests that public policies

**Table 9.14. Number of Weeks for Most Recent Absence, by Type of Absence (Years 1989–1992)**

| Variable | Illness | | Accident | | Maternity/Parental | |
|---|---|---|---|---|---|---|
| | B (Standard Error) | Beta | B (Standard Error) | Beta | B (Standard Error) | Beta |
| Weeks of Unemployment Insurance Benefits | .83 (.02)*** | .48 | .81 (.03)*** | .30 | .68 (.02)*** | .61 |
| Weeks of Full Pay from Employer | .70 (.02)*** | .35 | .73 (.04)*** | .25 | .44 (.11)*** | .09 |
| Weeks of Partial Pay from Employer | .48 (.03)*** | .14 | .17 (.05)*** | .05 | .21 (.05)*** | .10 |
| Weeks of Worker's Compensation Received | .63 (.03)*** | .18 | .78 (.01)*** | .71 | N/A | N/A |
| Weeks of Group Insurance | .84 (.010)*** | .60 | .78 (.03)*** | .33 | N/A | N/A |
| Weeks Other Compensation | .63 (.03)*** | .23 | .31 (.06)*** | .06 | N/A | N/A |
| Post-Law (1991–1992) | -.11 (.15) | -.01 | -.20 (.23) | -.01 | .47 (.44) | .02 |
| Weeks Worked Full-Time in the Past Year | -.05 (.01)*** | -.07 | -.04 (.01)*** | -.04 | -.03 (.02) | -.03 |
| *Province* | | | | | | |
| Newfoundland | -.01 (.39) | .00 | -.68 (.57) | -.02 | -3.13 (1.15)*** | -.06 |
| Prince Edward Island | .22 (.54) | .00 | -.70 (.92) | -.01 | -1.96 (1.15)* | -.04 |
| Nova Scotia | -.26 (.32) | -.01 | -.46 (.54) | -.01 | -.31 (.94) | -.01 |

| | | | | | | |
|---|---|---|---|---|---|---|
| New Brunswick | .32 (.31) | .01 | .32 (.49) | .01 | -1.70 (1.04) | -.04 |
| Quebec | -.30 (.22) | -.02 | -.90 (.34) | -.04 | 2.16 (.61)*** | .09 |
| Manitoba | -.33 (.34) | -.01 | .13 (.50) | .00 | .07 (.93) | .00 |
| Saskatchewan | -.40 (.36) | -.01 | -.04 (.51) | -.00 | -.26 (.85) | -.01 |
| Alberta | .00 (.29) | .00 | -.25 (.42) | -.01 | 1.39 (.75) | .04 |
| British Columbia | -.09 (.29) | -.00 | .36 (.39) | .01 | .51 (.92) | .01 |
| *Age* | | | | | | |
| 17 to 19 | -.22 (.56) | -.00 | 2.01 (.69)*** | .04 | 3.22 (1.55)** | .05 |
| 20 to 24 | -.22 (.34) | -.01 | .19 (.39) | .01 | .29 (.61) | .01 |
| 35 to 44 | -.14 (.21) | -.01 | -.22 (.29) | -.01 | .10 (.71) | (.00) |
| 45 to 54 | .31 (.23) | .02 | .14 (.37) | .01 | -6.16 (7.98) | -.02 |
| 55 to 65 | .22 (.27) | .01 | -.48 (.49) | -.01 | N/A | |
| *Gender* | | | | | | |
| Male | .11 (.19) | .01 | -.51 (.31) | -.03 | N/A | N/A |

*(continued)*

**Table 9.14. (continued)**

| | Illness | | | Accident | | | Maternity/Parental | | |
|---|---|---|---|---|---|---|---|---|---|
| Variable | B (Standard Error) | Beta | | B (Standard Error) | Beta | | B (Standard Error) | Beta | |
| *Marital Status* | | | | | | | | | |
| Married | -.48 | -.03 | | -.15 | -.01 | | -.29 | -.01 | |
| | (.24)** | | | (.32) | | | (.98) | | |
| Widowed, Divorced, Separated | -.04 | -.00 | | .14 | .00 | | -1.35 | -.02 | |
| | (.32) | | | (.51) | | | (1.86) | | |
| *Educational Level* | | | | | | | | | |
| Grade School | -.12 | -.00 | | .18 | .01 | | .98 | .01 | |
| | (.31) | | | (.46) | | | ('.98) | | |
| Some Secondary | .05 | .00 | | .22 | .01 | | .2 | .02 | |
| | (.23) | | | (.33) | | | (.80) | | |
| Some Postsecondary | -.28 | -.01 | | .33 | .01 | | .37 | .01 | |
| | (.31) | | | (.44) | | | (.82) | | |
| Postsecondary Certificate | -.58 | -.03 | | .15 | .01 | | .44 | .02 | |
| | (.22)*** | | | (.33) | | | (.59) | | |
| University | -.04 | -.00 | | .41 | .01 | | -.32 | -.01 | |
| | (.34) | | | (.69) | | | (.81) | | |
| | N= 3873 | | | N=2352 | | | N=1448 | | |
| | R²=.64103 | | | R²=.62268 | | | R²=.41175 | | |
| | F=145.36*** | | | F=80.93*** | | | F=23.43*** | | |

\* Statistically significant at .10 level.
\*\* Statistically significant at .05 level.
\*\*\* Statistically significant at .01 level.
Source: Absence from Work Surveys, 1990–1993, author's calculations.
Note: Seventeen control variables were also included for occupation and industry classifications.

do not displace private policies in the case of illnesses and accidents. Second, the evidence also suggests that the market does not respond well to the needs of workers for wage replacement during periods of absence on account of caregiving responsibilities. Within the United States in particular, arguments against mandated leave and benefits center on the ability of the market to provide the optimal mix of wages and fringe benefits. In its most simple form, this argument holds that the market will provide leave and wage replacements to those workers who value these benefits and who are willing to accept lower wages in return to finance the nonwage benefits. (See Trzcinski, 1991, 1994; and Trzcinski and Finn-Stevenson, 1991, for a detailed discussion and critique of this argument.)

Although market forces provide widespread but not universal coverage for wage replacement during leaves for sickness, the Canadian evidence suggests that the market is not as effective in providing widespread availability of leaves and wage replacement for caregiving needs. The next section addresses another question pertinent to the debate concerning the implementation of wage replacement for sickness, accident, and family leaves and examines how absence rates and lengths of leave vary in response to policy changes.

## VII. ABSENCE RATES AND LENGTH OF LEAVE

Table 9.15 provides data on the annual number of days lost per worker for all workers in Canada; while table 9.16 examines the differences in annual rates by gender for workers without children and with children under five years of age. Not surprisingly, women with children under 5 years of age had the highest absence rates, ranging from 11.2 percent in 1987 to 17.1 in 1995. These rates include absences for maternity and paternity leave. For full-time workers as a whole, absences for own illness far exceeded absences that occurred on account of personal or family reasons, including absences for maternity and parental leaves.

Tables 9.15 and 9.16 indicate that Bill C-21, which increased the availability of maternity/parental benefits, had small effects on overall absence rates in the labor market as a whole and on absence rates for women with children under age 5. Overall absence rates for illnesses consistently exceed absence rates for personal and family responsibilities. Before and after the introduction of parental benefits on December 30, 1990, the male and female absence rates for illnesses exceeded the female absence rate for personal and family responsibilities for all years in the period 1986 to 1996. These data strongly suggest the availability of fifteen weeks of benefits for maternity

**Table 9.15. Absence Rates and Annual Number of Days Lost per Worker by Cause and Sex, Canada (Full-Time Workers)**

| Year | Illness or Disability | | | | Personal or Family Responsibility | | | |
|---|---|---|---|---|---|---|---|---|
| | Rate (Percent) | | Number of Days | | Rate (Percent) | | Number of Days | |
| | Males | Females | Males | Females | Males | Females | Males | Females |
| 1987 | 4.0 | 4.4 | 6.4 | 6.4 | 1.3 | 2.7 | 0.9 | 4.4 |
| 1988 | 4.1 | 4.9 | 6.5 | 7.3 | 1.4 | 3.1 | 0.9 | 4.8 |
| 1989 | 3.8 | 4.9 | 6.3 | 7.1 | 1.3 | 3.4 | 0.9 | 5.3 |
| 1990 | 3.7 | 4.8 | 6.2 | 7.2 | 1.1 | 3.4 | 0.9 | 5.4 |
| 1991 | 3.4 | 4.7 | 5.9 | 7.1 | 1.0 | 3.3 | 0.9 | 5.7 |
| 1992 | 3.4 | 4.2 | 5.6 | 6.7 | 1.1 | 3.2 | 0.8 | 6.1 |
| 1993 | 3.2 | 4.2 | 5.4 | 6.6 | 1.1 | 3.6 | 0.9 | 6.7 |
| 1994 | 3.2 | 4.2 | 5.4 | 6.8 | 1.1 | 3.7 | 0.9 | 6.6 |
| 1995 | 3.2 | 4.1 | 5.0 | 6.6 | 1.2 | 3.7 | 0.9 | 6.8 |
| 1996 | 3.0 | 4.1 | 5.3 | 6.5 | 1.1 | 3.7 | 0.9 | 6.7 |

Source: Statistics Canada, 2002a.

**Table 9.16. Absence Rates of Full-Time Paid Workers, by Sex and Presence of Children, Computed Annual Average (Percent)**

| | Incidence Rate, Illness or Disability | | | | Incidence Rate, Personal or Family Responsibility, Including Maternity Leave | | | |
| | With Preschoolers, under 5 Years | | Without Children | | With Preschoolers, under 5 Years | | Without Children | |
| Year | Males | Females | Males | Females | Males | Females | Males | Females |
|---|---|---|---|---|---|---|---|---|
| 1987 | 3.5 | 4.7 | 3.8 | 4.1 | 1.6 | 11.2 | 1.0 | 1.5 |
| 1988 | 3.8 | 5.4 | 3.9 | 4.7 | 2.0 | 12.8 | 1.2 | 1.6 |
| 1989 | 3.9 | 5.0 | 4.2 | 4.8 | 2.0 | 13.8 | 1.2 | 1.8 |
| 1990 | 3.7 | 4.9 | 3.9 | 4.7 | 2.1 | 13.8 | 1.1 | 2.0 |
| 1991 | 3.6 | 4.7 | 3.6 | 4.5 | 1.8 | 15.4 | 0.9 | 1.5 |
| 1992 | 3.1 | 4.2 | 3.4 | 4.1 | 1.6 | 15.7 | 0.9 | 1.5 |
| 1993 | 3.4 | 4.1 | 3.3 | 4.3 | 1.8 | 16.8 | 0.9 | 1.5 |
| 1994 | 3.0 | 4.2 | 3.1 | 4.0 | 2.1 | 17.0 | 1.0 | 1.6 |
| 1995 | 2.9 | 3.8 | 3.3 | 4.0 | 1.8 | 17.1 | 1.0 | 1.7 |
| 1996 | 2.7 | 5.1 | 3.1 | 4.1 | 1.8 | 16.7 | 0.9 | 1.7 |

Source: Statistics Canada, 2002a.

leave and ten weeks of parental leave do not have large consequences for the economy as a whole.

In terms of the specific effects of the introduction of parental benefits, administrative data from Statistics Canada indicate the average number of weeks of parental benefits per beneficiary was approximately 4.4 weeks per year following the introduction of these benefits (table 9.12). Table 9.17, which is based on Absence from Work Surveys for years 1989 to 1992, indicates that the average length of completed maternity/parental leaves was 3.5 weeks longer after the implementation of parental benefits. Average number of weeks of UI benefits received for these leaves was 4.4 weeks greater following the implementation of parental benefits—a result that corresponds exactly with the administrative data.

These findings have two direct implications for the debate surrounding the introduction of parental benefits in the United States. First, parents do adjust their leave-taking behavior in response to policy changes. This result undermines the premise that the market produces the optimal level of benefits desired by employees. If the market had been providing the optimal wage-fringe package for women, then the implementation of new benefits should have had no effect. Employees who are parents of newborn children are not compelled by the legislation to make use of the benefits and should not adjust their behavior in response to benefits that they do not want. Second, when attempting to predict future behavior as a result of changing the number of weeks of benefits available, evidence suggest that other demographic, social, and economic factors must be examined in addition to the weeks of benefits available.

## VIII. CONCLUSIONS AND POLICY IMPLICATIONS

The Canadian experience provides an answer to a number of questions concerning the potential impact of wage replacement during family and medical leave. The first centers on the issue of whether a public plan for temporary disability insurance would replace private plans. In the Canadian case, despite the availability of wage replacement during medical leaves, a far greater percentage of the most recent absences from work on account of illness are compensated through private-sector rather than through public-sector policies.

In comparison, however, the private sector is far less effective in providing for wage replacement during maternity and parental leaves. Wage replacement through the unemployment insurance program is much more prevalent than through private policies. The evidence also suggests that Canadian women do not simply adjust their labor supply after childbirth to the weeks of wage replacement under the UI/EI system. In the first two years

**Table 9.17. Number of Weeks for Most Recent Absence and Number of Weeks of Unemployment Insurance Benefits, Most Recent Completed Absence, Maternity/Parental (Years 1989–1992)**

| Received | Length of Last Absence | | Number of Weeks UI | |
|---|---|---|---|---|
| Variable | B (Standard Error) | Beta | B (Standard Error) | Beta |
| Post-Law (1991–1992) | 3.56 (.53)*** | .17 | 4.40 (0.47)*** | .24 |
| Weeks Worked Full-Time in the Past Year | 0.04 (.03) | .03 | 0.08 (0.03)*** | .09 |
| *Province* | | | | |
| Newfoundland | −3.50 (1.43)*** | −.07 | 0.09 (1.28) | .00 |
| Prince Edward Island | −2.80 (1.43)** | −.05 | −0.50 (1.28) | −.01 |
| Nova Scotia | −0.91 (1.17) | −.02 | −1.01 (1.04) | −.03 |
| New Brunswick | −2.10 (1.30)* | −.04 | −0.47 (1.16) | −.01 |
| Quebec | 3.11 (0.76)*** | −.12 | 1.18 (0.67)* | .05 |
| Manitoba | 1.54 (1.17) | .04 | 2.16 (1.04)** | .06 |
| Saskatchewan | −0.01 (1.06) | −.00 | 0.54 (0.94) | .02 |
| Alberta | 0.95 (0.94) | .03 | −0.02 (0.83) | −.00 |

*(Continued)*

**Table 9.17.** *(continued)*

| Variable | Length of Last Absence | | Number of Weeks UI received | |
|---|---|---|---|---|
| | B (Standard error) | Beta | B (Standard Error) | Beta |
| British Columbia | -0.63 (1.14) | -.02 | -1.33 (1.02) | -.04 |
| *Age* | | | | |
| 17 to 19 | -0.13 (1.94) | -.00 | -4.70 (1.72)*** | -.08 |
| 20 to 24 | 0.53 (0.76) | .02 | 0.68 (0.68) | .03 |
| 35 to 44 | -0.10 (0.88) | -.00 | -0.55 (0.78) | -.02 |
| 45 to 54 | -12.38 (9.97) | -.03 | -8.44 (8.87) | -.02 |
| *Marital Status* | | | | |
| Married | 0.99 (1.23) | .03 | 1.83 (1.09)* | .05 |
| Widowed, Divorced, Separated | -0.97 (2.33) | -.01 | 0.74 (2.07) | .01 |

*Educational Level*

| Educational Level | | | | |
|---|---|---|---|---|
| Grade School | −0.39 | −.00 | −1.70 | −.02 |
| | (2.47) | | (2.20) | |
| Some Secondary | 0.74 | .02 | 0.39 | .01 |
| | (1.00) | | (0.89) | |
| Some Postsecondary | 0.26 | .01 | 0.17 | .01 |
| Secondary | (1.02) | | (0.91) | |
| Postsecondary | 1.03 | .05 | 1.01 | .05 |
| Certificate | (0.74) | | (0.66) | |
| University | 0.06 | .00 | 0.50 | .02 |
| | (1.01) | | (0.90) | |
| | $N = 1448$ | | $N = 1448$ | |
| | $R^2 = .08$ | | $R^2 = .11$ | |
| | $F = 3.07467^{***}$ | | $F = 4.27395^{***}$ | |

\* Statistically significant at .10 level.
\*\* Statistically significant at .05 level.
\*\*\* Statistically significant at .01 level.
Source: Absence from Work Surveys, 1990–1993, author's calculations.
Note: Seventeen control variables were also included for occupation and industry classifications.

following the passage of Bill C-21, the mean number of weeks received under the UI system increased by 4.4 weeks per beneficiary per year, while the
mean weeks of leave increased by 3.5 weeks.

The Canadian experience with wage replacement during medical and
parental leave provides a basis with which to examine potential impacts of
wage replacement in the United States. At the national level, U.S. workers
have job protection under the Family and Medical Leave Act (FMLA). However, no wage replacement is provided under the FMLA. Since its enactment
in 1993, the Family and Medical Leave Act has enabled more than 24 million
Americans to take up to twelve weeks of unpaid leave to care for a newborn,
child, spouse, or parent. According to the Department of Labor, however,
about two-thirds of those who desire to take leave are unable to do so because of financial reasons. This fact prompted President Clinton, in a commencement address at Grambling State University on May 23, 1999, to call
upon the Labor Department to encourage states to develop policies that will
enable them to use unemployment insurance surpluses to provide paid
leave. As a result of this directive, the U.S. Department of Labor formulated
a regulation that allows each state to decide individually whether to use its
unemployment system to provide some income during family leave.

During the 2001–2002 legislative period, twenty-eight states considered policy options that would provide for some kind of wage replacement during
family and/or medical leave. According to the National Partnership for Women
and Families (2002), the state alternatives included initiatives that would:

- extend unemployment insurance benefits to new parents during leave
  or to employees taking leave to care for a seriously ill family member,
- extend temporary disability insurance systems, where they exist, to
  cover some or all types of family and medical leave,
- establish a new temporary disability family-leave insurance fund out of
  which family-leave benefits are financed,
- allot general-fund money (money from the state's budget) to provide income during parental or full family and medical leave,
- establish tax credits for employers who provide paid leave, and
- establish studies of the costs and benefits of providing paid family
  leave.

On September 23, 2002, California became the first state to enact any wage
replacement legislation for family leave. This legislation (SB 1661) expands
the state's disability insurance program to provide up to six weeks of wage replacement benefits to workers who take time off work to care for a seriously
ill child, spouse, parent, or domestic partner or to bond with a new child. The
act uses California's existing disability insurance program to provide benefits
for family- and medical-leave purposes. This milestone in U.S. state policy

will likely increase efforts in other states to assess the impacts of wage replacement. Hence an international comparison that draws on Canada's long and changing experience with paid medical, maternity, and parental leave can provide a rich and dynamic source of information for U.S. policy makers.

## REFERENCES

*Daily*. 1999. "Employment Insurance Support to Families with Newborns." October 23. Ottawa: Statistics Canada. At http://www.statcan.ca/Daily/English/.

Drolet, Marie, and Morissette, Rene. 1998. *Recent Canadian Evidence on Job Quality by Firm Size*. Analytical Studies Branch, Research Paper Series, 11F0019MPE, no. 128, Business and Labour Market Analysis, Statistics Canada.

Fudge, Judy. 1987. "The Public/Private Distinction: The Possibilities of and the Limits to the Use of Charter: Litigation to Further Feminist Struggles." *Osgoode Hall Law Journal* 25, no. 3: 483–553.

Housing, Family and Social Statistics Division, Statistics Canada. 2002. *Women in Canada: Work Chapter Updates*. April. Catalog no. 89F0133XIE. Ottawa: Minister of Industry.

Human Resources Development Canada. 2000a. "2000 EI Premium Reduction Means Billion Savings for Workers and Employers." At http://www.hrdc.drhc.gc.ca/common/news/insur/.

———. 2000b. *Changes to Maternity and Parental Benefits December 31, 2000*. At http://www.hrc-drhc.gc.ca/insur.

———. 2000c. *Employment Insurance and the Family Supplement*. Ottawa: HRDC. At http://www.drhc.gc.ca.

———. 2000d. *EI Monitoring and Assessment Report, 2000*. At http://www.hrdc-drhc.gc.ca.

———. 2000e. *Information on Supplemental Unemployment Benefit (SUB) Plans*. At http://www.hrdc-drdc.gc.ca/insur.

———. 2002a. *History of Unemployment Insurance*. At http://www.hrdc-drhc.gc.ca/ae-ei./hist/chapter9.

———. 2002b. *Supplements to EI Maternity and Parental Benefits*. Ottawa: HRDC. At http://www.hrdc.-drhc.gc.ca.

Lin, Zhengxi. 1998. *Employment Insurance in Canada: Recent Trends and Policy Changes*. Analytical Studies Branch, Research Paper Series, no. 11F0019MPE, no. 125, Statistics Canada.

National Partnership for Women and Families. 2002. "State Family Leave Benefit Initiatives in the 2001–2002 State Legislatures. Making Family Leave More Affordable." Available at http://www.nationalpartnership.org.

Pal, Leslie A., and Morton, F. L. 1986. "Bliss v. Attorney General of Canada: From Legal Defeat to Actual Victory." *Osgoode Hall Law Journal* 24, no. 1: 141–60.

Picot, Garnett, Myles, John, and Pyper, Wendy. 2002. "Markets, Families, and Social Transfers: Trends in Low-Income among the Young and Old, 1973–95." Pp. 11–50 in *Labour Markets, Social Institutions and the Future of Canada's Children*, ed. Miles Corak. Ottawa: Statistics Canada.

Schwartz, Laurie. 1988. "Parental and Maternity Leave Policies in Canada and Sweden." Paper no. 18. Kingston, Ontario: Industrial Relations Centre, Queens University at Kingston.

Statistics Canada, Annual Absence from Work Surveys, 1990–1993. Data available from Human Resources Development Canada,. Special Surveys Division. Available at www.statcan.ca/english/IPS/Data/75M0007XCB.htm#abstract.

Statistics Canada. 2001. *Workplace and Employee Survey Compendium, 1999 Data.* Catalogue no. 71-585-XIE. Ottawa.

———. 2002a. CANSIM II. *Labour Force Survey.* At http://cansim2.statcan.ca/cgi-win/cnsmcgi.exe. (CANSIM II is an online statistical-analyses program that, for a fee, provides extensive access to data collected by Statistics Canada.)

———. 2002b. CANSIM II. *Employment Insurance Statistics.* At http://cansim2.statcan.ca.

Trzcinski, Eileen. 1991. "Separate versus Equal Treatment Approaches to Parental Leave: Theoretical Issues and Empirical Evidence." *Law and Policy* 13, no. 1: 1–33.

———. 1994. "Family and Medical Leave, Contingent Employment, and Flexibility: A Feminist Critique of the U.S. Approach to Work and Family Policy." *Journal of Applied Social Sciences* 18, no. 1 (Fall/Winter): 71–88.

Trzcinski, Eileen, and Alpert, William T. 1994. "Changes in Pregnancy and Parental Leave Benefit in the U.S. and Canada: Judicial Decisions and Legislation." *Journal of Human Resources* 30, no. 2 (Spring): 534–54.

Trzcinski, Eileen, and Finn-Stevenson, Matia. 1991. "A Response to Arguments against Parental Leave: Findings from the Connecticut Survey of Parental Leave Policies." *Journal of Marriage and the Family* 52, no. 3: 445–60.

Women's Legal Education and Action Fund. 1992a. "Schachter: Court Can Extend Benefits to Remedy Discriminatory Laws but Powers Limited." *Leaf Lines* 5, no. 2: 5–12.

———. 1992b. *Factum of the Respondent/Intervenor.* Submitted in the Supreme Court of Canada between Her Majesty the Queen and Canada Employment and Immigration Commission (Appellants) and Shalom Schachter and Women's Legal Education and Action Fund (Respondents).

## CASES CITED

*Andrews v. Law Society of British Columbia.* 1989. Supreme Court of Canada, 91 National Reporter.

*Bliss v. Attorney General of Canada.* 1978. Supreme Court of Canada, October 31, 1978, 23 National Reporter.

*Brooks, Allen, and Dixon et al. v. Canada Safeway Ltd.* 1989. Supreme Court of Canada, May 4, 1989, 94 National Reporter.

*Schachter v. Canada et al.* 1990. Federal Court of Appeal, February 16, 1990, 108 National Reporter.

———. 1992. Supreme Court of Canada, July 9, 1992, Judgment.

# 10

## Erosion of the Male-Breadwinner Model? Female Labor-Market Participation and Family-Leave Policies in Germany[1]

*Katherine Bird and Karin Gottschall*

### INTRODUCTION

At the start of the twenty-first century the legacy of the German welfare-state model is under economic and political pressure. Not only the state's empty coffers and the continuing labor-market crisis are responsible. In addition to long-term financing problems that have become even more acute as a consequence of German unification, the German welfare state is only able to fulfill its socially redistributive function to a limited extent. An illustration of this can be found in the increasing number of households with children that are counted among the "new poor." Women play a special role in this scenario: not only are they affected by cuts in welfare spending, for example as lone parents, but through their increasing and more constant employment participation they are also promoters of a modernization process that has exposed the structural weaknesses of a welfare-state model oriented around the male breadwinner.

In the 1950s and 1960s labor-market participation and employment patterns of men and women fitted the institutional structure. Since the 1970s, with an expansion of the service sector and a decline of the industrial sector, female employment rates have been growing, especially among working mothers. This trend has continued throughout the eighties and nineties, fueled by higher educational levels of women, a pluralization of household forms, and German unification. With the decline of male-breadwinner employment patterns and a continuously high unemployment rate, female supplemental earnings gained more importance for the income of family households and put the question of combining work and family on the agenda.

Policy responses in West Germany to this process of socioeconomic modernization and individualization mainly have centered on family-leave policies and have been combined with a symbolic and modest financial upgrading of family child care for nonworking women. Given the fact that the continuous and rising labor-market participation of women is a more or less secular modernization trend, as well as a general political and economic quest of welfare capitalism, the question is whether the policies in Germany are sufficient to meet the needs of working mothers/parents. As we will argue in this chapter, the outcome and innovative effects of family-leave policies since the eighties are questionable.

The chapter is structured in four sections. The first section links theories of labor-market structures and the life course. We adopt a life-course approach that seems especially helpful to identify discrepancies between the strong institutional shaping of labor-market participation in the German welfare system on the one hand, and social change in individual action, challenging this institutional framework, on the other. The second section discusses how education and family policies regulate and influence maternal labor-market participation. The third section presents longitudinal empirical data on labor-market participation of different cohorts of women who are entitled to different forms of parental leave. This analysis allows for the identification of the distinctive effects of single policy measures on the life course and on work and life arrangements. We find that these regulations have led to the institutionalization of a "baby break" for younger women and to the promotion of labor-market exclusion. In the last section the sociopolitical implications of these outcomes are discussed.

## 1. THE LABOR MARKET AND THE LIFE COURSE

The structuring of the labor market by means of rules governing access, retention, remuneration, and promotion opportunities and the structuring of the life course by means of status passages are closely related to each other and vary considerably between different countries. In German welfare capitalism the linkage is chiefly achieved by a corporative regulation of employment relations in the industrial core sectors and an associated employment-oriented social policy, including labor-market policy (Gottschall and Dingeldey, 2000). This form of welfare regime has been referred to as a strong male-breadwinner model (Lewis and Ostner, 1994; Gottfried and O'Reilly, 2002). A correspondence exists between the "standard employment relationship," which has been firmly anchored in the German employment system for decades, and the "normal biography," which describes a standardization of the life course by institutionally defined status passages. Both the structuring of the labor market and the structuring of the life course are gendered. It is only recently that a sensitivity to gender as a master status has been evident in German labor market and life-course research (Krüger and Levy, 2000, 2001).

If we turn to the functioning of labor markets first, segmentation theory is particularly relevant. While the theory of the dual labor market (Doeringer and Piore, 1971) distinguishes a primary labor-market segment, with comparatively stable and well-paid jobs linked to corporate promotion tracks, and a secondary segment, characterized by unstable jobs requiring few qualifications and with a low level of integration into the company, for the situation in West Germany a tripartite labor-market structure has been specified. The third segment is called the occupationally specialized (*berufsfachlich*) segment that is based on the wide-ranging system of vocational training and maintained by close links between the training system and the labor market (Sengenberger, 1978, 1987).

Although this theoretical approach emphasizes the role of both corporate personnel strategies and the transcorporate state regulation of occupational training in the structuring of the labor market, it cannot adequately explain the gender segregation[2] of the German labor market. The main reason is that it ignores the existence of a two-class system within the general system for vocational training. While the so-called dual, firm- *and* school-based vocational training, deriving from the historically male-dominated apprenticeship system, is regulated by national law, guaranteeing unified training standards and inclusion in corporate codetermination, the school-based training system for the stereotypical female occupations within the service sector (for example, nurse, physiotherapist, child minder), historically deriving from the idea of "natural vocations" for women, is regulated by the individual states and characterized by a high degree of heterogeneity in qualification standards and privatization of costs. This institutionalized arrangement distributes the majority of the male certificate holders into an occupationally organized labor market in the field of industry and commercial services with credential-based claims and career patterns and the majority of female credential holders into a less regulated feminized employment sector in the broad field of social support services with low-income work and a sharp separation of semiprofessionals and professionals (Krüger, 1999).

So far we see close linkages between the training and employment systems and the role of continuous full-time employment for achieving social security. These linkages have been related to the life course. The dominant conceptualization ascribes a central role to the labor market, which, in modern societies, structures the life course in three phases on the basis of age: preparation for employment, employment itself, and withdrawal from employment (Kohli, 1985). A more gender-sensitive alternative approach does not only focus on participation in the labor market but assumes the simultaneous relevance of different institutions, with different regulations, expectations, and requirements (Levy, 1996). In this view, individuals can *participate* in several social fields simultaneously (for example, the labor market and the family). During their participation they take on certain *positions* within these fields (for example, an ordinary employee or a woman on maternity leave). Both participation and position are evaluated by the individual actors themselves, those around them, and society at large, in terms of their correspondence to culturally acceptable or deviant configurations of participation and position. The normatively dominant participation and position profile forms the socially expected "normal biography." At least two major variants ascribe a male normal biography and a female normal biography, with further differentiation possible (for example, nonmothers and mothers).

In the preunification Federal Republic of Germany (as in Austria and Switzerland) the major distinction between the female normal biography and the male normal biography was the relationship between paid employment and the family. Whereas marriage or the birth of the first child was usually associated with increased income through promotion and/or overtime for men, this status passage in the female life course usually implied a break from employment or a reduction in hours (Krüger, 2001). This gendered structuring of life courses is not only institutionally supported by the previously mentioned sociopolitical regulation of employment relationships, but also by a specific arrangement of education and family policies in Germany. This is the topic of the next section.

## 2. PUBLIC EDUCATION AND CHILD-CARE POLICIES: THE SEPARATION OF STATE AND FAMILY

In contrast to other western European states, in particular France and the Scandinavian countries, West German welfare capitalism is known as transfer intensive rather than service intensive. This means that the state more readily gives direct financial assistance to those taking on the tasks of child or elder care *in the family*, rather than investing in an expansion of public social services. This is accompanied by a limitation of women's/parent's availability to the labor market and therefore a reduction of the labor supply. The historical roots of this situation reach back to the Bismarck era when the division of labor between the family and the state (or its welfare establishments) was legally and institutionally established. This legacy implies a strict separation of child care and education. The care and upbringing of children is the "natural right" and "highest duty" of the family, whereas the state is responsible for education. "Education" is interpreted in a relatively narrow fashion, defined as imparting knowledge at school, which is also evident in the historical establishment of the system of half-day schooling without lunch. After the Second World War the newly founded German Democratic Republic departed radically from this tradition. Taking as a role model the centrally steered Soviet welfare system, it provided supervision for nursery-, preschool-, and school-aged children outside of school hours on a universal basis. As a result, the female employment rate was extremely high, even in comparison with other socialist countries. In contrast, postwar West German politicians clung to the institutional separation of child care and education, with the former remaining the firm responsibility of the family, or the wife and mother. Child-care facilities for preschool children or for supervision outside of school hours remained poor even though the employment rate of mothers began to rise.

It is only since unification and under pressure from the extremely different starting situations in the two parts of Germany that notable reforms in the area of elementary and primary schooling have taken place. In the early 1990s the Child and Youth Assistance Law (*Kinder- und Jugendhilfegesetz, KJHG*) was revised and amended so that at least on paper local authorities are required to provide an adequate level of public child-care facilities. Furthermore, in 1996 children between three and six years received the *right* to attend kindergarten for half a day, which has caused an expansion of facilities so that 80 percent of this age group can now be accommodated. However, in West Germany there are still very few facilities for children under three years and the number of all-day facilities for preschool and school children trails far behind the demand. In particular, the extension of school supervision to at least six hours a day and the provision of a meal are long awaited, but not yet realized, reforms (Gottschall, 2001).

Although the family's responsibility for child care enjoys a long tradition in Germany, actual family policy can be described as "symbolic" (Kaufmann et al., 2002). The esteem enjoyed by the family in the constitution and in public rhetoric is certainly not matched by adequate social safeguards. In the conservative welfare model, women's work in the family is considered an alternative to paid employment. However, it permits no access to the insurance system available to paid employees, nor does the financial compensation offered by the family allowance offset the costs associated with bringing up children. Even the principle of differential taxation for spouses does not benefit couples with children; instead it promotes either nonemployment or part-time employment of one partner (Dingeldey, 2001).[3]

The institutional protection of the strong male-breadwinner model with all its contradictions entered the cross fire of public criticism prior to German unification. The employment rate among mothers has been rising since the 1970s in West Germany. Women increasingly asserted their claims to egalitarian employment opportunities, to the reconciliation of work and the family, and to social insurance for wives and mothers. Against this background a hesitant reform started in the 1980s under a conservative government. The primary objectives were the recognition of child care in the family[4] and improving the compatibility of paid employment and family responsibilities. To achieve this second objective the entitlement to leave after the birth of a child has been extended considerably. In the following section the effects of changing parental-leave regulations on female employment participation will be considered.

## 3. MATERNITY-LEAVE REGULATIONS AND FEMALE EMPLOYMENT PARTICIPATION IN WEST GERMANY

The forerunners of parental-leave regulations in West Germany were the earlier maternity-leave regulations, *Mutterschutz* and *Mutterschaftsurlaub*,[5] which were only available to women in employment at the time of the birth. During their time off work they received an earnings-related benefit, intended as a compensation for lost earnings. Leading conservative politicians regarded these regulations as discriminatory against nonemployed women. As a result, the *Erziehungsurlaub* was introduced in 1986. This reform departed from previous legislation in the extension of leave to men and the entitlement to remuneration for a stay-at-home parent who had not previously been employed (*Erziehungsgeld*). The relatively modest financial remuneration (which was not increased during the fourteen years in force) was intended as a symbol of social recognition for the work of child care and child rearing within the family (Bird, 2001a, 2003). For this reason, *Erziehungsgeld* was a universal benefit. Since 1986 the period for which *Erziehungsgeld* was paid and the duration of the *Erziehungsurlaub* were increased several times, but not always equally. As a consequence, after 1992 the third year of leave received no financial remuneration, unless the leave taker worked part-time. From the introduction of the *Erziehungsurlaub* in 1986 until its replacement in January 2001, the number of fathers taking leave never exceeded 2 percent, so we concentrate our analysis on female leave taking. We will now take a closer look at the effects of these regulations on the employment participation of mothers during the past forty years.

### 3.1 Outline of the Study

The empirical investigation was conducted by the B1 Project ("Occupations in the Female Life Course and Social Change") of the Special Research Centre 186.[6] Throughout its fourteen years of research, a central focus of this project has been to study how women's life courses in Germany are structured by the first occupation they are trained for. The final phase involved the collection and analysis of the family and employment histories of a large sample of skilled female workers. These were women who formally had all attained qualifications at the same level by completing an apprenticeship as a skilled worker in one of ten occupations most frequently chosen by women.[7] Three cohorts were questioned to ensure that significant social changes could be taken into consideration. So that the employment histories had a common starting point and would be affected by labor-market or economic fluctuations at the same stage, the cohorts were defined by the date of completion of occupational training (1960, 1970, or 1980). A total of 2,130 women returned usable questionnaires providing details of their employment and family histories on a half-yearly basis from the completion of their occupational training until the date of the survey at the end of 1997 (Bird, Born, and Erzberger, 2000).

The analyses were conducted with a subsample of women selected in accordance with two criteria. First, they had to be mothers, since the life courses of women without children are unlikely to be affected by leave regulations. Second, the women had to be in paid employment shortly before the birth of their child, otherwise they would not be eligible for leave. This resulted in a subsample of 1,471 mothers.

During the time frame under investigation, three different types of maternity leave were available to mothers. Since these did not exactly correspond with the dates for apprenticeship completion that defined the cohorts, it was considered more meaningful to depart from the original structure of the data and to construct "motherhood cohorts."[8] Membership in one of the four motherhood cohorts is defined by the regulations in force at the time of a child's birth as shown in box 1.

### 3.2 Patterns of Leave Taking and Homemaking

In considering how maternity-leave regulations and occupation affect women's behavior, we will investigate their actions both on the birth of their first child and in the time following this event.[9] The first issue considered is whether or not women took leave or quit their jobs, and if the type of leave or occupation influenced this decision. The second point is how long mothers stayed at home and how this is related to the length of leave. Then we focus on the role of different occupations in the length of leave taken. Finally, we consider the return to work and the factors that influence the timing and likelihood of this move.

#### 3.2.1 *Taking Leave and Quitting Work*

Since the introduction of the *Mutterschaftsurlaub* in 1979 a legal framework has enabled women to *interrupt* their employment, which has led to

**Box 1. The Motherhood Cohorts**

- The ***Mutterschutz*** cohort: mothers whose first child was born before July 1, 1979.
- The ***Mutterschaftsurlaub*** cohort: mothers whose first child was born between July 1, 1979, and December 31, 1985.
- The short ***Erziehungsurlaub*** cohort: mothers whose first child was born after January 1, 1986, and before December 31, 1991.
- The long ***Erziehungsurlaub*** cohort: mothers whose first child was born after January 1, 1992.

increased standardization, as will be shown below. The additional security offered by the job guarantee appears to have prompted more mothers to stop work on the birth of their first child (see table 10.1).

Considering first the *Mutterschutz* cohort, just over half stopped work on the birth of the first child.[10] Slightly more than one-fifth stopped later (usually on the birth of the second child) and another fifth continued working. The introduction of the *Mutterschaftsurlaub* marked a turning point in the timing and frequency of homemaking periods in women's lives. Suddenly, the proportion of mothers becoming homemakers on the birth of the first child rose to 81.1 percent, the proportion becoming late homemakers was halved to 10.9 percent, and the number who continuously worked fell considerably. This trend continues in both the *Erziehungsurlaub* cohorts, where even more mothers took time off (nearly 90 percent on the first birth), and the proportion who worked without interruption drops further from the short to the long *Erziehungsurlaub*. These figures are the first evidence of the standardizing effect of maternity-leave regulations.

A more complex multivariate analysis of the transition from employment to homemaking found that in the *Mutterschutz* cohort the likelihood of stopping work on the birth of the first child was influenced by a range of factors, including occupation, age, and marital status. In particular, women trained as bank employees, retail sales assistants, industrial office employees, and nurses are significantly less likely to quit their jobs than women who trained for other occupations, whereas older and married women are more likely to quit. In the *Mutterschaftsurlaub* cohort the influence of these factors declines and they are completely absent in the combined *Erziehungsurlaub* cohort. Differences between the women, which in the past accounted for variations in behavior, are no longer important. Since the introduction of the *Erziehungsurlaub* birth is no longer one of several necessary conditions for stopping work, but in itself it has become the sole sufficient condition (Bird, 2003).

### 3.2.2 How Long Do Women Stay at Home?

The introduction and extension of maternity leave has resulted in increased uniformity of behavior after childbirth, such that taking a "baby break" has become a virtually universal phenomenon. The various regulations also imposed a limit on the duration of this break. Whether or not this was adhered to will be investigated in this section.

Survivor functions were calculated to describe how long women stayed at home following the birth of their first child.[11] These start with the birth of the first child, when the women either quit work or took leave. Women who stayed at home for longer than their leave entitlement either received an extension to their leave because they had another child or they quit their jobs. The time spent at home ended with commencement of an employment-related activity. This could be paid employment, registering as unemployed, or

**Table 10.1. Timing and Frequency of the Labor-Market Exits According to Motherhood Cohort**

| Motherhood Cohort | Mothers Who Stopped Working on the Birth of the First Child | | Mothers Who Stopped Working Later | | Mothers Who Did Not Stop Working | | Total |
|---|---|---|---|---|---|---|---|
| | n | % of cohort | n | % of cohort | n | % of cohort | N |
| Mutterschutz | 399 | 56.7 | 153 | 21.7 | 152 | 21.6 | 704 |
| Mutterschaftsurlaub | 283 | 81.1 | 38 | 10.9 | 28 | 8.0 | 349 |
| Erziehungsurlaub (short) | 293 | 89.0 | 14 | 4.3 | 22 | 6.7 | 329 |
| Erziehungsurlaub (long) | 80 | 89.9 | 6 | 6.7 | 3 | 3.4 | 89 |
| Total | 1055 | 71.7 | 211 | 14.3 | 205 | 13.9 | 1471 |

furthering education or training.[12] The four survivor functions, one for each motherhood cohort, are shown in figure 10.1. The curves show how long the mothers "survived" at home. At the start of the observation all of the women are at home. As time passes, more and more leave this status to take up new activities and so the curve declines towards the x-axis.

The effects of the different leave regulations on the length of time mothers spent at home can be best illustrated by considering the example of the *Erziehungsurlaub*. The two motherhood cohorts entitled to *Erziehungsurlaub* only vary in the length of leave available to them; all other aspects were equal. Nevertheless, the courses taken by the curves for these two cohorts vary considerably. If the length of leave available was relatively short, then a large proportion of the mothers returned to the labor force quickly. This is the case for the short *Erziehungsurlaub* cohort (and also for the *Mutterschaftsurlaub* cohort). The time periods leading up to and following the expiration of leave are characterized by a large proportion of mothers returning to the labor force. Eighteen months after the birth of their first child 40 percent of the short *Erziehungsurlaub* cohort had started a new activity. Following this initial high rate of return, the curve flattens out considerably, which means that in each following time interval only a small proportion of mothers took up a new activity.

The initial part of the curve for the long *Erziehungsurlaub* cohort is very different. The decline is very shallow, which means that only a small proportion of mothers returned to the labor force in the first two years. This parallels the *Mutterschutz* cohort that was not entitled to any extended leave. After this point the proportion of mothers from the long *Erziehungsurlaub* cohort end-

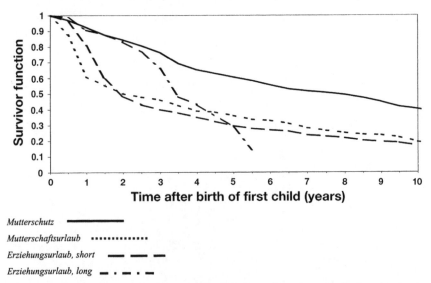

**Figure 10.1. Duration of the Homemaking Episodes of the Four Motherhood Cohorts**

ing leave starts to increase, slowly at first but then much more rapidly as the three-year-leave entitlement expires. After two-and-a-half years at home 23 percent of the mothers in the long *Erziehungsurlaub* cohort had returned to the labor force; after three-and-a-half years this figure had risen to 52 percent.

If the pattern of ending homemaking observed in the *Mutterschutz* cohort is considered typical for mothers with no leave entitlement, then it can be seen clearly that the introduction of fixed periods of extended maternity leave has led large numbers of mothers to spend less time at home. A fixed period of leave introduces more uniformity into the duration of employment interruptions, which end, primarily, around the expiration of the leave entitlement.

Further analyses indicated that in both *Erziehungsurlaub* cohorts the women who had a second child before their leave expired took longer to return to the labor market than those with only one child. With the birth of the second child a new period of leave starts, so that women in the long *Erziehungsurlaub* cohort could stay at home for an additional three years (Bird, 2003). This was, however, not the case for all mothers. A small proportion of mothers returned to work between births, a trend that until now has been identified in East Germany only (Falk and Schaeper, 2001).

### 3.2.3 The Role of Occupation in Mothers' Employment Prospects

Occupation played a minimal role in determining which mothers stayed at home longest. In all cohorts nurses and industrial office workers return to the labor market faster and in greater numbers than women who trained in other occupations. Part-time working is very common among the nurses returning to work, and, contrary to popular beliefs, it would appear that working night shifts makes it easier to combine family and employment responsibilities. Furthermore, it is not uncommon for larger hospitals to provide child-care facilities for employees' children. This removes the need to search for an appropriate nursery or kindergarten before returning to work, and it saves working mothers an extra journey before and after work to drop off or collect their children.

Due to their pronounced attachment to not only the labor market but also to their occupation, the nurses' pattern of labor-market participation highlights three significant features of the German labor-market. First is the consistent relevance of the occupation trained for, second is the standardizing influence of a fixed period of leave, and the third is the increase in part-time employment. Previous research has shown that the occupation in which women start their employment careers has a significant impact on their labor-market prospects in the long run (Born, 2000; Born et al., 1996; Kurz, 1998; Lauterbach, 1994). Even within the relatively narrow spectrum of typically female occupations there is variation with respect to the ability of occupations to retain both young women after training and mothers. In this study nursing emerged as the occupation that could best offer acceptable long-term employment prospects to both mothers and nonmothers. In the following set of charts the nurses' patterns of labor-market participation after the birth of their last child is shown. A comparison of the working patterns of mothers who had children under different leave regulations highlights both the effects of these regulations and wider trends during the historical period under investigation.

The charts show the proportion of mothers participating in each type of employment or family work following the birth of their youngest child.[13] Even a brief glance at the charts in figure 10.2 reveals the importance of employment in the first occupation for the nurses. The two shaded areas at the bottom of the graphs represent full-time and part-time employment in the first occupation and these two activities account for up to 70 percent of all activities. The second notable development is the shift from full-time to part-time employment. Whereas around 25 percent of the nurses in the *Mutter-*

a) *Mutterschutz* cohort

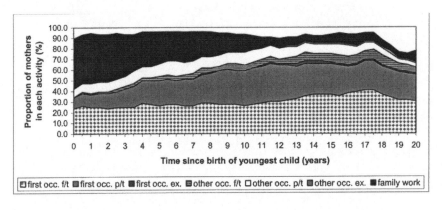

b) *Mutterschaftsurlaub* cohort

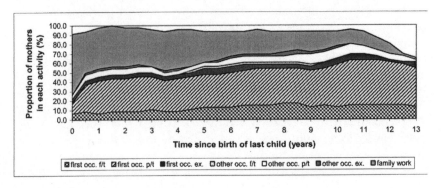

c) short *Erziehungsurlaub* cohort

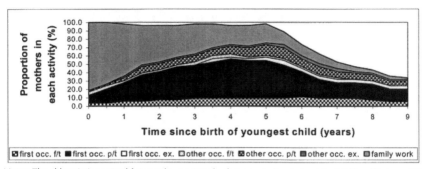

Notes: The abbreviations stand for: employment in the first occupation trained for full-time (first occ. f/t), part-time (first occ. p/t), or social-insurance exempt (first occ. ex.); employment in other occupations full-time (other occ. f/t), part-time (other occ. p/t), or social-insurance exempt (other occ. ex.)

**Figure 10.2. Paid Employment and Family Work among the Nurses**

*schutz* cohort worked full-time in the ten years after the birth of their youngest child, the comparable figure in the *Mutterschaftsurlaub* cohort for the same time period is closer to 10 percent and never exceeds this in the short *Erziehungsurlaub* cohort. Furthermore, the proportion of full-time employment remains virtually constant in all cohorts during the observation, only starting to increase in the *Mutterschutz* cohort after ten years. Part-time working, on the other hand, starts at a low level but then increases during the observation. The increase in part-time working mirrors, to a large extent, the decrease in family work, which leads to the conclusion that many of the nurses who return to work after a period at home return on a part-time basis, whereas those who work full-time were less likely to stop when they had children.

With the introduction and extension of a fixed period of leave the proportion of women who did not stop working declined dramatically, from 42 percent in the *Mutterschutz* cohort to 26 percent in the *Mutterschaftsurlaub* cohort and 19 percent in the short *Erziehungsurlaub* cohort. Nevertheless, it is clear that many of the mothers who did stop working only stopped for the period of leave and returned to work when it expired. The *Mutterschaftsurlaub* cohort best illustrates this behavior; nearly one-quarter of the mothers (22 percent) only stopped work for six months and then returned to nursing on a part-time basis. The same pattern of taking leave and returning to nursing part-time is also evident in the short *Erziehungsurlaub* cohort, but less clear-cut because the leave entitlement of this cohort varied between ten and eighteen months.

The final point to note is the high proportion of mothers who return to some form of employment and that this has become faster over the cohorts.

After thirteen-and-a-half years, 87 percent of the *Mutterschutz* cohort were engaged in some type of employment and only 7 percent were homemakers. After ten-and-a-half years, the comparable figures for the *Mutterschaftsurlaub* cohort were 80 and 15 percent, respectively, and after only five years 75 percent of the short *Erziehungsurlaub* cohort were already in some type of employment. To put these figures into a wider context, the aggregate employment rate of all mothers with children under fifteen years of age was only 40 percent in the 1970s, increasing gradually to top 50 percent in the early 1990s (Klammer et al., 2000). In comparison, it is quite clear that women who trained as nurses display a high degree of attachment not only to the labor market but, in particular, to their occupation.

### 3.2.4 The Relative Power of Maternity-Leave Regulations and Social Change

The analysis of the survivor functions revealed a distinct change in women's behavior over time. The introduction and extension of fixed-term maternity leave has had a twofold effect. First, the length of leave taken corresponds closely to the length of leave available. Second, a greater proportion of mothers have returned to the labor force since the introduction of fixed-term leave. However, the different maternity-leave regulations are not the only source of variation between these mothers. They have also been affected by wider aspects of social change over the past forty years, of which two are of particular relevance: the changes in when and how women work, and attitudes towards this.

Turning first to women's, and in particular mother's, patterns of labor-market participation. Since the 1960s more mothers engage in paid work. Numerous studies and official statistics show that younger generations spend less time at home following the birth of a child.[14] For example, the proportion of mothers in paid employment whose youngest child was between six and fourteen years of age rose from 44 percent in 1972 to 62 percent in 1996 (BMFSFJ, 1998). The rise in part-time employment is responsible for this change. In fact, fewer mothers with children of minority age were in full-time employment in 1996 than in 1972 (16 percent as opposed to 21 percent). Labor shortages during the 1960s led to the introduction of measures to encourage the reserve of qualified homemakers to return to employment. The wide-scale introduction of part-time and social-insurance-exempt positions enabled mothers to return to a job but, at the same time, to still fulfill their family responsibilities.[15] With the support of trade unions, the employers' offers of reduced hours for women with families became widely accepted (Eckart, 1986; Oertzen, 1999). Attitudes to the employment of women and mothers changed, and acceptance for life-long female employment (with breaks for children) grew. It is, however, questionable whether mothers' desire to return to work was really new, or whether it was just the opportunities and the greater social acceptance that changed (Born et al., 1996).

Given these wider social changes the question arises of whether the different durations of the homemaking episodes shown in figure 10.1 are really the result of changing maternity-leave policies, or can they simply be attributed to the wider process of social change? An investigation of the mothers who completed their occupational training in 1970 should answer this question. Most of these women had their children under either the *Mutterschutz* or the *Mutterschaftsurlaub* regulations. This means that within one cohort, that is, a group of women confronted with similar labor-market conditions and similar attitudes towards women, work, and children, two different types of maternity leave were available. This is ideal for testing the effects of the different leave regulations. By keeping apprenticeship-completion cohort constant we can control the role of changing labor-market conditions, norms, and attitudes. Therefore, variations in the duration of homemaking episodes among these women must be due to other factors, such as the maternity-leave regulations in force at the time.

A comparison of the survivor functions for the duration of the time at home following the birth of the first child for the women from the 1970 apprenticeship-completion cohort[16] shows that many of the women entitled to a *Mutterschaftsurlaub* ended their homemaking episode far more quickly than those entitled to *Mutterschutz*. Of the former group, 40 percent had returned to a new activity by one year after the birth. Of the latter group, only 7 percent had made this transition by this time (Bird, 2001b, 2003).

Although this result seems fairly conclusive, it should be remembered that there could be other differences between these women that could also affect the length of time spent at home. Age could be one such factor, since women eligible for the *Mutterschaftsurlaub* only started having children in 1979, whereas those eligible for *Mutterschutz* had children from 1970 onwards. To investigate the influence of a wider range of factors a model for the transition rate of a return to the labor force was estimated. The greatest influences on the likelihood of a return to the labor force were the birth of another child and the expiration of leave. These effects work in opposite directions, so that a further birth dramatically reduces the likelihood of a return (by 80 percent), leading to longer periods at home, but in the half year when leave expires the likelihood of a return is three-and-a-half times greater than at other times. Once these effects and the role of characteristics such as marital status and employment history had been discounted, the major factor found to affect the time spent at home was the *type* of leave. Mothers who were entitled to either a short or long *Erziehungsurlaub* were twice as likely to return to the labor force as the women entitled to *Mutterschutz* (Bird, 2003).

The effects of increasing age on the rate of return to the labor force follow a U-shape, such that younger women are likely to leave homemaking quickly, and as they get older this likelihood drops before starting to rise again for older women. Consequently, younger and older women have similar, higher rates of return, whereas those in between have a lower rate. Returning to the example of the 1970 apprenticeship-completion cohort, the older women in this cohort (entitled to *Mutterschaftsurlaub*) would have a similar transition rate to the youngest women (entitled only to *Mutterschutz*). Therefore, the differences between the younger and the older women cannot merely be attributed to age at first birth, nor to other characteristics such as being married or having another child, since these are just as common amongst both groups. Since all these women are members of one apprenticeship-completion cohort these differences cannot be attributed to wider processes of social change—but the most plausible explanation for them is the maternity-leave regulations the women encountered.

## 4. CONCLUSIONS

We have seen that the introduction of and successive increases in the length of maternity leave have had a profound effect on mothers' labor-market participation. In the areas investigated—leaving employment, time at home, return to the labor force—the degree of standardization in the behavior of women eligible for different types of leave has increased. This standardization accords with the provisions of the maternity-leave regulations that they encountered and is to such an extent that the relevance of other distinguishing features, such as age, marital status, or occupationally specific labor-market factors have disappeared. Furthermore, this standardization cannot be explained away by reference to social change; in fact only counterevidence is found for the frequently asserted increased diversity and differentiation of life courses that is to be found in modern societies. In this one particular area of the reconciliation of employment and family commitments a startling degree of uniformity can be observed.

The simple explanation for this is that mothers abide by the institutional steering of their life courses prescribed for them by legislation and backed up by normative expectations of colleagues, friends, and families. These dual measures—the external policy instrument and the expectations of their normative environment—combine to produce a nearly insurmountable prescribed pattern for the labor-market participation of mothers with children under three years old; that is, they stay at home. Furthermore, there is also recent evidence (Born, 2001; Hopf and Hartwig, 2001) to suggest that women's attitudes toward staying at home with young children are changing so that a three-year interruption from employment is becoming a norm that features in the life plans of young women.

A further consequence of the establishment of a new phase in the female life course is its corresponding effect on men's life courses. A woman on *Erziehungsurlaub* does not have sufficient income to support herself and her child. Consequently, she is dependent on either a partner or the state to provide for her. Since the majority of mothers live with a male partner, if she stays at home to look after the child, he will have to work to support his family. In this way the *Erziehungsurlaub* has cemented the traditional gendered division of labor.[17] To deviate from the accepted practice of a mother taking *Erziehungsurlaub* requires nonconformity from both the mother *and* the father. Whereas one parent may be able to tolerate the disapproval of family, friends, and work colleagues, expecting both to do so would imply overcoming even greater hurdles. It is these constraints of institutionalized leave taking that explain why a supposedly gender-neutral policy has only succeeded in perpetuating traditional gender relations.

The findings presented here are based on retrospective data covering the period from 1960 until 1997. Since then there have been changes in the institutional framework regulating female employment. The most immediately relevant change is that of parental leave that came into force in January 2001. The new regulation, called *Elternzeit*, retains the old structure of the *Erziehungsurlaub* but also introduces the new option of both parents reducing their working hours and caring for their child. However, there are no incentives for couples to choose this option and in the past the number of women who did work a few hours a week while in *Erziehungsurlaub* was small (8–10 percent; see Engelbrech and Jungkunst, 2001). Given that the old norms and structures have not been affected by this change, the likelihood of a significant increase in either the number of men taking leave or the number of women working during leave is low (Koch, 2001).

A second measure that may have a greater impact on working patterns is the new right for workers to request a reduction in their hours, introduced in January 2001. This can be achieved in one of two ways. At the end of a period of *Elternzeit* an employee in a company with more than fifteen employees has the right to request a part-time position on their return. Only if the employer can show that there are serious business reasons (which have not yet been defined) against such a reduction can they refuse the request. Second, under the new law for part-time working (*Teilzeitgesetz*) that came into force in January 2001, this same right to request a reduction in hours is open to all employees in firms of the same size who have been employed for more than six months. As yet it is too early to tell how many people will make use of this right, and whether they are men or women. It is likely that women returning after a period of leave will predominate, since surveys have repeatedly shown that many (more in the West than in the East) already work part-time after an *Erziehungsurlaub* (Beckmann and Kurtz, 2001; Engelbrech and Jungkunst, 2001; Engelbrech et al., 1997). This measure also carries a symbolic message. Expressly giving mothers the right to work fewer hours implies that this is what they should be doing. It is interesting here to consider the differences between East and West Germany. Before unification it was normal for all East German women to be in full-time employment. The high degree of labor market attachment even among mothers has survived over the last ten years, as has repeatedly been shown (e.g., Falk and Schaeper, 2001; Klammer et al., 2000; BMFSFJ, 1998). Even with the same institutional framing conditions the different normative expectations still exert a major influence on behavior, a fact that is also seen in the area of day care for young children, which enjoys far higher acceptance in the East than the West.[18]

Both of these reforms, that of parental leave and the extension of opportunities for part-time working, have met resistance from the corporate sector concerned about the cost implications of these new measures. Furthermore, the fact that in expanding service industries, such as multimedia, cultural occupations, and software production, there is a tendency to long and unregulated working hours implies that the principle of the "ever ready" worker, unhindered by private responsibilities, has changed little (Gottschall and Betzelt, 2001). It is only in individual companies keen to retain highly qualified young personnel that openness to more family-friendly working arrangements or offers of active support for child care (for example, company kindergarten or procurement of child minders) is evident (Moliter, 2001).

From the perspective of the welfare state, the growth of structural unemployment, particularly in East Germany, and changes in labor-market policy have led to the erosion of "standard employment contracts," the principle of lifelong full-time employment that forms the basis for the breadwinner-homemaker family model. Increasing uncertainty on the part of employees has not been met with increased security on the part of the welfare state, which is coming under ever greater pressure. The dissonance between the realities of the labor market and normative images of an outdated ideal are becoming more profound. To solve these problems it would be necessary to finally dispense with traditional notions of the family and develop measures to help all types of families participate in paid employment (Gottschall and Dingeldey, 2000). As this chapter shows, there is little evidence that such a change is occurring within the field of family and educational policy. However, a comparison of Germany with other EU and OECD countries reveals increasing social pressure for an effective reform of the institutions of the German welfare state. In closing, two examples will be presented that illustrate the danger of increasing social disintegration.

The recently published results of an OECD comparison of school students' performance revealed structural weaknesses of the German educational system (Baumert et al., 2001) that provoked intense public debate in an election year. In addition to the poor performance of the German children, the study also revealed the resilience of the reproduction of social inequality. In the debates and commentaries on the results, explanations have focused on the lack of linkages between the elementary and primary sectors, and the shortcomings of the half-day system of schooling. These are the foundations of the German system of child care that undervalues public education, but sociopolitically supports the responsibility of the mother or the family for child care. The victims of this development are not only the women who face structural disadvantages in accessing the labor market, but also the children from underprivileged (and often immigrant) families (Allmendinger and Leibfried, 2002).

The present institutional framework not only reconstructs traditional gender roles, but it also enhances new forms of social inequality among women and among childless households and households with children. There is a long-term trend among well-qualified women to either delay or forgo completely having children (Klammer et al., 2000). Since these are the women who have a high earnings potential, and their partners often have similar qualifications and career prospects, income disparities between highly qualified dual-earning couples and those with lower resources are increasing (Blossfeld et al., 2001). When children enter the picture, the situation becomes even more extreme. Well-qualified women tend not to take parental leave in its full length and are able to employ other women to take over many household and child-care tasks, which enables them to work full-time. Women with lower-status jobs (in West Germany) tend to take their full entitlement of leave and adopt the classical homemaker role. When they return to work, it is more likely to be part-time and to jobs with lower qualification demands. Consequently, such households have reduced earnings and higher poverty risks once they start having children. The income of academic families is less affected by the presence of children (Kirner, 1999).

As we have tried to show, the German institutional system is suffering from a modernization deficit in assuming traditional patterns of work and life while at the same time economic and cultural trends are weakening the male-breadwinner model. Women departing from the lifelong-housewife career might try to meet the norms of the traditional male "ever ready" worker, but apart from a highly qualified professional group with options for individual solutions the majority of women as working mothers will find themselves dependent on a male breadwinner or the state. Thus a more sustainable transformation of the German welfare model remains on the agenda.

## NOTES

1. We would like to thank Heidi Gottfried for her helpful and thorough comments on an earlier draft.

2. The term "segregation" will be used to refer to the gendered divisions of the labor market in order to avoid confusion with the term "segmentation" as used in labor-market segmentation theory.

3. Instead of being taxed as individuals, married couples can choose for one partner (with a high income) to pay a low rate of income tax and the other partner (with a low income) to pay a high rate, thus maximizing their joint net income.

4. Since the beginning of the nineties, depending on the mother's age, up to three years of nonemployment per child are considered equivalent to employment in calculating pension entitlements.

5. The literal translations of *Mutterschutz* and *Mutterschaftsurlaub* are "protection of mothers" and "motherhood leave," respectively.

6. The center's overall research objective was "Status Passages and Risks in the Life Course." It was funded by the Deutsche Forschungsgemeinschaft and supported by the University of Bremen from 1988 to 2001.

7. The full titles of the occupations are: doctor's clerical and medical assistant, hairdresser, hotel receptionist, office employee in industry, nurse, qualified bank employee, qualified office employee, specialist sales assistant in a baker's or butcher's shop, qualified retail sales assistant (in other branches), and wholesale and export office employee.

8. These can be considered cohorts insofar as membership is based on a defining event, in this case giving birth on a certain date. The range of dates within the cohorts is, however, rather large for these to be strictly considered true cohorts. Consequently, the term is used rather loosely to denote the different groups of women who gave birth when different laws were in force.

9. Comparable analyses relating to the second and further children produced virtually identical results, but from a much reduced sample. Thus the results relating to the first child can be considered typical for employed women in the sample.

10. The statutory prohibition on mothers working in the eight weeks following a birth is not considered leave.

11. The product limit estimator was used, as this is temporally more sensitive and less arbitrary than the life-table method.

12. These last two activities indicate a willingness to participate in the labor market that cannot currently be satisfied by reason of labor-market fluctuations, skill depreciation, availability of child-care facilities, or other structural factors. Consequently, including such activities as valid reasons for terminating homemaking restricts the homemaking period to a "voluntary" devotion to the family and not to difficulties in reentering employment (see also Falk and Schaeper, 2001, and Kirner and Schulz, 1992).

13. No distinction was made between the first, second, or further children.

14. For example, Kurz, 1998; Lauterbach, 1991, 1994; Kirner and Schulz, 1992; BMFSFJ, 1998; Klammer et al., 2000.

15. Until 1976 married women in West Germany were, by law, only permitted to be in paid employment if this did not lead them to neglect their household duties.

16. In this cohort 164 women fell into the *Mutterschutz* cohort, 99 were in the *Mutterschaftsurlaub* cohort, and 8 were in the short *Erziehungsurlaub* cohort. This last cohort is not included in this analysis due to its small size.

17. Vaskovics and Rost (1999) come to the same conclusion from studying *fathers* in *Erziehungsurlaub*.

18. In answer to the question of whether day care for children under three was damaging to their development, 62 percent of West Germans and 40 percent of East Germans agreed (BMFSFJ 1997).

# REFERENCES

Allmendinger, Jutta, and Stephan Leibfried. 2002. "Bildungsarmut im Sozialstaat." In *Lebenszeiten. Erkundungen zur Soziologie der Generationen,* ed. Günter Burkhard and Jürgen Wolf, 287–316. Opladen: Leske + Budrich.

Baumert, Jürgen; Eckhard Klieme, Michael Neubrand, Manfred Prenzel, Ulrich Schiefele, Wolfgang Schneider, Petra Stanat, Klaus-Jürgen Tillmann, Manfred Weiß. 2001. PISA 2000: Basiskompetenz von Schülerinnen und Schülern im internationalen Vergleich. Opladen: Leske + Budrich.

Beckmann, Petra, and Beate Kurtz. 2001. "Die Betreuung der Kinder ist der Schlüssel." *IAB Kurzbericht,* Bundesanstalt für Arbeit no. 10, June 15.

Bird, Katherine. 2001a. "Parental Leave in Germany: An Institution with Two Faces?" In *Institutionen und Lebenslauf im Wandel. Institutionelle Regulierung von Lebensläufen,* ed. Lutz Leisering, Rainer Müller, and Karl Schumann, 55–87. Weinheim and München: Juventa.

———. 2001b. "The Institutional Shaping of Female Life Courses: How Maternity-Leave Regulations Affect Female Employment Participation." Paper presented to the international symposium "Institutions, Interrelations, Sequences: The Bremen Life-Course Approach," University of Bremen, September 26–28.

———. 2003. "Reconciling Work and the Family: The Impact of Parental Leave Policies and Occupation Trained for on the Female Life Course." Ph.D. diss., University of Bremen.

Bird, Katherine, Claudia Born, and Christian Erzberger. 2000. "Ein bild des eigenen Lebens zeichnen. Der Kalender als Visualisierungsinstrument zur Erfassung individueller Lebensverläufe." Working Paper no. 59, Bremen: Sonderforschungsbereich 186.

Blossfeld, Hans-Peter, Sonja Drobnič, and Gotz Rohwer. 2001. "Spouses' Employment Careers in (West) Germany." In *Careers of Couples in Contemporary Society: From Male Breadwinner to Dual-Earner Families,* ed. Hans-Peter Blossfeld and Sonja Drobnič, 53–76. Oxford: Oxford University Press.

Born, Claudia. 2000. "Erstausbildung und weiblicher Lebenslauf. Was (nicht nur) junge Frauen bezüglich der Berufswahl wissen sollten." In *Übergänge. Individualisierung, Flexibilisierung und Institutionalisierung des Lebensverlaufs,* ed. Walter Heinz, 50–65. Zeitschrift für Soziologie der Erziehung und Sozialisation. Beiheft.

———. 2001. "Family Images of Women in an Intergenerational Comparison: An Indicator for Modernization Processes in Gender Relations?" Paper presented to the international symposium "Institutions, Interrelations, Sequences: The Bremen Life-Course Approach," University of Bremen, September 26–28 (to be published in W. R. Heinz, V. W. Marshall, eds., *The Social Dynamics of the Life Course: Transitions, Institutions, and Interrelations.* Berlin/New York: Aldine de Gruyter, 2003.).

Born, Claudia, Helga Krüger, and Dagmar Lorenz-Mayer. 1996. *Der unentdeckte Wandel. Annäherung an das Verhältnis von Struktur und Norm im weiblichen Lebenslauf.* Berlin: edition sigma.

Bundesministerium für Familie, Senioren, Frauen und Jugend (BMFSFJ). 1997. *Gleichberechtigung von Frauen und Männern—Wirklichkeit und Einstellung in der Bevölkerung.* Bonn: Kohlhammer.

———. 1998. *Die Familie im Spiegel der amtlichen Statistik.* Bonn: Kohlhammer.

Dingeldey, Irene. 2001. "European Tax Systems and Their Impact on Family Employment Patterns." *Journal of Social Policy* 30, no. 4: 653–672.

Doeringer, Peter, and Michael Piore. 1971. *International Labour Markets and Man Power*. Lexington: Heath.

Eckart, Christal. 1986. "Halbtags durch das Wirtschaftswunder. Die Entwicklung der Teilzeitarbeit in den 60er Jahren." In *Grenzen der Frauenlohnarbeit. Frauenstrategien in Lohn- und Hausarbeit seit der Jahrhundertwende*, ed. H. Kramer, C. Eckart, I. Riemann, and K. Walser, 183–249. Frankfurt: Campus.

Engelbrech, Gerhard, Hannelore Gruber, and Maria Jungkunst. 1997. "Erwerbsorientierung und Erwerbstätigkeit ost- und westdeutscher Frauen unter veränderten gesellschaftlichen Rahmenbedingungen." In *Mitteilungen aus der Arbeitsmarkt- und Berufsforschung*, ed. K. Bolte and U. A. Martin, 150–169. Stuttgart: Verlag W. Kohlhammer.

Engelbrech, Gerhard, and Maria Jungkunst. 2001. "Wie bringt man Beruf und Kinder unter einem Hut?" *IAB Kurzbericht*, Bundesanstalt für Arbeit, no. 7, April 12.

Falk, Susanne, and Hildegard Schaeper. 2001. "Erwerbsverläufe von ost- und westdeutschen Müttern im Vergleich: ein Land ein Muster?" In *Individualisierung und Verflechtung*, ed. C. Born and H. Krüger, 181–210. Weinheim: Juventa.

Gottfried, Heidi, and Jacqueline O'Reilly. 2002. "Re-regulating Breadwinner Models in Socially Conservative Welfare Systems: Comparing Germany and Japan." *Social Politics* 9, no. 1 (Spring): 29–59.

Gottschall, Karin. 2001. "Erziehung und Bildung im deutschen Sozialstaat. Stärken, Schwächen und Reformbedarfe im europäischen Vergleich." *Arbeitspapier des Zentrums für Sozialpolitik der Universität Bremen.* September.

Gottschall, Karin, and Sigrid Betzelt. 2001. "Self-Employment in Cultural Professions: Between De-gendered Work and Re-gendered Work and Life-Arrangements?" Paper presented at the Gender Conference on "Changing Work and Life Patterns in Western Industrial Countries," Wissenschaftszentrum Berlin, September 20–21, Berlin. Retrieved September 21, 2001, from http://www.zes.uni-bremen.de/~kgs/vorträge.htm.

Gottschall, Karin, and Irene Dingeldey. 2000. "Arbeitsmarktpolitik im konservativ-korporatistischen Wohlfahrtsstaat: Auf dem Weg zu reflexiver Deregulierung?" In *Der deutsche Sozialstaat: Bilanzen, Reformen, Perspektiven*, ed. S. Leibfried and U. Wagschal, 306–339. Campus: Frankfurt.

Hopf, Christel, and Myriam Hartwig, eds. 2001. *Liebe und Abhängigkeit. Partnerschaftsbeziehungen junger Frauen*. Weinheim: Juventa.

Kaufmann, Franz-Xaver, Anton Kuijsten, and Hans-Joachim Schulze, eds. 2002. "Family Life and Family Policies in Europe." *Problems and Issues in Comparative Perspective*, Vol 2. Oxford: Oxford University Press.

Kirner, Ellen. 1999. "Entscheidung des Bundesverfassungsgerichts erfordert Reform der staatlichen Förderung von Ehe und Familie." *DIW-Wochenbericht* 8: 163–173.

Kirner, Ellen, and Erika Schulz. 1992. "Unterbrochene Erwerbsverläufe von Frauen mit Kindern. Traditionelles familienpolitisches Leitbild fragwürdig." *DIW-Wochenbericht* 19: 249–257.

Klammer, Ute, Christina Klenner, Christiane Ochs, Petra Radke, and Astrid Ziegler. 2000. *WSI—FrauenDatenReport*. Berlin: edition sigma.

Koch, Angelika. 2001. "Neubewertung der Familienarbeit in der Sozialpolitik? Die Neuregelung von Erziehungsgeld und Erziehungsurlaub und alternative Reformkonzepte." *Feministische Studien* 1: 48–61.

Kohli, Martin. 1985. "Die Insitutionalisierung des Lebenslaufs." *Kölner Zeitschrift für Soziologie und Sozialpsychologie* 37, no. 1: 1–29.

Krüger, Helga. 1999. "Gender and Skills. Distributive Ramifications of the German Skill System." In *The German Skills Machine. Sustaining Comparative Advantage in a Global Economy,* ed. P. D. Culpepper and D. Finegold, 189–227. New York: Berghahn Books.

———. 2001. "Social Change in Two Generations. Employment Patterns and Their Costs for Family Life." In *Restructuring Work and the Life Course,* ed. V. W. Marshall, W. R. Heinz, H. Krüger, and A. Verma, 401–23. Toronto: University of Toronto Press.

Krüger, Helga, and René Levy. 2000. "Masterstatus, Familie und Geschlecht. Vergessene Verknüpfungslogiken zwischen Institutionen des Lebenslaufs." *Berliner Journal für Soziologie* 3: 379–401.

———. 2001. "Linking Life Courses, Work, and the Family: Theorizing a Not So Visible Nexus between Women and Men." *Canadian Journal of Sociology/Cahiers Canadiens de Sociologie* 26, no. 2: 145–166.

Kurz, Karin. 1998. *Das Erwerbsverhalten von Frauen in der intensiven Familienphase. Ein Vergleich zwischen Müttern in der Bundesrepublik und in den USA.* Opladen: Leske + Budrich.

Lauterbach, Wolfgang. 1991. "Erwebsmuster von Frauen. Entwicklungen und Veränderungen seit Beginn dieses Jahrhunderts." In *Vom Regen in die Traufe: Frauen zwischen Beruf und Familie,* ed. K. U. Mayer, J. Allmendinger, and J. Huinink. 23–56. Frankfurt am Main: Campus.

———. 1994. *Berufsverläufe von Frauen. Erwerbstätigkeit, Unterbrechung und Wiedereintritt.* Frankfurt am Main: Campus.

Levy, René. 1996. "Toward a Theory of Life Course Institutionalization." In *Society and Biography. Interrelationships between Social Structure, Institutions and the Life Course,* ed. A. Weymann and W. R. Heinz, 83–108. Weinheim: Deutscher Studien Verlag.

Lewis, Jane, and Ilona Ostner. 1994. *Gender and the Evolution of European Social Policy. Arbeitspapier des Zentrums für Sozialpolitik der Universität Bremen.*

Molitor, Andreas. 2001. "Wirtschaftswunder. In einer Münchner Computer-Firma wird die Arbeit so ungewöhnlich organisiert, dass die Chefin anfangs nicht darüber redete—bis sie Preise erhielt." *Berliner Zeitung* (April 5): 3.

Oertzen, Christine von. 1999. *Teilzeitarbeit und die Lust am Zuverdienen. Geschlechterpolitik und gesellschaftlicher Wandel in West Deutschland 1948–1969.* Goettingen: Vandenhoeck & Ruprecht.

Sengenberger, Werner. 1978. *Der gespaltene Arbeitsmarkt: Probleme der Arbeitsmarktsegmentation.* Frankfurt am Main: Campus.

———. 1987. *Struktur und Funktionsweise von Arbeitsmärkten im internationalen Vergleich.* Frankfurt am Main: Campus.

Vaskovics, Laszlo, and Harald Rost. 1999. *Väter und Erziehungsurlaub.* Stuttgart: Verlag W. Kohlhammer.

# 11

## Globalization and Work/Life Balance: Gendered Implications of New Initiatives at a U.S. Multinational in Japan

*Glenda S. Roberts*

From 1999 to 2002, I was engaged in research on the implementation of flexible work arrangements (FWAs) among highly educated white-collar employees at a large-scale U.S. multinational financial-services corporation in Tokyo, Japan, which I shall call MNF.[1] MNF has a long history in Japan, having established its first office in the first part of the twentieth century. Over 95 percent of its employees in Japan are Japanese. Currently the firm has operations in numerous countries worldwide, with thousands of workers. MNF is one of many U.S. financial-services firms in Japan's market. In this chapter, I seek first to introduce the concept of work/life policy as it was formulated in the United States. Next I will briefly discuss the Japanese cultural environment for work, the state's social-policy framework, and how these "fit" with the notion of balancing work and life across gender. Last, I will discuss the corporation's stake in this endeavor, and what workers' responses reveal about MNF's initiatives to date.

### WORK/LIFE POLICY IN THE UNITED STATES

In the past two decades, the United States has seen increasing variegation and complexity in family patterns. While U.S. culture was never fully represented by the breadwinner father, the homemaker mother, and two children, it is ever less so (Coontz, 1993). More importantly, we have seen a paradigmatic shift in which we recognize the legitimacy of women's role in the workplace throughout their life course, regardless of marital status.

As the United States moves away from the gendered male-breadwinner/female-homemaker division of labor we encounter an increasing number of

parents in the workplace who have sole or shared responsibilities for dependents, be they children, disabled family members, or elderly family members.
Indeed, the labor-force participation rate of married women with children under the age of six climbed from 18.6 percent in 1960 to 30.3 percent in 1970
and 63.5 percent in 1995 (Blau, 1998: 117). Recognition of the difficulties
workers have in dealing with life-course-related events, be they maternity and
childbirth or care for infirm dependents, led the U.S. government to pass the
Family and Medical Leave Act in 1993 (Blau, 1996; Ruhm and Teague, 1997).

Some corporations have come to realize that in this new social environment, rigid and rule-bound work schedules invite problems of absenteeism
and lowered productivity. In response to this, from about the 1980s there has
been an increase in policies, known as "work/family friendly policies" or
"work/life policies," to give employees more discretion over their work
schedules. Among them are reduced hours for regular workers, telecommuting, flextime, compressed workweek, family leave, and job sharing. Research on U.S. corporations with work/life policies has shown employees'
use of such policies leads to more satisfied, more productive, and more dedicated workers. Such policies are said to improve worker retention, and also
act as a way to attract recruits to the firm (Rapoport et al., 1998; Bailyn,
Fletcher, and Kolb, 1997).

While work/life policies may sound like a panacea for workers' problems
in the postmodern age, researchers have found many difficulties at the implementation stages. Prime among them are informal, unspoken "rules" of
work culture that see as slacking anything less than 100 percent effort, made
visible by one's presence at the company (what Perlow [1997] refers to as
"face-time"). When employees make use of flexible work arrangements they
may be taken off the promotion track, and indeed their jobs themselves may
be endangered (Perlow, 1997). Hence, workers are reluctant to make use of
the policies, lest they be branded as disloyal for lacking commitment to the
firm. Managers, for their part, hesitate to grant use of the policies for a variety of reasons. Among them are disbelief that such policies could really improve productivity, fear of being seen as a patron (the "fairness" issue), fear
of loss of control, and anxiety over head count (Bailyn, 1993; Perlow, 1997).

Why are these policies so tough to implement? Fletcher and Bailyn point to
the cultural view that family is adversarial to the needs of work as the fundamental problem, what they identify as the "last boundary" of a new "boundaryless" way of doing business. That is, whereas the business world recognizes
the value in bridging barriers between various boundaries that had previously
been kept distinct, such as those between marketing, engineering, and research
and development, it has yet to realize the necessity of questioning the barrier
between work and family (Fletcher and Bailyn, 1996: 256). In my reading of
them, Fletcher and Bailyn are not advocating that work life envelop private life,
but that concerns in one's private life have a legitimate place in influencing

one's work schedule, that one's life apart from work should have an above-board presence. This last boundary between public and private, work and family, often goes unchallenged, by corporations, managers, and by workers.

## THE CULTURE OF WORK IN JAPAN

Unlike U.S. workplaces, Japanese workplaces have not undergone either the revolution in the gender role paradigm or the variegation in family patterns discussed above. Although women have steadily increased their labor-force participation in the past four decades, and while it is has become commonplace for married Japanese women to reenter the workforce after their children are of school age, their reentry is usually restricted to part-time work. The postwar pattern in large corporations has been that employers allot the stable "regular" jobs to men, the "corporate warriors," and from them they expect total commitment, expressed in long hours of work and loyalty to the firm. Women, because they are viewed by employers as ephemeral and peripheral employees, are not generally expected nor encouraged to remain in the workplace for the span of their careers. Rather, they take on the entire responsibility for managing the home, their children's educations, and the health of their families (Lock, 1996; Osawa, 1994; Roberts, 1994, 1996). This gendered division of labor, together with other socio-institutional frames (education, tax system, social-welfare system, legislation) that support large corporations, has been termed the "corporate centered society" (*kigyou chu-ushin shakai*) (Osawa, 1993). Gordon (1998: 56) notes,

> Workplaces in large private corporations eventually became citadels of Japan's corporate-centered society. The ascendance of the institutions of capitalism was common to many parts of the globe by the 1950s and 1960s, in particular Western Europe and North America, but in the long run, for better and for worse, the Japanese version has proved unusually total and durable.

In fact, Japan was the only postindustrial nation where we saw no correlation between higher educational status and attachment to work for women: holding a college degree does not necessarily mean commitment to a career (Brinton, 1993; Tsuya and Mason, 1992).

While the Equal Employment Opportunity Law of 1986 did result in some corporations allowing a few women to become female corporate warriors, it did nothing to change the baseline masculine standard of the "regular employee" job, which requires the counterpart of a "professional housewife" to make family life possible. Because of the incompatibilities of career and home life in Japan, many Japanese women reject this "corporate warrior" model, and put more emphasis on their roles as mothers, homemakers, and community activists, in which they have considerable authority and for which they garner a strong measure of cultural respect (Lebra, 1984; Iwao, 1993; LeBlanc, 1999). At the same time, however, Japan's increasingly highly educated young women are demonstrating their dissatisfaction with the status quo, by delaying marriage or eschewing it altogether. An example of this can be seen in the MNF employee statistics: MNF Japan is composed of over 1,500 employees, about 60 percent women. The norm for marriage among male employees appears very strong, with 75 percent of men aged 31 to 40, 90 percent of men aged 41 to 50, and 96 percent of men aged 51 to 60 married. For women, marriage is less prevalent: only 37 percent aged 31 to 50, and 27 percent aged 51 to 60, are married. The women's marriage rate is markedly lower than that for Japanese women in general. One could infer that for a man, a career without a spouse is a challenge, while the opposite is true for a woman.

## WORK/LIFE POLICY AND THE JAPANESE STATE

The strategic role of the Japanese state in coordinating industrial strategy such that Japan achieved global success in challenging European and American domination has been much discussed in the literature on the political economy and society of Japan (Johnson, 1983; Hamada, 1991; Waters, 1995). This coordination reached to the domestic realm as well. Gordon (1998: 54) states that in 1955, the Japanese government sponsored a campaign called "The New Life Movement," whereby "Women were to run 'rational' and 'efficient' homes, and this would allow men to realize the same ideal at work. By playing these complementary roles, women and men were expected to raise productivity and bring prosperity to all." This sort of coordination, termed "social management" by Garon (1997), can be seen clearly in the Ministry of Labour's current efforts to change the workplace to one that is more "family friendly."

Waters, in discussing globalization, asserts:

> In seeking to develop strong cultures, firms become receptive to ideas and seek them out. Global flows of business ideas have therefore increased very rapidly. This provides the second effect which is that the very act of looking outside the company and outside the nation for ideas encourages a consciousness of global events and consequences (1995: 85).

Indeed, Japan has been looking outside the nation to take the best from Western technology, *wakon yosai* (Japanese ethics, Western skills), for well over a century, and has also done her share of globalizing Western manufacturing processes. Furthermore, global flows of another kind, what Waters refers to as cultural globalization, inevitably accompany technological globalization and affect cultural practices and hence, lifestyles.

One could argue that the legal frameworks the Japanese state has established since 1986 aimed at creating equal opportunity for men and women in the society are an example of cultural globalization. While the impetus of the initial Equal Opportunity Employment Law (EEOL) came substantially from foreign pressure, *gaiatsu* (Hanami, 2000; Bishop, 2000), I and others have argued that there is also significant indigenous demand for creating a legal and social infrastructure supportive of gender equality (Roberts, 2002). In brief, in recent years, women have "voted with their feet" by marrying increasingly late, due mainly to reluctance to assume the burdens marriage entails. This in turn has caused a steady decline in the total fertility rate of the nation, now at 1.34.[2] The government, heeding this trend with alarm, is strategically beginning to foster the development of "family-friendly" and gender-bias-free workplaces in order to try to convince young people that marriage does not mean that a woman must lose her career goals and quit her job to raise a family. In large part in Japan, the impetus for family-friendly and "gender-equal" workplaces, then, springs from population policy of a state that is anxious about a future (2050) where one worker will have to support two elderly pensioners.

The most salient recent laws include:

### The Child-Care/Family-Care Leave Law (1999)

Child-Care Leave (CCL) was established in 1992 and family care followed in 1999. CCL allows a one-year child-care leave after childbirth for mother or father or shared; 25 percent of salary is paid by social insurance (to be raised to 40 percent in 2001). Family-Care Leave (FCL) allows three months' unpaid leave to care for family members in need of care.

### The Basic Law for a Gender-Equal Society (1999)

The law obliges the government (including local self-governing bodies) to devise a "basic plan for a gender-equal society." Furthermore it requires the government to establish a procedure for handling complaints concerning its measures to establish a gender-equal society and to aid those whose human rights are violated (JIL, 1999: 4).

### Revised EEOL

Enacted in June 1997; enforced, April 1999: prohibits employment discrimination against women workers, provides for settlement of disputes, punishes corporations that violate the law (by publishing their names), provides measures against sexual harassment.

## Revised Child Welfare Law (1997)

Rendered parents clients with "choice" in day-care services; rendered local governments as service providers; required day-care centers to respond to the child-care concerns of people in the locale; altered fee scales to reflect varied costs depending on age level of children; raised the position of after-school care programs.

The Labour Ministry and the Ministry of Health and Welfare keep very well informed about U.S. and European nations' policies and corporate practices regarding gender equality, employment, and child welfare. In fact, in June of 2000, twenty employees of the Japan Institute of Workers Evolution, an organization that undertakes contract work from the MOL, went on a study tour of the top ten firms on the "Best 100" list of *Working Mother* magazine (interview at the JIWE, October 18, 2000).[3] Furthermore, in 2000, the Ministry of Labour sponsored an international symposium entitled "Thinking about Family and Firms in the Age of a Low Birthrate," to which they invited specialists on flexible work arrangements and family policy from France, the United States, Great Britain, Sweden, and Japan to present their ideas on ways to "harmonize" work and family life.[4]

## SYNERGY BETWEEN THE STATE AND THE CORPORATION

There is a synergistic effect between corporate initiatives and governmental initiatives in Japan, and this synergy is both intentional and coincidental.

It is *intentional* in at least three ways: first, the MOL has created linkages between itself and corporations it considers to be "family friendly," both Japanese and multinational, and asks these firms to cooperate in mentoring other firms that have yet to establish such policies. For instance, the Ministry of Labour, in its efforts toward "administrative guidance,"[5] recently asked the American multinational firm I am studying to host a meeting with three small-to-medium-sized Japanese firms from the city of Nagoya, to brief them on the sorts of policies it has established regarding child-care and family-care leave, reduced hours for regular workers, and so on. None of these smaller firms had any such policies in place. What they really wanted advice on, however, was not how to implement the more elaborate flexible work arrangements, but simply how to get their employees to use their vacation days. This speaks worlds to the nature of the current recession work environment in Japan, wherein hours tend to be long, and people are not taking even their fully allotted time off.[6]

Second in the government-corporate link is the practice of requesting that employees from private enterprises be seconded to government-related offices for periods of two years or so in order to create networks between government and business, and to foster shared knowledge and cooperation between the sectors.[7]

Third, so-designated "Family Friendly Firms" are given awards by the MOL and are advertised at national symposia and in newspapers and other media. Hence, their profile is raised and the notion that the government is interested in having all firms follow suit becomes commonplace. While this is not a speedy means to full compliance, it does give people in firms that do not comply a slightly better footing on which to legitimately argue—whether through the union or through other means—that the firm ought to be a good "corporate citizen" and comply with the law.

In sum, while the state sees family-friendly policies as a necessary population policy measure, most firms are not eager to embrace them and have no strong business reason to do so in the current recession economy. In fact, the recession is aggravating the already long hours of work with "service" overtime, and holiday taking is down. Since the legal framework is deliberately weak, firms can ignore it with relative impunity.

I mentioned above that family-friendly initiatives are also *coincidental*. To explain this, let us visit another player in the "family-friendly policy" camp, MNF corporation.

## MNF JAPAN AND THE INTRODUCTION
## OF FLEXIBLE WORK ARRANGEMENTS

Unlike many Japanese firms, who have not been quick to implement the legislation I earlier mentioned, MNF has a corporate policy to the effect that it must comply with the laws of the state in which it is sited. Thus, it has offered CCL since 1992, and FCL was introduced in 1999. Furthermore, career female employees report that MNF's attitude toward women in terms of training and promotion improved during the later 1980s, when the EEOL came into effect.

In 1999, MNF decided to implement some of the flexible work arrangements (hereon FWAs) already in place in its U.S. operations, as a pilot study, and to expand them if they proved successful. Up to this time, flextime was the only FWA offered at MNF Japan. The firm was expanding in Japan despite the recession, and needed to both attract and retain good workers. The management expressed concerns that they had been losing some talented female staff due to their difficulties balancing work and family lives. This was especially important because MNF had been treating female and male employees on an equal basis,[8] and had hired many female four-year-college graduates as well as MBA holders. They had a strong interest in retaining them.[9] Hence, the top management decided to take action along several lines, and announce it as "Managing with Flexibility." "Reduced hours for regular staff" was billed as a new tool that managers could use to retain workers who needed shorter hours.

Extended provision of Child-Care Leave and the new Elder-Care Leave were also announced, and it was suggested that reduced hours could be used in combination with these leaves as appropriate for the worker and work site. In addition, a website on child care was established, a "Bring Your Children to Work Day" was institutionalized (once a year), and, most recently, a half-day vacation-day policy was announced. Pilots of telecommuting were launched in 2001. Job sharing and compressed workweeks have not been taken up as of now.

While some of MNF's flexible work arrangements can be termed "family friendly," the intent is not to only target people with families, but to offer more flexibility to all employees. This departs from the government discourse with its population agenda.

The top managers were willing to introduce these measures, but they also noted that there could be resistance to flexibility at the mid-managerial level, for a couple of reasons. One is that many mid-managers are head-hunted in from previous employment in Japanese firms, and they lack the mind-set of the MNF culture, which tends to be oriented more toward an individual's targets and getting the job done at an intense pace during the work day. In contrast, the Japanese white-collar work culture is seen as one where the day is much longer, interspersed with socializing, and workers are not expected to leave if others in the section still have jobs to finish.

Another roadblock to implementation that top managers noted is that MNF's culture tends more toward gender equality, and managers from more traditional Japanese banking environments will not be used to this and may not feel that retaining female employees is desirable. In a similar vein, MNF has recently made some acquisitions of Japanese companies that are perceived to have a very different, more conservative managerial culture as compared to MNF's. MNF Japan's top personnel manager expressed doubt as to whether these new acquisitions would be convinced of the efficacy of flexible work initiatives. The long hours of overtime evidenced in some sectors of MNF were also seen as strong barriers to the implementation of FWAs.[10]

Finally, the notion of "fairness" came up. This has also been a concern in the United States (Bailyn, 1993), but I would argue that it is even more strongly a concern in Japan, where social institutions (such as contracts) are less individually tailored and more vague. As I found in my study of a factory in western Japan in the 1980s, if a person's working conditions vary significantly from those of the rest of her reference group, the "unfairness" of this will be a cause for comment. Nagata (2000) points out that the Prime Minister's Commission on Japan's Goals in the Twenty-First Century has even coined a new phrase in recognition of this, *atarashii kouhei no gainen* ("fair disparity"). The Commission states, "We should bid farewell to equal outcomes and introduce a new concept of fairness, what we might call "fair disparity," which appreciates performance and growth potential, accepting differences and disparities in individual abilities and talents as a given" (Prime Minister's Office, 2000: 12–13).

For all the above reasons, top management took a gradual approach to implementation, especially on the reduced-hours policy. Perhaps this is obvious, but the corporation, especially in a multicultural environment, meets with a number of obstacles in trying to change the work culture. Each manager has his or her own experiences and challenges, and one training session on managing with flexibility is not sufficient to convince a person to take the risk and encourage what amounts to a very different relationship between worker and manager, worker and team, and worker and home. Nagata notes that some Japanese managers have a visceral reaction when workplace flexibility is raised—they tense their bodies as if under assault. This leads to compliance in name only—that is, the manager's body language is enough to communicate his or her disapproval of a worker who desires flexible work arrangements:

> If a manager believes with every fiber of his being that all his regular employees should be in the office during the same hours and share equally in any overflow of work that requires overtime, he is likely to be physically uncomfortable . administering a new reduced work hours policy that only a few people will be using. His disapproval of a woman who requests to work only 60% will be communicated to her and her colleagues so clearly, even if only nonverbally by posture, gesture, and expression, that few Japanese working in large companies will be able to withstand their own resultant discomfort and possible group ostracism (Nagata, 2000: 6).

Resistance to flexible work arrangements for one's subordinates is not restricted to Japanese nationals, however. One interviewee told me that her American boss was surprised to hear that maternity leave is so long in Japan (six weeks before and eight weeks after birth), let alone the optional child-care leave one may request after that until the child is one year of age. He made it clear that he was not comfortable with a long leave, and she, fearing for her job, did not take child-care leave. This same boss had fits of rage when, upon returning to work, she would leave the office at 6 P.M. to pick up the baby from day care. She eventually left the company for a position elsewhere.[11]

## IMPLEMENTING FLEXIBILITY: INCREMENTAL CHANGE?

In the beginning of this chapter, I noted that flexible work arrangements may create the potential for female employees to remain at work throughout marriage and child-rearing years, while they could give men the time to participate more fully in the lives of their families. In other words, the corporation, through the introduction of such policies, could be acting as a positive-change agent in the Japanese urban setting. Is it?

The answer to this question is not so simple. Married women with children strongly welcome these initiatives, but they are also skeptical about what it will take to really "change the culture." As I mentioned above, many mid-level managers are not eager to implement policies that go against the style of work they have embraced up to now. There may not be anything particularly cultural about this hesitance; researchers of U.S. workplaces also point to mid-managers as being the strongest roadblocks to implementation.[12]

- The long hours of overtime in some sections render FWAs meaningless. Commutes in Tokyo average over an hour each way; some are more than two hours each way. Overtime is an issue for women with family responsibilities since most of their husbands cannot be relied on to do housework or child care during the week. If one works an eight-hour day in such sections, it is as if one is working a part-time job.
- In sections where teamwork is prevalent, it is particularly difficult to implement FWAs such as reduced hours for regular staff. Japanese workers in particular are educated to have a strong team consciousness. Many people I interviewed told me that to leave the team early to go home makes one feel as if one is causing a great inconvenience to others (*meiwaku*). This is considered to be inexcusable behavior (*moshiwakenai*). It might be accepted for emergencies, but on a regular basis it is very difficult to maintain amicably.
- Day-care centers generally close at 6 P.M., although a few remain open until 7 P.M. Most women choose a center near their home rather than face a crowded commute by train to the office with a baby in tow. This means they must leave work in the late afternoon in order to meet the day-care closing time. Women devise various means of handling this problem, including moving close to the company, asking relatives to pick up the child from day care, or hiring a professional baby-sitter or home day-care provider to pick up the child and wait at home. A few even hire nannies, a very costly option in Japan.
- Women's responsibility as mother is aggravated by lack of domestic work on their husbands' part. Most women we interviewed are virtually single parents during the week; their husbands do not return home until very late. Some husbands also go to work on the weekend. Most husbands work for Japanese corporations that have less flexibility than MNF has. Unless most corporations make similar plans to give their workers more flexibility, such policies in a minority of firms will certainly not suffice to alter the household division of labor for working couples in this country. If this cannot be altered, then FWAs have the potential to be turned into a female "mommy track" ghetto. The women I am studying are not unlike Hochschild's (1989) American women who do the "second shift" of household labor, except that the amount of

household labor they can expect from their spouses is less.[13] Furthermore, until now most workers on reduced hours are doing so to care for family. Unless more workers make use of flexibility for non-family-related reasons (such as study goals or community service), workers who do not have children may feel resentment.

- Women with children can be divided into two groups; those with family help and those with none. Some women with family help get considerable assistance, as with one worker whose retired father came to live with her and her husband for the first year of the baby's life (leaving her mom watching her brother's child in another city) until he could be placed in a day-care center. The flip side of depending on close relatives for child care is the felt obligation and desire to then care for one's relatives should they need assistance in old age. While elder-care leave should be useful in such circumstances, it is at this point rather short (three months) and unpaid. Nursing homes are insufficient in number as well as being culturally unacceptable alternatives for elderly people needing assisted care.

- Those with no family help may have a difficult time as there are long waiting lists for day care for babies in many of Tokyo's wards. Day care for mildly ill children is not readily available, and casual baby-sitting by neighborhood teenagers or neighbor women is generally not done. While public and private licensed day care is affordable and of high quality, at present it is insufficient to meet the demand. Outsourcing of other household tasks, such as housecleaning, is costly and not the usual practice.

- Some women we have interviewed have complained that upon returning from child-care leave they were assigned tedious jobs and were no longer given challenging work, due to the perception of management that challenging work could not be completed in the course of a normal work day. Such boring work saps motivations and causes these women to wonder if they would not be performing more "value-added" work by staying at home minding their own child instead. So far one woman has resigned over this problem.

- As in other countries, men hesitate to take CCL or reduced hours for regular staff. So far no man at MNF has taken CCL. We held a focus group for working fathers, but only two men came. More did, however, participate in the Bring Your Children to Work Day. The regular practice in Japan of dispatching employees to far-flung branches of the company for years at a time (*tanshinfunin*), unaccompanied by spouses, also makes "flexibility" seem a bit inflexible for the working partner left at home.

- Female employees we interviewed have been very positive about FWA initiatives, and they also have been positive about government policies to expand spaces in day-care centers and increase the hours of care provided. Most women are dissatisfied with the little time their husbands participate in child care and housework, but they also recognize that their husband's work environments do not allow them to participate.

- The Bring Your Children to Work Day, in which both boys and girls come to the office and are hosted with activities, was initiated as a means of getting people to recognize that their fellow workers may also be moms and dads, to try to bridge this divide between private life and corporate life. It has been well received, but it is not a "natural" at MNF, where workers hesitate to bring up family matters in small talk, and pictures of family are not usually placed prominently on desks. The exception to this is that some workers now use screen savers featuring their children's faces.

- While it might not seem like a revolution, most of the women we have interviewed report that their spouses were present at their children's birth, and some were able to arrange to take some paid holidays off. Several women told me that their husbands take the child to the day-care center in the morning, something rarely seen a generation ago. One woman remarked that her husband had more flexibility in the first year of the baby's life than she did, because he had been seconded to a different workplace for this period. When it was over, though, he had to go back to working until 3 A.M. every morning, and he no longer sees his son during weeknights. She said he and the baby are going through withdrawal. My point is that at least some men in Japan now want to spend time caring for their families but are constrained by their workplace environments.

## CONCLUSION

In this chapter I have attempted to weave the actions of three players in a bid to alter the work environment in Japan: the state, MNF, and MNF's employees. The state, because of its concerns over the low birthrate, appears to be highly interested in the notion of flexibility, but is adopting a very soft approach in educating corporations to embrace it. MNF has put substantial resources behind introducing FWAs and is continuing to explore new flexible options. It is too early to tell how much of an impact the flexible initiatives will have on worker recruitment, retention, satisfaction, and gender equality at MNF. I hope to view this firm longitudinally to follow the workers who have started making use of these policies.

The external cultural and social-institutional environment is gradually changing toward acceptance of dual-career families, although the obstacles remain high. Primary among them is the male work standard and gender role that sees time spent at work as a man's commitment to his family. Public and private are being continually negotiated in the lives of MNF workers, but the negotiation is mostly between female workers, their managers, and the relatives, institutions, and others who care for their children. For the most part, male spouses (who work at other corporations) are not negotiating. Moreover, very few employees are taking advantage of FWAs for reasons other than caring for family members. We have yet to see anyone, male or female, come forth to request reduced hours for a year of volunteer work or to gear up for some sports challenge, for instance. It will be interesting to see whether these first steps toward flexibility at MNF eventually embolden male employees, as well as singles, to make use of flexibility in their lives. At the present time, however, one is left asking, "Where is the balance?"

## NOTES

1. I began research at MNF Japan in 1999 after learning that it was about to pilot flexible work arrangements. I was successful in obtaining an exploratory grant for the project in an international grant competition. The research consists of soliciting interviews from top managers, mid-managers, and employees who are interested in taking, who are taking, or who in the past have taken flexible work arrangements of some sort. I have also interviewed some who resigned from the corporation after having made use of an FWA. Interviews are thematic and open-ended, intended to elicit employees' views of the current work environment, their strategies for work/life balance, their response to corporate initiatives, and so on. Working closely with me and wearing two hats is a vice president of personnel, whose job it is to implement the FWA initiatives. She is also a doctoral candidate, specializing in human development and cross-cultural communication. She acts as my research assistant, and is often, although not always, present and involved in interviewing; many of the mid-managerial interviews were conducted by her alone. From MNF's perspective, her role is as a "change agent" and this research is "action research." From my perspective, I have free rein over the interview content and analysis, I benefit tremendously from the perspective of someone whose knowledge of the company is deep and far-reaching, and I am able to learn a great deal about how workers are actually coping with work and life. Complementing the interviews is my ongoing study of Japan's governmental policy environment regarding population and labor (1996–), my interviews in 1997 with women who sought employment after a period of child rearing, and my previous study of female blue-collar workers at a Japanese manufacturer in the early 1980s (see Roberts, 1994). By now the FWA programs are well under way, and we have interviewed sixteen top managers, thirty managers, nine staff on reduced hours, six who have recently taken maternity leave and/or child-care leave, four interested in taking MCL or CCL, eleven working mothers, nine employees taking reduced hours, and ten who resigned, as well as held two focus groups with working mothers and one with working fathers.

2. Women have also been leaving the country to seek careers abroad. According to the *Japan Times*, in 1999 the number of Japanese women living abroad (402,500) exceeded that of men (393,200) for the first time since 1976 when the first such survey was taken. The article quotes an official of the Foreign Ministry's Consular and Migration Affairs Department as saying, "In the past, most Japanese women (living abroad) were accompanying their husbands on overseas assignment, but now there is a growing number of women who go overseas alone for work" (*Japan Times*, 2000).

3. Perhaps here we should ask the question: Why the U.S.? Why is Japan so interested in U.S. corporate-policy initiatives on flexible work and family-friendly arrangements? Although it is beyond the scope of this paper to fully address this question, the answer may be threefold: First, Japan is trying not to develop a strong welfare-state approach to child care and elder care but to encourage privatization of such services; second, the work environments in the two countries have some compelling similarities (both have longer work hours and fewer holidays as compared with other OECD countries), and third, firms in the U.S. have been experimenting with work/life policies for over a decade now.

4. Interestingly, and, I think, against the Ministry of Labour's intent, the representative from Japan, a corporate executive from Kikkoman corporation, expressed the opinion that while his company had established child-care leave in the early 1980s along with other programs to help women maintain their employment, he himself thinks that a child needs its *mother* for "skinship" (close skin contact) during the first year of life, so encouraging fathers to take CCL is not necessarily a good idea. He backed up his opinion by citing a recent popular psychology book by a Japanese psychologist.

5. Hanami Tadashi (2000: 9) argues that "the Japanese way of administrative guidance with advice, suggestions, recommendations, consultation, and persuasion—including through implication and bestowal of favor and disfavor—could be to some extent effective in implementing a policy goal. . . . However, such a method of enforcing policy goals very much depends on voluntary compliance by companies, and does not work for those companies unwilling to change long-held prejudices."

6. According to the *Nikkei Weekly*, people at small firms (thirty to ninety-nine employees) took only seven vacation days in 1999, less than half of their allotted (sixteen) days. This is down 1.3 percent from the previous year, and follows the trend of decreasing rates of taking holiday since 1995. The *Nikkei Weekly* owes the trend to corporate restructuring during recession: "A ministry official attributed the decline in the execution rate mainly to the fact that even though paid holidays have increased, workers cannot take them at their own discretion as the number of workers at plants and offices is decreasing due to corporate restructuring" (2000: 17).

7. At the Japan Institute of Worker's Evolution, for example, a managerial-level employee of an American multinational is currently serving a two-year stint as department head of the Career Woman Support Section. Presumably when she returns to her company, she will have extensive firsthand knowledge of government services supporting home and work nationwide, while the foundation in which she currently serves will benefit from her expertise as a member of a firm that is known as a leader in this area. Under such arrangements, salaries are paid by hosting firms.

8. This is unlike the practice of many Japanese large corporations, which, in response to the EEOL, put in place dual-track systems of *ippan-shoku* (noncareer) track and *sogo-shoku* (career) track, and proceeded to hire most female graduates in the noncareer track. See Mori (1998) and Shire (2000: 39). Shire notes, "While officially the two-track employment system should allow for the employment of qualified women in career-track roles, in 1995 only 28 percent of the companies with such a system actually employed women in the career track (Japan Institute of Labor, 1996). Instead, a trend toward recruiting university-educated women into the non-career track became more prevalent" (Shire, 2000).

9. MNF Japan's workforce is composed of over a thousand people, with women making up just over half. The norm for marriage among male employees appears very strong, with 75 percent of men aged 31–40, 90 percent of men aged 41–50, and 96 percent of men 51–60 married. For women, marriage is much less prevalent: only 37 percent aged 31–40, 37 percent of those aged 41–50, and 27 percent aged 51–60 are married. The women's marriage rate is vastly lower than that for Japanese women in general. One could speculate that for a man, a career without a spouse is a challenge, while the opposite is true for a woman.

10. Overtime varies depending on the section and depending on one's particular job. In interviews, managers noted that one reason for long hours of overtime in some sections is the MNF environment in Japan. It is seeking to be on the forefront of new innovations in financial services, so the systems used in the work process are often being redesigned. Moreover, the regulatory environment frequently changes and they must respond immediately. Expectations of customer service are also extremely high. Last, MNF is in expansion mode and finds itself short staffed because the head count for the country has been set at a very tight level. Several non-Japanese top managers expressed dismay at the hours some workers put in and could not put their finger on the cause. One sector of MNF is now experimenting with paying people not to do overtime.

11. She remarked to me after she left the company that she feels some Japanese firms are now well under way in implementing Child-Care Leave, and that there is no problem with taking it, because the companies have a long-term perspective, expecting the career woman to stay twenty or thirty years on the job. What's one year in twenty? Not so long. But American firms have a much shorter timeline of expectation for their employees, she noted.

12. As of yet there are no explicit disincentives or incentives in place for managers to be active proponents of these policies.

13. A 1998 campaign sponsored by the Ministry of Health and Welfare, aimed at getting men to contribute more to child care, noted that the average amount of time men spent per day on household tasks was seventeen minutes (Roberts, 2002).

## REFERENCES

Bailyn, Lotte. 1993. *Breaking the Mold: Women, Men and Time in the New Corporate World*. New York: The Free Press.

Bailyn, Lotte, Joyce Fletcher, and Deborah Kolb. 1997. "Unexpected Connections: Considering Employees' Personal Lives Can Revitalize Your Business." *Sloan Management Review* 38, no. 4 (summer): 11–19.

Bishop, Beverly. 2000. "The Diversification of Employment and Women's Work in Contemporary Japan." Pp. 93–109 in *Globalization and Social Change in Contemporary Japan*. Melbourne: Trans Pacific Press.

Blau, Francine. 1996. "Comment," on Aileen Leibowitz, "Childcare: Private Cost or Public Responsibility?" In *Individual and Social Responsibility: Child Care, Education, Medical Care, and Long-term Care in America*, ed. Victor Fuchs. Chicago: University of Chicago Press.

———. 1998. "Trends in the Well-Being of American Women, 1970–1995." *Journal of Economic Literature* 36 (March): 112–65.

Brinton, Mary. 1993. *Women and the Economic Miracle: Gender and Work in Postwar Japan*. Berkeley: University of California Press.

Coontz, Stephanie. 1993. *The Way We Never Were: American Families and the Nostalgia Trap*. New York: Basic Books.

Fletcher, Joyce, and Lotte Bailyn. 1996. "Challenging the Last Boundary: Reconnecting Work and Family." In *The Boundaryless Career: A New Employment Principle for a New Organizational Era*, ed. Michael B. Arthur and Denise M. Rousseau. New York: Oxford University Press.

Garon, Sheldon. 1997. *Molding Japanese Minds: The State in Everyday Life*. Princeton, N.J.: Princeton University Press.

Gordon, Andrew. 1998. *The Wages of Affluence: Labor and Management in Postwar Japan*. Cambridge, Mass.: Harvard University Press.

Hamada, Tomoko. 1991. *American Enterprise in Japan*. Albany: SUNY Press.

Hanami, Tadashi. 2000. "Equal Employment Revisited." *Japan Labor Bulletin* 39, no. 1 (January): 5–10.

Hochschild, Arlie R. 1989. *The Second Shift*. New York: Avon.

Iwao, Sumiko. 1993. *The Japanese Woman: Traditional Image and Changing Reality*. New York: The Free Press.

*Japan Times*. 2000. "Expats Hit Record High; Women Outnumber Men." May 21.

JIL (Japan Institute of Labor). 1999. "Public Policy: Fundamental Law for a Gender-Equal Society." *Japan Labor Bulletin* 38, no. 9 (September): 4.

Johnson, Chalmers. 1983. *Miti and the Japanese Miracle: The Growth of Industrial Policy, 1925–1975*. Stanford: Stanford University Press.

LeBlanc, Robin. 1999. *Bicycle Citizens: The Political World of the Japanese Housewife*. Berkeley: University of California Press.

Lebra, Takie S. 1984. *Japanese Women: Constraint and Fulfillment*. Honolulu: University of Hawaii Press.

Lock, Margaret. 1996. "Centering the Household: The Remaking of Female Maturity in Japan." Pp. 73–103 in *Reimaging Japanese Women*, ed. Anne Imamura. Berkeley: University of California Press.

Long, Susan, and Phyllis Brady Harris. 2000. "Gender and Elder Care: Social Change and the Role of the Caregiver in Japan." *Social Science Japan Journal* 3, no. 1.

Mitchell, Olivia S. 1997. "Work and Family Benefits." Pp. 269–76 in *Gender and Family Issues in the Workplace*, ed. F. Blau and R. Ehrenberg. New York: Russell Sage Foundation.

Mori, Masumi. 1998. "Kosu betsu Koyo Kanrika no Shokumu no Jenda Bunri to Togo [Gender Segregation and Integration of Jobs under the Employment Track System]." In *Josei Rodo Kenkyu* (The Bulletin of the Study of Working Women), no. 33, January. Tokyo: Domesu.

Nagata, Adair. 2000. "Shifting the Bodymindset." Unpublished paper, The Fielding Institute.

*Nikkei Weekly*. 2000. "Weekly Window: Paid Holidays." October 23, p. 17.

Ogasawara, Yuko. 1998. *Office Ladies and Salaried Men: Power, Gender and Work in Japanese Companies*. Berkeley: University of California Press.

Osawa Mari. 1993. "Kigyō Chūshin Shakai wo Koete: Gendai Nihon wō 'Jenda' de Yomu [Overcoming the Corporate-Centered Society: Reading Contemporary Japan through Gender]." Tokyo: Jiji Tsūshin.

———. 1994. "Bye-Bye Corporate Warriors: The Formation of a Corporate-Centered Society and Gender-Biased Social Policies in Japan." In *University of Tokyo Institute of Social Science Occasional Papers in Labor Problems and Social Policy*, no. 18 (March).

Perlow, L. A. 1997. *Finding Time: How Corporations, Individuals, and Families Can Benefit from New Work Practices*. Ithaca, N.Y.: Cornell University Press.

Prime Minister's Office. 2000. Report of the Prime Minister's Commission on Japan's Goals in the Twenty-First Century: *"The Frontier Within: Individual Empowerment and Better Governance in the New Millenium."* January.

Rapoport, Rhona, Lotte Bailyn, Deborah Kolb, and Joyce Fletcher. 1998. *Relinking Life and Work: Toward a Better Future*. Innovations in Management Series. Waltham, Mass.: Pegasus Communications.

Roberts, Glenda S. 1994. *Staying on the Line: Blue-Collar Women in Contemporary Japan*. Honolulu: University of Hawaii Press.

———. 1996. "Careers and Commitment: Azumi's Blue-Collar Women." In *Reimaging Japanese Women*, ed. Anne Imamura. Berkeley: University of California Press.

———. 2002. "Pinning Hopes on Angels: Reflections from an Aging Japan's Urban Landscape." Pp. 54–91 in *Family and Social Policy in Japan*, ed. Roger Goodman. Cambridge: Cambridge University Press.

Ruhm, Christopher J., and Jackqueline L. Teague. 1997. "Parental Leave Policies in Europe and North America." Pp. 133–56 in *Gender and Family Issues in the Workplace*, ed. Francine Blau and Ronald Ehrenberg. New York: Russell Sage Foundation.

Shire, Karen. 2000. "Gendered Organization and Workplace Culture in Japanese Customer Services." *Social Science Japan Journal* 3, no. 1: 37–58.

Tsuya, Noriko, and Karen Mason. 1992. "Changing Gender Roles and Below-Replacement Fertility in Japan." Paper presented at the IUSSP Seminar on Gender and Family Change in Industrialized Countries, Rome, Italy, January 26–30, 1992.

Wakisaka, Akira. 1997. "Women at Work." Pp. 131–50 in *Japanese Labour and Management in Transition: Diversity, Flexibility and Participation*, ed. Mary Sako and H. Sato. New York: Routledge.

Waters, Malcolm. 1995. *Globalization*. New York: Routledge.

# IV

## SPECIFIC APPLICATIONS OF WORKPLACE POLICIES: GENDER EQUITY IN THE WORKPLACE

# 12

# Europeanizing the Military: The ECJ and the Transformation of the Bundeswehr[1]

*Ulrike Liebert*

Compared to the armed forces of her NATO partners, the German Bundeswehr until recently remained a relic with regard to gender homogeneity. Whereas by the beginning of 2000, most member states of the European Union had military forces with sizable minorities of female soldiers ranging between 4 percent and 10 percent, the Bundeswehr continued to marginalize women.[2] Women were conceived as the "weaker gender" in need of protection and not as equal partners in arms, working shoulder to shoulder with their male comrades. Though some 4,300 women among 340,000 Bundeswehr soldiers represented 1.3 percent of the whole, they remained restricted to two domains—the health service and the music band—and were completely invisible in public representations. The combination of women's defenselessness and exclusion from armed forces, and a Bundeswehr limited by the German Constitution to defense purposes and prohibited to take part in offensive ventures, was suddenly challenged by a young woman. In 1996, Tanja Kreil, an electronic technician, applied for service in the weapon electronics maintenance section of the Federal Armed Forces (Bundeswehr). Her application was rejected on the ground that German law bars women from military posts involving the use of arms. Two years later, Ms. Kreil brought an action in the Hanover Administrative Court, claiming that the rejection of her application only on the grounds of sex was contrary to the 1976 EU Equal Treatment Directive. This matter then turned to the European Court of Justice (ECJ) in Luxembourg for a preliminary ruling about whether the German government had a right to claim that EU equal-treatment norms did not apply to national military forces.

The ECJ, depicted by law scholars as the driving force behind legal integration in the EU, took its time. Finally, with its judgment issued on January

11, 2000, the ECJ opened a new era for the Bundeswehr. Every soldier had to cope with fundamental consequences as a result of this judgment, affecting "the very nature and character of the German armed forces" (Kümmel and Biehl, 2000: 9). This statement by two researchers of the Social Research Institute of the Bundeswehr is not an exaggeration. In fact, the EU Court left no doubt that it backed Tanja Kreil's case against the German government. Regarding *Case C-285/98 Tanja Kreil v. Federal Republic of Germany [2000] ECR I-69*, the ECJ ruled that German legislation generally barring women from military posts involving the use of arms was contrary to the Community principle of equal treatment between men and women, although derogations concerning certain special combat units were possible.

Even more important, the ECJ's judgment also obliges member states to implement EU gender equality laws not only within the civilian realm but also in those core state institutions invested with the monopoly of legitimate violence. Up to now, the scope of the EU's working women's rights[3] has been restricted to the civilian—public and private—sector. Cases of women claiming rights to inclusion in the police forces in Northern Ireland or in the Marine Corps in Britain had been turned down by the ECJ. In the case pressed by Tanja Kreil against the German government, the ECJ judges dared for the first time to break a breach for European legal integration, affecting also the military as a core institution of nation-state sovereignty. In this process, the Bundeswehr—among EU militaries arguably the least sovereign—served as a test case.

The ECJ judgment and its impact on military change in EU member states, including Italy as well as Germany, are part of an accelerated process of Europeanization. This is to be understood here as a process triggered by European norms and enhancing changes at the domestic level, involving in some cases conflict and stubborn resistance, in others adaptation and convergence towards European shared norms. I will test these two propositions for the case of Germany, by examining the adjustments made by the government in response to the ECJ's *Kreil* judgment. In so doing, three questions are at center of this inquiry:

First, how pervasive are the impacts of the *Kreil* judgment on the Bundeswehr in light of the adjustments made by the German legislature and government? Has the Bundeswehr, in answer to the challenge to integrate women, simply adopted superficial adjustment measures, or did it embark on profound institutional change?

Second, what role did the European Court of Justice play relative to other mechanisms pushing for and resisting transformation of the gender arrangements in the Bundeswehr?

Finally, will domestic adjustments to EC norms, as a consequence of ECJ decisions in the domain of the military forces, contribute to the emergence of a European identity vis-à-vis the national identity?

This chapter aims to use the case of the *Kreil* judgment and the German Bundeswehr in order to explore the type of impact which EC gender equality norms can have on state institutions,[4] and to explain why the ECJ was able to play such a vital role in what I will describe as quite a profound transformation of the institutional identity of the Bundeswehr. My account of Germany's exceptional compliance in this case emphasizes the interaction of three sets of explanatory mechanisms (see Liebert and Sifft, 2003): First, the ability of the ECJ to justify its claim by drawing on common European aims and global values. Second, the long- as well as the short-term strategic goals of the German defense policy in the context of European cooperation. Third, the politicization of the issue of women's exclusion from the Bundeswehr in Germany. In contrast to the 1970s, the 1990s are shaped by widely diffused egalitarian attitudes about gender.

Put in a nutshell, I claim that ECJ judgments may provoke a collision of norms at the domestic level that serves as a catalyst in making the legal and institutional setup of the Bundeswehr adjust to externally and internally changing political, social, and cultural realities. In my conclusion, I will speculate why the *Kreil* judgment would contribute to enhancing the Europeanization of the military in a specifically European way.

In the following I will:

First, discuss the scope and depth of the gendered transformations of the Bundeswehr in the aftermath of the ECJ judgment;

Second, assess the role of the ECJ vis-à-vis other opportunities and constraints on domestic change; and

Third, examine the discursive frames and mass public attitudes and in what sense they contribute to the Europeanization of the military.

## 1. TRANSFORMATIONS OF THE BUNDESWEHR IN RESPONSE TO THE ECJ *KREIL* JUDGMENT

The ECJ's judgment on the *Kreil* case argued clearly that member-state governments must ensure that women are granted equal treatment not only in the civilian public sector but also in military working places. The question is: to what extent might ECJ judgments trigger effective changes in the institutionalized practices that rule gender relations within the state, and to what extent, if any, might they be conducive to profound institutional transformations?

ECJ preliminary rulings clarify how and to which degree public and private actors in member states are expected to comply with EC norms, such as regulations or directives. In the domain of gender equality jurisdiction, the ECJ issued 133 "preliminary rulings" between 1970 and 2000 (Ketelhut, 2003). Among the fifteen EU member states, German courts were directly affected in thirty-three of these cases. But in the majority of these gender equality conflicts that German courts brought to the ECJ, only two of the ten gender equality directives issued between 1975 and 2002 as well as Article 119 of the EEC treaty on equal pay were in question: in no less than twenty-one rulings, the ECJ was asked to interpret the treaty article and the directive on equal pay (75/117/EEC) and in ten rulings the directive on equal treatment of women and men (76/207/EEC). The *Kreil* judgment represents a further case for inclusion in the latter category of legal conflicts. By contrast, the EEC social security directive was of interest for women mostly in member states other than Germany: Of forty judgments, fourteen came from the Netherlands and sixteen from Great Britain, but none from Germany.

To date, systematic empirical studies on how member states transpose and implement EC norms in the area of gender equality and how they adjust their legal and institutional settings in order to align with ECJ interpretations of primary and secondary EC law are rare (Duina, 1997; Tesoka, 1999; Caporaso and Jupille, 2001; Liebert and Sifft, 2003; Falkner, 2002). *Gendering Europeanisation* presents a systematic comparative analysis of the patterns of implementation of EC gender directives in six member states. This study finds that in the area of gender equality Germany belongs to the laggards among member states that have been most out of sync with the deadlines stipulated by the respective EC provisions within which domestic adjustments are expected to take place. For the period of 1975–1998, Germany can be described not only as a "laggard" but also as an example of legislators choosing the strategy of "minimizing impact" of EC norms in the domestic realm (Kodré and Müller, 2003), at least at the national level.[5]

To explain patterns of underperformance or even outright noncompliance, alternative accounts have been put forward. Following a legal-political approach to compliance, Michael Zürn distinguishes between four sources of noncompliance (Zürn, 2000: 11):[6] the ambiguity of the EC norm; because the member state challenges the supranational norm on legal or constitutional grounds; intentional "cheating" by the member state, without challenging the norm; and the lack of state capacity for implementing the EC norm at the domestic level. By contrast, if we adopt the framework of comparative Europeanization analysis, institutional, cognitive, and agency-related mechanisms and their combinations need to be explored to account for different modes of Europeanization, ranging from resistance towards EC norms, formal compliance, and domestification to transformation (Liebert, 2003a).

The account developed here is based on the framework of Europeanization and will therefore go beyond the notion of formal compliance. It aims at assessing the scope and depth of domestic adjustments and, possibly, institutional transformations that result from the transposition of EC norms into the domestic realm. In the present context of the ECJ judgment on women in the military, we will therefore ask whether in the German case governments complied at all, and if they did, whether their compliance was formal and restricted to domestic legal and legislative adjustments to EC norms; or whether Europeanization triggered domestic changes, including discursive shifts and elite learning, conducive to a "domestification" of the relevant EC gender norm, or even to profound and sustainable institutional transformations.

Hence, for assessing the impact of the EC's equal-treatment norms on changes in the German military that emerged from the ECJ *Kreil* judgment, it is necessary to explore legislative as well as discursive and institutional adjustments. For Europeanization to transform the Bundeswehr, three conditions were necessary: first, the EC's equality norms needed to be formally transposed into the German constitutional and legislative framework governing the Bundeswehr; second, there had to be organizational changes in order to integrate women practically into the military infrastructure; and, finally, cultural or "discursive" shifts had to occur legitimizing the inclusion of women in the military.

In which of these three different dimensions did the German government, military leaders, and public-opinion formers cope with EC equal-treatment norms regarding the gender composition of the Bundeswehr in the aftermath of the ECJ *Kreil* judgment? Were they restricted to only formally including women, or were the organizational prerequisites created and even the cultural frames constructed for effectively and legitimately integrating women into the armed forces, as the symbol of sovereign state power?

In all these three dimensions, including legal, organizational, and discursive, changes can be detected:

1. First, the ECJ judgment urged the German government to change the Basic Law provision in force for more than fifty years that had banned women from the armed forces. Within less than ten months, by November 2000, the German government adjusted the German Constitution and, thus, the legal bases of the Bundeswehr. Although the governing coalition of Social Democrats and the Green Party initially considered not changing that part of the Basic Law prohibiting women from serving under arms but only reinterpreting it, both parties finally agreed to constitutional change in order to prevent recourse to the German Constitutional Court. With an impressive cross-party near unanimity, the Bundestag dropped the restrictive Article 12a of the Basic Law that had stipulated, "Women . . . in no case may be drawn to serve the arms." Since January 2001, women have unrestricted access to all careers within the German Bundeswehr.

2. Simultaneously, the ECJ norm of equal treatment for women and men was implemented by organizational changes in the Bundeswehr necessary for including women into Bundeswehr practice. In the Ger-

man Ministry of Defense, a steering committe, "Women in the Armed Forces," was created under the leadership of Brigade General Jörg Sohst. Its tasks comprised: (1) legal questions such as changes in the soldier law and the soldier carrier regulations; (2) infrastructural and logistic-organizational requirements regarding uniform, accommodation, or hygiene; (3) ergonomic aspects such as the adjustment of arms and equipment to women soldiers; (4) changes in the guidelines for education and formation; (5) information for and preparation of interested women; and (6) the problem of the degree to which the army should open its ranks to women (Kümmel and Biehl, 2000: 7).

3. Finally, also in terms of both cultural and cognitive dimensions, studies were launched about the ambivalent attitudes held by male soldiers toward opening the military to women, and their underlying notions of masculinity, femininity, and gender relations (Kümmel and Biehl, 2001). Courses in "gender-sensitive training" were developed to dismantle resistance on the part of male soldiers based on "justified or unjustified" gender stereotypes (Kümmel and Biehl, 2000).

As a result, the number of women in uniform between 1999 and 2002 nearly doubled, from 4,173 to 7,734. Among these, 2,752 women soldiers serve in the armed troops, while 4,982 form part of the health service and music corps. To summarise, the approach adopted by the German government towards implementing the ECJ judgment on women in the military was to transform the Bundeswehr profoundly. This response is particularly exceptional, if compared to the pattern of noncompliance or underperformance characteristic of Germany with respect to implementing EC gender equality law between 1975 and 1998. Although Germany clearly still belongs to the "laggards" with respect to the percentage of women included in other national armies, the impact of Europeanization is unusual, since it was not limited to the formal level, but included organizational as well as cultural changes. Thus, traditional cognitive frames were questioned and training programs developed to trigger learning processes necessary to challenge the male exclusiveness of the Bundeswehr effectively.

The question is how it can be explained that the German government was eager to pave the way for women in the Bundeswehr as much or even more than in the state bureaucracy, the courts, or state universities, especially considering that in these various state branches "gender training" for removing cognitive constraints and informal impediments to equal treatment have hardly ever been contemplated. Hence, why was the Bundeswehr a pioneer in the area of egalitarian gender relations?

In the following section, I will discuss some rational accounts for why the ECJ could have an important impact on transforming the Bundeswehr. Then, in the last section, I will adopt an interpretative perspective to capture some of the underlying cognitive and discursive aspects of this puzzle.

## 2. INSTITUTIONAL MECHANISMS AND
## AGENCY IN EUROPEANIZING THE BUNDESWEHR

The traditional debate on the driving forces of European integration provided alternative clues to the question of why the German government adjusted to the ECJ judgment by transforming the Bundeswehr. The controversial issue in this debate involved the role of the ECJ in relationship to national institutions: whether to treat the ECJ as a supranational agent acting in alliance with national courts and interest groups, or whether to view the ECJ as only a catalyst where member governments are in control of domestic adjustments to legal integration. The Europeanization framework bridges this artificial dichotomy, by exploring the interactions of supranational with domestic mechanisms, including institutional provisions, frames, and agents.

(1) With the expansion of EC jurisdiction, supranational law gradually penetrates the domestic legal realm, due to an interplay between "functional" and "political spillovers" that are conducive to an "incremental upgrading of common European interests" (Burley and Mattli, 1993). Following this argument, the central actors who pursue the aim of including women in the military in the EU are located above and below the nation-state: the ECJ judges in their role as arbiters serve their own institutional interests; and domestic courts and interest groups support the ECJ because of their complementary self-interests. Both categories of actors are engaged in processes of reciprocal empowerment, while limiting their operations to a legal context that is neatly separated from the political.

In the case of the Bundeswehr, the ECJ proved a powerful mediator since (a) it confirmed domestic critics of the German government's constitutional, legal, and normative justifications for the exclusion of women in the Bundeswehr (Reich 1999; von Münch 1999); and (b) it enforced EC norms in Germany through an unambiguous judgment. In this case, the ECJ was an important mechanism for transforming the Bundeswehr, and, hence, for domestic change. Regarding subnational allies, the court could rely on two groups: the Bundeswehrverband, an association of military personnel, on one hand, and the Liberal Party (FDP), on the other. Furthermore, the *Kreil* case stirred up an intense public debate in practically all of the major German mass media. When the ruling was announced on January 11, 2000, it even superseded for some days the attention devoted to the party finance scandal of the Christian Democratic Union.

At the domestic level, the German government acted as a crucial agent as well, working hand in hand with the ECJ. In the *Tanja Kreil* case, the ECJ ruling fit in with changed national German interests as much as the other way round. The renewed national interest in including women in the military can be explained, in part, as the result of a government change in 1998. The German government had changed its position on the issue of women in the armed forces. Appearing in front of the European Court in June 1999, only a few months after taking office, the representative of the German Social Democratic Party (SPD)-Green coalition government defended the exclusion of women by traditional gender norms, emphasizing differences between men and women, where the latter needed to be protected by the former. Yet after January 2000, Rudolf Scharping, the SPD Minister of Defense, endorsed the mission to open the Bundeswehr for women. He became the most visible actor in the reform process, although some of his actions were concealed by the press and only published on the Internet: for example, a "hearing" held with fifty women soldiers to discuss women's problems in the Bundeswehr health corps. The introduction of "gender training" programs in the armed forces was initiated by the "brain trust" of the "Social Scientific Research Institute of the Bundeswehr" (Kümmel, Klein, and Lohmann, 2000; Kümmel and Biehl, 2000) to effect cognitive changes of the traditional Bundeswehr culture.

(2) In two debates about the revision of the Basic Law in the Bundestag, the representatives of the governing Social Democratic and Green parties deployed a radically changed discourse.[7] The Christian Democrats, the governing party in 1996 when Tanja Kreil's case was brought to the ECJ, also changed their position. These shifts facilitated the passage of the new article of the Basic Law that allowed women to join the Bundeswehr on a voluntary basis by a near unanimous vote of the MPs. There were two pragmatic motives for German legislators opting in favor of the provision: First, women were seen as a resource to offset the shortage of male candidates volunteering for a professional career in the Bundeswehr. In this context, the norm of equal treatment of men and women promises to make the Bundeswehr "more attractive" in competition with civilian workplaces. Second, women's inclusion in the Bundeswehr was seen as a strategy to create a new appeal and image to counter the bad press the Bundeswehr had suffered in recent years.

Previous governments, primarily the SPD-led governments between 1969 and 1984, had sought to include women in the Bundeswehr, but without success. To understand why these former attempts failed while they succeeded in 2000, an "instrumental" account may highlight two major contextual changes: First, the pressure on the Bundeswehr to function effectively in out-of-area actions grew with NATO obligations increasing after the Gulf War, and especially with the Kosovo War. Second, in the 1970s, women's organizations successfully mobilized against attempts to draw women into the armed services; for instance, the initiative of 1979 supported by public figures and intellectuals, "Women into the Bundeswehr—We say NO" (Janßen, 1980). Bearing this historical antecedent in mind, one could expect that any renewed attempt to "militarize women" would have been blocked again, if not by the women's movement then by the German peace movement. Ultimately, during the seventies and eighties, both movements repeatedly rallied against attempts by German elites to "legitimate militarism" by including women, instead of abolishing the Bundeswehr altogether.

To understand why in the aftermath of the ECJ's judgment on women in the military a countermobilization did not materialize, it appears necessary to include public opinion into the account. Arguably the changing patterns of public attitudes toward the issue of women and the military created the strikingly new constellation to overcome the old stalemate, that is, a social democratic–liberal government coalition trying to "promote" women in the army, but women activists resisting it. By 2000, German mass publics displayed an overwhelmingly positive attitude toward the issue of women in the Bundeswehr. As a representative survey conducted by EMNID in March 2000 revealed, 79 percent of men and women viewed a woman applying for a job in the Bundeswehr positively, and 34 percent extremely positively; 59 percent of the women welcomed the decision of the European Court of Justice to open the Bundeswehr to women, and 33 percent were in favor of opening all units of the army to voluntary female soldiers (Bundesministerium der Verteidigung, 2000: 18–21). This change was the result of a diffusion of egalitarian attitudes among German mass publics.

## 3. GENDER EQUALITY, EUROPEANIZATION, AND THE REFRAMING OF THE BUNDESWEHR

Europeanization comprises, apart from promoting equal treatment of men and women, also the project of building EU rapid-intervention forces, serving as crisis intervention troops, as well as a common security and defense policy, seen as "a logical consequence of the process of European integration" (Berlin, forty-sixth annual meeting of the Parliamentary Assembly of NATO, November 2000). If Europeanization helps to diffuse European norms and common frameworks across a diversity of domestic contexts, this will be the result not only of institutional and interaction mechanisms, but will require also cognitive and discursive shifts. Is there evidence in the German case that cognitive frames changed in domestic discourses related to the issue of women in the armed forces? Can newly dominant cultural frames be identified that help to explain the transformation of the Bundeswehr? More specifically, has a "European," egalitarian gender frame replaced traditional and masculinist notions in German public debates about women in the Bundeswehr?

One question is whether in German public debates the issue of women's inclusion in the military is reframed by referring to the "normal situation" typical of other EU member states. Do discourses draw on cognitive, normative, or emotional symbols with a European dimension? Are there arguments legitimizing the ECJ judgment, or conversely protesting against the intrusion of the ECJ in domestic affairs? "Norm collisions" will result from competing and incompatible normative frames of the issues at stake in situations of "misfit" between European regulations and national practices. Women's inclusion in the military will be a controversial issue of public debate to the extent to which people frame this issue in contrasting terms, in particular, if they draw on differing conceptions of "gender" and "equality."[8] The question is to what extent the gender equality discourses of the ECJ and Germany converge, thus explaining the Europeanization of the Bundeswehr, or whether they continue to differ or even clash.

## (1) The Legal Discourse of the European Court of Justice

In the June 1999 court deliberations on the case *Tanja Kreil v. Federal Republic of Germany* held in Luxembourg, the ECJ backed Tanja Kreil's claim that the denial of a job by the Bundeswehr represented direct discrimination because of her gender and therefore was in conflict with the EC equal-treatment norm. The court also adopted the argument of the European Commission that the norm of equal treatment applied to all public employment relations and hence was valid for the armed forces. The court concluded that, "a stronger protection of women against the dangers that affect men and women in the same way cannot be justified" (4). The EC treaty would only allow for exceptions from Community law in cases of war or serious tensions, but not during peace times. Exceptions were legitimate only if it was deemed "necessary" that men perform a specific function. It was the business of national courts to establish which activities fell under the exemption. The courts had to examine whether women's exclusion from the armed service had disadvantages, and balance these against the claim to serve the protection of the women. In particular, excluding women from "crisis-resistant" workplaces and chances of qualification, such as the military provided to men, could be a handicap also with respect to competing in the civil labor market.

In their judgment as well as in the report accompanying it, the ECJ judges reaffirmed the principle that the inclusion and promotion of women in the military helped to upgrade common interests held by the EU in its entirety. Although the EU left it to member states to adopt adequate measures for assuring their internal and external security, this did not necessarily imply that national defense and security policy was completely detached from Community law and, in particular, from equal-treatment norms for women and men. Exceptions are limited to extraordinary cases. For instance, member states have the right to exclude professional activities for which gender constitutes an undeniable prerequisite from the domain to which gender equality regulations apply. But such exceptions may not go beyond that which is necessary for the relevant aim. The court has to examine whether national state institutions do in fact guarantee public security and whether their measures are adequate and necessary to reach these aims. Given that women are excluded from nearly all branches of the military, this no longer can justify an exception of unequal treatment admissible for protecting women.

## (2) The Defensive Discourse by the German Government

In 1956, in the parliamentary debate on the constitutionalization of the new German Army, Christian Democrat Elisabeth Schwarzhaupt argued that, "our conception of the nature and destination of women prohibits women to serve with arms." Social Democrat Annemarie Renger saw women in uniform "in contradiction to the feminine." The stereotype of women as the physically weak gender was the basis for the introduction of provision 11a in the German Basic Law: "Women are in no case admitted to serve with arms." By 1999, Germany was one of only three European Union member states where women were not admitted to all branches of the armed forces, and where with its 340,000 soldiers the Bundeswehr represented the largest public employer practicing a "Berufsverbot" (job prohibition) against women. This "misfit" of German practices with EU equal-treatment norms also contradicted the constitutional reform of 1994 where Article 3, paragraph 2, sentence 2, stipulates, "The state promotes the effective realization of equal rights of women and men and contributes to the abolition of existing disadvantages" (von Münch, 1999: 7).

Still in 1999, in the proceedings of the ECJ case in Luxembourg on June 29, the German government continued to argue that this "disadvantage" was justified, since Community law should not apply to the domain of defense, as part of the common foreign and security policy which remained in the sovereignty of the member states. Furthermore, it held that experiences with the National Socialist Regime dictated that legislators had a "moral obligation" to protect women from being exposed to combat and the arms of enemies, without considering whether women were willing to expose themselves to such dangers.

In the October 2000 Bundestag debate on the revision of the German Constitution to extend women's access to military careers, few complained about the "intrusion" of the ECJ in domestic affairs. Only Rupert Scholz, the speaker of the CDU opposition party in the Bundestag, judged the ECJ judgment to be "a clear transgression" (*Kompetenzenverstoß*). The domain of the military, he argued, did not belong to the competences of the EC. Citing a number of decisions by German courts, he affirmed that women's service in the armed forces even on a voluntary basis was unconstitutional. Finally, Scholz had to admit that the "protection norm in favor of women" that had become state practice was in contradiction with the "meanwhile changed societal consciousness" in Germany that required that the "women citizens in uniform" become an integral part of a democratic society (DBT, 2000e).

Apart from this, the Bundestag debate confirmed the legitimacy of the ECJ judgment in several aspects (DBT, 2000e):

a. Changing public attitudes toward "women citizens in uniform" was acknowledged to have become an "integral part of democratic society" (Rupert Scholz, CDU);
b. A high proportion of women applying for jobs in the Bundeswehr were found to achieve higher scores on the "performance tests" than male candidates (H. P. Bartels, SPD);
c. In new peacekeeping tasks, women would supply specific capabilities in out-of-area ventures;
d. Regarding the improvement of the public image of the Bundeswehr, women would contribute to making it a model site where liberal democracy, responsibility, and the rule of law were "confirmed" (Margot von Renesse, SPD);
e. The Bundeswehr as a major workplace site required combating discrimination against women (Volker Beck, Greens); in particular, it mandated dismantling "the last 'Berufsverbot' supported by the constitution" (Jörg van Essen, FDP);
f. However, the equal-treatment norm for women and men was seen as violated by giving women the choice, and keeping conscription for men, as reform communists (PDS) argued (Petra Bläss, PDS). In the view of Christian Democrats, by contrast, women should be excluded from conscription because they provided sufficient "community service" to society by working in the family, in the child's education as well as by their "Ehrenamt" (Irmgard Karwatzki, CDU);
g. Finally, even female patriotism was invoked to back women's admission into the army: Women needed the right to participate in the "responsible task of providing security to their country" (Karwatzki).

In view of this range of arguments voiced in the parliamentary debate to pave the way for women into the Bundeswehr we can conclude with a mixed balance: German legislators adopted constitutional and legislative changes necessary to Europeanize the Bundeswehr. But they supported this fundamental change for quite different reasons: ranging from instrumental interests, to ideas about the possible effects of women on improving the Bundeswehr, to varying norms about gender and equality.

## CONCLUSION: THE BUNDESWEHR ON

## THE WAY TOWARD A EUROPEAN IDENTITY?

Before the *Kreil* judgment was issued by the ECJ, high courts in the U.S. in numerous cases served as catalysts for promoting women's access to the U.S. armed forces by facilitating their careers and combating multiple forms of internal discrimination (see Katzenstein, 1998). It can be therefore assumed that, once the national barrier of sovereignty around the military has been perforated by an international and European norm such as gender equality, this process of erosion will continue. The ECJ as well as the International Criminal Court will continue to make inroads for civil and human rights in a territory where military logics and chains of command operate. In that respect, women in uniform who feel treated unequally and seek redress at the court are pioneers. Generalizing from the first few military cases, the ECJ could continue to function as a catalyst making internal military affairs more transparent and stimulating mass public debates.

Two questions remain open in this account: Will expanding transnational military operations—such as NATO or, more recently, EU-led joint ventures—further promote convergence towards norms of gender equality framed as "sameness" modeled after male norms? Or will military in the EU progressively pursue a slightly different path? Following the third generation of equal-treatment directives developed during the 1990s, and with their orientation toward a variety of "gender integrating" militaries, "family friendliness" of the military is becoming an always more important issue of making it attractive as a workplace by safeguarding parental, and even marital rights. Thus the reconciliation of work and family life, and even of foreign service and marital sex life, has become an issue in the evolution of public debates about the inner life of the Bundeswehr since 2000.[9] If in the future, the gender-mainstreaming approach to public policy in the EU (Shaw and Beveridge, 2002) will also expand to the armed forces, we might expect notions about gender identities and gender relations in European militaries will further depart from traditional masculinist norms.

## NOTES

1. This article originates in a paper given at the Conference "Europeanization in Transatlantic Perspective," Institute for European Studies (IES), Cornell University & Jean Monnet Centre for European Studies (CEuS), University of Bremen; Bremen, December 8–9, 2000. I am grateful for comments by Mary Fainsod Katzenstein, Peter Katzenstein, and Heidi Gottfried, and for research assistance by Henrike Müller.

2. While in 2000, in Great Britain women constituted 7.4 percent, in the Netherlands 7.2 percent, in Belgium 7.2 percent, in France 6.3 percent, in Portugal 5.1 percent, in Denmark 4.8 percent, and in Greece 4.0 percent of the military forces; within the Eu-

ropean Union only Luxembourg and Italy until 2000 excluded women completely, and outside the EU Turkey (0.9 percent) and Poland (0.1 percent). At the same time, 14 percent of 1.4 million American and 11.3 percent of Canadian soldiers were recruited among women (Bundesministerium der Verteidigung, 2000: 22)

3. The body of EC gender equality law includes treaty provisions (Art. 119 of the 1958 Treaty of Rome, the protocol and agreement on social policy of the 1992 Maastricht Treaty, and articles 2, 3, 13, and 141 of the 1997 Amsterdam Treaty), as well as nine Council Directives (CD 75/117/EEC on Equal Pay; CD 76/207/EEC on Equal Treatment; CD 79/9/EEC on Social Security; CD 86/378/EEC on Occupational Social Security; CD 86/613/EEC on Self-Employment; CD 92/85/EEC on Pregnant Workers; CD 96/34/EC on Parental Leave; CD 96/97/EC on Second Occupational Social Security; CD 97/80/EC on Burden of Proof), and most recently a joint European Parliament and Council Directive, D 2002/73/EC, amending CD 76/207/EEC on the implementation of the principle of equal treatment for men and women regarding access to employment, vocational training and promotion, and working conditions (source: http://europa.eu.int/comm/employment_social/equ_opp/rights_en.html).

4. As a consequence of the _Kreil_ judgment of the ECJ, Italy, Luxembourg, and to some degree also Great Britain will have to face similar changes.

5. However, there are also opposite cases of women-friendly Länder in Germany—such as Bremen—that sought to advance gender equality by adopting affirmative action measures for their public sector, but that have been constrained by the ECJ judgment on the _Kalanke_ case (1995).

6. Voluntary noncompliance would take the form of cheating if it did not challenge the rule, while it would challenge the rule openly if the norm were considered wrong. Involuntary noncompliance would not challenge the norm if ambiguous. It would challenge the norm in case of a lack of capacities to implement (Zürn, 2000).

7. See German Bundestag, 107th session, June 7, 2000; and 128th session, October 27, 2000.

8. At least five conceptions of "gender equality" can be distinguished in European policy and legal discourse: the egalitarian norm of "gender sameness"; the norm of gender neutrality; the formal norm of equality of opportunity; the conception of substantial equality as an outcome; and equality understood as gender equity, depending on individual needs, resources, and rights.

9. Thus, _Der Spiegel_ reports that, "With strange regulations the high command seeks to control the sex life of German soldiers. But court cases show that out of area service and the rising number of women in the Bundeswehr create problems that commanders are hardly capable of solving" ("Verführerische Situationen" ["Seductive Situations"], November 4, 2002, no. 45, p. 78ff).

## REFERENCES

Bläss, Petra. 1999. "Frauen an die Waffen? Gleichberechtigung?" _Neues Deutschland_, November 10.

Bundesministerium der Verteidigung. 2000. _Frauen in der Bundeswehr_. July. Bonn.

Bundeswehr aktuell: Gleiche Rechte—gleiche Pflichten? Anmerkungen zur Entscheidung des Europäischen Gerichtshofes in Sachen Tanja Kreil. Von Peter Dreist. No. 2, 2000.

Burley, Anne-Marie, and Mattli, Walter. 1993. "Europe before the Court: A Political Theory of Legal Integration." Deutsche Friedensgesellschaft - Vereinigte KriegsdientsgegnerInnen (DFG-VK): Frauen und Bundeswehr. Keine Frage- Gleiches Recht für alle! Niemand und Keiner zur Bundeswehr. At http://www.dfg-vk.de/bundeswehr/frauen.htm.

Caporaso, James A., and Jupille, Joseph. 2001. "The Europeanization of Gender Equality Policy and Domestic Structural Change." Pp. 21–43 in *Transforming Europe*, ed. Maria Green Cowles, James A. Caporaso, and Thomas Risse. Ithaca, N.Y.: Cornell University Press.

Deutscher Bundestag. 2000a. Unterrichtung durch die Wehrbeauftragte (Claire Marienfeld). Jahresbericht 1999 (41. Bericht). Drucksache 14/2900, March 14.

———. 2000b. Entwurf eines Gesetzes zur Änderung des Grundgesetzes Artikel 12a. (Antrag der FDP, Bundestagsdebatte) Drucksache 14/1728 (neu).

———. 2000c. Bundestagsdebatte zur "Zukunft der Bundeswehr" - Drucksache 14/3454.

———. 2000d. Gesetzentwurf der Fraktionen SPD, CDU/CSU, Bündnis 90/DIE GRÜNEN und F.D.P.. Drucksache 14/4380. October 24.

———. 2000e. Beratung eines Gesetzes zur Änderung des Grundgesetzes, Artikel 12a. 128. Sitzung des Bundestages. October 27. (Protokoll: www.bundestag.de/pp/9000501.htm).

Duina, Francesco. 1997. "Explaining Legal Implementation in the European Union." *International Journal of the Sociology of Law* 25: 155–79

Eifler, Christine. 2000. "Militär, Gender und 'Peacekeeping'—zu einem widersprüchlichen Verhältnis." *Femina Politica* 9, no. 1.

Emnid-Institut. 2000. Ergebnisse einer Telefon-Umfrage unter 1000 befragten Frauen über 14 Jahren. January 17–22.

———. 2000. Meinungsbild zur Sicherheitspolitischen Lage (SPL).

European Commission. 1995. *The Utilisation of Sex Equality Litigation Procedures in the Member States of the European Community: A Comparative Study.* Directorate-General V/D5 Equal Opportunities Unit. June.

European Court of Justice. 1999. Schlussanträge des Generalanwalts Antonio La Pergola. Rechtssache C -285/98. Tanja Kreil gegen Bundesrepublik Deutschland. October 26.

———. 2000. Urteil des Gerichtshofes vom 11. Gleichbehandlung von Männern und Frauen. Beschränkung des Zugangs von Frauen zum Dienst mit der Waffe in der Bundeswehr (C-285/98). Tanja Kreil gegen Bundesrepublik Deutschland. January.

Falkner, Gerda, Miriam Hartlapp, Simone Leiber, and Oliver Treib. 2002. "Transforming Social Policy in Europe? The EC's Parental Leave Directive and Misfit in the 15 Member States." MPIfG Working Paper 02/11, October 2002, Max Planck Institute for the Study of Societies, Cologne.

Garrett, Geoffrey. 1995. "The Politics of Legal Integration in the European Union." *International Organization* 49, no. 1: 171–81.

Katzenstein, Mary Fainsod. 1998. *Faithful and Fearless: Moving Feminist Protest inside the Church and Military.* Princeton, N.J.: Princeton University Press.

Ketelhut, Jörn. 2003. "EU Gender Equality Law, Gender Disparities in Domestic

Labour Markets, and Public EU Support." Appendix, pp. 308–24 in *Gendering Europeanisation*, ed. U. Liebert, with S. Sifft. Brussels: Peter Lang.

Kodré, Petra, and Müller, Henrike. 2003. "Shifting Policy Frames: EU Equal Treatment Norms and Domestic Discourses in Germany." In *Gendering Europeanisation*, ed. Ulrike Liebert, with Stefanie Sifft. Brussels: Peter Lang.

Kümmel, Gerhard, and Biehl, Heiko. 2000. *Die weitere Öffnung der Bundeswehr für Frauen aus der Sicht männlicher Soldaten. Eine erste Zwischenbilanz in Auszügen.* July/August. Strausberg: Sozialwissenschaftliches Institut der Bundeswehr.

———. 2001. *Warum nicht? Die ambivalente Sicht männlicher Soldaten auf die weitere Öffnung der Bundeswehr für Frauen.* February. Strausberg.

Kümmel, Gerhard, Klein, Paul, and Lohmann, Klaus. 2000. *Zwischen Differenz und Gleichheit. Die Öffnung der Bundeswehr für Frauen.* Strausberg: Sozialwissenschaftliches Institut der Bundeswehr, Mai.

Liebert, Ulrike, with Sifft, Stefanie, eds. 2003. *Gendering Europeanisation.* Brussels: Peter Lang.

Liebert, Ulrike. 2003a. "Causal Complexities: Analysing Europeanisation." In *Gendering Europeanisation*, ed. Ulrike Liebert, with Stefanie Sifft. Brussels: Peter Lang.

———. 2003b. "Gendering Europeanisation: Patterns and Dynamics." In *Gendering Europeanisation*, ed. Ulrike Liebert, with Stefanie Sifft. Brussels: Peter Lang.

Louis, Chantal. 2000. Kreil gegen Deutschland. *Emma.* January/February.

PDS im Bundestag. 2000. Bundeswehr. Postionen der PDS im Bundestag. Berlin. March.

Reich, Norbert. 1999. "Europarechtlich kaum haltbarer Frauen-Ausschluß." *FAZ*, July 28, S. 9.

Rottmann, Heiko. 2000. "Die Männer müssen vorbereitet sein. Der Verteidigungsminister diskutiert mit Soldatinnen über die Folgen des Urteils des Europäischen Gerichtshofes." In: Aktuell. Zeitung für die Bundeswehr 36, no. 8 (February 28).

Shaw, Jo, and Beveridge, Fiona, eds. 2002. "Gender Mainstreaming in the European Union." *Feminist Law Studies*, special issue.

Sohst, Jörg. 2000. "Alle Laufbahnen stehen offen." *Truppenpraxis/Wehrausbildung* (June): 387–93.

Tesoka, Sabrina. 1999. "The Differential Impact of Judicial Politics in the Field of Gender Equality: Three National Cases under Scrutiny." Working Paper, RSC No. 99/18, Florence, European University Institute.

von Münch, Ingo. 1999. "Ein Widerspruch zum Gleichbehandlungsgebot." *FAZ*, July 22, 7.

Zürn, Michael. 2000. "Introduction: Law and Compliance at Different Levels." First draft of an introductory chapter for a volume, *Compliance in Modern Political Systems*, presented at the workshop of the German Science Foundation DFG, Humboldt University, Berlin, May 10.

# 13

## Implementing Sexual Harassment Law in the United States and Germany

*Kathrin Zippel*

This chapter compares the implementation of policy approaches to sexual harassment in Germany and the United States. Legislation and enforcement practices of sex equality law are embedded in German labor law in the form of workers' protection laws and in the United States in civil rights law. In the United States, the dynamics of implementation have emphasized individuals' legal redress, individual reporting, and lawsuits, which have affirmed employers' responsibilities to prevent harassment by institutionalizing policies and educational programs. By contrast, in the absence of strong antidiscrimination laws in Germany, the implementation process of policies against sexual harassment depends on the political will of unions, employers, and emerging state equality offices for women.

This comparative analysis of the dynamics of implementation examines the implications of these different paths for institutionalizing policy measures against sexual harassment. German employers and unions have redefined sexual harassment as an issue of "mobbing" or "bullying" in the workplace. While this move turns sexual harassment into a gender-neutral issue, discussions around "mobbing" do address "fairness in the workplace," and have led to broader attempts to challenge unfair, disrespectful (gender) cultures in the workplace. For example, the German Ministry of Women has sponsored projects of "structural mediation" as a "collective solution" to gender inequality in the workplace. By contrast, because sexual harassment in the workplace has been primarily addressed as a legal issue in the U.S., solutions based on individual reporting and complaint procedures have been emphasized. The implications of these policy responses on gender equality and gender relations in the workplace will be discussed.

## INTRODUCTION

Legal and policy changes regarding sexual harassment have been described as a feminist success story.[1] The evolution of employers' policies against sexual harassment is seen as a response to the second wave of the women's movement. Countries around the world have looked at the U.S. model to deal with the issue.[2] This model of legal and policy change has been promoted by international women's organizations, endorsed by the European Union, and diffused by other supranational bodies like the International Labor Organization (ILO) (Collins, 1996; Hodges, 1996; Husbands, 1992; Mazur, 1994; Rubenstein, 1988; Zippel, 2000). However, little research has explored cross-national differences in policy approaches and implications for gender equality and relations in workplaces (Cahill, 2001; Saguy, forthcoming).

The main questions of this chapter are: How do policy approaches differ in their orientation to individual versus collective rights in the United States and Germany? What implications do these different orientations have on gender relations? Because laws differ across countries and are similarly vague on what constitutes sexual harassment and what employers' obligations are, there is much variation in policy profiles across workplace organizations and countries. I distinguish between policy approaches focused on sexual harassment as a conflict between individuals and group-based, collective approaches (see table 13.1). The United States and Germany represent these two different models (see table 13.2). Work organizations in Germany tend to emphasize collective rights and group-based approaches to training and broader awareness over individuals' redress. Since the new labor law against sexual harassment, the *Bundesbeschäftigtenschutzgesetz* (Federal employee protection law) in 1994, employers and works councils have negotiated collective agreements that subsumed sexual harassment as one incident of "unfair workplace" practices alongside non-gender-specific discrimination and "mobbing." There are only sporadic training efforts, yet these tend to be group-oriented, antimobbing, or women-only seminars on gender-sensitive assertiveness training.

In contrast, employers in the United States, complying with the Civil Rights Act of 1964 and following case-law developments[3] on sexual harassment, have adopted policy approaches that emphasize individuals' (legal) rights and individual internal redress, defining sexual harassment as sex discrimination. This is also evident in training programs that focus on the legal (individual) dimensions of sexual harassment only. Group-based approaches of team building and general sensitivity training programs are the exception.

This chapter addresses the trade-offs and implications of these two models for gender relations. Both models lack an explicit concern with gender equality and with changing workplace cultures. I suggest a third model based on a synthesis of individual- and group-based approaches that explicitly takes into account gender inequality as the underlying cause of sexual harassment.

Drawing on feminist theories of sexual harassment, gender, organizations, and the welfare state, I use a cross-national, comparative approach to highlight variations in policy profiles and point out the particularities of the United States. I discuss the context in which these models are emerging based on country-specific laws, industrial relations, and institutionalized gender equality politics. Then, I examine the trade-offs and implications of these approaches for gender relations in the workplace.

Since policies against sexual harassment are a fairly recent phenomenon, this study contributes to the development of feminist policy assessment criteria to identify gender dimensions of variation in the adoption, implementation, and enforcement of public policies. The comparative research design is particularly useful to develop these criteria to study policy profiles and implications of policy responses.

## POLICY DISCOURSES ON SEXUAL HARASSMENT

The implementation of sexual harassment laws remains one of the most contentious issues of gender politics in the workplace. The issue itself is highly controversial, and views on sexual harassment fall along gender lines (Reese and Lindenberg, 1999). The very definition of what constitutes sexual harassment has triggered conflict. The power to "name" reflects the power struggles over definitions of "sexual harassment." Policy discourses in workplace organization vary nationally and internationally, ranging from individual-rights frames to moral issues (good behavior), workplace conflict, abuse of power, "mobbing," or violence against women (Saguy, forthcoming; Bernstein, 1994; Zippel, 2000).

In policy discourses in the United States, the dominant frame is that of sex discrimination (Cahill, 2001; Saguy, forthcoming). This frame draws on the legal definition of the violations of individual rights to equal treatment. The interviewees in the United States defined sexual harassment in line with the Equal Employment Opportunity Commission (EEOC) definition, referring to harassment as "unwanted attention of a sexual nature." In contrast, German interviewees defined sexual harassment most often as the "violation of boundaries" and "stepping over the line."

In Germany, the notion of "sexual harassment" was borrowed from the United States. In the first publicized sexual harassment case a group of women filed a complaint against a newly elected Green Party parliamentarian with the party leadership in 1982. Sybille Plogstedt explained: "One of the harassed women had been in the U.S. She knew what one calls it." (Interview with Plogstedt, 1999). The German notion of "sexuelle Belästigung" is a direct translation from the English "sexual harassment."

The U.S. legal definition of "unwanted" behavior strengthens the subjective perspective of the harassed person. By contrast, the German legal definition is explicitly gender neutral and not set in the context of sex discrimination, because it defines sexual harassment as the "violation of dignity." Furthermore, sexual harassment is defined as "intentionally, sexually motivated behavior" that is "recognizably rejected" by the person. This definition reflects the perspective of the harasser and observers of the situation rather than the harassed person. In contrast to the legal definition, the women I interviewed clearly used subjective notions such as "what offends me, bothers me," and so on. As in other policy areas, these legal frames shape employers' and employees' definitions of the problem and the solutions proposed. In the United States, the legal definitions of harassment have, however, permeated everyday language and discourse in workplaces more than the German legal definitions have. In part, this reflects the gap between the legal definition and how women define harassment based on their experience, but also, indicates that legal concerns are less prevalent in dealing with the issue in the German context.

## MOBBING

Mobbing has become the European model to address "diversity issues" in the workplace. The notion of mobbing describes the violation of a person's rights (*Persönlichkeitsrechts*) through intimidation and degradation that includes bullying and harassment. In the United States, the closest concept to mobbing is bullying or "hostile environment." The important difference in U.S. concepts of discrimination is that "mobbing" can happen to everybody, independent of a person's sex, race/ethnicity, age, or sexual orientation.

Mobbing, a term originating in Sweden, describes conflict-laden communications among colleagues or among superiors and employees, in which the attacked person is treated as inferior. It is a situation in which one or more persons systematically, and over a long time period, attack someone directly or indirectly with the goal of marginalizing and driving out (Holzbecher and Meschkutat, 1999). In Germany, no specific law defines mobbing. However, the Federal German Labor Court has defined mobbing as systematic hostility, harassment, or discrimination between employees or by supervisors (Decision January 15, 1997, NZA 1997, p. 781 f). And most recently, a state-level labor court ruled that mobbing can be a violation of *allgemeine Persönlichkeitsrechte* (general personal freedoms).[4] Employers need therefore to protect employees from mobbing.

## POLICY ADOPTION AND IMPLEMENTATION

Cross-national studies of policy approaches to sexual harassment have primarily examined differences in legal dimensions (Baer, 1995; Bernstein, 1994; Cahill, 2001; Elman, 1996; Hodges, 1996; Husbands, 1992; Saguy, forthcoming; Valiente, 2000). While national laws are an important dimension of cross-national variation, employers' practices do not merely mirror these laws. Because employers have leeway in how to comply with and implement these laws, we need to examine employers' practices to understand what happens at the workplace level (Cahill, 2001).

The adoption of workplace policies is an important "first step," reflecting at a minimum the acknowledgment of sexual harassment as a problem. They signal to employees that management is aware of the issue. Because putting the issue on the agenda triggers debates on the relevance of the issue, on questions of definitions, appropriateness of procedures and sanctions, and so forth, the adoption process itself contributes to awareness of the issue. However, more important is the second step, the implementation and enforcement of these policies, as employers could be adopting policy statements to comply with the law that would be merely symbolic or "toothless" paper tigers (Cockburn, 1991). Even well-designed policies can be ineffective if they are not publicized or enforced. Therefore, employers need to implement and enforce policies and develop effective informal and formal grievance procedures that provide redress to those who have been harassed, and to sanction perpetrators.

We know surprisingly little about the implementation process or the effectiveness of policies and educational awareness programs in changing both gender workplace culture and employers' responses to women's complaints (Gutek, 1997; Magley et al., 1999; Grundmann, O'Donohue, and Peterson, 1997). What we know is that there are significant gender differences in attitudes about sexual harassment and the implementation of policies (Reese and Lindenberg, 1999; Gutek, 1997). In addition, gender relations within workplace organizations shape the adoption and implementation of these policies (Hawkesworth, 1997; Zippel, 1994).

## MODELS TO ANALYZE POLICIES AGAINST SEXUAL HARASSMENT

Policy profiles themselves are "gendered." Feminist policy studies supply us with the following tools to identify gender dimensions of policy approaches to sexual harassment. Policy approaches to combat sexual harassment can be divided into two categories: individual versus collective and group-oriented approaches (see table 13.1). Model 1 is characterized by defining sexual harassment as a conflict between two or more individuals, the harassed person and the perpetrator. Thus, employer policies and efforts focus on improving procedures to handle complaints. Individuals are informed about their "rights" and the procedures in place. Organizational change is limited to adding sexual harassment as one form of workplace conflict that needs to be resolved.

Model 2 is characterized by a focus on groups. Policy statements depict sexual harassment as an organizational problem beyond its effect on the individuals involved. Individual complaints are the basis for group interventions. Training programs focus on sensitivity, team building, respectful partnership, and cooperative teamwork. Organizational change is oriented toward improving workplace culture.

Yet, because both models lack explicit consideration of gender relations, I suggest model 3 as the combination of both approaches with an explicit focus on gender relations. In this feminist approach, an incident of sexual harassment between individuals is interpreted as an indicator of problems caused by organizational and cultural gender inequality. Sexual harassment is defined in gender-specific terms and policies take power differentials (hierarchical and gender power) into account. Both improving the handling of individual complaints *and* effecting broader changes in gender workplace culture are at the core of this approach. Interventions in workplace organizations are oriented toward changing gender inequality. Training programs focus on gender-power sensitivity training, including the assertion of, and respect for, the right to sexual self-determination.

As we will see the first two models are prevalent to different degrees in Germany and in the United States: while the U.S. leans towards the individual-based model 1, Germany's approach can be characterized by the model 2 group-based approach (see table 13.2).

## METHODS, DATA, AND CASE SELECTION

The cross-national comparative method is particularly appropriate for exploratory studies allowing us to highlight the variation in policy profiles. The data for this research project are based on fieldwork and content analysis of a variety of documents in the U.S. and Germany between 1994–1999. Primary documents include employers' policies and brochures and publications by state officials, unions, and women's organizations. Secondary documents include social science, policy, legal, and human resource and management studies in both Germany and the U.S. In the U.S., I conducted a case study of a public educational institution, including interviews with Affirmative Action and Equal Employment Officers (AA/EEO) personnel, consultants, and women's groups. In addition, I

**Table 13.1. Models of Anti-Sexual-Harassment Policies**

| | Model 1:<br>Individual Based | Model 2:<br>Group Based | Model 3:<br>Combined Model 1 and 2 with<br>Focus on Gender Equality |
|---|---|---|---|
| *Policy statements* | Protection of the rights of the individual employee | Protection of employee as collective group right | Protection of women's rights to sexual self-determination and nondiscrimination |
| *Interventions* | Procedures for complaint handling of conflict between individuals: harasser and harassed. | Intervention in workplace unit:<br>Group-based sensitivity training, group mediation, team building. | Both individual and group focused: First, immediate help for individuals: advocates, support systems for complainant, such as legal and psychological consultation. Second, group-based intervention in workplace units with focus on dynamics of gender power. |
| *Form of complaints* | Individual, formal complaints:<br>Interest-based quasi-legal rights.<br>Confrontational strategy between accuser and accused.<br>Information of legal rights | Class action.<br>Needs based: informal complaints, informal consultation. | Multiple forms: formal and informal (needs and interest based).<br>Multiple routes: multiple offices to handle complaints. |
| *Training goals* | | Change of workplace culture to respect and fairness<br>Group dynamics awareness<br>Cooperative teamwork, team building, partnership<br>Power-sensitive training | Goal: Change of gender workplace culture<br>Empowerment of women, equality for women<br>Gender sensitivity training |

**Table 13.2 National Approaches to Sexual Harassment**

|  | U.S. (Liberal Welfare State) | Germany (Corporatist Welfare State) |
|---|---|---|
| Claims | Individually formulated claims of civil rights | Collective, group-based claims of social rights |
| Laws against Sexual Harassment | Civil Rights Act, 1964, 1991; case law; Supreme Court rulings, 1986, 1993, 1998; state-level laws | Law for the Protection of Employees, 1994, both public and private sector |
| Antidiscrimination | Stronger laws Civil Rights Act 1964, covering different forms of discrimination | Weaker laws Second Gender Equality Law, 1994, covering discrimination based on sex only in public sector |
| Implementation Dynamic | Liberal-legal Compliance with case law Pressure from women's groups as informal/ formal watchdog groups | Corporatist-collective Employer–union-negotiated collective bargaining agreements Agenda setting from women, including equality officers, women within unions, and other organized women's groups |

participated in and observed training and awareness programs as an intern in the Office for Human Resources.[5] In Germany, little research exists on sexual harassment in general. I conducted seventy in-depth face-to-face and telephone interviews with legal and policy experts, including lawyers specializing in sexual harassment issues, equality officers, union stewards, and feminist activists.[6] Among the interviewees were thirty equality officers in public and private employers.[7] Finally, I had access to a number of reports and materials through the Federal Ministry of Women in Germany, the private collections of court rulings and documents of a prominent legal scholar and lawyer, Dr. Barbara Degen, and the archive of the *Arbeitsstelle für Diskriminerung im Erwerbsleben* (ADE) (Office for Discrimination in the Workplace) in Bremen.

Germany and the U.S. are compelling cases through which to explore the variation across policy developments that address sexual harassment. Sexual harassment in the workplace is similarly prevalent in both countries (Zippel, 2000). In both countries, increasing numbers of women have joined the workforce. Yet, these two countries exemplify two contrasting models to address sexual harassment (see table 13.2).

Gathering data at the organizational level is problematic due to employers' hesitance regarding legal liability and sensitivity of the issue. Because of the highly politicized nature of the issue, many respondents asked me not to reveal their names. To protect the confidentiality of these intervie-wees, I cite here only those who explicitly gave me the permission to use their names.

## LAWS AND EMPLOYERS' POLICIES

Two main factors have shaped these different national models of sexual ha-rassment policy: first, national laws against sexual harassment and the legal system, and second, the system of workplace regulation and the representa-tion of (women) workers' interests within workplaces. These institutional factors contribute to different political opportunity structures that women's movements have encountered in raising the issue of sexual harassment (Zip-pel, 2000).

In both Germany and the U.S., there were significant legal changes re-garding sexual harassment in the 1980s and 1990s. In 1986, both the U.S. Supreme Court and the *Bundesarbeitsgericht* (German Federal Labor Court) ruled on cases of sexual harassment. While the German court ruled that a su-pervisor could be dismissed for taking advantage of his authority (Degen, 1999), the Supreme Court affirmed in *Meritor vs. Savings Bank*[8] that sexual harassment constitutes sex discrimination, and thus is actionable under the Civil Rights Act of 1964. U.S. feminist legal scholars, most prominently Catherine MacKinnon (1979), were successful in changing jurisprudence by supporting civil rights litigation. The U.S. approach can be characterized as one of *individually formulated claims* in the U.S. liberal welfare state (Esp-ing-Andersen, 1990; O'Connor, Orloff, and Shaver, 1999). This individual-le-gal model mirrors the approach to sex discrimination based on individual civil rights, which was developed in analogy to race discrimination.

In contrast, the German approach can be characterized as "corporatist-collective, group based." In the early 1980s, in the absence of strong anti-discrimination legislation, feminists realized that unions had to become their allies: "This was part of the political work. It was obvious, if one insti-tution should be interested, then it was the unions, because of the works councils" (Interview with Sybille Plogstedt, 1999).

Women demanding changes regarding how employers handled sexual ha-rassment made an explicit political demand toward protection of women as a social right. As one union woman explained: "If we don't make politics around the issue, then each individual woman will have to see how she deals with it. But what are organizations for: to have collective protection. And not that each individual woman will have to claim her rights. Naturally, individual rights are important. But there has to be a political shield of pro-tection. This is typical for social rights. Otherwise they are not realized" (In-terview with union leader, 1999).

Some exceptional local workplace organizations were on the forefront of policy developments, by adopting collective agreements preceding legal developments.[9] Yet, mobilizing women within unions and finding political support took more time than the legal route. Consequently, it took until 1994 to pass the *Bundesbeschäfitigtenschutzgesetz* (Federal employee protection law) as a new labor law against sexual harassment. The law is an amendment to the Federal Second Gender Equality Law, but the tradition is based on collective, group rights of workers vis-à-vis their employers. The law emphasizes the responsibility of employers to protect employees from the non-gender-specific "violation of dignity" in the workplace.

In both countries these laws are similarly vague in what employers' responses to sexual harassment should be and what procedures and prevention efforts should be taken. Only recently the U.S. Supreme Court clarified how employers should comply with the law. The 1998 cases of *Burlington Industries v. Ellerth*[10] and *Faragher v. City of Boca Raton*[11] allow employers to make an affirmative response. Demonstrating that an employer has taken action to prevent sexual harassment by institutionalizing policies and training programs can reduce the legal liability of an employer for a supervisor's inappropriate behavior. In addition, these cases have emphasized plaintiffs' use of internal grievance procedures. Based on these legal developments, employers have strong incentives to design internal grievance procedures and to make individual employees aware of them.

In contrast to the United States, the German law is specific in that employers are to designate an office where incidents can be reported and to develop training and prevention measures (Baer, 1995). Yet, sanctions against employers for noncompliance are very weak, as legislators were hesitant to interfere in an area normally regulated by workplace agreements. Instead of imposing sanctions for violating the law, the preferred solution is that employers and unions will negotiate policies and procedures to handle sexual harassment. The unions favor group-based claims and formulations of collective rights of protection, rather than individual rights of (minority) groups.

No matter how one might interpret the role of the Equal Employment Opportunity Commission (EEOC) in implementing and enforcing equal opportunity politics in the U.S., there is no equivalent agency in Germany. Instead, similar to the U.S. Women's Bureau in the Department of Labor, "femocrats" or equality offices throughout the public sector have been created to deal with "women's issues" since the mid-1980s. Their power and influence depend, however, on the federal, state, or communal level, as well as on the ruling political parties. In the case of sexual harassment, offices at the local and communal level were indeed often initiators of policies and prevention efforts against sexual harassment (Zippel, 2000), however, they lack significant implementation and enforcement authority.

In both countries, women's groups within workplaces have used these laws to raise sexual harassment as a serious issue and to demand changes. With the law on their side, women's groups, including feminist activists in university task forces, took part in the development and formulation of these policies. And legal developments were crucial in both countries: management was ultimately more convinced by arguments of their legal liability in cases of sexual harassment than feminist arguments about the necessity to improve women's equality in the workplace (Hawkesworth, 1997; Zippel, 1994).

Even with the new law in place, unions were hesitant to put the issue on the agenda and women who raised the issue encountered strong resistance.[12] For example, within the teachers' unions, a woman recalls:

> And that was the first major dispute, when I made it an issue in the union at the state level. When I was later vice chair of the union at the state level, [I] made the law for the protection of employees a topic. . . . There were counter arguments: "This is a problem on the construction sites, but not here among us!" And this was an argument from women, from full-time union women. "We are coming from higher education." . . . I made a press release on the issue, and I was afraid to get in trouble because of this press release. I was new in my position. And it turned out to be that way. There were resignations within the unions. There were wild letters. The chair was OK, he supported me. But internally, they put the issue down.

The position unions take on the issue of sexual harassment and whether they promote or resist policies and grievance procedures is likely to vary according to a number of factors, such as the percentage of women organized in the union. Yet, workplace policies such as policies against sexual harassment can compete with unions' interests in preserving collectively negotiated grievance procedures. In fact, policy adoption and new procedures to handle sexual harassment complaints depend not only on legal considerations, but also on the existing systems of workers' representation. In both countries, informal/formal women's groups argued that the existing works councils and stewards were ill equipped to handle harassment cases. Unions were criticized for not helping victims of harassment but for supporting perpetrators' rights to stay in the workplace. Yet, if workplaces are unionized, conflicts arise between demands for specific procedures against sexual harassment and union-negotiated grievance procedures around conflicts in workplaces in general.

According to women in German union leadership positions, it was also difficult to find union support for specific grievance procedures for cases of sexual harassment. In part, this is because these procedures compete with union–employer-negotiated grievance procedures. Agencies such as the equality officers or EEO/AA officers that handle complaints against sexual harassment are seen as competitors to collective representation of workers' interests. In both countries, systems of workplace regulation shape the models of implementation of sexual harassment law. However, in the United States, only the public sector has significant degrees of unionization.[13] By contrast the German system of "works councils"[14] is a firmly institutionalized system of workers' representation at the company level. As we will see, these works councils and unions have been more important in the implementation process in Germany.

Thus, both countries leave room for the interpretation of employers' compliance with laws. The implementation process itself becomes a political process in which gender and workers' interests are negotiated. The policy models lead to considerable differences in the employers' practices, workplace policies, and prevention efforts in both countries. In the following sections, I discuss the trade-offs and implications of these different models on gender relations.

## THE INDIVIDUAL-LIBERAL-LEGAL MODEL OF THE U.S.

The majority of employers in the U.S. covered by the Civil Rights Act of 1964 have developed policies to comply with these legal developments. By 1997, 95 percent of mid- and large-sized public and private employers had adopted policies against sexual harassment (Dobbin and Kelly, 2001). This policy adoption process began in the late 1970s and continued throughout the 1980s and 1990s. Given that the individual-liberal-legal model drives sexual harassment law, policy statements of employers formulate sexual harassment as sex discrimination and interpret sexual harassment as the violation of the rights of an individual. Furthermore, because of increased legal pressures, employers have designed and improved procedures to handle complaints internally. In line with risk-minimization strategies, these policies are oriented toward assuring legal rights of both the harassed and the harasser while preventing the employer from being sued by either of these parties.

Legal discourse based on case law has shaped employers' approaches to sexual harassment. Previously institutionalized EEO/AA offices, which implement the Civil Rights Act of 1964, have become central in adopting policies (Edelman et al., 1999). These offices interpret legal changes for employers. While interpretations of the Civil Rights Act allow for both individual pursuit of rights against sex discrimination and group-based arguments, individualized claim making fits more easily into workplace organizations than collective claims. Collective, group claims would be supported by Catherine MacKinnon's argument that sexual harassment is an abuse of gender power and women are harassed because they belong to the group that is discriminated against (Cahill, 2001).

Particularly in educational institutions, informal networks and coalitions around civil rights mobilized in the 1980s and 1990s with a broader understanding of discrimination, demanding broader antiharassment policies. While most employers have adopted policies specifically against sexual harassment, only 60 percent of employers have general antiharassment policies (Dobbin and Kelly, 2001). Thus, even though the majority of employers have specific policies against sexual harassment, management discourses depict sexual harassment as a gender-neutral problem of morality—of "good" or "appropriate" behavior (Cahill, 2001). Sexual harassment as an expression of gender inequality and power becomes invisible.

In the U.S. system, in the absence of union representation in workplace organizations, organized women did not have to negotiate with existing workers' representation. Yet, formulating "collective" claims is more difficult than in the German case. For example, employers argued that in the absence of individual complaints of sexual harassment they could not take any action. Some interviewees formulated the demand that employers create an environment free of harassment. "Our goals ought to be . . . to make people feel comfortable in the workplace versus a hostile climate where people feel unsafe" (Interview with affirmative action officer, 1994). Without a strong tradition to base "collective" or social rights in the workplace on, demanding that employers take preventive measures is a more difficult task to undertake than in the German system of workers' representation. Instead, precedent-setting U.S. court rulings have raised the expectation that employers take preventive measures: in the form of training and awareness programs. Over 60 percent of medium- and large-sized employers have some form of training (Dobbin and Kelly, 2001). However, courts expect little beyond informing employees of their legal rights and the employer's policy in place.

Thus, training programs emphasize individuals' rights and encourage victims to use internal procedures rather than file lawsuits against the company.

> We are making sure that people are well informed about the policy and the procedures. So there is ongoing training that we provide. We have training programs that we actually offer for people so they can understand what the policy means, what it means for them personally (Interview with director of dispute resolution, 1994).

Employers' training programs focus on managers and supervisors because of legal liabilities for employers if the harasser has supervisory functions over the harassed person. In addition, supervisors are responsible for handling complaints and taking action and are seen as the key to setting and enforcing new behavioral standards. As one of the interviewees pointed out: "We have training programs for managers and supervisors, so they understand what their obligations are to make sure the climate is free of sexual harassment" (Interview with director of dispute resolution, 1994). Thus, training programs are oriented towards employers' under-standings of compliance with the law. More expensive group-based inter-ventions or training programs oriented toward team building, and so on, are left to the employers' discretion and constitute an exception rather than the rule.

On the positive side, U.S. employers adopted policies at a faster pace than in Germany. Using arguments of legal threat as the cornerstone of imple-mentation efforts, the orientation toward individual-based solutions empha-sizes individual redress and raises expectations of those harassed that indeed their employer cares and will act appropriately.

The U.S. model of individual redress is not without problems. Even though workplace organizations have spent much time considering effective strategies and procedures to handle complaints according to legal expecta-tions, women who have been harassed (still) do not take advantage of these procedures. The reality of outcomes of complaints casts doubt on how effi-ciently workplace organizations are willing to or can handle cases of sexual harassment. As one interviewee pointed out:

> What we see as the biggest problem is the official mechanisms have absolutely no credibility. And so women will not go and use them, because they have no credibility. Because for years all they've done is to protect management. So you go file a sexual harassment claim, and they use that to protect the harasser and to harass the women some more. And that's the perception. It's widespread. So that's the biggest problem with this institution. People don't believe in the ad-ministrator. They don't believe in their integrity, they don't believe in their commitment, they don't believe in their understanding. They see them as sim-ply as pro-management, and they do everything they can to protect manage-ment. And management is oftentimes the ones accused (Interview with women's activist, 1994).

Much of the institutions' reputation for dealing with complaints is based on rumors. Confidentiality concerns for the perpetrators bring about a lack of transparency of results which in turn undermines the trust that the ad-ministration handles complaints fairly. There is considerable controversy about appropriate responses in terms of the level of sanctions. According to administrators, the most likely outcome of a complaint is the written repri-mand of the harasser. Yet, for many victims of harassment this punishment seems not severe enough.

Instead of empowering victims of harassment to choose among multiple ways to deal with a situation of harassment, an unintended consequence of the focus on individuals is the "pressure to report" (Zippel, 1994). Employ-ers have an interest in solving issues of sexual harassment internally in order to shield the organizations from lawsuits.

It's in the interest of the institution to have people file an official complaint because that's the one way you have to get a result. And to prevent a later, maybe upcoming complaint. What I talked about was protection of the institution, which doesn't really address the concerns of the individual (Interview with director of dispute resolution, 1994).

As a result, training and awareness programs encourage individuals to report harassment. There is a great deal of ambivalence from feminist administrators who on the one hand, see that women should speak up, report, and complain about the behavior, and on the other hand are very aware of the risks associated with reporting, such as institutional revictimization including disappointment with the institutional response. EEOC statistics indicate increasing numbers of retaliation claims; 15 percent of civil rights cases are complaints about retaliation demonstrating that complaining about harassment has often negative consequences for the victim. Yet, the underlying assumption is that organizational improvements in handling sexual harassment can only be achieved if individuals come forward and use the policies (Reese and Lindenberg, 1999). Thus the individual victim becomes responsible for effecting institutional change.

Paradoxically then, instead of an organizational openness for reporting, the pressure to report puts the burden on those most affected by harassment and exposes them to further risks. As a consequence, we now discuss and know more about why victims do not report than why individuals harass, or what organizational factors contribute to harassment. Making victims politically responsible for stopping the social problem ignores the sociocultural factors that contribute to sexual harassment, such as status differences, gender power, organizational hierarchies, and so on. One might ask, how many individual women then will need to go through the grueling process of reporting harassers before harassment will stop? Training programs that focus on individual behavior changes tell men what not to do, how not to behave inappropriately. Yet, the challenge is to encourage men to see and treat women as equals in the workplace. This requires explicit awareness of gender and hierarchical power and organizational changes.

The individual-legal discourse is more prevalent than group-based, collective rights of employees. Alternatives to formal reports such as informal complaints or "dispute resolution" through mediation, an approach promoted by the EEOC in the 1990s, still focus on solving individual cases. Furthermore, in the absence of strong labor protection law in the U.S., employers can use measures against sexual harassment to erode workers' rights. For example, zero-tolerance policies give little protection or internal redress to individuals and, thus, diminish collective, group-based unions' rights.

Fitting easily with corporate interests of productivity and efficiency, managerial discourses of risk minimization, productivity, and efficiency have the advantage of speedy implementation. However, from a feminist perspective, using this model of implementation is highly problematic since it comes at the cost of emphasizing individual cases and behaviors, while silencing organizational and gender dimensions of the problem of sexual harassment. If organizations handle sexual harassment primarily as a conflict between individuals, more structural problems of gender inequality in organizational hierarchies will not be addressed. Grauerholz et al. argue "the network would displace responsibility for resolving systemic problems by treating sexual harassment as an individual problem to be resolved through customary remedies" (Grauerholz et al., 1999: 966). The focus on individual behaviors and making individual victims responsible to effect changes ignores systemic aspects of sexual harassment as rooted in unequal gender (power) relations and the gender workplace culture become difficult to address.

## THE CORPORATIST-GROUP-BASED MODEL IN GERMANY

Because the adoption of workplace policies in Germany depends on the political will of employers and unions, anti-sexual-harassment policies have developed slowly. While some employers adopted specific policies against sexual harassment in the context of the *Frauenfördermassnahmen* (women's equality measures) in the early 1990s, the majority of employers have ignored the federal law of 1994. Public employers at the local level, including cities and universities, were the first to develop policies. However by 1999, only two out of the sixteen federal ministries had anti-sexual-harassment policies (BMFSJ, 1999). In 1996, Volkswagen (VW) was the first private company to adopt antimobbing and discrimination policies. Policies against sexual harassment in the private sector in general are still the exception rather than the rule. Even companies otherwise known for "women-friendly" workplace policies have not adopted any kinds of policies against sexual harassment.[15]

Since the mid-1990s, most employer policies against sexual harassment have been antimobbing/antiharassment and discrimination policies that subsume sexual harassment as one form of unfair workplace practices. The development of these gender-neutral policies is striking, because there are no specific laws that prohibit "mobbing" in the workplace, nor had courts defined "mobbing" at that point. Therefore, these policies are the result of a political process of implementation preceding legal developments.

The participation of workers' representatives in the development of anti-sexual-harassment policies explains this formulation as antimobbing policies. Because these policies against sexual harassment are the result of collective bargaining between employers and works councils, rather than solely shaped by legal discourse, there is leeway for the kinds of policies workplace organizations adopt. The formulation of collective rights is more prevalent than in the U.S., and policies reflect organized workers' interests in addition to employers' interests.

Because works councils prefer general employee protections and group-based solutions, they broaden concerns of sexual harassment to issues relevant to all employees. Unions were therefore mobilizing around issues of gender-neutral "mobbing" and "unfair workplace practices." The concept of mobbing itself reflects a group orientation. The attack of a "mob" on a person shows the lack of fairness and respect in the broader collective or team. The goal of mobbing is to get rid of this person. Thus, the exclusion of an individual through group dynamics is emphasized as opposed to a conflict among individuals.

Mobbing and sexual harassment have certain aspects in common: both can lead to intrigue, victimization, insults, and threats that cause psychosocial stresses. Both phenomena reflect the lack of respect and dignified treatment of employees. The German notion emphasizes the generalizability of experiences of groups treated without fairness and respect by others in the workplace. Mobbing furthermore focuses on the group dynamics of abuse of power and exclusion. Yet, because mobbing is silent on the specific differentials of power it fails to indicate why a person is seen as inferior and treated unfairly. While sexual harassment is rooted in unequal gender relations, the notion of mobbing does not make visible power differentials between men and women. Despite this important difference, sexual harassment in Germany has been subsumed under mobbing.

Furthermore, the German equality officers told me that they had strategically adopted managerial discourses to define harassment to draw the attention of employers to the issue. For example, they would emphasize that both phenomena—sexual harassment and mobbing—signal broader organizational problems that employers should be concerned with: the lack of leadership and bad management. Defining the problem of sexual harassment in this way implies that supervisors are to blame if harassment occurs among their supervisees. The solution, thus, is "better management," which fits into current German management discourse to reform and restructure workplace relations by introducing and emphasizing teamwork, flat hierarchies, and so forth.

Even though the law requires employers to specify an office responsible for accepting complaints, policies most often state only the usual units: supervisors, personnel offices, and works councils. Yet, harassed women prefer to seek out women who they expect will be more sympathetic to their complaint. In the federal ministries, only 12 percent of complaints were filed with works councils, 27 percent were with personnel offices, and the overwhelming majority (almost two-thirds) were filed with women's equality offices. Thus, the newly created women's offices are the obvious preferred units to provide support for complainants. These offices of gender equality have become key agents in implementing sexual harassment law.[16]

While the latest revisions of gender equality law covering public-sector employers state that equality officers should be involved in cases of sexual harassment, they do not have enforcement or investigative powers, which are left to supervisors and human-resource personnel. Structurally speaking, these women's offices are in competition with structures of works councils, similar to the EEO/AA offices. Works councils are the main formal negotiation partners for employers to adopt and implement policies. Their responsibilities lie with representing both the complainant and the accused. Thus, works councils will insist on using already existing grievance procedures in which they play an important role. Conversely, they will prefer procedures that do not jeopardize the rights of the accused. For this reason, women who feel harassed often do not trust works councils even though stewards have frequently more formal powers than equality officers.

Prevention efforts are rare in most German workplaces, despite the fact that the law explicitly demands employers to institutionalize prevention and awareness programs. The lack of management's concern with prevention is reflected in these infrequent training efforts. In the early 1990s, the newly institutionalized offices for gender equality printed and publicized brochures and information on sexual harassment. A number of training seminars were held within the public sector, organized primarily by equality officers, some by unions for works council members, and by general educational divisions. The new law of 1994 gave an increased impetus to introduce or update information on the issue. Yet, in the late 1990s these educational and awareness efforts dwindled. One explanation is that participation in these training programs is not mandatory. According to public officials I interviewed, "interest" in the seminars was not very high and few participants came to the seminars offered. The problem is obvious. If these prevention efforts are based on voluntary participation, and the "interest" of participants determines the frequency with which seminars are held, it is not surprising that training and awareness efforts have fallen short. Furthermore, those who would need the training most because of their unawareness or ignorance of sexual harassment are unlikely to participate voluntarily. The discussion in the United States about voluntary/mandatory training is controversial, too. However, employers have a strong interest today in educating their employees about the policies and procedures in place due to the recent Supreme Court decisions.

In contrast to the United States, where managers and supervisors have been a primary target group for educational efforts, employers in Germany provide little training for these groups. The German system of civil servant training is structured. Seminars on sexual harassment could become obligatory, but only in exceptional cases have employers required employees to attend these seminars. Most often, information on the new law of 1994 has been included in sections on other types of labor law, without specific attention paid to this issue.

Moreover, the voluntary nature of these workshops provides obstacles for women to obtain information on sexual harassment. In order to sign up, for example, women have to ask permission from their supervisors. The ridicule and stigma attached to the issues can discourage women from participation. If women have been harassed by their supervisor, asking him for the approval to attend the seminar will be very difficult. Therefore, organizers of workshops offer "women's seminars" or "mobbing seminars" instead, which are far less stigmatized.

The existing training programs are surprisingly feminist in their orientation and content. Provided by outside trainers, women's advocates, and women within works councils and unions, they go beyond informing participants about legal rights (Meschkutat et al., 1995). Structured around feminist principles of empowerment, seminars use methods of consciousness raising, and include assertiveness training. So far, it is women who are considered the experts who "own" the issue of sexual harassment (Interview with Dr. Barbara Degen, February 19, 1999).

An alternative strategy has been to make sexual harassment part of "antimobbing seminars." These seminars focus on group-based processes of discrimination and exclusion of employees. Antimobbing seminars focus on team building and cooperative leadership styles and have become an integral part of changes in workplace culture in general.

An alternative project focused on gender-specific, group-based training is that of "structural mediation" initiated by Barbara Degen. The project is based on the assumption that changes in the broader gender workplace culture are necessary to combat sexual harassment. Male and female employees first discuss issues separate from one another and then come together to develop group-based solutions to gender conflict. One of the most prominent issues for women was that they felt men did not respect women's expertise and would not take them seriously.

The German approach emphasizes group dynamics that contribute to sexual harassment as a conflict in the workplace. Because policies and measures are employer–employee negotiated there is an orientation toward collective, group-based solutions over individual conflict solutions. Even managerial discourses are focused on modernizing organizational structures to flat-hierarchies that emphasize team building and cooperative leadership styles. Thus, future developments have the potential to focus on preventing sexual harassment by effecting broader changes in workplace culture and organizational structures.

The disadvantage is that political will is the motor of implementation rather than strong incentives to comply with laws. Mobilization of women's pressure groups and alliance building with works councils is necessary to pressure employers to adopt policies. For this reason, the adoption process has been slower in Germany than in the U.S.

In addition, for victims of sexual harassment, individual redress is weak. Legal threats and sanctions for noncompliance are less serious than in the United States; thus, employers have had little incentive to improve internal grievance structures. Works council structures have existed to represent individual employees' interests. Yet, the challenge is to reform these, to increase awareness, and to make these structures available for women who have been harassed. In the public sector, the expectation is that women's offices are responsible for harassed women. Since the new law of 2001, equality offices are supposed to be "involved" in cases of harassment. Yet, they lack the formal power to investigate or sanction harassers. Moreover, because of their mandate to represent women's interests, some equality officers do not feel responsible for handling reports by men.

The most problematic aspect of having union/works councils negotiate the policy approaches of "mobbing," however, is the danger that concerns about mobbing eradicate the gender dimension of sexual harassment. Power differentials based on unequal gender relations are invisible when considering group dynamics of mobbing. Because the notion of "mobbing" is gender neutral, it becomes a challenge to "gender" the concept in order to confront and change the male-dominated gender workplace cultures.

## CONCLUSION

This chapter has contrasted two models of dealing with sexual harassment in the workplace. Model 1 is focused on sexual harassment as a conflict among individuals, while model 2 is based on a collective-group orientation, as exemplified by the U.S. and Germany, respectively. Legislation and enforcement practices of sex equality law are embedded respectively in German labor law in the form of workers' protection laws versus civil rights law in the U.S. In the U.S. the dynamics of implementation have emphasized individuals' legal redress, individual reporting, and lawsuits that have affirmed employers' responsibilities to prevent sexual harassment by institutionalizing policies and educational programs.

In the absence of strong antidiscrimination laws in Germany, the implementation process of policies against sexual harassment depends on the political will of unions, employers, and emerging state equality offices for women (Zippel, 2000). Since the process in Germany is predominantly based on political will, many German employers have been able to resist the adoption of policies. In addition, the model that is emerging is a gender-neutral one relying on collective rights and group-based approaches emphasizing broader changes in workplace culture.

Neither country, however, has developed a gender-power-based model for dealing with sexual harassment. Feminist discourses that emphasize unequal gender power compete with workers' representation discourses on the one hand, and with managerial discourses on the other. While works councils and unions will prefer gender-neutral group-based discourses, managerial discourses will emphasize gender-neutral, individual behaviors, and (legal) risk minimization. Thus, the process of negotiation has led to a predominance of group-based approaches in Germany, while in the U.S. individualized approaches are more prevalent.

The ideal third model would be a combination of both models, individual *and* collective approaches that both take unequal gender relations into account. Because sexual harassment is rooted in gender inequality in sexuality and work, employers' responses need to strengthen (economic) nondiscrimination rights and the right to sexual self-determination. A gender-sensitive strategy focuses on the needs of harassed persons, including having support systems for harassed employees in place, with legal and psychological consultation. Furthermore, multiple forms of complaints, informal, formal, and mediation approaches, should be in place. Interventions need to be group based, focused on team building, and encouraging partnership. Training efforts should go beyond presenting information of legal rights, gender sensitivity, and assertiveness. Finally, the goal of prevention needs to be based on change to the gender workplace culture.

In conclusion, adopting the U.S. model with a focus on individual rights will be difficult in countries with legal systems other than case-law systems. Implementation paths based on convincing unions that they indeed have an interest in adopting sexual harassment policy as an important tool to mobilize women workers, are an important alternative, viable particularly in countries where unions are stronger than in the United States. Embracing broader antimobbing policies, however, needs to be combined with strengthening structures supporting women's interests. Future studies need to compare what changes have indeed occurred in gender culture in workplaces to evaluate which of the models is more effective in empowering women individually and collectively.

## NOTES

I would like to thank for a critical reading and constructive criticism of the dissertation research leading to this paper the members of my dissertation committee, Ann S. Orloff, Erik O. Wright, Myra Marx Ferree, Pam Oliver, Phil Gorski, and Virginia Sapiro. In addition, I would like to thank Kimberly Morgan, Silke Roth, and Tom Koenig, for their comments and suggestions. This research was supported by the European Union Center of the University of Wisconsin, Madison (1999, 2000), a fellowship at

---

the European University Institute in Florence, Italy (1996–1997), and a Travel Award from the Department of Sociology at the University of Wisconsin, Madison.

1. See for example Susan Estrich (1991): "The very existence of such a cause of action is a triumph for feminist scholars and practitioners, as well as for victims of sexual harassment."

2. Some as an example to imitate or to avoid (Zippel, 2000; Saguy, forthcoming; Cahill, 2001; Valiente, 2000).

3. The first Supreme Court ruling on sexual harassment was *Meritor vs. Savings Bank* in 1986.

4. This ruling affirmed that mobbing can violate the general personal freedoms expressed in the German Constitution: Article 1 human dignity and/or Article 2 personal freedoms (LAG Thuringia: Decision April 10, 2001).

5. I chose this particular institution for its large size which allowed me to study institutional responses to sexual harassment both as a workplace issue and as an issue within educational settings.

6. I identified the legal experts through pertinent publications in legal journals and combined this with a snowball sample: there are fewer than ten lawyers in Germany with expertise in labor law and sexual harassment. Based on national directories, I selected and interviewed all sixteen equality officers at the German *Länder* level (state) and contacted all ten women's units of nationwide unions.

7. I selected these equality officers through pertinent publications of "best practices" companies, known for women-friendly workplace policies, and an availability sample at the *Frauenmesse Top '99* (Top: Perspectives for Women), a nationally recognized convention in Düsseldorf April 15–18, 1999. The interviewees included equality officers from large national and international corporations and public administrators at city and communal levels. This selection is likely to overrepresent employers most active in women's issues, and thus those likely to be most concerned with issues of sexual harassment. My findings of the lack of policies and awareness programs among these employers is thus even more striking.

8. 477 U.S. 57 (1986).

9. The early regulations were most often initiated by active women's groups in works councils and/or gender equality officers. For example, even in the conservatively ruled city of Stuttgart, one of the *Dienstanweisung* was passed in 1991.

10. 524 U.S. 742 (1998).

11. 524 U.S. 775 (1998).

12. For the U.S. Reese and Lindenberg (1999) make similar observations.

13. Only around 14 percent of wage and salaried workers are members of unions in the U.S. in the 1990s. While less than 10 percent of private-sector employees are unionized, public employees have significantly higher rates with 37.3 percent of employees in unions. Thus, the public sector in the U.S. is more similar to German rates of unionization with 35 percent. Women make up between 30–40 percent of union membership in both countries (Sources: U.S. Department of Labor's Bureau of Labor Statistics, 2000; Statistisches Bundesamt, 1998).

14. Employers with fifty or more employees must comply with the law that constitutes workplace regulations, the *Betriebsverfassungsgesetz* (BetrVG), to allow the establishment of a *Betriebsrat* (works council), or *Personalrat* in the public employment sector. These systems of representation are empowered to represent workers'

interests on the company level. Works councils have a say in personnel decisions and, by law, may challenge unfair dismissals of workers. Yet, less than one quarter of elected workers' representatives are women (BMFSFJ, 1998:142).

15. Instead, in my telephone inquiries I was told that a comprehensive anti-mobbing policy was "in progress."

16. The Second Gender Equality Law requires public-sector employers to institutionalize *Gleichstellungsbeauftragte* (offices for gender equality) or *Frauenbeauftragte* (women's advocates). This "state feminism" developed simultaneously with public attention on sexual harassment in the aftermath of the Anita Hill–Clarence Thomas hearings in the 1990s.

## REFERENCES

Baer, S. 1995. *Würde oder Gleichheit? Zur angemessenen grundrechtlichen Konzeption von Recht gegen Diskriminierung am Beispiel sexueller Belaestigung am Arbeitsplatz in der Bundesrepublik Deutschland und den USA.* Baden-Baden, Germany: Nomos Verlagsgesellschaft.

Bernstein, A. 1994. "Law, Culture, and Harassment." *University of Pennsylvania Law Review* 142, no. 3: 1227–311.

BMFSFJ (Bundesministerium für Familie, Senioren, Frauen und Jugend). 1998. *Frauen in der Bundesrepublik Deutschland.* Bonn: BMFSFJ.

———. 1999. "Die Umsetzung des Bundesbeschäftigtenschutzgesetzes in Bundesministerien [The Implementation of the Employee Protection Law in Federal Ministries]." Unpublished report.

Cahill, M. 2001. *The Social Construction of Sexual Harassment Law: The Role of National, Organizational and Individual Context.* Aldershot: Ashgate.

Cockburn, C. 1991. *In the Way of Women: Men's Resistance to Sex Equality in Organizations.* Ithaca, N.Y.: ILR Press.

Collins, E. 1996. "European Union Sexual Harassment Policy." Pp. 23–34 in *Sexual Politics and the European Union: The New Feminist Challenge*, ed. R. A. Elman. Providence, R.I., and Oxford: Berghahn Books.

Degen, Barbara. 1999. "Neue Rechtsprechung zu Sexueller Belästigung am Arbeitsplatz." *Der Personalrat* (1): 8–13.

Dobbin, F., and Kelly, E. 2001. "Case Law and Corporate Politics: The Spread of Harassment Policies." Unpublished paper. Princeton University.

Edelman, L. B., Erlanger, H. S., and Lande, J. 1993. "Internal Dispute Resolution: The Transformation of Civil-Rights in the Workplace." *Law and Society Review* 27, no. 3: 497–534.

Edelman, L. B., Uggen C., and Erlanger, H. S. 1999. "The Endogeneity of Legal Regulation: Grievance Procedures as a Rational Myth." *American Journal of Sociology* 105, no. 2: 406–54.

Elman, R. A. 1996. *Sexual Subordination and State Intervention: Comparing Sweden and the United States.* Oxford: Berghahn Books.

Esping-Andersen, G. 1990. *The Three Worlds of Welfare Capitalism.* Cambridge, U.K.: Polity Press.

Estrich, Susan. 1991. "Sex at Work." *Stanford Law Review* 43: 813–20.

Fraser, N. 1997. *Justice Interruptus: Critical Reflections on the "Postsocialist" Condi-tion*. New York: Routledge.

Grauerholz, E., C. Stohl, N. Gabin, and H. Gottfried. 1999. "There's Safety in Num-bers: Creating a Campus Advisers' Network to Help Complainants of Sexual Ha-rassment *and* Complaint-Receivers." *Violence against Women* 80: 950–77.

Grundmann, E., O'Donohue, W., and Peterson, S. 1997. "The Prevention of Sexual Harassment." Pp. 175–84 in *Sexual Harassment: Theory, Research, and Treatment*, ed. W. O'Donohue. Boston: Allyn and Bacon.

Gutek, B. 1997. "Sexual Harassment Policy Initiatives." Pp. 185–98 in *Sexual Harass-ment: Theory, Research, and Treatment*, ed. W. O'Donohue. Boston: Allyn and Bacon.

Hawkesworth, M. 1997. "Challenging the Received Wisdom and the Status Quo: Cre-ating and Implementing Sexual Harassment Policy. *NWSA Journal* 9, no. 2: 94–102.

Hodges, J. A. 1996. "Sexual Harassment in Employment: Recent Judicial and Arbitral Trends." *International Labour Review* 135, no. 5: 499–533.

Holzbecher, M., and Meschkutat, B. 1999. *Mobbing am Arbeitsplatz*. Dortmund and Berlin: Bundesanstalt für Arbeitsschutz und Arbeitsmedizin.

Husbands, R. 1992. "Sexual Harassment Law in Employment: An International Per-spective." *International Labour Review* 131, no. 6: 535–59.

MacKinnon, C. A. 1979. *Sexual Harassment of the Working Women: A Case of Sex Discrimination*. New Haven, Conn.: Yale University Press.

Magley, V. J., Zickar, M., Salisbury, J., Drasgow, F., and Fitzgerald, L. F. 1999. "Evalu-ating the Effectiveness of Sexual Harassment Training." International Coalition Against Sexual Harassment.

Mazur, A. G. 1994. "The Formation of Sexual Harassment Policies in France: Another Case of French Exceptionalism?" *French Politics and Society* 11, no. 2: 11–32.

Meschkutat, B., M. Holzbecker, G. Richter. 1995. *Strategien gegen sexuelle Belästi-gung am Arbeitsplatz*. Germany: Bund-Verlag.

O'Connor, J., Orloff, A., and Shaver, S. 1999. *States, Markets, Families: Gender, Lib-eralism and Social Policy in Australia, Canada, Great Britain and the United States*. Cambridge: Cambridge University Press.

Reese, L. A., and Lindenberg, K. E. 1999. *Implementing Sexual Harassment Policy: Challenges for the Public Sector Workplace*. Thousand Oaks, Calif.: Sage.

Rubenstein, M. 1988. *The Dignity of Women at Work: A Report on the Problem of Sex-ual Harassment in the Member States of the European Communities*. Brussels/Luxembourg: Office for Official Publications of the European Communities.

Saguy, A. C. Forthcoming. *What is Sexual Harassment?: From Capitol Hill to the Sor-bonne*. Berkeley: University of California Press.

Statistisches Bundesamt. 1998. *Datenreport: Zahlen und Fakten über die Bundesre-publik Deutschland*. Available at www.destatis.de/.

U.S. Department of Labor Bureau of Labor Statistics. 2000. Available at www.bls.gov/ (keyword: Union Membership).

Valiente, C. 2000. "Left or Right: Does It Make Any Difference? Central-State Sexual Harassment Policies in Spain." Twelfth International Conference of Europeanists.

Zippel, K. 1994. "Institutional Responses to a Social Problem: Sexual Harassment in a Large University." Master's thesis, Ohio State University, Columbus, Ohio.

———. 2000. "Policies against Sexual Harassment: Gender Equality Policy in Ger-many, in the European Union, and in the United States in Comparative Perspec-tive." Doctoral dissertation, University of Wisconsin at Madison.

# 14

## Sexual Harassment Policies and Employee Preferences in Local U.S. Government

*Laura Reese and Karen E. Lindenberg*

While human-resource specialists, legal analysts, and academics have reached a basic consensus on what constitutes "model" sexual harassment policies, the subjects of those policies—employees themselves—are often uncertain, unclear, or simply dissatisfied with policies, procedures, and outcomes. This only serves to increase the innumerable challenges personnel practitioners face in trying to implement sexual harassment policies. And, because research has indicated that there is a connection between satisfaction with policy and process and willingness to use workplace sexual harassment policies, uncertainty and conflict become all the more critical (Riger, 1991; Reese and Lindenberg, 1999, 2002a).

This chapter explores employee satisfaction with sexual harassment policies in public-sector workplaces in the United States, using a survey of municipal employees to address the following research and policy questions:

- What types of sexual harassment policies do employees want?
- How would employees handle complaints of sexual harassment?
- How satisfied are employees with current workplace policies?
- What appears to enhance employee satisfaction with policy and process?
- Does gender matter in addressing any of the foregoing questions?

## POLICY, PROCESS, AND SATISFACTION

### Model Policy

Recommendations for model sexual harassment policies have remained remarkably uniform over two decades (see, for example, Stringer et al., 1990; Remick et al., 1990; Riger, 1991; American Association of University Professors, 1995; Gutek, 1997; Reese and Lindenberg, 1999; among many others). The consensus is that effective sexual harassment policies should include:

- A clear statement of what sexual harassment is and that it will not be tolerated;
- Strong commitment to and understanding of the policy by supervisors and top management;
- Training programs for both employees and supervisors regarding the nature of sexual harassment to increase awareness of unacceptable behaviors;
- Sensitivity training for supervisors to improve interaction with all parties involved;
- Training for supervisors on the proper processes for conducting investigations;
- Clear procedures for dealing with sexual harassment complaints;[1]
- Clear lines for reporting sexual harassment that offer options for remedies yet avoid too many different actors;
- Trained, neutral investigators to deal with sexual harassment complaints;
- Investigative teams composed of both men and women;
- Procedures which safeguard the confidentiality of both accused and claimant, including sanctions for breaches of confidentiality;
- Timelines for various policy processes—interviews, investigations, findings, reporting;
- Specific procedures for reporting, to both the complainant and accused, the findings and outcomes of the investigation on at least some level;
- Serious sanctions for inappropriate behaviors (treatment, leave, dismissal); and,
- Inclusion of supervisor handling of sexual harassment complaints in supervisory evaluation procedures.

Fewer studies have examined the extent to which these "model" elements are actually incorporated into sexual harassment policies in public-sector workplaces. A recent content analysis of municipal policies in Michigan indicated that most municipalities had sexual harassment policies (73 percent), policies basically followed EEOC guidelines (67 percent), policies required that supervisors report all complaints of sexual harassment (84 percent), and offered multiple reporting options for employees (70 percent). However, there were a variety of issues on which most policies were silent. For example, only 29 percent of municipalities evaluated supervisors on how they handle complaints, only 14 percent of policies included time frames for processing complaints, only 3 percent included sanctions for retaliation, only one city had a policy that specified the gender composition of the investigation team, and no policies included sanctions for breaches of confidentiality. The faults of existing municipal sexual harassment policies, we argue, tend to be those of omission (failure to codify regulations) rather than commission (having bad policy) (Reese and Lindenberg, 2002b). Still, there were a number of municipalities that appeared to have very high-quality policies and procedures and the existence of sexual harassment policies is widespread.

### Implementation and Employee Satisfaction

Irrespective of the presence of "model" policies in organizations, however, employees indicate a number of areas of uncertainty and dissatisfaction, particularly with implementation (Pierce et al., 1997). For example, having a supervisor *blame* a complainant for sexual harassment has significant negative effects on policy satisfaction (Reese and Lindenberg, 1999). Perceptions, based on past experience, that the organization will not seriously address complaints of sexual harassment will reduce reporting rates (Perry et al., 1998). Employees seem particularly "uncertain" about whether current policies operate in such a way as to reduce future harassment and provide a sense of closure for victims by offering feedback on the findings of investigations and possible repercussions for the harasser (Reese and Lindenberg, 1999). Generally, employees support a central role for the organization in sexual harassment cases, including formal investigations and interviews with all parties, though many do not think dismissal is an appropriate "punishment" for harassment (O'Hare Grundmann, 1997). In short it appears that:

- there is considerable uncertainty about current policy processes but evaluation of policy is less negative than evaluation of implementation;
- supervisor reaction to and handling of sexual harassment complaints appears particularly problematic;
- being blamed when reporting has very serious negative consequences;
- confidentiality is of particular concern; and,
- even given the above concerns, formal procedures are preferred over informal.

Given the apparent uncertainty and dissatisfaction with extant sexual harassment policies, exactly what do employees want regarding process and procedure? Previous research on this issue has suggested that many employees are equally uncertain about what they want. Some specific suggestions for policy improvement have included:

- the need to better protect confidentiality of the accused or accusers;
- the need for victims of sexual harassment to be informed about what actions were taken to deal with perpetrators;
- recommendations to limit the number of individuals involved in investigating complaints;
- the need for improved implementation, particularly better follow-up on complaints by line supervisors, and more vigorous enforcement of penalties for those found to have harassed (particularly if they are "management");
- clear and progressive disciplinary steps;
- clearer definitions of sexual harassment; and,
- greater effort to publicize the current policy and its use (Reese and Lindenberg, 1996).

However, these findings were drawn from a study of only two organizations with very similar policies. Obviously an assessment of employee satisfaction under a wider array of policy alternatives is desirable.

## Is It Really All about Gender?

Four major theories have been posited to "explain" sexual harassment: the natural/biological model; the organizational-power model; the sociocultural model; and, the sex-role spillover model (Paludi, 1990). The *natural/biological* explanation rests on the assumption that gender-based differences in sexual responses are dependent on "human nature" and are inherently bound to occur in the workplace as well as other social environments (Saal, 1996: 68). The *organizational-power* model focuses on the demographic/historical reality of work organizations; males dominate at the top, and in many workplaces, males dominate throughout the structure. Dziech and Weiner (1984) and Fitzgerald (1990) have identified organizational climates stressing hierarchy and authority relations as providing supportive environments for sexual harassment. A logical extension of this model is the *organizational-culture* perspective that suggests that hostile work environments, often rooted in power inequities, impact all personnel issues including sexual harassment. The *sociocultural* model is derived from a comparison of the work environment to the influences of the larger society. Essentially, it argues that socialization to roles of power, status, and hierarchy differ between the sexes and this learning is reflected in the work environment. In short, "sexual harassment of women by men is best understood as a mechanism by which existing disparities in these two groups' access to social and economic power and status are maintained throughout a society" (Saal, 1996: 68). The *sex-role spillover* model is a variant of the sociocultural model and focuses specifically on gender roles related to sex as the basis of harassing workplace behavior. Thus, women are "expected" to act submissive and feminine while males are authoritative and dominant. These roles then open the door for sexualized interactions between employees that keep female employees in a subordinate position. Which of the models best "explains" workplace sexual harassment? It is hard to say. The biological model has not received much empirical support. To the extent that both organizational and cultural models are accommodated by the sex-role spillover theory, the latter may present the most robust "explanation."

The issue of the accuracy of the different theories is not just an academic exercise since each has different implications for choosing effective policy and procedural "solutions" to sexual harassment. For example, the biological and sex-role spillover theories imply that extensive training and education programs must take place to make employees aware of the impact of social sexual roles in the workplace. This training would focus on helping employees of both sexes know when stereotypical sexual interactions are occurring and how to defuse such situations when they do. Policy and procedure would then focus on processes and remedies for dealing with problematic behaviors when they occur. Indeed, it is on this model that much model sexual harassment policy in the United States is based.

However, if the organizational-power or culture theories are more accurate then root changes in the organization power structure must occur for sexual harassment problems to be addressed. Women must receive the education, training, experience, and promotional opportunities necessary to balance men in workplace power structures. Finally, the sociocultural theory suggests changes in both organizational and work-group dynamics to enhance the representation of women in power and to alter the interactions or culture of work groups. This latter approach is more akin to the "mobbing" policies employed in Germany (Zippel, this volume). Understanding the dynamics of the causes of sexual harassment has direct implications for the creation and implementation of effective workplace policy.

Regardless of which theory is accurate in explaining gender relationships that "cause" sexual harassment, research has found a variety of gender differences that appear important from a policy implementation perspective. For example, general uncertainty surrounds major issues related to gender relations in the workplace including whether the whole issue is overrated, whether men and/or women use their sexual attractiveness to gain advantages at work, whether the workplace is an appropriate venue for establishing sexual relationships, and whether employees of different ranks should engage in "romantic" relationships. Male and female feelings about being harassed are different, with men more likely to feel flattered. Women are more likely to avoid reporting sexual harassment due to concerns that nothing will be done, fear of retaliation, and knowledge of failure to act in other cases. And, for women, there are two conceptually different aspects of policy process satisfaction/dissatisfaction; confidentiality and perceiving the process as "fair" to all parties determine overall satisfaction with the outcome of a complaint (Reese and Lindenberg, 1999). Finally, women appear to characterize more behaviors as sexual harassment than men, particularly those that occupy a "gray area" of ambiguity (see Reilly et al., 1982; Gutek, 1985; and Frazier et al., 1995). For example, women are more likely to define complimentary looks, staring, pinups, comments about the body, and unwelcome staring as sexual harassment (Reese and Lindenberg, 1999).

Yet other studies have found substantial gender agreement on definitions of sexual harassment (Gutek and O'Conner, 1995; Frazier et al., 1995). Surveys have indicated widespread agreement (over 90 percent of respondents) that physical assault, demands for sex accompanied by threats (quid pro quo harassment), unwanted pressure for sexual activity and/or dates, unwelcome touching, and subtle pressure for sex constitute sexual harassment. Over 80 percent of respondents indicated that sexual remarks about clothing or body and pressure for dates were sexual harassment, and over 70 percent classified unwelcome staring and sexually related language as sexual harassment. More moderate numbers—53 to 65 percent—defined the following as sexual harassment: excessive eye contact, pinups, touching, and jokes with sexual content (Reese and Lindenberg, 1999). These high rates of consensus suggest that male and female employees agree on the basic parameters of the definition of sexual harassment even though women may classify more behaviors as harassment. This doesn't necessarily mean that agreement on definitions will affect behaviors nor willingness to use or implement sexual harassment policies.

It appears that other factors besides gender come into play in determining definitions of sexual harassment. For example older employees are more likely to define sexual jokes and pinups as sexual harassment, indicating possible generational differences in tolerance for such activities/items. Similarly, those with more tenure on the job are more likely to define jokes with sexual content as harassment. African-American employees are significantly more likely to consider unwelcome pressure for sexual activity to be harassment. And, having been sexually harassed is correlated with broader or more inclusive definitions of sexual harassment (Reese and Lindenberg, 1999). Thus, while gender plays a role in how employees define sexual harassment, it is probably not the barrier to effective policy implementation that many lamenting the perceptual nature of the policy area would have us believe. Clearly, more exploration of the relationship between gender and sexual harassment policy processes as well as other factors that may affect attitudes about policies is warranted.

## METHODOLOGY

### Stage 1

Data for this research were collected in several stages employing different methodologies. The first stage of the research involved a content analysis of municipal sexual harassment policies in the state of Michigan. All cities in the state are members of the Michigan Municipal League (MML) and serve as the population for the study (N=273). A single-state focus was chosen for several reasons. First, examination of municipal policies within one state controls for enabling legislation. Michigan has a strong tradition of municipal home rule and local governments have independence in creating and implementing personnel policies such as those related to sexual harassment. Second, a single-state focus allows for a more comprehensive examination of policies, implementation issues, training, and the like across a number of local governments. Third, ensuring the cooperation of local governments, and stimulating response rates, requires working through state municipal associations.[2]

All MML member municipalities were sent a brief questionnaire under the auspices of the league that asked if they had a sexual harassment policy and, if so, to provide a copy of the policy. Respondents were also asked to describe the nature and extent of training to support the policy and whether evaluations of supervisory personnel take into account how they handle sexual harassment complaints or hold supervisors accountable for proper policy implementation.

### Stage 2

Because the focus of this research is on satisfaction and outcome differences emanating from sexual harassment policies and training systems, a method was needed to sort the policies in the database by the nature of policy and training. While many public- and private-sector organizations now have sexual harassment policies that follow EEOC guidelines in their major components, previous research has indicated that policies vary along the following lines (Reese and Lindenberg, 2002b):

- Confidentiality protections and sanctions for breach of confidentiality;
- Nature and number of reporting avenues;
- Information provided to the complainant regarding findings and outcome of investigation;

- Time-frame requirements for investigation and findings;
- Provision for external versus internal investigative bodies;
- Extent of supervisor evaluations of complaint processing; and,
- Composition of investigator teams particularly including gender.

In addition, municipalities differ in training formats and intensity. Training modalities in particular could vary along a number of lines, including:

- Frequency and comprehensiveness (regarding who is trained) of training;
- Single- versus mixed-gender workshops;
- Single-position (supervisors only) versus mixed-position workshops; and,
- Passive (movies/written materials) versus active (role play/simulations) modes of training (Gutek, 1997).

Using factor analysis on the policy attributes noted above, two indexes were created. One represents the extent and coverage of sexual harassment training as well as the policy and procedures. The other measures the extent that procedures are codified in the policy (see Reese and Lindenberg, 2002b, for more discussion of these indexes). Policies that provide more detailed processes increase the likelihood that all complaints are investigated, ensure that all cases are treated in a similar fashion, provide employees with a sense that the organization takes sexual harassment seriously, and may increase the willingness of employees to file complaints in the first place. Such codified policies have time frames for starting, completing, and reporting the findings of investigations; requirements that particular information be reported back to the person filing the complaint; include explicit confidentiality protections; and include evaluation of supervisors on handling sexual harassment complaints (Reese and Lindenberg, 2002b).

Cities scoring high and low on both the training and policy indexes were identified. Cities high on the "good policy" index included those with an f-score of .89 or higher, while "bad policy" cities scored −.93 or lower. High training cities were those scoring above .61 and low training was anything below that.[3] Cities with high and low training and good and bad policy were then arrayed on a four-by-four grid to create four "types" of municipalities: good policy and good training (type A), good policy and bad training (type B), bad policy and good training (type C), and bad policy and bad training (type D) cities. For further analysis only cities with at least seventy employees were targeted.[4]

**Policy and Training Matrix**

|  | Good Training | Bad Training |
|---|---|---|
| Good Policy | TYPE **A**<br>N = 15 / 3 | TYPE **B**<br>N = 14 / 3 |
| Bad Policy | TYPE **C**<br>N = 6 / 3 | TYPE **D**<br>N = 9 / 4 |

N = Number of cities in type / Number participating

Based on this methodology there were fifteen type A cities, fourteen type B, six type C, and nine type D. Each city was contacted by letter and phone with a request to permit employees to be surveyed by a mailed questionnaire and for the cooperation of local officials in face-to-face interviews. Of these, four type D cities and three of each of the other types agreed to participate further in the study.

All employees in each of these thirteen cities were surveyed; questionnaires were distributed via internal mail systems but returned directly to the researchers by regular mail. Key personnel in each city were interviewed in person to obtain information on the history of the sexual harassment policy, to confirm how complaints were actually handled, to identify if there were any other procedures in place, to explore the cooperation of unions and elected bodies, and to secure more detail on the nature of training.

It is interesting to note that population size and the size of the public-sector workforce are related to the nature of existing sexual harassment policies. Population and public-workforce size are proxies for each other, relating to the policy attributes in the same way. Large communities and those with more governmental employees are significantly more likely to have sexual harassment policies, to provide training for their entire workforce, to have broader topic coverage in their training (including definitions of harassment, how to handle complaints, and how to conduct investigations), to have confidentiality protections with sanctions, to impose sanctions for false complaints, and to include sanctions for retaliation against complainants.

### Sample Profiles and Response Rates

The response rate to the stage 1 request for policies and the brief survey was quite high; of 273 cities in the state, 177 or 65 percent responded. Average population size of the cities responding is 19,624, ranging from 385 to 189,126. The average size of the population of cities in the state is 19,555, so the responding municipalities appear to be representative of the population size of all cities in the state. Cities responding are most likely to have a city-manager form of government (75 percent), also mirroring patterns generally in the state. The mean number of employees is 151.

The employee survey achieved a 30 percent response rate varying from 16 percent to 41 percent among the targeted municipalities. A total of 595 completed surveys were returned. Response rates to previous mailed employee sexual harassment surveys have ranged from 26–39 percent (Reese and Lindenberg, 1999).[5] It should be noted that this rate was obtained with no follow-up to nonrespondents since human-subjects review would not permit code numbers to be placed on surveys.

The survey included a number of questions related to respondent traits, providing another way to profile survey responses. Sixty-two percent of respondents are male, the modal age of respondents is 40–49 (36 percent), and almost half of respondents have been in their current place of employment for over ten years (49 percent). Ninety-two percent of respondents are Caucasian, four percent are African-American, and other racial groups comprise less than 1 percent of the sample. The majority of respondents are line employees (55 percent), 20 percent are middle managers, 18 percent are supervisors, and 8 percent are top managers.[6]

## FINDINGS

### Preferences for Model Policy

Respondents were asked about their perceptions of the importance of nine attributes commonly identified as aspects of model policy; the responses are presented in table 14.1. At least 56 percent of respondents felt that all of the attributes of model policy were "very important" and almost all (at least 86 percent) thought they were somewhat important. Thus, it is clear that large numbers of employees agree with the importance of central elements of what the literature identifies as "model policy." Of the individual elements of model policy the greatest importance is given to confidentiality protections including sanctions for violation of confidentiality, sanctions for false reporting, and providing the individual complaining with information about the findings of the investigation. Over 80 percent of respondents felt that these were very important. There was less agreement that timelines for reporting harassment and publicizing the types of punishments that might be used were very important (56 percent in each case).

There appear to be several correlations between the attributes of individual respondents and their preferences for model policy (also in table 14.1). For example, women are significantly more likely to want the policy to encompass confidentiality statements including sanctions, timelines for processing complaints, requirements that outcomes and punishments be reported to the complainant, supervisor evaluations on complaint handling, detailed definitions of harassment, and publicizing the types of punishment possible. In other words women are more interested than men in greater codification

**Table 14.1. Model Policy Percent Frequencies**

| | Mean[a] | Very Important | Somewhat Important | Somewhat Unimportant | Not Important at All |
|---|---|---|---|---|---|
| Confidentiality protections | 3.81 | 84 | 13 | 2 | 1 |
| Sanctions for false reports | 3.77 | 81 | 15 | 2 | 1 |
| Informing on outcome | 3.76 | 80 | 18 | 1 | 1 |
| Informing on discipline | 3.61 | 68 | 27 | 4 | 2 |
| Timelines for processing complaints | 3.60 | 66 | 30 | 3 | 1 |
| Detailed definitions of harassment | 3.60 | 68 | 26 | 4 | 2 |
| Evaluating supervisors | 3.59 | 65 | 30 | 3 | 2 |
| Timelines for reporting | 3.45 | 56 | 36 | 6 | 2 |
| Publicizing possible punishments | 3.37 | 56 | 30 | 11 | 4 |

[a]Mean response on a four-point scale.

*Correlations with Model Policy*

| | Female | Older | Tenure | Race | Manager | Harassed | Reported |
|---|---|---|---|---|---|---|---|
| Confidentiality protections | .20* | -.02 | -.06 | -.08 | -.04 | -.06 | -.01 |
| Sanctions for false reports | .07 | .02 | -.05 | .00 | -.05 | -.16* | -.06 |
| Informing on outcome | .18* | .00 | -.01 | -.08 | -.01 | -.01 | .02 |
| Informing on discipline | .20* | -.01 | .04 | -.04 | -.06 | -.01 | .06 |
| Timelines for processing complaints | .17* | -.03 | -.05 | .00 | -.04 | -.06 | -.02 |
| Detailed definitions of harassment | .11* | -.05 | -.01 | -.11* | -.08 | -.10* | -.07 |
| Evaluating supervisors | .18* | -.01 | .00 | -.07 | -.10* | .01 | .02 |
| Timelines for reporting | .00 | .02 | .05 | -.01 | .02 | -.05 | .00 |
| Publicizing possible punishments | .17* | -.01 | -.10* | -.09* | -.06 | -.04 | .01 |

* Significant at .05.

of procedural elements within the policy itself. The only exceptions are sanctions for false reports and time requirements for reporting harassment. Thus, although there is general agreement among employees that all of the elements of model policy are desirable, women feel more strongly almost across the board.

There are no significant correlations between age of employee and desired policy, although employees of color and those with longer tenure in their cities are less likely to support publicizing possible punishments. Managers, not surprisingly, are less likely to want to be evaluated on how they handle complaints of sexual harassment. Actually having used a city's sexual harassment complaint process is not related to any preferences for model policy. However, respondents indicating they have been sexually harassed are significantly less likely to support sanctions for false accusations (logical) and less likely to desire detailed definitions of harassment within the policy, perhaps because they are more sensitive to the perceptual nature of sexual harassment.

### Preferences for Model Process

Respondents were also asked to indicate what actions should be taken when a complaint of sexual harassment is made (see table 14.2). Here there is less agreement among employees in what would be preferred. Conducting an investigation with a team of trained individuals and basing discipline on the severity of the harassment were felt to be the most important elements of the process (48 percent and 41 percent saw these as very important respectively). At least 80 percent of respondents saw these two elements as being at least *somewhat* important. Between 28 and 30 percent of respondents felt that the use of progressive discipline prior to dismissal, a codified system of discipline for specific offenses, and a case-by-case application of discipline were very important parts of a sexual harassment process (between 70 and 78 percent found these to be at least somewhat important). It should be noted that the latter two elements are mutually exclusive. If a policy outlines specific disciplines to be applied for specific offenses of sexual harassment then discipline cannot be applied on a case-by-case basis.

It appears that several features of the sexual harassment implementation process are not perceived as important by employees: dismissal if charges of sexual harassment are substantiated, requiring that mediation occur when complaints are made, and having investigations performed by one individual. Fewer than 50 percent of respondents identified these as even somewhat important. Offering mediation as an option is preferred above requiring it and a team is seen as more desirable than investigation by a single person, even given the widespread concerns about confidentiality.

**Table 14. 2.  Model Process Percent Frequencies**

| | Mean[a] | Very Important | Somewhat Important | Somewhat Unimportant | Not Important at All |
|---|---|---|---|---|---|
| Investigation team | 3.36 | 48 | 43 | 8 | 2 |
| Discipline on severity | 3.27 | 41 | 48 | 8 | 3 |
| Progressive discipline | 3.05 | 30 | 51 | 14 | 5 |
| Codified disciplines | 3.01 | 28 | 50 | 18 | 4 |
| Case-based discipline | 2.89 | 28 | 42 | 22 | 9 |
| Offer mediation | 2.79 | 13 | 61 | 18 | 8 |
| Handle informally | 2.71 | 19 | 40 | 28 | 13 |
| Conduct an investigation | 2.70 | 20 | 43 | 26 | 12 |
| Dismiss if substantiated | 2.53 | 16 | 24 | 50 | 9 |
| Require mediation | 2.45 | 11 | 37 | 38 | 14 |
| Investigation by individual | 1.88 | 5 | 11 | 51 | 33 |

[a]Mean response on a four-point scale.

Correlations with Model Process

| | Female | Older | Tenure | Race | Manager | Harassed | Reported |
|---|---|---|---|---|---|---|---|
| Investigation team | .10* | .00 | -.06 | .05 | -.11* | .08 | -.01 |
| Discipline on severity | -.06 | .01 | .02 | .00 | .08* | .07 | -.01 |
| Progressive discipline | -.18* | -.02 | .01 | -.05 | .03 | -.06 | -.04 |
| Codified disciplines | .07 | -.03 | -.11* | .03 | -.12* | -.02 | -.07 |
| Case-based discipline | -.21* | .06 | .05 | -.04 | .06 | .00 | .05 |
| Offer mediation | .02 | .11* | .07 | -.08 | -.01 | -.02 | .03 |
| Handle informally | .01 | .08* | .03 | .02 | .00 | -.05 | .01 |
| Conduct an investigation | .04 | .09 | .05 | -.02 | .26* | -.18* | -.01 |
| Dismiss if substantiated | .12* | -.08 | -.01 | -.06 | -.07 | .02 | -.01 |
| Require mediation | -.07 | -.02 | -.06 | .08 | -.15* | -.04 | -.01 |
| Investigation by individual | -.03 | -.06 | -.05 | -.06 | .08 | -.14* | -. |

* Significant at .05.

There are also several significant correlations between respondent traits and preferences for particular procedures. Female employees are more likely to prefer an investigation team but are less supportive of the use of progressive discipline and a case-by-case disciplinary approach. Rather, they are more supportive of dismissing the accused if charges are substantiated. Older employees are more likely to prefer more informal solutions including offering (although not requiring) mediation and handling the whole situation informally if possible. Employees with longer tenure are less likely to want specific disciplines linked to particular offenses.

Managers appear to have different attitudes about several aspects of process. First, they are significantly less likely to want a team of investigators, perhaps because it may limit their ability to conduct an investigation on their own. Similarly, they are less likely to want specific disciplines tied to particular offenses. And, they are less likely to support mandatory mediation. Managers are significantly more likely to want a disciplinary system that varies based on the severity of the incident and would like to see an investigation conducted in all cases. In short, managers appear to want to preserve their own discretion and/or flexibility in dealing with the situation and female managers appear to feel even more strongly that discretion is desirable.

Finally, respondents who indicated that they had experienced sexual harassment are significantly less likely to support an investigation in all circumstances. They may not have been satisfied with the nature of the previous investigation or they may prefer to have options to handle the situation informally. Since there are no significant correlations between actually reporting harassment and any of the process elements, the latter explanation is more likely.

The survey also included an open-ended question asking respondents to indicate how they would handle a complaint if they had the chance to determine the most desirable policies and procedures; 305 individuals responded. The most frequent responses (10 percent) closely followed standard model practices for sexual harassment investigations: interviews with all parties would take place, the situation would be investigated, affirmative efforts made to find out the "truth," and formal reports compiled. Another 9 percent indicated that their actions would depend on the severity of the purported situation, the history of the individuals involved, and an examination of pertinent personnel records. In short, the reaction would depend on the parties and behavior involved. Seven percent of respondents indicated that they would "follow the policy" or act in a "professional manner" and another 7 percent had no idea what they would do. Six percent of respondents focused on the particular types of discipline they would use, with no particular emphasis on process, and 3 percent indicated that they would seek outside assistance, from the EEOC for example. Thus, while many employees would follow typical investigative procedures there are almost as many who would vary procedures depending on the circumstances and many are more focused on discipline rather than process.

Responses to the open-ended question were cross-tabulated with several independent variables to assess any differences in attitudes due to gender, age, race, job, tenure, and experience of sexual harassment. There are no significant differences in what employees would do to address complaints of sexual harassment and their personal or job characteristics. Differences in attitudes between male and female employees almost reach statistical significance (at .07) with women being more likely to indicate they would follow standard procedures and more interested in discipline and men more likely to prefer to deal with situations on a case-by-case basis.

### Satisfaction with Current Policy and Process

Table 14.3 contains response data for questions relating to satisfaction with existing policy and the implementation of that policy. Responses are very dispersed here; no longer is there clear consensus on local policy and process. And, although satisfaction with existing policy is relatively high, satisfaction with policy implementation is lower. Indeed, the six highest satisfaction scores based on means all relate to policy. Employees tend to feel that their policy is fair to all parties, serves to reduce further harassment, and contains provisions to make the complainant aware of the outcomes (over 78 percent of respondents are satisfied or very satisfied on these points). However, fewer feel that their policy protects the confidentiality of the complainant and the accused (60 percent and 59 percent respectively are at least somewhat satisfied with this).

Satisfaction with how policy is implemented is lower. Between 50 and 59 percent of respondents are at least somewhat satisfied with the timeliness of the investigation, how the complainant was treated, the findings of the investigation, and the solution or remedy applied to the situation.[7] Less than half of the respondents were satisfied with how the accused was treated, with the quality of the investigation, and with the extent to which confidentiality was actually protected for both parties. In short, then, employees appear to be relatively satisfied with the content of existing sexual harassment policies (with the exception of confidentiality protections), but are less satisfied with the application of those policies.

Table 14.3 also provides the correlation coefficients between satisfaction with policy and procedures and other respondent traits. Women are significantly more likely to think that their policy is fair to the accused individual and more likely to feel that the policy protects confidentiality for the accused. Other than these two policy issues, there are no significant differences between men and women in satisfaction with the process of implementing sexual harassment policy. Employees with longer tenure are

**Table 14.3. Policy and Process Satisfaction Percent Frequencies**

| | Mean[a] | Very Satisfied | Somewhat Satisfied | Somewhat Dissatisfied | Very Dissatisfied |
|---|---|---|---|---|---|
| Policy fair to complainant | 2.99 | 15 | 72 | 10 | 3 |
| Policy fair to accused | 2.84 | 11 | 68 | 17 | 5 |
| Policy reduces harassment | 2.83 | 14 | 63 | 17 | 7 |
| Complainant aware of outcome according to policy | 2.80 | 9 | 68 | 17 | 6 |
| Policy protects confidentiality for complainant | 2.66 | 10 | 50 | 30 | 10 |
| Policy protects confidentiality for accused | 2.59 | 9 | 50 | 32 | 9 |
| Timely investigation | 2.54 | 23 | 36 | 13 | 28 |
| Complainant treated well | 2.54 | 25 | 33 | 12 | 30 |
| Findings were appropriate | 2.53 | 24 | 28 | 24 | 24 |
| Solution was appropriate | 2.44 | 23 | 27 | 21 | 29 |
| Accused treated well | 2.31 | 17 | 29 | 22 | 32 |
| Quality investigation | 2.28 | 19 | 25 | 20 | 36 |
| Confidentiality was protected | 2.21 | 17 | 23 | 23 | 36 |

[a]Mean response on a four-point scale.

Correlations with Policy and Process Satisfaction

| | Female | Older | Tenure | Race | Manager | Harassed | Reported |
|---|---|---|---|---|---|---|---|
| Policy fair to complainant | -.00 | .01 | -.12* | -.02 | .16* | -.24* | -.11* |
| Policy fair to accused | .22* | -.01 | -.09* | -.04 | .09* | -.13* | -.05 |
| Policy reduces harassment | .02 | -.03 | -.15* | -.03 | .14* | -.36* | -.12* |
| Complainant aware of outcome according to policy | -.01 | .08 | -.10* | .06 | .18* | -.27* | -.06 |
| Policy protects confidentiality for complainant | .07 | -.03 | -.10* | -.01 | .05 | -.15* | -.07 |
| Policy protects confidentiality for accused | .17* | -.01 | -.14* | -.10* | .10* | -.13* | -.05 |
| Timely investigation | -.10 | .17 | .00 | -.17* | .42* | -.17* | -.10 |
| Complainant treated well | .02 | .11 | -.06 | -.05 | .33* | -.17* | -.07 |
| Findings were appropriate | .00 | .13 | .05 | .03 | .31* | -.22* | -.11 |
| Solution was appropriate | .01 | .14 | .02 | .02 | .31* | -.19* | -.05 |
| Accused treated well | .02 | -.02 | -.06 | -.04 | .32* | -.14 | -.03 |
| Quality investigation | -.03 | .15 | .06 | -.12 | .37* | -.25* | -.09 |
| Confidentiality was protected | .01 | .03 | -.01 | -.12 | .39* | -.18* | -.05 |

* Significant at .05.

less likely to think that the policy is fair to or protects the confidentiality of either the complainant or the accused, do not think that the policy serves to reduce harassment, and do not think that the complainant is sufficiently made aware of outcomes. Thus, as a group, employees with longer tenure tend to be more negative about existing policies overall. Respondents of color are significantly less likely to think that investigations are timely and that the policy protects the confidentiality of the accused. Individuals who have actually reported harassment are significantly less likely to feel that the policy is fair to the complainant, but there are no other significant differences in attitudes about either policy or process based on having filed a complaint.[8]

The primary individual traits that appear to differentiate respondent satisfaction with policy and process are whether or not they are managers and whether they have been harassed. Managers are significantly more positive on most aspects of policy and process. Indeed, the only attribute on which they are not more positive is whether the policy protects confidentiality for the complainant. Conversely, respondents indicating that they had experienced sexual harassment are significantly less positive about policy and process, again almost across the board. It does not appear that experience with the policy is particularly important in assessing that policy. Experiencing harassment is sufficient to increase negative feelings. This raises concerns from an organizational perspective since it suggests that there is little a city can do to improve the satisfaction levels of those experiencing harassment, given that they appear to be independent of policy and process. The only plausible solution would be a general effort to reduce the incidence of harassment; changing policy and/or process does not appear to "cut it" as far as satisfaction is concerned.

Another open-ended question asked respondents to indicate how they would improve current policies; 321 individuals responded. The most frequent response (17 percent) was that although they were not satisfied with current policy and procedure they were uncertain about how it should be improved. The next largest group of respondents (13 percent) indicated that the policy and procedure were fine but more training, workshops, information, and education were needed. Six percent of respondents indicated that greater codification was needed in the policy in the form of specific timelines, more detail on how to report incidents, more detail on how the investigation should be conducted, and so on. Another 4 percent of respondents indicated that the policy was fine but that the individuals implementing it were the problem. Comments such as "supervisor conducting investigation disliked accused personally, supervisor should have recused themselves" and "the personnel director was not adept at handling these situations and the complaint was swept under the rug" are examples of the concerns with personality over process. Two percent each suggested that greater confidentiality protections were needed, that external bodies should investigate complaints, and that the old policy was so flawed that the organization should throw it out and start over. Five percent indicated that the current policy was working well and needed no revisions.

Again, various respondent traits were cross-tabulated with attitudes about current policy and procedure. Male and female employees were significantly different in their attitudes. Men were more likely to feel that the policy was satisfactory but that more training and information were required. Women were significantly more likely to feel that confidentiality protections were insufficient and were concerned about the individuals implementing the policy. Males and females were not different in their desires for greater codification. There were no differences in attitudes regarding policy and procedure based on age, race, tenure, and job status. Experiencing sexual harassment, however, has a significant impact on attitudes about policy and process. Those who had experienced sexual harassment were more likely to indicate that while the policy was satisfactory, the individuals implementing it were not and they preferred external bodies or actors to implement policy. This suggests that those closest to the process itself—complainants—were unhappy with how current policy was interpreted and implemented by individuals within the organization. Concomitantly those who had experienced harassment were more likely to indicate that the policy needed greater codification. Greater specificity of deadlines, procedures for investigation, interviewing processes, and so on presumably would lead to less discretion for those implementing policies and hence would also address concerns about how policies are carried out.

### Policy Preferences and Policy and Process Satisfaction

It is possible that policy preferences affect satisfaction with policy and procedure. In other words, expectations and preferences for certain policies may well color evaluation of existing municipal policies. To facilitate analysis by reducing the number of variables considered, these various elements of policy and process preferences were entered into a factor analysis, providing four preference factors (see table 14.4).[9] These factors represent a preference for policies that include "teeth," sanctions, and timelines (codification), a preference for processes that are open and/or more transparent with regard to findings and punishment (openness), a preference for a disciplinary focus (discipline), and a preference for informal processes (informal). Similarly, the several policy and process satisfaction variables were also subjected to factor analysis, resulting in the two indexes presented in table 14.4. In short, there are two conceptually different aspects to satisfaction; satisfaction: with elements of the policy and satisfaction with the process of handling a complaint.

**Table 14.4.  Factor Analysis**

|  | Factor Loading |
|---|---|
| *Codification Index* | |
| Sanctions for breach of confidentiality | .74 |
| Sanctions for false reporting | .78 |
| Timelines for reporting | .75 |
| Timelines for investigation | .66 |
| | |
| *Openness Index* | |
| Claimant is informed of findings | .82 |
| Claimant is informed of punishment | .83 |
| Supervisor evaluation | .78 |
| Detailed definitions | .77 |
| Publicize potential punishments | .65 |
| | |
| *Disciplinary-Focus Index* | |
| Progressive discipline | .71 |
| Discipline based on severity | .82 |
| Outline specific disciplines | .61 |
| Case-by-case discipline | .60 |
| | |
| *Informal-Process Index* | |
| Handle situation informally | .68 |
| Offer mediation | .49 |
| Require mediation | .80 |
| | |
| *Policy Satisfaction Index* | |
| Fair to complainant | .79 |
| Fair to accused | .71 |
| Protects confidentiality for complainant | .77 |
| Protects confidentiality for accused | .51 |
| Complainant is made aware of outcome | .76 |
| Policy operates to reduce sexual harassment | .82 |
| | |
| *Outcome/Process Satisfaction Index* | |
| Satisfaction with findings of investigation | .87 |
| Satisfaction with methods to address situation | .91 |
| Satisfaction with protection of confidentiality | .85 |
| Satisfaction with how the complainant was treated | .90 |
| Satisfaction with how the accused was treated | .81 |
| Satisfaction with quality of investigation | .90 |
| Satisfaction with timeliness of investigation | .84 |

**Table 14.5.   Correlations between Policy/Process Preference and Policy/Process Satisfaction**

|                              | Sanctions | Openness | Discipline | Informal |
|------------------------------|-----------|----------|------------|----------|
| Policy satisfaction          | .21*      | .16*     | .13*       | .13*     |
| Outcome/process satisfaction | .13       | .13      | .07        | .12      |

*Significant at the .05. level.

As indicated in table 14.5, it appears that respondents with strong feelings on all of the policy and preferences indexes are more satisfied with existing policies. Current public sexual harassment policies seem to meet employee expectations for codification, openness, discipline, and even in providing informal options. However, policy and process preferences have nothing to do with satisfaction with the actual implementation of the sexual harassment policy. Again, as suggested above, attitudes about process are quite different than those about policy.

### What Leads to Satisfaction?

How important are employee policy preferences to satisfaction with existing policies and procedures? Are there other variables that appear to be more important? Do employee preferences on policy really matter to the implementation of sexual harassment policies? To answer these questions regression analyses were run with policy satisfaction and process or outcome satisfaction as the dependent variables. Independent variables included the four policy/process preference indexes, the various traits of respondents previously discussed, and several other variables that have been shown to affect policy satisfaction: effectiveness of training, knowledge of existing policies and procedures, and the extent to which individuals hold traditional gender values—opinions that women should stay in the home and that women use their gender or looks to exact special benefits at work (see Foulis and McCabe, 1997; Reese and Lindenberg, 1999; and De Judicibus and McCabe, 2001, for more detail on these variables). Regression results are presented in table 14.6.[10]

**Table 14.6.   Regression Analysis**

|                               | $R^2$ | B     | Beta  | Significance |
|-------------------------------|-------|-------|-------|--------------|
| *Policy Satisfaction*         | .42   |       |       |              |
| Effective training            |       | .48   | .47   | .00          |
| Harassment                    |       | −.21  | −.16  | .00          |
| Tenure                        |       | −.11  | −.12  | .02          |
| Process knowledge             |       | .15   | .12   | .04          |
| Traditional gender values     |       | −.12  | −.12  | .01          |
| Constant                      |       | .24   |       | .41          |
| *Outcome/Process Satisfaction*| .97   |       |       |              |
| Poor supervisor reaction      |       | −.60  | −.66  | .01          |
| Effective supervisor training |       | .46   | .5    | .01          |
| Constant                      |       | .20   |       | .15          |

The five variables in the equation account for 42 percent of the variation in satisfaction with existing policies.[11] First, none of the policy preference indexes remained significantly correlated with policy satisfaction in multiple regression. This implies that when accounting for other variables in the model, policy preferences are relatively unimportant in whether employees are satisfied with current policies. The best predictor of policy satisfaction is the extent to which training in the city is viewed as being effective. Knowledge of the policy and process also significantly increases satisfaction and is the likely result of training. More recent employees tend to be more satisfied with policies. Respondents who have experienced sexual harassment and those who hold traditional gender values are less satisfied. In addition to the absence of policy preferences in this model, other variables such as age and gender are also missing. Thus, it appears that policy satisfaction is most dependent on training and familiarity with the policy itself.

None of the policy/process preference indexes were significantly correlated with process or outcome satisfaction in bivariate analysis, so it makes little sense to include them in a regression equation. However, to provide a sense of what might contribute to satisfaction with policy implementation and the outcome of investigations, table 14.6 presents the most robust regression model with process satisfaction as the dependent variable. Only two variables remain significantly correlated with process/outcome satisfaction in multiple regression and alone they account for 97 percent of the variation in satisfaction.[12] It appears that the critical factors in satisfaction with implementation are effective training for supervisors on how to handle sexual harassment complaints and the absence of negative reactions when complaints are initially filed. Previous research has indicated that how supervisors respond when complaints or concerns are initially raised is critical to satisfaction (Reese and Lindenberg, 1999), and this analysis bears this out. Obviously, effective training of those taking complaints will have a strong impact on the quality of those reactions. Thus, how supervisors treat those involved in complaints is the critical link in the process and is more important than any policy or process preferences as well as any individual traits such as gender, age, or job status.

## CONCLUSIONS AND POLICY IMPLICATIONS

There are several conclusions that can be drawn from these findings with direct implications for more effective sexual harassment policies and procedures. Each of the questions posed at the beginning of the chapter is revisited and specific policy implications are identified.

## What Policies Do Employees Want?

Several summary points are important. First, there is substantial consensus among employees that all aspects of model policies included in the survey are important. There is a good deal of agreement on what policies employees want. While there are significant differences in intensity of feelings about desired policy between men and women (with women consistently more committed to model policy elements), there remains agreement on substance. Thus, it should not be difficult to gain consensus around the elements of the sexual harassment policy itself. And, it should be noted that the aspects of policy deemed most important by employees tend to follow sex-role spillover and biological theories of sexual harassment in that they focus on greater codification of processes after violations occur as well as on training to both inform employees about the policy and increase awareness of which behaviors and actions constitute sexual harassment. Given the individual-legal focus of U.S. sexual harassment policy (see Zippel, this volume), it is not surprising that there is little concern with policy changes to address organizational power inequities or work-group dynamics.

There are three aspects of model policy that employees feel most strongly about: clear confidentiality statements that include sanctions for breach of confidentiality, requirements that feedback be provided to the claimant, and sanctions for false reports. Recent research examining the content of public-sector sexual harassment policies suggests that these aspects of model policy are not widely in place, however. No policies from Michigan cities included sanctions for breach of confidentiality, only 14 percent required that claimants be informed of the findings of an investigation, 12 percent required that remedies be reported, and 13 percent included statements or sanctions about false reports (Reese and Lindenberg, 2002b). From this it seems clear that by adding these elements organizations could create policies that more closely reflect the desires of employees.

## How Would Employees Handle Complaints?

There is less consensus on how complaints should be handled than there is on more abstract policy issues. Indeed, open-ended questions revealed that many respondents are unsure about what should happen when a complaint is made. The greatest consensus is that investigations should be handled by teams of trained personnel rather than by just one individual and that discipline should vary based on the severity of the harassing behavior. Beyond this there are mixed messages regarding discipline; many employees appear to want both greater codification of discipline for specific behaviors and the application of discipline on a case-by-case basis. Obviously these are mutually exclusive because greater specificity in the policy would lead to less discretion in application. Thus, it appears that employees have mixed emotions about appropriate discipline. Further, there are some gender differences in this area. Women are more likely to support dismissal if the severity of the offense warrants it, while men are not comfortable with this. Female employees also appear to be more focused on disciplinary options when considering how they would deal with a complaint of sexual harassment. Older employees are more likely to prefer that the whole process—including discipline—be handled informally.

As a practical matter, organizations face less consensus in desired processes overall and ambiguity regarding discipline in particular. The fact that policy and process preferences appear to have little to do with feelings about policy implementation supports the conclusion that trying to address employee preferences as far as process is concerned may not be the most productive approach.

An alternative focus is suggested in the significantly different attitudes of managers or supervisors and employees. Supervisors have significantly different views on most aspects of policy process; they do not want to be evaluated on how they handle sexual harassment complaints, they do not want investigation teams, and they do not want codification of discipline. In other words they are less supportive of any policy elements or processes that limit their discretion in handling complaints of sexual harassment. However, the quality of supervisor reaction to complaints is critical to employee satisfaction with policy implementation. This is where organizations should focus their attention.

## How Satisfied Are Employees with Current Policies and Procedures?

There is even less consensus on policy and process satisfaction than there is on desired processes. Satisfaction with existing policies is higher than satisfaction with processes or outcomes. Obviously, the "devil is in the details" of policy implementation.

The greatest areas of dissatisfaction are the lack of confidentiality protections and sanctions, the extent to which confidentiality is protected during investigations, how the accused is treated during the whole process, and the quality of the investigation itself. While managers tend to be happier with all aspects of policy and procedures, employees with more tenure are dissatisfied and employees of color are not comfortable with the timeliness of investigations and confidentiality protections for the accused in particular. And, having experienced sexual harassment makes employees more negative across the board.

## What Increases Satisfaction?

Satisfaction with existing policies is increased by training, particularly to the extent that it leads to greater knowledge of policy and procedures. In short, employees will be more comfortable with sexual harassment policies if they are made aware of them and are trained on sexual harassment issues more generally. A need for more training appears to be more critically felt among male employees. Beyond this, satisfaction with the implementation of sexual harassment policies is almost completely dependent on how effectively supervisors react to initial complaints. Effective reactions can be increased by training supervisors on all aspects of handling complaints. This makes clear that, despite supervisor preferences, sexual harassment investigations cannot be left to their discretion. And, because so few supervisors receive complaints of sexual harassment, relying on "on the job training" is simply not going to suffice. Training supervisors on all aspects of processing sexual harassment complaints and evaluating them on how well they deal with this aspect of their job should lead to uniformity in the treatment of complaints, should improve the response to all parties involved, and should improve the quality of investigations. In short, training supervisors is probably the most important thing organizations can do to improve satisfaction with sexual harassment policy and procedure. Very simply, the policies themselves do not guarantee effective outcomes.

A final observation is that the experience of sexual harassment appears important in satisfaction with existing sexual harassment policies as well as in policy preferences. But, being harassed operates independently from the experience of reporting harassment. This is the case because so few incidents of harassment are actually reported (Kidder et al., 1995). Thus, experiencing harassment causes victims to form preferences apart from actually being involved in policy implementation. Since there is no direct connection between satisfaction and actually having filed a report, improving process alone may not produce greater satisfaction with policy and procedure. However, reducing overall levels of sexual harassment will also lead to greater policy satisfaction. And, what will lead to this ultimately desired outcome? Again, previous research has indicated that training of both employees and supervisors is related to reduced levels of sexual harassment and that the training appears to predate changes in harassment levels (Reese and Lindenberg, 2002a).

## What Are the Extent of Gender Differences?

There are gender differences in perceptions of sexual harassment policy although they tend to relate more to process than evaluation of effects. For example, women are more interested than men in greater codification of all elements of the policy process. Men prefer a more case-by-case approach and more lenient discipline. In evaluating policy, women feel that processes are more fair to and better protect the confidentiality of the accused—most likely a man. Other than these two issues, however, there are no significant differences between men and women in satisfaction with the actual process of applying sexual harassment policy. Ultimately how supervisors react to complaints is more important than individual traits such as gender.

# NOTES

This research has been supported by the Michigan Municipal League, the State Policy Center at Wayne State University, the Fraser Center for Workplace Issues at Wayne State University, and by Eastern Michigan University. The authors would like to acknowledge the research assistance of Kristofer Kazmierezak, Heather Kahn, and Tammy Croxall and thank colleague Joe Ohren for helpful comments and suggestions.

1. While there is agreement in the literature that procedures should be clear there are mixed arguments about whether both formal and informal options should be provided. Some authors have argued that informal options are beneficial in increasing complaints and making complainants more comfortable with the process (Riger, 1991) but others have argued that all complaints should be formal to provide an institutional tracking system and to ensure uniformity (Reese and Lindenberg, 1999).

2. Michigan as a case study represents several ideal factors that permit generalizing survey results. While often characterized as a classic "rust belt" state, there are many areas of Michigan which remain rural and/or where the primary source of income is tied to tourist dollars and agriculture. Michigan also has a high percentage of minorities or ethnic groups concentrated in distinct geographical regions of the state. There are areas of the state which are distinctly more liberal, while others are conservative in both political and lifestyle preferences. Many blue-collar communities in Michigan experienced in-migration from the South only a generation or two ago and remain distinctly blue-collar communities, while other areas in Michigan have seen a suburban explosion of middle- and upper-middle-class wealth. Thus, Michigan presents a microcosm that is sufficiently heterogeneous to provide a good snapshot of public-sector practices in high-profile policy areas such as sexual harassment.

3. Scores on the policy and training indexes were converted to standardized scores (f-scores) to assure that all responses were comparable. The cut points identified in the text were chosen because they represented visible breaks or skips in the data and hence seemed to best distinguish between cities with poor policies below the cut and those with exceptionally good policies above it. For the good policy index there was a jump from two cities to twelve cities at .89 and there were thirty-five cities identified as having highly codified policies; there was another large group of fifty-four that did not have any of the effective policy elements. For training there was a large jump from twenty-one cities to one city at .62 and this was chosen as the dividing line between good and bad training. This resulted in 106 cities with poor training and 85 with good training.

4. It only made sense to survey employees in cities that had relatively large numbers of employees. For example, if a city had only twenty employees it would be difficult to get a generalizable sense of the effects of its policies. While the initial preference was only to include municipalities with 100 or more employees this would have resulted in only one or two cities in some of the quadrants. By using a minimum employee size of 70, a reasonably large set of eligible cities resulted for each quadrant. The analysis was limited to cities to control for form of government but also because villages tended to have substantially fewer employees.

5. The response rates for the individual cities are as follows (response rates do not appear to vary systematically with city characteristics such as size of workforce or nature of policy):

- Light Blue city – 210 surveys distributed, 50 returned = 24% response rate
- Light Green city – 84 surveys distributed, 21 returned = 26% response rate
- Yellow city – 332 surveys distributed, 135 returned = 41% response rate
- Cream city – 118 surveys distributed, 28 returned = 24% response rate
- Pink city – 118 surveys distributed, 43 returned = 36% response rate
- Orange city – 111 surveys distributed, 44 returned = 40% response rate
- Dark Blue city – 82 surveys distributed, 13 returned = 16% response rate
- Purple city – 154 surveys distributed, 48 returned = 31% response rate
- Red city – 197 surveys distributed, 51 returned = 26% response rate
- Brown city – 107 surveys distributed, 39 returned = 36% response rate
- Orchid city – 180 surveys distributed, 33 returned = 18% response rate
- Dark Green city – 140 surveys distributed, 44 returned = 31% response rate
- Gold city – 164 surveys distributed, 46 returned = 28% response rate

6. This sample composition is representative of many surveys on workplace sexual harassment, which tend to have lower responses from nonwhite employees. This results in a more limited ability to assess the experiences and attitudes of employees of color and appears to be a consistent limitation to sexual harassment surveys. The thirteen cities surveyed differ significantly on only a few respondent traits. Respondents from the Pink city are significantly younger and are more likely to be nonwhite (mirroring the population profile in the community, roughly 50 percent nonwhite). Respondents from the Cream city were significantly more likely to be female and less likely to be supervisors. Respondents from the Orange and Red cities were significantly more likely to be male (and older in the latter). Finally, respondents from the Orchid and Light Blue cities were significantly younger.

7. Only respondents who had used the policy or knew of others who had responded to these questions.

8. Because the data are drawn from thirteen different cities with different policies and procedures it is possible that satisfaction rates are better explained by city than by respondent traits. These relationships have been explored in other research (see Reese and Lindenberg, 2002a) and results can be provided by the authors. However, in summary form, only three cities had significantly different employee satisfaction rates; the Dark Blue and Orchid cities significantly higher and the Light Blue city significantly lower. And, regarding the two cities with significantly higher satisfaction rates, one came far closer to matching model policy than the other so the differences are more likely to emanate from the process and/or the extent of training (see Reese and Lindenberg, 2002a, for a full discussion of the importance of training) as opposed to the policy.

9. For the factor analysis, the standard SPSS default modes were employed including varimax rotation, listwise deletion of missing data, and principle components analysis. A .50 or higher loading was the criteria used for inclusion in a factor. No variable loaded on more than one factor. Factor scores were converted to f or standardized scores and added to create an index score.

10. Initial regressions were run with all independent variables significantly correlated with policy and process satisfaction in bivariate correlation analysis. Only those variables that remained significantly correlated to policy and process satisfaction in multiple regression are included in the equations. The models presented are the most parsimonious yet have the highest explanatory ($R^2$) value.

11. Of the independent variables the effectiveness of training and knowledge of sexual harassment processes are correlated at a relatively high level (.48); thus the $R^2$ is likely inflated somewhat due to multicollinearity. When knowledge of the policy is removed from the equation the $R^2$ remains at .40. When training is removed it drops to .25. This suggests that the presence of both variables is not inflating the $R^2$ but that training is by far the more critical factor.

12. The two independent variables in this equation are not significantly correlated with each other.

## REFERENCES

American Association of University Professors. 1995. "Sexual Harassment Suggested Policy and Procedures for Handling Complaints." *Academe* (July/August): 62–63.

De Judicibus, M., and McCabe, M. P. 2001. "Blaming the Target of Sexual Harassment: Impact of Gender Role, Sexist Attitudes, and Work Role." *Sex Roles* 44: 401–17.

Dziech, B. D., and Weiner, L. 1984. *The Lecherous Professor*. Boston: Beacon Press.

Fitzgerald, L. F. 1990. "Sexual Harassment: The Definition and Measurement of a Construct." Pp. 21–44 in *Ivory Power: Sexual Harassment on Campus*, ed. M. A. Paludi. Albany: State University of New York Press.

Frazier, P. A., Cochran, C. C., and Olson, A. M. 1995. "Social Science Research on Lay Definitions of Sexual Harassment." *Journal of Social Issues* 51 (Spring): 21–37.

Foulis, D., and McCabe, M. P. 1997. "Sexual Harassment: Factors Affecting Attitudes and Perceptions." *Sex Roles* (November): 773–98.

Gutek, B. A. 1985. *Sex and the Workplace*. San Francisco: Jossey-Bass.

———.1997. "Sexual Harassment Policy Initiatives." Pp. 185–98 in *Sexual Harassment*, ed. W. O'Donohue. Boston: Allyn and Bacon.

Gutek, B. A., and O'Connor, M. 1995. "The Empirical Basis for the Reasonable Woman Standard." *Journal of Social Issues* 51 (Spring): 151–66.

Kidder, L. H., Lafleur, R. A., and Wells, C. V. 1995. "Recalling Harassment, Reconstructing Experience." *Journal of Social Issues* 51 (Spring): 53–67.

O'Hare Grundmann, E., O'Donohue, W., and Peterson, S. H. 1997. "The Prevention of Sexual Harassment." Pp. 175–84 in *Sexual Harassment*, ed. W. O'Donohue. Boston: Allyn and Bacon.

Paludi, M. A., Grossman, M., Scott, C. A., Kindermann, J., Matula, S., Oswald, J., Dovan, J., and Mulcahy, D. 1990. "Myths and Realities: Sexual Harassment on Campus." Pp. 1–13 in *Ivory Power: Sexual Harassment on Campus*, ed. M. A. Paludi. Albany: State University of New York Press.

Perry, E. L., Kulik, C. T., and Schmidtke, J. M. 1998. "Individual Differences in the Effectiveness of Sexual Harassment Awareness Training." *Journal of Applied Social Psychology* 28: 698–723.

Pierce, E. R., Rosen, B., and Hiller, T. B. 1997. "Breaking the Silence: Creating User-Friendly Sexual Harassment Policies." *Employee Responsibilities and Rights Journal* 10: 225–43.

Reese, L., and Lindenberg, K. E. 1996. "Sexual Harassment Policy: What *Do* Employees Want?" *Policy Studies Journal* (Autumn): 387–403.

———. 1999. *Implementing Public Sector Sexual Harassment Policies.* Thousand Oaks, Calif.: Sage.

———. 2002a. "It's the Training Stupid." Paper presented at the annual meeting, Midwest Political Science Association, Chicago, Ill.

———. 2002b. "Assessing Local Government Sexual Harassment Policies." *The American Review of Public Administration* 32: 295–311.

Reilly, T., Carpenter, S., Dull, V., and Bartlett, K. 1982. "The Factorial Survey: An Approach to Defining Sexual Harassment on Campus." *Journal of Social Issues* 38: 99–109.

Remick, H., Salisbury, J., Stringer, D., and Ginorio, A. B. 1990. "Investigating Complaints of Sexual Harassment." Pp. 191–212 in *Ivory Power: Sexual Harassment on Campus,* ed. M. A. Paludi. Albany: State University of New York Press.

Riger, S. 1991. "Gender Dilemmas in Sexual Harassment Policies and Procedures." *American Psychologist* (May): 497–505.

Saal, F. E. 1996. "Men's Misperceptions of Women's Interpersonal Behaviors and Sexual Harassment." Pp. 67–84 in *Sexual Harassment in the Workplace,* ed. M. S. Stockdale. Thousand Oaks, Calif.: Sage.

Stringer, D. M., Remick, H., Salisbury, J., and Ginorio, A. B. 1990. "The Power and Reasons behind Sexual Harassment: An Employer's Guide to Solutions." *Public Personnel Management* 19 (Spring): 43–52.

# Index

# About the Contributors

**Heidi M. Berggren** is a doctoral candidate in political science, specializing in American politics and public policy, at the University of Colorado, Boulder. She is primarily interested in U.S. social policy, with a particular focus in her dissertation research on work-family policies such as family and medical leave and child care.

**Katherine Bird** is a Researcher at the University of Bremen, where she recently completed her Ph.D. She has studied business in London (1985–1989) and sociology in Bremen (1992–1997), and served as research assistant in the project entitled "Occupations in the Female Life Course and Social Change" of the Special Research Centre at the University of Bremen. Research interests include the development of and influences on female employment from a gender perspective as well as longitudinal methodology in life-course research. She recently completed a dissertation on "Reconciling Work and the Family: The Impact of Parental Leave Policies and Occupation Trained for on the Female Life Course."

**Heidi Gottfried** is Associate Professor of Labor Studies in the College of Urban, Labor, and Metropolitan Affairs at Wayne State University. Her M.A. in sociology is from the University of Michigan, Ann Arbor, and her Ph.D. was received in 1987 from the University of Wisconsin, Madison. Over the past several years her work, funded by ASA/NSF, DAAD, and SSRC-Abe, has focused on comparative analysis of flexible employment practices and regulation in the United States, Germany, Sweden, and Japan.

**Karin Gottschall** is Professor of Sociology at the Center for Social Policy Research, University of Bremen. She has written extensively on women's work, labor-market segmentation, and social inequality. Previous research concerns the rationalization of office work from a feminist perspective and the effects of the service-sector expansion on gender-specific labor-market segregation. This empirical research is complemented by a focus on theorizing gender, class relations, and social change. Current empirical research focuses on the impact of the flexibilization of work on gender relations and social security.

**Linda Haas** is Professor of Sociology and Adjunct Professor of Women's Studies at Indiana University in Indianapolis, Indiana. She regularly teaches courses on gender, family policy, and families and work. Her research interests focus on the linkages between gender, family, and work in postindustrialized societies. Publications include *Equal Parenthood and Social Policy* (SUNY Press, 1992) and *Organizational Change and Gender Equity* (with P. Hwang and G. Russell, Sage, 2000).

**Wendy L. Hassett** has nine years of experience in local-government management, currently as the assistant city manager of Auburn, Alabama. She holds a master of public administration degree and a Ph.D. in public administration and public policy from Auburn University. She is the coauthor of articles published in *Public Administration Review*, *Public Works Management & Policy*, and other journals. She is also coauthor of a chapter in *Innovative Governments: Creative Approaches to Local Problems* and is coeditor of a forthcoming book, *Local Government Management: Current Issues and Best Practices*.

**Ilse Lenz**, Professor of Gender Studies and Social Structure at Bochum University, has published extensively on gender and work, gender and politics, and gender and the women's movement in Germany and Japan. Further aspects of her research concern gender and ethnicity and gender and globalization (twelve books, seventeen articles). She has coedited books on gender and computer technologies, on gender and ethnicity, and on gender and society in Japan. She has a long-standing interest in comparative research.

**Ulrike Liebert** is Coordinator of the Jean Monnet Centre for European Studies, Professor of Political Science, and Jean Monnet Chair of Comparative European Integration Research, all at the University of Bremen, Germany.

**Karen E. Lindenberg** is Professor Emeritus of political science at Eastern Michigan University and was formerly Director of the Master of Public Administration Program. Her research has focused on public personnel management issues and labor arbitration. She has over twenty-five years of experience as a grievance and arbitration advocate, as well as experience in collective-bargaining negotiations, and she is a trained mediator. Her most recent publication, *Implementing Sexual Harassment Policy* (Sage, 1999), coauthored with Laura Reese, focused on sexual harassment policy and implementation issues. She has retired from academia to allow time for a second career as a labor arbitrator.

**Jacqueline O'Reilly** is Senior Research Fellow at the WZB and acting coordinator of the TRANSLAM project with Professor Günther Schmid. She edited the *International Handbook for Labour Market Policy and Evaluation* (Edward Elgar) with Professor Günther Schmid and Dr. Klaus Schömann (1996), and published an edited volume, *Part-Time Prospects* (Routledge), in 1998 with Dr. Colette Fagan (Manchester University), and another, *Working Time Changes,* edited with Professor Inmaculda Cebrian and Professor Michel Lallement. Another book due out soon is *Time Rules.* She is currently working on a new book, *Changing Welfare and Work: Revising the Social and Gender Contract in Europe* (Oxford University Press).

**Laura Reese**, a political scientist, is Professor in the Urban Planning Program and Fellow in the Fraser Center for Workplace Issues, College of Urban, Labor, and Metropolitan Affairs, at Wayne State University. She has published articles on urban politics, local economic development, comparative urban policy, and public personnel management. Her most recent books are *The Civic Culture of Local Economic Development* (with Raymond Rosenfeld) and *Implementing Sexual Harassment Policy* (with Karen E. Lindenberg), both with Sage. Her current research interests focus on further exploration of local civic cultures in the United States and Canada, comparative studies of urban consolidation and metropolitan governance, and the identification and implementation of effective sexual harassment policy.

**Glenda S. Roberts**, a sociocultural anthropologist, is Professor at the Graduate School of Asia-Pacific Studies of Waseda University in Tokyo. Among her publications are *Staying on the Line: Blue-Collar Women in Contemporary Japan* (University of Hawaii Press, 1994), *Japan and Global Migration: Foreign Workers and the Advent of a Multicultural Society* (coedited with Mike Douglass, Routledge, 2000), and *Pinning Hopes on Angels: Reflections from an Aging Japan's Urban Landscape*, in Roger Goodman, ed., *Family and Social Policy in Japan* (Cambridge University Press, 2002). She is currently continuing to research issues of work/life balance and Japan's low-birthrate society from the perspective of gender.

**Eileen Trzcinski** received her Ph.D. in economics and social work from the University of Michigan. She is currently Associate Professor in the School of Social Work and a coordinate faculty member in the College of Urban, Labor, and Metropolitan Affairs. Her areas of research center on family policy and labor-market policy, both on the national and international level. She has written extensively on how family-leave policy affects the employment of women and has conducted analyses of family-leave policy both nationally and cross-nationally. She has worked as Visiting Research Scholar at the German Institute for Economic Research and at the Fachhochschule fuer Wirtschaft, Berlin. In 2001–2002, she received a fellowship from the Kosciuszko Foundation and worked as Visiting Research Professor at the Institute of Sociology, Jagiellonean University, Krakow, Poland.

**Sylvia Walby**, Professor, School of Sociology and Social Policy, University of Leeds, has published several seminal books on gender and work. She has previously been Professor and Head of the Department of Sociology at the University of Bristol, U.K., and founding Director of the Gender Institute at the LSE. She was founding President of the European Sociological Association, 1995–7. Her books include *Gender Transformations* (Routledge, 1997), *Theorising Patriarchy* (Blackwell, 1990) and *Patriarchy at Work* (Polity, 1986). Her next book will be *Modernities/Globalization/Complexity* (Sage, 2003).

**Steven K. Wisensale**, Ph.D., is Professor of Public Policy in the School of Family Studies at the University of Connecticut. He teaches courses in family policy, family law, comparative family policy, planning and managing human-service programs, and aging policy. Most of his research has focused on work and family issues and aging concerns. His recent book, *Family Leave Policy: The Political Economy of Work and Family*, was published by M. E. Sharpe in 2001. He received his Ph.D. in social-welfare policy from the Heller School at Brandeis University.

**Alison Woodward** is Professor and Chair of the International Affairs and Politics Program of Vesalius College at the Free University of Brussels (VUB) and cofounder of the Center for Women's Studies. Her primary research interest is in the field of comparative European public policy and organization, especially in the areas of equal opportunities policies, housing, and alternative energy. Her current research is on transnational social movements and public policy and the role of regional parliaments in European governance. Recent publications include *Inclusions and Exclusions in European Societies* (edited with Martin Kohli), Routledge, 2001, and *Going for Gender Balance* (Council of Europe, 2002).

**Kathrin Zippel** is Assistant Professor of Sociology at Northeastern University and a faculty affiliate at the Center for European Studies at Harvard University in Boston. Her research interests are in the areas of public and social policy, gender politics, social movements, law, and the welfare state.